Complete

**Civic Center**

# Complete
# Portuguese
Manuela Cook

The publisher has used its best endeavours to ensure that the URLs
for external websites referred to in this book are correct and active
at the time of going to press. However, the publisher and the
author have no responsibility for the websites and can make no
guarantee that a site will remain live or that the content will remain
relevant, decent or appropriate.

For UK order enquiries: please contact Bookpoint Ltd,
130 Milton Park, Abingdon, Oxon, OX14 4SB.
*Telephone:* +44 (0) 1235 827720. *Fax:* +44 (0) 1235 400454.
Lines are open 09.00–17.00, Monday to Saturday, with a 24-hour
message answering service. Details about our titles and how to
order are available at www.teachyourself.co.uk

For USA order enquiries: please contact McGraw-Hill Customer
Services, PO Box 545, Blacklick, OH 43004-0545, USA.
*Telephone:* 1-800-722-4726. *Fax:* 1-614-755-5645.

For Canada order enquiries: please contact McGraw-Hill
Ryerson Ltd, 300 Water St, Whitby, Ontario, L1N 9B6, Canada.
*Telephone:* 905 430 5000. *Fax:* 905 430 5020.

Long renowned as the authoritative source for self-guided
learning – with more than 50 million copies sold worldwide –
the *Teach Yourself* series includes over 500 titles in the fields of
languages, crafts, hobbies, business, computing and education.

British Library Cataloguing in Publication Data: a catalogue record
for this title is available from the British Library.

Library of Congress Catalog Card Number: on file.

First published in UK 2008 by Hodder Education, part of
Hachette Livre UK, 338 Euston Road, London, NW1 3BH.

First published in US 2008 by The McGraw-Hill Companies, Inc.

This edition published 2010; previously published as
Teach Yourself Portuguese.

The *Teach Yourself* name is a registered trade mark of
Hodder Headline.

Copyright © 1987, 2003, 2008, 2010 Manuela Cook

Typeset by MPS Limited, A Macmillan Company.

Printed in Great Britain for Hodder Education, an Hachette Livre
UK Company, 338 Euston Road, London, NW1 3BH, by CPI
Cox & Wyman, Reading, Berkshire, RG1 8EX.

Hachette Livre UK's policy is to use papers that are natural,
renewable and recyclable products and made from wood grown
in sustainable forests. The logging and manufacturing processes
are expected to conform to the environmental regulations of the
country of origin.

Impression number    10 9 8 7 6 5 4 3 2 1
Year                 2014

# Contents

| | | |
|---|---|---|
| *Meet the author* | | ix |
| *Author's introduction* | | xi |
| *Only got a minute?* | | xii |
| *Only got ten minutes?* | | xiv |
| *How to use this book* | | xxiii |
| *Introduction* | | xxix |
| 1 | **Muito prazer** *Delighted to meet you* | 1 |
| | Greeting people and saying goodbye | |
| | • Asking someone's name and giving your name | |
| 2 | **Onde é a saída?** *Where is the exit?* | 8 |
| | Asking the way and understanding main directions • Seeking clarification and help | |
| 3 | **Ida e volta, por favor** *A return ticket, please* | 23 |
| | Buying travel tickets and understanding simple public notices • Asking for what you need on arrival | |
| 4 | **Um quarto simples ou duplo?** *A single or double room?* | 37 |
| | Booking in at a hotel • Finding your way around town and locating shops and services | |
| 5 | **Tem pão e leite?** *Do you stock bread and milk?* | 51 |
| | Asking for what you want in a shop • Asking whether what you want is available • Booking in at a caravan or camping site | |
| 6 | **Tudo bem** *All is well* | 66 |
| | More practice on speaking to the people you meet on arrival • Working out your route, using different forms of transport • Getting what you need | |
| 7 | **Você está de férias?** *Are you on holiday?* | 79 |
| | Introducing a friend or relation • Saying where you are from, talking about yourself • Finding out about others | |

**8**    **Quando começa a excursão?** *When does the tour start?*    **94**
Talking about time and the days of the week
• Finding out when a service is available
• Identifying a person you are going to meet
for the first time

**9**    **Vou encontrar-me com ela amanhã** *I am going to meet
her tomorrow*    **109**
Saying what you are going to do • Describing
clothes as a form of identification • Following
the route described to you

**10** **Ontem fui de carro** *Yesterday I went by car*    **123**
Describing your daily routine or someone else's
• Talking about the months, seasons and the
weather • Talking about something you did or
what happened in the past

**11** **Lugares e pessoas** *Places and people*    **137**
More practice on what you have learned
about moving around and meeting people
• Talking about times, dates and weather
• The past and the future

**12** **Siga em frente** *Go straight on*    **149**
Receiving and giving directions and instructions
• Being specific about what you want in a shop and
talking about weights, measures and quantities

**13** **Quando estará pronto?** *When will it be ready?*    **164**
Practising with currency including large figures
• Alternatives to self-service • Finding different
ways of expressing yourself about the future

**14** **Eu costumava calçar 43** *I used to wear shoe size 43*    **179**
Making comparisons and choices • Talking about
what something is made of, design and pattern
• Finding different ways of expressing yourself
about the past

**15** **Fazendo isto e aquilo** *Doing this and that*    **194**
Meeting someone socially and fitting in with
local life and times • Talking about what is
happening and expressing the idea of progression

**16 Ontem, hoje e amanhã** *Yesterday, today and tomorrow* **209**
More practice across the different topic
areas you have studied in a variety of new
ways • More practice on what you have learned
about expressing yourself in the present, past and future

**17 Espero que a consulta seja hoje** *I hope you can book me
in for today* **228**
Coping in the event of illness or injury
• Distinguishing between wishes, invitations,
suggestions and orders • Using a new way of
expressing yourself about the future

**18 Se os acharem, telefonem logo** *If you find them,
phone right away* **245**
Trying to recover missing property • Coping in the case
of road accident and car breakdown
• Solving a variety of other problems

**19 Gostaria muito de viajar mais** *I'd love to travel more* **261**
Expressing likes and dislikes • Comparing
interests, leisure pursuits and sporting activities
• Talking about conditions, wishes and hopes

**20 Se fosse uma coisa diferente** *If it were something different* **279**
Exploring local cuisine and drink • Explaining
what a place is like and what is special about it
• Giving details about your home town and area

**21 Ao voltarmos, abrirei conta bancária** **294**
*On our return, I shall open a bank account*
Opening and using a bank account • Accepting
or declining an invitation to a social event • Talking
and writing about the place where you are staying

**22 Tenciono visitar esse país** *I'm intending to visit your country* **311**
Further use of services, from hairdressing
to e-mail • Sightseeing and getting to know
the country • More on expressing yourself
both verbally and in writing

**23 Tomara que eles telefonem** *I wish they would phone* **324**
Becoming more involved • Replying to an
advertisement • Writing your CV and applying
for a job • Looking for property on the market

**24 Irei, se puder** *I shall join in, if I can*      **336**
Becoming more familiar with the country's
way of life, culture and shows • Joining in
at family celebrations and parties • Domestic
work • Cooking in local style

**25 Gostaria de praticar mais** *I should like to
practise further*      **346**
Taking stock of what you have achieved and
planning for the future

*Testing yourself*      **354**
*Key to the exercises*      **355**
*Glossary of grammatical terms*      **382**
*Pronunciation and spelling*      **386**
*Verb guide*      **403**
*Portuguese–English vocabulary*      **416**
*English–Portuguese vocabulary*      **442**
*Taking it further*      **463**
*Index to grammar and problem words*      **465**
*Index of topics*      **470**

# Meet the author

I combine two lines of professional activity. My academic pursuits centre on the Lusophone world in general. My language teaching addresses the needs of different learners of Portuguese.

As a Lusophone researcher, I have lectured and written in the area of linguistics, and others, and have had work published in academic journals in the UK, USA, Brazil, and France. I have delivered papers at several universities in the UK, and also in Portugal. In the UK I have held lecturing and examining posts at the University of Wolverhampton, the University of London and a number of other institutions.

I have produced texts for university students of Portuguese as well as other learning situations including both class and self-tuition. My Complete Portuguese course is available internationally, with UK and USA editions. It has also been adapted for French and German learners, these translated versions being available from Harrap Chambers / Larousse and Cornelsen, respectively.

Over the years, I have taught and examined Portuguese at all levels, from 'holiday' courses to under- and post-graduate programmes. My linguistic background and wide teaching experience have come together in the production of Portuguese learning materials that combine sound information with a flexible and user-friendly approach.

A web search on 'Portuguese' and 'Manuela Cook' will give you further details.

# Credits

........................................................................................

# Author's introduction

Dear Learner

Welcome to **Complete Portuguese**. We shall be working together, and for each page of the book you turn we shall take a few new steps in your learning of Portuguese.

No two learners have exactly the same requirements. English may be your only language or you have grown up bilingual or have acquired one or more foreign languages as an adult learner. You may want Portuguese just for basic communication or wish to take it further. You may be an absolute beginner or have come back after a break.

Whatever your circumstances and learning style, this course is right for you. My wide teaching experience – from 'holiday' Portuguese to postgraduate programmes – has enabled me to enhance general teaching principles with special features and produce a flexible method that caters for different learning requirements.

This course consists of a number of progressive modules. The first six units will give you an all-round package at an elementary level designed for you to get by in everyday situations as a visitor. The remaining units will take you on your journey further into the language, and you can go as far as you choose to go.

I hope you will find learning Portuguese an enjoyable and rewarding experience.

Remember, it takes time and practice.

**Força!** *Take heart!*

**Boa sorte!** *All the best!*

Manuela Cook

# *Only got a minute?*

## What is Portuguese like?

Portuguese is a Romance language, as are Spanish, Italian and French, and they all have a lot in common.

For instance, a noun, or naming word, is either masculine or feminine, be it the name of a living being or not. This grammatical gender is shown by the particle for *the*, **o** (masculine) or **a** (feminine). Both **o homem**, *the man*, and **o carro**, *the car*, are masculine, and both **a mulher**, *the woman*, and **a cadeira**, *the chair*, are feminine.

Verbs, which tell us what the nouns are doing or are like, have personal endings for 'I', 'we', etc. – **eu** fal**o** Português, *I speak Portuguese*, and **nós** fal**amos** Português, *we speak Portuguese*. Equally, **eu sou** inglês, *I am English*, and **eles são** americanos, *they are American*. This means that the subject pronoun, 'I', 'we', etc., can be dropped – fal**o** Português, *I speak Portuguese*, fal**amos** Português, *we speak Portuguese*.

These features may be a new experience for an English-speaking learner but they are quite straightforward to grasp. Most vocabulary should also be easy to learn. In fact, even an absolute beginner must be using some Portuguese already! Take *banana*, **a banana**, and English *marmalade* comes from Portuguese **a marmelada**.

## Where is Portuguese spoken?

Portuguese has a wide geographical spread. This is as a result of the long voyages made by the Portuguese in the 15th and 16th centuries when they ventured far in their caravels and larger ships, and reached lands then unknown to the Europeans. These seafarers went as far west as the Americas and as far east as Australia and Japan. Today, Portuguese is the official language of Angola, Brazil, Cape Verde, Guinea-Bissau, Mozambique, Portugal – including the Azores and Madeira – and São Tomé and Príncipe. It is co-official with other languages in East Timor, Equatorial Guinea and Macau. The total estimate of native speakers of Portuguese is over 210 million.

# 10 Only got ten minutes?

Portuguese is a Romance language that evolved in what became Portugal in the 12th century. Later on it spread across the world. This is as a result of the long voyages made by the Portuguese in the 15th and 16th centuries when they ventured far in their caravels and larger ships, and reached lands then unknown to the Europeans. These seafarers went as far west as the Americas and as far east as Australia and Japan. Today Portuguese is one of the world's major languages, with speakers on six continents, and it ranks sixth according to the number of native speakers, estimated to be more than 210 million. It is the language of over 50% of South America and a major lingua franca in Africa.

## The origin of Portuguese

Portuguese is one of the six Romance languages which are also national languages, the others being Catalan, French, Italian, Romanian, and Spanish. Romance, meaning 'from Rome', designates the vernacular types of Latin speech, descending from the language of ancient Rome, which evolved in the territories of the Roman Empire.

Portuguese is the Romance language that evolved from the Latin brought by the Romans to what is Portugal today. More precisely, it originated in the geographical area of present-day Galicia, in north-west Spain, and northern Portugal.

In the Roman Empire, official documents used to be written in a more learned form of Latin. Gradually vernacular words crept in and eventually took over. From this process it is possible to determine when vernacular speech became dominant and a language in its own right.

A property agreement of the late 12th century, found in the monastery of Vairão, near Porto, has been traditionally regarded as the oldest official text in Portuguese. There are, however, earlier documents that display Portuguese words and phrases mixed with Latin. One example is a deed of 1008 found in the public notary's office of the Old Cathedral of Coimbra.

## Geographical distribution

The Portuguese language was subsequently spread across the globe in the 15th and 16th centuries as Portugal established a colonial and commercial empire which stretched from Brazil in the Americas to Timor, north of Australia. As a result, Portuguese is today the third most spoken European language in the world, after English and Spanish. Portuguese speakers across the world share a common language, and the different accents and local words are no obstacle to communication.

Portuguese has formal status in several international organizations such as the European Union (EU), the African Union (AU) and Mercosul. Of the countries where Portuguese is spoken, it is the official language in Angola, Brazil, Cape Verde, Guinea-Bissau, Mozambique, Portugal – including the Azores an Madeira – and São Tomé and Príncipe. It is co-official with other languages in East Timor, Equatorial Guinea and Macau. A Community of Portuguese-speaking Countries – Comunidade dos Países de Língua Portuguesa (CPLP) – was created in 1996.

There are significant Portuguese-speaking communities in the United States of America and Canada. Other countries and territories with a sizeable number of Portuguese speakers include Andorra, Argentina, Australia, Bermuda, the British Isles, France, Japan, Jersey, Luxembourg, Namibia, Paraguay, South Africa, Switzerland, Uruguay and Venezuela.

The Portuguese-speaking world is also termed the *Lusosphere* – Lusoesfera – and its members are *Lusophones* – Lusófonos. These 'Luso' words derive from 'Lusitania', an ancient Roman province which covered roughly the area of Portugal as we know it today, where the Portuguese language evolved and was subsequently taken to other lands. To be a 'Lusophone' is to be linked to the Portuguese-speaking world historically or by choice.

## Main semantic and grammatical features

As part of their common heritage, Romance languages share conceptualizations, ways of categorizing and organizing information through their vocabularies and grammars. Some learners of Portuguese already know another Romance language, often French, Spanish, or Italian. They will have experience of a Romance way of interpreting their surrounding world which they will also meet in Portuguese.

For What is your name? French asks *Comment vous appelez-vous?* and Portuguese *Como se chama?* – with the alternatives *Como se chama você?*, in Portugal, and *Como você se chama?*, in Brazil. Both French and Portuguese share the same way of thinking, 'How do you call yourself?'. For How old are you?, the French will ask *Quel âge avez-vous?* and the Portuguese *Que idade tem?* or *Quantos anos tem?* Both share the notion that age is something 'you have got' (in the sense of 'you have accumulated').

Equally as part of its Latin roots and Romance heritage, Portuguese has noun gender and agreement as well as a rich verb system. The paragraphs below will give you some insight into key aspects.

Concerning noun gender and agreement, there are two main points to consider. First, a naming word falls into one of two classes, either masculine or feminine, even when it stands for something inanimate. This grammatical gender is shown by the definite article, **o** (*the*), masculine, or **a** (*the*), feminine. Both **o homem**, *the man*, and **o carro**, *the car*, are masculine, and both **a mulher**, *the woman*, and **a cadeira**, *the chair*, are feminine. Although noun ending **-o** is seen as the masculine marker – **o** menin**o**, *little boy*, **o** carr**o** – and **-a** as the feminine – **a** menin**a**, *little girl*, **a** cadeir**a** – they are not always present: **o** homem, **a** mulher. Secondly, noun gender triggers off agreement with adjectives and other words modifying the noun – **o** carr**o** vermelh**o**, **a** cadeir**a** pequen**a**. Grammatical gender is still preserved even if not all the words display the gender marker – **o** carr**o** azul, **a** cadeir**a** grande. Noun gender and agreement enables longer sentences to be built without meaning being blurred or lost.

There is no neuter gender as such, but there are forms that perform that function. For this effect, marker **o** tends to be used – **o** que é ist**o**?, *what is this?*; aquil**o** é meu, *that (thing) is mine*.

Verbs, which tell us what the nouns are doing or are like, have personal endings corresponding to *'I'*, *we'*, etc. – **eu** fal**o** Português, *I speak Portuguese*, and **nós** fal**amos** Português, *we speak Portuguese*. Equally, **eu sou** inglês, *I am English*, and **eles são** americanos, *they are American*. Since the concept of person is already conveyed in the verb flexions, the subject pronoun, *'I'*, *'we'*, etc., can be dropped – fal**o** Português, *I speak Portuguese*, fal**amos** Português, *we speak Portuguese*, s**ou** inglês, *I am English*, and s**ão** americanos, *they are American*.

An interesting characteristic of the Portuguese verb system is the personal, or inflected, infinitive. The subject pronoun (*I, you, s/he*, etc.) and/or a personal ending can be used with an infinitive to show who does what. In 'temos de encontrar a chave da porta para conseguir<u>mos</u> entrar' (*we have to find the key to the door for us to get in*), the '-mos' shows who will get in (*we*), in a simple way, without having to use a more elaborate rendering, as in '...para que possamos entrar' (*...so that we may be able to get in*).

## Vocabulary shared, given and taken

As members of the same family, Romance languages naturally share vocabulary. If you already know another Romance language, you will be able to recognize some words in Portuguese.

When it comes to decoding written Portuguese, if you have some French, you are likely to feel on familiar ground over words such as rua, for *street, urban road*, or chapéu, for *hat;* not too different from rue and chapeau. Better still, the perfect match will be occasionally found, as in tomate *(tomato)*, servir *(to serve)* or entre *(between)*. Perfect cognates with Portuguese will be found here and there also for those who speak Italian, as in porta *(door)*, terra *(land)* or posso *(I can)*. Portuguese, Spanish, Catalan and Italian share casa for house; with casă in Romanian.

However, not all lexical similarities are obvious. Parallel words in different Romance languages can be masked by the specific sound shapes they have taken.

The fall of the intervocalic -n- and -l- is one of the phonological transformations that contributed to make Portuguese a distinct language. For *moon*, the Latin **luna** remains almost undisturbed in most cases of modern usage: **luna** in Italian and Spanish, **lune** in French. It is different in Portuguese, where it changed to **lua**. For *to fly*, the Latin original survives in Italian **volare** (intact), in Spanish **volar**, and French **voler** with little change. In Portuguese we have **voar**.

Being aware of this phenomenon can help you work out the meaning of Portuguese words. For instance, with Spanish as your source language, remove the -n- from **moneda** *(coin)* and you will get Portuguese **moeda** *(coin)*; remove the -l- from **águila** *(eagle)* and you will get Portuguese **águia** *(eagle)*.

You can apply this same technique to Portuguese noun and adjective plurals. Spanish plural hospitales will give a clue to Portuguese plural hospitais *(hospitals)*. By the same token, Spanish pasteles, fáciles, patrones and panes correspond, respectively, to Portuguese pastéis *(pasties, cakes)*, fáceis *(easy (plural))*, patrões *(bosses)* and pães *(loaves)*. The diacritic (~) in patrões and pães, called a 'til', denotes a nasal presence left in the vowel by the fallen -n-.

However, similarities are to be explored with caution. This applies not only to words that look alike but also to those that sound alike. Spanish **tirar** means *to throw (away)* but Portuguese **tirar** means *to take*. Although sounding close enough to suggest being the same, Spanish **niño** means *child* and Portuguese **ninho** a *bird's nest*. Watch out for false friends!

Although most of the lexicon of Portuguese is derived from Latin, a few Portuguese words can be traced to the pre-Roman inhabitants of present-day Portugal. Examples include abóbora *(pumpkin)*, from the nearby Celtiberian language, and cerveja *(beer)*, from Celtic.

In the 5th century AD the Iberian Peninsula was invaded by the Germanic Suebi and Visigoths, who also contributed a few words such as guerra *(war)*, espora *(spur)* and a number of toponyms. In the early 8th century the Peninsula was invaded by the Moors, who stayed in the Algarve for over 500 years. They contributed about 800 words, often still recognizable by the initial Arabic article a(l)-, such as alface *(lettuce)*, aldeia *(village)*, arroz *(rice)*, azeite *(olive oil)*.

Starting mainly in the 15th century, with the Portuguese maritime explorations, the Portuguese language was taken to far-off lands but also received loan words from all over the world. From Asian languages came, for example, catana *(cutlass)*, from Japanese, and chá *(tea)*, from Chinese. From South American languages came batata *(potato)*, from Taino, ananás and abacaxi *(types of pineapple)*, from Tupi-Guarani and Tupi. Words of African origin include caçula *(youngest offspring)* and tanga *(loincloth, short bikini pants)*, both from Kimbundu.

More recently there have also been loanwords from Portuguese 'sibling' Romance languages. For instance, fiambre *(wet-cured ham)* and melena *(lock of hair)*, from Spanish, paletó *(jacket)* and batom *(lipstick)*, from French, and macarrão *(type of pasta)* and piloto *(pilot)*, from Italian. To these can be added the borrowing of lexical items from English, especially in information technology and the 'Coca-Cola culture'.

In this give and take of loanwords are there any English words of Portuguese origin? Yes, there have been several Portuguese imports into the English language throughout the centuries.

Take banana, **a banana**. Cobra comes from the Portuguese generic name for *snake*, **a cobra**. Some words have changed a bit, in meaning or form. When you talk about a glass of *port*, this is **o porto**. *Cashew* is **o caju**. *Breeze* is **a brisa** and *monsoon* is **a monção**. *Marmalade* comes from **a marmelada**, quince jam, the name for *quince* being **o marmelo**. The term *massage* is believed to come from **a massa**, *dough,* and **amassar**, to *knead* (bread). A number of Portuguese words that have entered the English language have done so via French. This is the case with *marmalade*, *massage* and others, such as *caravel*, **a caravela** – a small, fast ship of the 15th and 16th centuries.

---

## Portuguese east and west of the Atlantic

When comparing European and Brazilian Portuguese, a parallel can be drawn with British and American English. First, what tends to be meant by European Portuguese is the standard practised east of the Atlantic, not just in Portugal but also in Africa and Asia. Secondly, as for the United States in North America, for Brazil in South America one needs to consider a different accent, some different lexical choices and other aspects.

In Brazil you will be walking on the calçada *(pavement)* and travelling by ônibus *(coach)*, not walking on the passeio *(pavement)* and travelling by autocarro *(coach)*, as you would hear in Portugal.

But what other kind of differences are there between European and Brazilian Portuguese? For an objective view we need to look at standard practice rather than regional variations.

A main difference can perhaps be seen in the formation of continuous tenses. The gerund is the normal practice in Brazil while in European Portuguese preposition **a** + infinitive has become the first choice – Ele está falando Português (Br.) and Ele está a falar Português (Eur.).

Concerning word order and object pronouns, in Brazil there is a tendency to resist inversion after an interrogative while in European Portuguese inversion tends to occur – Onde você trabalha? (Br.), but Onde trabalha você? (Eur.).

In the Portuguese language in general, the object pronoun is in principle enclitic and hyphenated to the preceding verb, but there is a 'pull' towards the beginning of the sentence which is stronger in Brazil. For *'Can you tell me where he is?'*, in European Portuguese you may hear both Você pode dizer-me onde ele está? and, more colloquially, Você pode me dizer onde ele está? In Brazil you may hear the latter or Você me pode dizer onde ele está?

There are instances in the Portuguese language in which the subject form of the personal pronoun is also used as object – ele/ela *(he/she)* as in para ele *(for him)*, para ela (for her). This is taken further in Brazil, where colloquially ela/ela can replace the weak pronouns o/a *(him/her)* after a transitive verb – Ela viu ele instead of Ela viu-o *(She saw him)*.

Finally, there are some differences of practice in relation to the second person subject, the word for 'you', and respective verb form. Below there is some detailed background information on this issue.

The Portuguese language inherited from Latin tu and vós and respective verb endings – tu falas *(you speak)*, for one person, and vós falais *(you speak)* for more than one person. The latter was also a ceremonial form of address, directed to one individual or more. In the Renaissance, following a vogue that spread across part of Europe, honorific titles became popular in Portugal when addressing someone of high standing. The Portuguese king was then addressed as *Your Mercy,* Vossa Mercê. Being a noun, Mercê enabled the use of the verb in the third person singular, that is, the same as for *s/he* – Vossa Mercê fala *(Your Mercy speaks,* for *You speak)*. The format became established but moved down the social scale. A corrupted form of the dignified Vossa Mercê is today the simple você, a common word for *'you'* with its plural vocês when addressing more than one individual – você fala *(you speak)*, for one person, and vocês falam *(you speak)* for more than one person.

The two second-person systems in the Portuguese language – tu, vós (tu falas, vós falais) and você, vocês (você fala, vocês falam) – coexisted for a long time but the latter has become the dominant one on both sides of the Atlantic. Today, for politeness, subject indicator você(s) can be replaced with o(s) senhor(es) or a(s) senhora(s) *(gentleman/men or lady/ladies)*. For Do you speak Português?, one can say O senhor fala Português? (courteous) or Você fala Português? (neutral, informal).

Vós, with its verb ending, survives in a few geographical pockets, for example in northern Portugal and in Rio Grande do Sul in Brazil. It has otherwise become archaic, used only in some special circumstances such as liturgical prayer. The singular tu, with its verb ending, continues in circulation as a more informal and intimate alternative to você. Here is where we come across a different practice depending on which side of the Atlantic you are. The actual tu paradigm is not much heard in Brazil but its oblique form te is – <u>Você</u> estava no aeroporto? Eu não <u>te</u> vi lá *(Were you at the airport? I didn't see you there.)*

This comparison of Portuguese east and west of the Atlantic presents the standards of Portuguese in Africa and Asia as being closer to that of Portugal than to that of Brazil. This is so in general, though in some aspects of their phonetics, especially the pronunciation of unstressed vowels, the Portuguese of some speakers from Africa resembles that of Brazilian Portuguese speakers.

# How to use this book

The Portuguese you will learn in this course is centred round realistic everyday situations. The emphasis is on communicating in Portuguese. To that purpose you are also given the necessary tools that will enable you to know how the language works and create sentences of your own.

Progression is done in stages. The course consists of four modules where each further stage revisits and builds up on the previous one.

The first six units are for someone who is looking for means of getting by as a visitor. You can then consolidate and expand on what you have learned by moving up to subsequent units as far as you wish to go in the course.

## Units 1–6

In Units 1–6 the following topics are introduced, at an elementary level:

Greeting people
Speaking to the people you meet on arrival
Seeing to what you may need on arrival
Buying food and what else you may need
Finding where to exchange currency
Using a taxi, train or other public transport
Sending an email back home
Asking someone's name and giving your name
Asking the way and working out your route
Understanding simple directions
Seeking clarification and help
Buying travel tickets
Driving a car or other vehicle
Understanding simple public notices

Booking in at a hotel or other form of accommodation
Booking in at a caravan or camping site
Finding your way around town
Locating shops and services
Asking whether what you want is available
Finding a doctor, dentist or car mechanic
Saying 'thank you' and other courtesy words

At this stage, grammar will be minimal. Only rudimentary notions are taught. This includes gender (masculine and feminine words) and verbs as they are shown in a dictionary.

### Units 7–11
Units 7–11 build up on the previous level and have the following new topic input:

Introducing a friend or relation
Explaining where you are from
Talking about your nationality
Talking about what you do for a living
Saying whether you are married or not
Talking about your age
Saying whether you are a parent
Giving your address and phone number
Explaining where you are staying
Finding out personal information about others
Talking about time and the days of the week
Finding out when a service is available
Identifying a person you are going to meet for the first time
Saying what you are going to do
Talking about what is expected to happen in the future
Talking about colours
Describing what someone looks like or is wearing
Understanding more complicated road directions
Describing your daily routine or someone else's
Talking about the months, seasons and the weather
Talking about something you did or what happened in the past

Grammar at this stage builds up and expands on the first level. The new main features introduced include subject pronouns, the present indicative, preterite (past tense) and colloquial future.

## Units 12–16

Units 12–16 build up on the previous level and have the following new topic input:

Using vending machines
Ordering food for a group
Using the post office and other services
Having your car checked at a garage
Receiving and giving directions and instructions
Explaining what you want as an alternative to self-service
Being specific about what you want in a shop
Talking about weights, measures and quantities
Dealing with currency involving large figures
Finding different ways of expressing yourself about the future
Making comparisons and choices
Discussing clothes and shoe sizes
Talking about what something is made of, design and pattern
Finding different ways of expressing yourself about the past
Meeting locals socially
Fitting in with local life and times
Talking about what is happening and express the idea of progression
Ordering a hotel breakfast in bed
Discussing alternative means of transport
Discussing bills and receipts
Enjoying a sunny day on the beach

Grammar builds up and expands on the previous level. Some main features introduced are 'command' forms, the future tense, emphatic future, imperfect indicative, and continuous present and past.

## Units 17–25

This is the top level in the course, designed mainly for learners who have more than a passing interest in the language. It builds up on the previous levels and has the following new topic input:

Explaining in detail what you want done at the hairdresser's
Sorting out a variety of problems
Providing details when reporting lost property
Providing details when coping in the case of illness or injury
Providing details when coping with a road accident and car breakdown
Using a new way of expressing yourself about something in the future
Expressing likes, dislikes and preferences
Talking about interests, leisure pursuits and sport
Expressing a condition, a wish or a hope
Distinguishing between a wish, an invitation, a suggestion and an order
Exploring local cuisine and drink
Describing the place where you are staying
Explaining what a place is like and what is special about it
Giving detailed information about your home town and area
Opening and using a bank account
Increasing your competence in using post office and other services
Writing informal and formal letters
Replying to an advertisement
Writing your CV and applying for a job
Looking for property on the market, to let or for sale
Talking about your house or apartment
Explaining what domestic work you want done
Getting to know the country better and its cultural heritage
Going to the cinema or theatre and attending local shows
Accepting or declining an invitation to a social event
Joining in at local family celebrations and parties
Talking about the Portuguese you have learned
Making the most of your Portuguese now and always

Grammar builds up and expands on material previously taught and adds to it some new features, including the following: present subjunctive, future subjunctive, perfect tenses, conditional, imperfect subjunctive, and personal infinitive.

### Communicative phrases

In the units, phrases are provided for immediate use in everyday interaction. This is done under the headings **Expressions** (E) and **Cultural information** (CI).

## Language structure
The incremental grammar notes in the units have the heading
**How it works** (HIW). They will help you create your own
sentences and evolve beyond the communicative phrases you have
learned. Additionally there is a **Verb guide** (VG) at the end of the
book, with verb tables and notes.

## Pronunciation
In **How to pronounce it** (HTPI) special assistance is given on
pronunciation in each unit up to Unit 10, with details of Portuguese
sounds that you may find difficult. You can listen to the Portuguese
sounds on your audio.

There is also a **Pronunciation and spelling** guide (PSG) at the end
of book with a list of Portuguese sounds you can listen to on your
audio. This section contains additional information for extra help,
including English sound-alikes.

You can use the audio to the best of your advantage. The Portuguese
native voices on your audio are male and female, from Portugal and
Brazil. This way you can develop an ear for different intonations
and at the same time choose the speaker you wish to model yourself
on, male or female, from Brazil or from Portugal.

## Exercises
The exercises provided in each unit are dual-purpose. In them you
will apply structures you have come across before to a number of
different situations. This way you will be enlarging your vocabulary
with new words but doing so within the comfortable framework of
a familiar ground. The exercises also serve the purpose of helping
you monitor your progress. You can see how well you have done
by comparing your results with the **Key to the exercises** at the end
of the book. Units 6, 11, 16, and 22–25 are revision units where
you will find extra opportunities for self-assessing your progress.

## Glossary of grammatical terms
Grammar explanations are supported with a **Glossary of
grammatical terms** at the end of the book. These will give you
extra help.

## Vocabulary lists

New vocabulary is generally presented as it occurs. There is also a Portuguese-English and an English-Portuguese reference **Vocabulary list** at the end of the book which you may find particularly useful if you need to refresh your memory on a word you have forgotten.

## Cross-reference indexes

For quick location of grammar points and topics you have two cross-reference indexes at the end of the book, **Index to grammar and problem words** and **Index of topics**. There you will be directed to the relevant pages, often more than one unit sub-section where information is revisited and built up upon.

# Introduction

## Welcome to **Complete Portuguese!**

### Is this the right course for you?

If you are an adult learner with no previous knowledge of Portuguese and studying on your own, then this is the course for you. Perhaps you are taking up Portuguese again after a break from it, or you are intending to learn with the support of a class? Again, you will find this course very well suited to your purposes.

### Developing your skills

The language introduced in this course is centred around realistic everyday situations. The emphasis is first and foremost on **using** Portuguese, but this course also aims to give you an idea of how the language works, so that you can create sentences of your own.

The course covers all four of the basic skills – listening and speaking, reading and writing. If you are working on your own, the audio recordings will be all the more important, as they will provide you with the essential opportunity to listen to Portuguese and to speak it within a controlled framework. You should therefore try to obtain a copy of the recordings if you haven't already got one.

## The structure of this course

The course book contains **25 course units** plus a **reference** section at the back of the book. There is also a two-hour **audio recording** which you really need to have if you are going to get maximum benefit from the course. A number of icons will signpost the listening material and will help you find your way through the different sections in each unit.

**The course units** The course units can be divided roughly into the following categories, although of course there is a certain amount of overlap from one category to another.

**Statement of aims** At the beginning of each unit you will be told what you can expect to learn to do in Portuguese by the end of the unit.

**Presentation of new language** In most units this is in the form of two or more initial dialogues. These are recorded on the audio ◀) and also printed in the book. They introduce the main **topic area and language features** dealt with in the unit. Assistance with new vocabulary is given in vocabulary boxes **Quick vocab**. The language is presented in manageable chunks, building carefully on what you have learned in earlier units.

**Practice of the new language** Under the heading **Exercises**, practice is graded, so that activities which require mainly **recognition** come first. As you grow in confidence in manipulating the language forms, you will be encouraged to **produce** both in writing and in speech. Some of these activities also involve your response to audio recorded material ◀). At the end of the book you will find a **Key to the exercises** so that you can check your answers.

**Pronunciation and spelling** The best way to acquire good pronunciation and intonation is to listen to native speakers and to try to imitate them. But most people do not actually notice that certain sounds in Portuguese are pronounced differently from their English counterparts, until this is pointed out to them. For this reason specific advice and practice are included under **How to pronounce it** within the course units. There is also a **Pronunciation and spelling** guide at the end of the book which includes a table of Portuguese sounds. You will also find it at the end of the recording.

**Expressions** Under this heading you are given new vocabulary and groups of words that you can use in different situations related to the aims of the unit. At the end of the book there is a cross-reference index of the several **Topics** covered in the different units, so that you can locate quickly phrases and vocabulary of particular interest to you in each topic.

**Description of language forms and grammar** In the section **How it works** you learn about the forms of the language, thus enabling you to construct your own sentences correctly. For those who are daunted by grammar, assistance is given in various ways, with 'handy hints' and extra help. This also includes the following, at the end of the book: a **Glossary of grammatical terms**; additional information on verbs and **Verb tables**; and a cross-reference **Index to grammar and problem words**.

**Vocabulary** New vocabulary is generally presented as it occurs. There is also a Portuguese–English and an English–Portuguese reference **Vocabulary list** at the end of the book, and you will be given practice on how to look up Portuguese verbs and other words as you would do in a dictionary.

**Information on Portuguese-speaking countries** Throughout this course, you will find relevant information about aspects of the Portuguese-speaking world. This ranges from how to use the language for politeness, formality and informality, to material on cuisine, traditions and historical sights. Cultural notes appear in a variety of ways including dialogues, specific information items and 'real' texts from different sources.

**Monitoring your progress** To help you monitor your progress, exercises are provided at the end of each unit for you to check whether you have mastered the main points. You can see how well you have done by comparing your results with the **Key to the exercises** at the end of the book. After every fifth or fourth unit there is a revision unit that will give you extra opportunities of self-assessing your progress. The last four units in the course also contain revision material. Special guidance on how to monitor your progress is provided in **Testing yourself**.

## How to progress through this course

Make sure at the beginning of each course unit that you are clear about what you can expect to learn.

Read any background information that is provided. Then either read the initial dialogues or listen to them on the audio recording. With audio recordings try to get the gist of what is being said before you look at the printed text in the book. Then refer to the printed text and the boxed key words in order to study the dialogues in more detail. Listen to the dialogues again and try to imitate the speakers. First listen to and repeat each short set of words; then listen to and repeat each full sentence.

Don't fall into the trap of thinking you have 'done that' when you have listened to the audio a couple of times and worked through the dialogues in the book. You may **recognize** what you hear and read, but you almost certainly still have some way to go before you can **produce** the language of the dialogues correctly and fluently. This is why you are recommended to keep listening to the audio at every opportunity – sitting on the tube or bus, waiting at the dentist's or stuck in a traffic jam in the car, using what would otherwise be wasted time. Of course, you must also be internalizing what you hear and making sense of it – just playing it in the background without really paying attention is not enough!

Move on to the **Certo ou errado?** (*Right or wrong?*) and the **Perguntas e respostas** (*Questions and answers*) exercises. These are mainly recognition activities which will further help you internalize the contents of the initial dialogues. Always check your results against the **Key to the exercises** at the end of the book before moving on.

Next read the English sound-alikes and other tips in the section **How to pronounce it**. Listen to your recording and try to imitate the speakers. For extra help, refer to the **Pronunciation and spelling** guide at the back of the book.

Study the contents of the **Expressions** section. Don't rush through, but make sure you take in all the new information. Imagine yourself in a situation in which you would use any Portuguese expressions you see in this section and say them aloud even if they are the same as or close to what you met in the initial dialogues.

You can now study the **How it works** section. Grammar explanations have been made as user-friendly as possible. It is up to you just how much time you spend on studying and sorting out the points in this section. Some people find that they can do better by getting an ear for what sounds right, others need to know in detail how the language is put together. At this stage you may want to look up the relevant names in the **Glossary of grammatical terms** as well as the extra information on **Verbs** at the end of the book, where applicable.

You will then be ready to move on to the final set of **Exercises** and work through the exercises following the instructions that precede them. Do not forget to check your answers carefully at the back of the book. It is easy to overlook your own mistakes. If you have a 'study buddy' it's a good idea to check each other's answers.

As you advance through the course, use the cross-reference **Index of topics** to revise vocabulary, phrases and expressions in specific areas, at successive levels of progression. Also do not forget to follow the progress monitoring advice given in **Testing yourself**.

### Portuguese in the modern world

In the Age of Discoveries, 15th and 16th centuries, seafarers from Portugal reached lands unknown to the Europeans as far west as the Americas and as far east as Japan. As a result, today Portuguese is one of the world's major languages, with speakers on six continents, and ranks sixth according to the number of native speakers, estimated to be more than 210 million. It is the language of over 50% of South America and a major lingua franca in Africa.

Portuguese has official status in several international organizations such as the European Union (EU), the African Union (AU) and Mercosul. Of the countries where Portuguese is spoken, it is the official language in Angola, Brazil, Cape Verde, Guinea-Bissau, Mozambique, Portugal and São Tomé e Príncipe. It is co-official with other languages in East Timor, Equatorial Guinea and Macau. There are also significant Portuguese-speaking communities, from various geographic origins, in the United States of America and Canada; in South American countries such as Paraguay, Argentina and Venezuela; in Luxembourg, Andorra, France, Spain, other countries and regions in continental Europe and in the British Isles; in South Africa, Namibia and other African countries; and in Australia. Portuguese speakers across the world share a common language, and the different accents and local words are no obstacle to communication.

### What kind of Portuguese am I learning?

Similar to what happens in the English-speaking world, there are differences across the Portuguese-speaking world. Portuguese speakers from Africa and Asia tend to have the same linguistic preferences as those from Portugal, but some Portuguese accents from Africa are quite close to some Brazilian accents. Brazil itself is a huge country and equally there are variations between regions.

The language chosen for your **Complete Portuguese** course is common ground wherever the language is spoken. It is standard Portuguese that will enable you to communicate anywhere in the Portuguese-speaking world.

Differences between South American and European Portuguese are explained throughout the course and highlighted with the abbreviation **Br.** for Brazilian and **Eur.** for European which will also apply to Africa and Asia unless stated otherwise. Not all alternatives are mutually exclusive. For example, **comboio** (Eur.) / **trem** (Br.), for *train*, will mean that you should use the former east of the Atlantic Ocean and the latter in Brazil; but **vermelho** / **encarnado** (Eur.), for the colour *red*, will mean that the former circulates anywhere in the Portuguese-speaking world and you can also use the latter east of the Atlantic. The audio recordings were made by speakers from both Portugal and Brazil so that you can choose a model voice to follow depending on your destination.

## *Spelling agreement* **(acordo ortográfico)**

A spelling reform of the Portuguese language was in the making
for some time, and a spelling agreement (acordo ortográfico) is
now in place for a single common orthography among the different
Portuguese-speaking countries. In 2005 Brazil adhered to the new
requirements and in Portugal the changes were formally accepted
in 2008.

The Portuguese you will see in this course complies with the *acordo
ortográfico*. In the **Pronunciation and spelling guide** at the end
of the book, there is a list of s**pelling updates** where you will be
able to compare the 'new' against the 'old' orthography. You also
have a list of **spelling alternatives** which cater mainly for cases of
variation in vowel quality. For example, some speakers, typically
from Brazil, will pronounce Antônio *(Anthony)*, with a close 'o'
and others, typically from Portugal, António, with an open 'o'.

### Where can I find real Portuguese?

Don't expect to be able to understand everything you hear or read
straight away. If you watch TV programmes in Portuguese, surf
the web for a Portuguese-language site, or buy newspapers or
magazines written in Portuguese, you should not get discouraged
when you realize how quickly native speakers talk and how much
vocabulary there is still to be learned. Just concentrate on a small
extract – either a video/audio clip or a short article – and work
through a few words till you have mastered them. In this way,
you'll find that your command of Portuguese increases steadily.

When you visit a Portuguese-speaking country, make the most of
any notices and advertisements directed at the general public. They
can be good examples of everyday language presented in small
chunks. You will find some 'real' texts in this volume which have
been used with the kind permission of the respective organizations.
The author is grateful for their cooperation.

For more sources of 'real' Portuguese look at **Taking it further** section at the end of the book.

We hope you enjoy working your way through **Complete Portuguese**. Try not to let yourself get discouraged. Mastering a new language does take time and perseverance, and sometimes it can seem just too difficult. But then you'll come back to it another day and things will begin to make more sense again.

# Muito prazer
## Delighted to meet you

In this first unit you will learn how to
- **Greet people**
- **Ask someone's name and give your name**
- **Say goodbye**

---

### 1A Greeting people

◀) **CD1, TR 2**

You will hear a number of people greeting each other. The first exchange is printed for you.

1 Look at the drawings and listen to the different greetings on your recording.

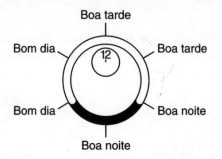

**Bom dia** *Good morning*

**Boa tarde** *Good afternoon / evening*

**Boa noite** *Good evening / night*

**2** Read the greetings above. Listen to the recording again and say each greeting, trying to imitate the speaker.

---

## Expressions

**O dia** means *the day*; **a tarde** is the part of the day between noon and sunset; **a noite** is *the night*. Say **bom dia** from daybreak to midday. Say **boa tarde** from midday until dark. Then switch over to **boa noite** until daybreak. Note that you will find a translation for *good evening* in both **boa tarde** and **boa noite**, depending on whether it is light or dark.

---

## Insight

*Hello!*

bom dia

boa tarde

boa noite

---

**3 a** Someone will meet you at the airport to take you to your hotel. You arrive at 11 p.m. Greet the person.

   **b** At about 10 a.m. you go into a bank to exchange currency. Greet the bank clerk.

   **c** It's 1 p.m. and you go into a restaurant. Greet the waiter.

4 You will hear some more people greeting each other. Listen to what they say and look at their mini-dialogues which are printed for you, below.

– Boa noite, Sr. José.
– Boa noite, D. Laura.
– Olá, boa noite.                    – Oi! (Br.)
– Olá!                               – Oi!
– Tudo bem?
– Tudo bem.

## Cultural information

You can add words to make your greeting more formal. This is the case when you address a woman as **dona** or a man as **senhor**, usually abbreviated in writing as **D.** or **d.** and **Sr.** or **sr.** respectively. It will be even more formal if you address José by his surname as **Sr. Santos** (*Mr Santos*).

For a very informal greeting, you can use **Olá!**, (*Hello!*, *Hi!*). **Oi!**, (*Hi!*), is a very informal greeting in Brazil.

In Brazil, **Seu** is a casual alternative to **Sr.** – **Olá, Seu José, tudo bem?**

**Tudo bem** is used both as a question and as a statement. When given a rising asking intonation, it corresponds to *How is it going? How are things?* (literally, *(Is) everything well?*). As a reply it means *Everything's fine (All (is) well)*.

## Insight

*Hello!*
**Olá!**
**Tudo bem?**

5 Listen to the formal and informal greetings again and repeat them after the speaker.
6 **a** Laura has greeted you formally. Reciprocate in the same manner. (It's 3 p.m.)

**b** Joana has greeted you very informally. Respond in the same way.

---

## 1B Asking someone's name and saying your name

◀) CD1, TR 4

QUICK VOCAB

**Qual é o seu nome?** (Eur.)
**Qual é seu nome?** (Br.) *What is your name?*
**O meu nome é...** (Eur.)
**Meu nome é...** (Br.) *My name is...*
**E o seu?** *And yours?*
**Muito prazer** *Delighted, Very pleased (to meet you)*
**Igualmente** *Likewise*

**1** You will hear some people who are meeting for the first time. They exchange names and shake hands. Listen to the recording and look at what they say, printed below.

▶ César Oliveira. Qual é seu nome?
▶ Fátima Rocha.
▶ Muito prazer.
▶ Muito prazer.

▶ Qual é o seu nome?
▶ Marcelo Ribeiro. E o seu?
▶ Catarina Silva.
▶ Muito prazer.
▶ Igualmente.

> ### Insight
> *How nice to meet you*
> **(O) meu nome é** (*your name*)
> **Qual é (o) seu nome?**
>
> ---
>
> **Muito prazer**
> **Igualmente**

**2** Listen again several times to the people who are meeting for the first time.

**3** When you feel confident, act out each one of the parts in the dialogues substituting your name.

---

## 1C Saying 'goodbye'

◀) CD1, TR 5

**1** You will hear four people saying goodbye. Look at the drawings and listen to what they say.

*Boa noite Boa tarde, adeus Tchau, até logo Até breve.*

**2** Now you will hear more goodbyes. Listen and tick the box(es) in the table below for each person. The first one is done for you.

| Parting words | 1 | 2 | 3 | 4 |
|---|---|---|---|---|
| a   bom dia | | | | |
| b   boa tarde | ✓ | | | |
| c   boa noite | | | | |
| d   até logo | | | | |
| e   até breve | | | | |
| f   adeus | | | | |
| g   tchau | | | | |

## Cultural information

**Bom dia, boa tarde** and **boa noite** are both greetings and parting words. Rather than formal, these expressions are neutral in tone. As with greetings, adding for example **dona Laura** or **senhor José** will add formality.

Particularly with people you know and friends, you may wish to use **adeus** in Portugal, where Brazilian **tchau** has become equally popular, also as **chau** *See you / talk to you soon*. These can be used on their own or in conjunction with the other expressions: **Adeus, até logo.**

You have **Até logo** or **Até mais logo** and, mainly in Brazil, **Até mais** for *See you / talk to you later*. **Até breve** translates *See you / talk to you soon*. Of course, both *'later'* and *'soon'* are relative concepts and may not mean the same to everyone. Some people may interpret **Até logo** as *See you / talk to you later* today. If what you mean is *See you / talk to you again* regardless of timescale, then you can say **Até a próxima**, literally, *Till next time*. In Portugal the **'a'** in this expression is often pronounced with an open sound, a bit like *a* in *arm*, and spelt **à, Até à próxima.**

**3** Listen again to the different parting words and repeat each goodbye after the speaker.

**4 a** It's mid-morning. You want to buy something and go to a shop. Say goodbye to the shop assistant when you leave.
 **b** You go to a restaurant for a meal in the early afternoon. Say goodbye to the waiter when you leave.
 **c** Say goodbye, see you again, to a Portuguese you have met.
 **d** Say bye to a Brazilian you have met.

---

## Summary

**1** Bom dia – Boa tarde / noite
**2** Olá! Tudo bem? – Tudo bem
**3** (O) meu nome é (*your name*) – Qual é (o) seu nome?
**4** Muito prazer – Igualmente
**5** Até logo / breve / mais / a próxima

# 2

**Onde é a saída?**
Where is the exit?

In this unit you will learn how to
- **Ask the way**
- **Understand simple directions**
- **Seek clarification and help**

This unit aims to help you find your way when you first arrive in a Portuguese-speaking country.

> **Onde é a saída?** *Where is the exit?*

Portuguese Pedro is in the airport terminal. He stops Isabel, another passenger, to ask where the exit is. Listen to what they say and study the printed dialogue with the help of the words in the box below.

◀ CD1, TR 6

| Pedro | Por favor, pode me dizer onde é a saída? |
| Isabel | Em frente, à direita. |
| Pedro | Como? |
| Isabel | Em frente, à direita. |
| Pedro | Obrigado. |
| Isabel | De nada. |

**por favor** *excuse me, please*
**pode me dizer...?** *can you tell me...?* **(literally** *can (you) + me + to tell)*

**onde** *where*
**é** *is, (it) is*
**a saída** *the exit, way out*
**em frente** *straight on*
**à direita** *on the right*
**como?** *pardon?*
**obrigado** *thank you (said by male)*
**de nada** *not at all*

**Onde são os telefones?** *Where are the telephones?*

Ana wants to make a phone call. She approaches Paulo to ask where the telephones are. Listen to them and study the new words.

| Ana | Desculpe, pode me dizer onde são os telefones? |
|---|---|
| Paulo | *(pointing to the steps)* Lá em cima, no correio. O correio é à esquerda, a seguir ao banco e em frente da farmácia. |
| Ana | Como? Mais devagar, por favor. |
| Paulo | Lá em cima…, no correio… O correio é à esquerda…, a seguir ao banco… e em frente da farmácia… |
| Ana | Obrigada. |
| Paulo | De nada. |

**desculpe** *sorry to trouble you*
**são** *are, (they) are*
**os telefones** *the telephones*
**lá em cima** *upstairs*
**no (= em + o) correio** *in the post office*
**à esquerda** *on the left*
**a seguir ao (= a + o) banco** *past the bank* (lit. *past + to + the + bank*)
**e** *and*
**em frente da (= de + a) farmácia** *opposite the chemist's* (lit. *in front of + the chemist's*)
**mais devagar** *more slowly*
**obrigada** *thank you (said by female)*

## Exercises

### 2.1 Certo ou errado? *Right or wrong?*

Tick the **C** or the **E** box for each statement below according to
whether it is correct or not. The first tick has been entered for you.

|   |   | C | E |
|---|---|---|---|
| **1** | A saída é à esquerda. | ☐ | ☑ |
| **2** | A farmácia é lá em cima. | ☐ | ☐ |
| **3** | O correio é em frente da farmácia. | ☐ | ☐ |

### 2.2 Perguntas e respostas *Questions and answers*

Choose the right answer and write it down.

**1** Onde é a saída?
   **a** À direita. **b** Em frente, à direita.

**2** Onde é a farmácia?
   **a** Lá em cima, à direita. **b** Lá em cima, a seguir ao correio.

**3** Onde são os telefones?
   **a** No correio, lá em cima, em frente da farmácia e do
   banco.
   **b** No correio, lá em cima, à esquerda, em frente da
   farmácia.

## How to pronounce it

🔊 **CD1, TR 8**

Pronounce the following words trying to imitate the speaker
on the recording. Pay special attention to the part highlighted
in bold.

**-ão:**

são ((*they*) *are*); estação (*station*); perdão! (*sorry!*). Say *ow* in *how*, through your nose.

**-ões:**

informações (*information services/desk*). Say *o* in *note* plus *y* in *yet* but through your nose.

**-lh-:** recolha de bagagem (*baggage reclaim*). Say *li* in mi*lli*on.

**-nh-:** senhora (*lady*). Say *ni* in o*ni*on.

For extra help, refer to the **Pronunciation and spelling** guide at the end of the book. There you will find more English sound-alikes and more information.

## Expressions
### a Directions and locations

Note that **lá em cima** and **lá em baixo** (Eur.) / **embaixo** (Br.) translate both *upstairs / downstairs* and *at the top / at the bottom.*

| | |
|---|---|
| **O banco é lá em cima.** | *The bank is upstairs or at the top of this slope.* |

Also, some words can be used for both direction and location:

| | | |
|---|---|---|
| **em frente** | *straight on* | *opposite* |
| **à direita** | *to the right* | *on the right* |
| **à esquerda** | *to the left* | *on the left* |

| | |
|---|---|
| **As lojas são em frente.** | *The shops are straight ahead.* |
| **As lojas são em frente da entrada.** | *The shops are opposite the entrance.* |

### b a seguir a *or* depois de?

**depois**, *after*, and **antes**, *before*, are for time and sequence but can also be used for location.

*(Contd)*

| O correio é depois do banco = o correio é a seguir ao banco. | *The post office is past / after the bank.* |
|---|---|
| O correio é antes do banco. | *The post office is before (you reach) the bank.* |

## Cultural information

### a 'Please' and 'thank you'

**Por favor** is literally a request for a favour. An alternative is **faz o favor** which in Portugal is reduced to **faz favor**, also in the version **se faz favor**. Use **por favor** or **faz (o) favor** when in English you would say *please* and / or *excuse me* to draw someone's attention or to accompany a request.

| **Por favor / Faz (o) favor, pode me dizer onde é a saída?** | *Excuse me, please, can you tell me where the exit is?* |
|---|---|

or simply,

| **Por favor / Faz (o) favor, onde é a saída?** | *Excuse me, please, where is the exit?* |
|---|---|

**Pode me fazer um favor?** (literally, *Can you do me a favour?*) is applicable when in English you would say *Can you help me?*

Both **desculpe** and **perdão** are an apology.

▶ Say **desculpe** instead of **por favor** or **faz (o) favor** to draw someone's attention or to precede a request, when you feel that you are inconveniencing the person.

| **Desculpe, pode me dizer onde são os telefones?** | *Sorry to trouble you, can you please tell me where the telephones are?* |
|---|---|

(You have, for example, interrupted someone's conversation to ask your question.)

► Say **perdão** or **desculpe** when in English you would say sorry to apologize:

**Perdão!** or **Desculpe!**          *Sorry!*

(You have, for example, bumped into someone.)

**Obrigado** or **obrigada** *thank you* (literally, *obliged, grateful*) is understood as *I am grateful to you*. (For the different ending **-o/-a**, please see Unit 2, How it works, a). **Muito obrigado** or **muito obrigada**, i.e., *much obliged,* corresponds to *Thank you very much*. **(Muito) agradecido** or **(Muito) agradecida** are alternatives with the same meaning.

**b Pardon?**

**Como?** is the abridged version of **Como disse?** or **Como é?** (lit. *How did you say?* or *How is it?*). This is what you say when you cannot understand, as *Pardon?* in English.

When someone speaks too fast for you, you can also add **mais devagar** to a **'favor'** expression as an easy way of asking the person to speak more slowly.

**Mais devagar, por favor.**          *More slowly, please.*

If you feel you need to apologize, you can always add **Desculpe** or **Perdão**.

**Como? Desculpe. Mais devagar,**  *Pardon? More slowly, please.*
  **por favor.**
**Como? Perdão. Mais devagar,**   *Pardon? More slowly, please.*
  **por favor.**

## How it works

**a Gender**
In Portuguese nouns are either masculine or feminine.

| masculine | feminine |
|---|---|
| **o homem** *(the man)* | **a mulher** *(the woman)* |
| **o banco** *(the bank)* | **a saída** *(the exit)* |
| **o câmbio** *(the foreign exchange)* | **a alfândega** *(the customs)* |

How can you tell whether a noun is masculine or feminine?

▶ By the meaning: masculine for male beings, feminine for female beings.
▶ By the ending: a noun ending in -o is likely to be masculine; a noun ending in -a is likely to be feminine, as also are nouns ending in -**gem**; -**dade**; -**tude**; -**ão** (when in the translation of the word the ending corresponds to the English -*ion*):

**a viagem** (*the journey*); **a verdade** (the truth); **a juventude** (*youth, the youth* (of the country)); **a estação** (*the station*).

There are, however, exceptions – e.g. o dia (*the day*), -**a** but masculine – and the only sure way of knowing the gender is to learn each noun with its definite article (its word for *the*) which will be either **o** or **a**:

> ## Insight
> the          the
> o homem – **a** mulher
> o banco – **a** saída
> o dia – **a** estação

o before a noun shows that it is masculine.
a before a noun shows that it is feminine.

Always memorize a new noun with the **o** or **a** before it. In the vocabulary lists at the end of the book, (m.) after a noun means that it takes an **o**, (f.) that it takes an **a**.

Adjectives, and some other words when used as an adjective, are also masculine or feminine. This explains why:

▶ you should say b**om** dia (m.) for *good morning* (*good day*) but b**oa** noite (f.) for *good evening / good night*.

▶ for *thank you* you should say **obrigado** if you are a male but **obrigada** if you are a female.

**Muito obrigado pela sua hospitalidade.** *Thank you very much for your hospitality.* (John talking to Janet)

## b 'The'

The definite article (*the*) agrees with the noun in both gender (masculine or feminine) and number (singular or plural). In English we have only *the* but in Portuguese there is **o** (m.), **os** (m. plural) and **a** (f.), **as** (f. plural).

**o** homem, **os** homens    *the man, the men*
**a** saída, **as** saídas    *the exit, the exits*

Note that Portuguese **a** does not mean the same as English *a/an* but corresponds to *the*.

## c De: saying 'of' and 'from'

**De** can often be translated by the English prepositions *of* and *from*:

em frente **do** (= de + o) banco    (lit. *in front of the bank*) *opposite the bank*
longe **do** (= de + o) aeroporto    *far from the airport*

**De** is often used to link a noun to another word (noun or other) which adds some meaning to the first noun:

a bagagem **de** mão
the baggage of hand

the hand baggage

o depósito de bagagem (*left luggage lockers / office*), o bilhete de passagem (*travel ticket*), o cartão de embarque (*boarding card*), a porta (Eur.) / o portão (Br.) de embarque (*boarding gate*), a carta de condução (Eur.) / a carteira de motorista (Br.) (*driving licence*)

## Insight

*opposite*
em frente de ...
em frente do banco
*far from*
longe de ...
longe do aeroporto
*hand baggage*
a bagagem de ...
a bagagem de mão

### d Contracted words

Some prepositions contract and combine with the definite article:

| | | | | |
|---|---|---|---|---|
| de + o | → do | de + a → da | *of / from the* |
| a + o | → ao | a + a → à | *to / at / on the* |
| em + o | → no | em + a → na | *in / on the* |

O hotel é **na** rua a seguir **à** estação, **no** centro **da** cidade.

*The hotel is on the road past the station, in the town centre.*

Note the following:

▶ The Portuguese word **no** does not translate English *no*.

## Insight

*Not no!*
**no** correio
**no** centro da cidade
**na** rua à esquerda

▶ Portuguese **a** as a preposition can translate English *for* and/or *to*, e.g., the Customs sign **'Nada a declarar'** (lit. *nothing + for + to declare*) for *Nothing to declare*.

## Insight
**a** saída
*the exit*
nada **a** declarar
*nothing to declare*

### e Plurals
Nouns, adjectives and some other words, when used as an adjective, follow the same basic rules.

Words ending with a vowel add -s in the plural:
telefone (*telephone*); telefones (*telephones*)

But note that some -ão endings (often corresponding to -*ion* in English) change to -ões:
estação (*station*); estações (*stations*)

Words ending in a consonant other than -m or -l add -es:
mulher (*woman*); mulheres (*women*)

Words ending in -m substitute -ns:
homem (*man*); homens (*men*)

Words ending in -al substitute -ais:
hospital (*hospital*); hospitais (*hospitals*)

### f Pode me dizer? *or* Pode dizer-me?

In principle the object pronoun (*me*, etc.) follows the second verb, that is, the verb it directly depends on (*tell*, etc.).

**Pode dizer-me…?** *Can you tell me…?*
**Pode fazer-me um favor?** *Can you do me a favour?*

However, particularly in the spoken language, this order tends to be reversed.

**Pode me dizer...?** *Can you tell me...?*
**Pode me fazer um favor?** *Can you do me a favour?*

---

## Exercises

### 2.3

◄) CD1, TR 9

You will hear five short dialogues in which the following places are mentioned.

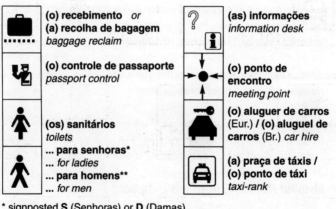

| | |
|---|---|
| **(o) recebimento** *or* **(a) recolha de bagagem** *baggage reclaim* | **(as) informações** *information desk* |
| **(o) controle de passaporte** *passport control* | **(o) ponto de encontro** *meeting point* |
| **(os) sanitários** *toilets* **... para senhoras\*** *... for ladies* **... para homens\*\*** *... for men* | **(o) aluguer de carros** (Eur.) / **(o) aluguel de carros** (Br.) *car hire* |
| | **(a) praça de táxis /** **(o) ponto de táxi** *taxi-rank* |

\* signposted **S** (Senhoras) or **D** (Damas)
\*\* signposted **H** (Homens) or **C** (Cavalheiros)

**2.3.1** In these dialogues people are asking the way and being given directions. Listen to what they say and look at the pictures opposite. Tick two boxes that will take each person to the place he or she is looking for. The first one has been done for you.

**i** A recolha de bagagem:

 A ✓   B ✓   C

**ii** As informações:

 A   B  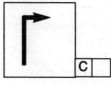 C

**iii** Os sanitários para senhoras:

 A   B  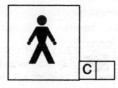 C

**iv** O aluguer (Eur.) de carros:

A  B  C

**v** A praça de táxis:

A  B  C

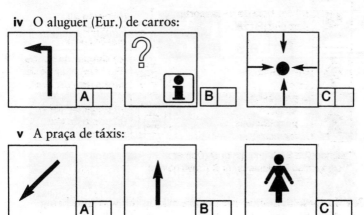

**2.3.2** Now listen again to the dialogues and write them down.

**2.4**

**2.4.1** Ask where the following is:

**a** the chemist's **b** the bank **c** the information desk **d** the men's toilets

**2.4.2** If you didn't quite catch what you were being told, what would you say to seek clarification?

**2.4.3** What would you say to thank for the help received?

**2.5**

◀) CD1, TR 10

It is your turn to help others. You are going to hear some people asking the way. Look at the notices and give the appropriate directions. But first listen to the example.

Example:

Your turn now:

i Partidas Internacionais, ii Partidas Domésticas

**2.6**

◆ CD1, TR 11

**(o) câmbio de divisas** *foreign currency exchange*

A woman is asking for the foreign exchange bureau. Listen to her on your recording and rearrange the words below so as to match what she is saying.

Por favor, / o câmbio? / onde / pode / é / me / dizer

**2.7**

◆ CD1, TR 12

You have overheard someone asking for Internet facilities:

Por favor, onde posso encontrar acesso à Internet?

Now rearrange the words below so as to ask for e-mail facilities.

Por favor, / email? / onde / posso / acesso a / encontrar

---

## Summary

1 Por favor – Desculpe
2 Onde é a saída / a entrada / o correio / o depósito de bagagem?
  Onde são os telefones / os sanitários / as informações?
3 Por favor, pode me dizer onde é a saída / a entrada /
  o correio / o depósito de bagagem?
  Por favor, pode me dizer onde são os telefones / os sanitários /
  as informações?
4 Por favor, onde posso encontrar telefones / táxis / acesso à
  Internet?

**5** em frente
à direita / esquerda
**6** lá em cima
lá em baixo /, embaixo (Br.)
**7** em frente do banco / da farmácia
a seguir ao banco / à farmácia *or* depois do banco /
da farmácia
antes do banco / da farmácia
**8** Como? – Mais devagar, por favor
**9** Desculpe! / Perdão!
**10** (Muito) obrigado – obrigada
De nada

# 3

# Ida e volta, por favor
## A return ticket, please

In this unit you will learn how to
- *Buy travel tickets*
- *Understand simple public notices*
- *Ask for what you need on arrival*

**Para o Porto** *To Oporto*

Clara is in a Portuguese railway station buying a ticket to Porto.

🔊 CD1, TR 13

| | |
|---|---|
| **Clara** | Queria um bilhete para o Porto. |
| **Empregado** | Ida e volta? |
| **Clara** | Sim, ida e volta, por favor. |

**Para São Paulo** *To São Paulo*

Beatriz is in a Brazilian railway station buying a ticket to São Paulo.

| | |
|---|---|
| **Beatriz** | Queria uma passagem para São Paulo. |
| **Empregado** | Ida e volta? |
| **Beatriz** | Não, somente ida, por favor. |

**queria** *I would like* (lit. *(I) wanted*)
**um bilhete para** (Eur.) *a/one ticket to*
**(a) ida e volta** *return* (lit. *way there and back*)
**(a) ida** *single*
**sim** *yes*
**uma passagem para** (Br.) *a/one fare to*
**não** *no*
**somente** *only*

### Para Coimbra *To Coimbra*

Alice is in a Portuguese coach station buying tickets to Coimbra.

| | |
|---|---|
| **Alice** | Queria dois bilhetes de ida para Coimbra. |
| **Empregado** | Como? Quantos? |
| **Alice** | Dois, faz favor. |

### Para o Rio *To Rio*

Rosana is in a Brazilian coach station buying tickets to Rio de Janeiro.

| | |
|---|---|
| **Rosana** | Queria duas passagens para o Rio, ida e volta. |
| **Empregado** | Como? Para onde? |
| **Rosana** | Para o Rio de Janeiro. |
| **Empregado** | Para hoje ou reserva? |
| **Rosana** | Como? Desculpe. Faça o favor de falar mais devagar. |
| **Empregado** | Para hoje… ou… reserva? |
| **Rosana** | Para hoje, por favor. |

**dois bilhetes** (Eur.) *two tickets*
**quantos?** *how many?*
**duas passagens** (Br.) *two fares*
**para onde?** *where to?* (lit. *to where*)

**para hoje** *for today*
**ou** *or*
**(a) reserva** *reservation*
**faça o favor de falar** *would you please speak* (more lit. *would (you) do the favour of + to speak*)

---

## Exercises

### 3.1 Certo ou errado? *Right or wrong?*

|                                         | C | E |
|-----------------------------------------|---|---|
| **1** Para o Porto é ida e volta.       | ☐ | ☐ |
| **2** Para Coimbra são dois bilhetes.   | ☐ | ☐ |
| **3** Para São Paulo são duas passagens.| ☐ | ☐ |

### 3.2 Perguntas e respostas *Questions and answers*

**1** Quantos são os bilhetes para o Porto?
   **a** Um.  **b** Dois.

**2** Como são os bilhetes para Coimbra?
   **a** De ida.  **b** De ida e volta.

**3** Quantas e como são as passagens para o Rio?
   **a** Uma de ida e volta.   **c** Duas de ida e volta
   **b** Duas de ida.

---

## How to pronounce it

◄) **CD1, TR 14**

Say the English word *anchor* and see how you use the back of your mouth to obtain the *an* sound. Then practise these sounds with your recording.

**vowel + -n:**

banco; centro; frente; cinco (*five*); cinto (*belt*); onde; longe; ponto; encontro.

**vowel + -m:**

bem; sem (*without*); viagem; bagagem; passagem; sim; fim (*end*); simples (*simple, single*); bom; com (*with*); um.

## Expressions
**a Queria** *I'd like*

By adding different words to **Queria** (*I would like*), you can ask for whatever you may first need, be it a train ticket or a cup of coffee.

| | |
|---|---|
| **Queria um bilhete para o Porto.** | *I would like a ticket to Oporto.* |
| **Queria uma passagem para São Paulo.** | *I would like a fare to São Paulo.* |
| **Queria um café.** | *I would like a coffee.* |

An even easier way of asking for something, when you expect it to be available, is just to say **Um** _____ or **Uma** _____ , accompanied by a **'favor'** expression.

| | |
|---|---|
| **Um bilhete para o Porto, por favor.** | *Please, … a ticket to Oporto.* |
| **Por favor, uma passagem para São Paulo.** | *a fare to São Paulo.* |
| **Um café, por favor / faz favor (Eur.).** | *a coffee.* |
| **A conta, por favor / faz favor (Eur.).** | *the bill.* |

Similarly, when you take a taxi, you can tell the driver **Queria ir para** (*…to go to*) _____ , or simply **Para** _____ , adding where you want to go to, please.

| | |
|---|---|
| **Para o Hotel Sol-Mar, por favor.** | *To the Hotel Sol-Mar, please.* |

### b O bilhete de passagem *The travel ticket*

When purchasing **um bilhete de passagem**, *a travel ticket*, the Portuguese prefer asking for a ticket (**um bilhete**) and the Brazilians for a fare (**uma passagem**). In both cases, the word for ticket or fare can be omitted and often the whole sentence is shortened.

|  | *Please …* |
|---|---|
| **Um de ida para o Porto, por favor.** | *one single to Oporto.* |
| **Um, ida, para o Porto, faz favor** (Eur.). | *one single to Oporto.* |
| **Por favor três, ida e volta, para o Rio.** | *three returns to Rio.* |

In some areas the word simples is also used for a single ticket.

|  | *Please …* |
|---|---|
| **Por favor, um, simples, para Cascais.** | *one single to Cascais.* |

### c empregado ou funcionário?

For practical purposes, in this course the ticket clerk and other individuals in the services sector are referred to as **(o) empregado**. Where a state-owned company is implied, the term **(o) funcionário** is also applicable, i.e., '**(o) empregado do Estado**'. The respective feminine forms are **(a) empregada** and **(a) funcionária**.

## Cultural information
### a Favor *Favour*

In addition to **por favor** and **faz (o) favor**, there are **faz o favor de** and **faça o favor de**. Common to all is the word **favor** (*favour*). Except for **por favor**, they also all share a form of **fazer** (*to do*).

**Faça o favor de** is an elegant alternative version of **faz o favor de**.

| | |
|---|---|
| **Faça o favor de falar mais devagar.** | *Would you please speak more slowly? or, more freely translated, Could you please speak slowly?* |
| **Faça o favor de me dar um mapa.** | *Could you please give me a map?* |
| **Faça o favor de chamar um táxi para mim.** | *Could you please send for a taxi for me?* |
| or | |
| **Faça o favor de me chamar um táxi.** | |

**Faça o favor de...** can also be used in public notices. A more impersonal but still courteous alternative is **É favor...** (lit. *it is (a) favour...*).

**É favor esperar aqui.** for *Please wait here.*

**b Importa-se...?** *Can / could you please...?*

This is an alternative to the **'favor'** expressions. Literally translated, it corresponds to *do you mind...?* but it corresponds to a polite approach as conveyed by *can / could you please... / would you kindly...?* when asking for something.

| | *Can / could you please ...* |
|---|---|
| **Importa-se de repetir?** | *... say that again.* |
| **Importa-se de falar mais devagar?** | *... speak more slowly.* |
| **Importa-se de me dar um café com leite e açúcar?** | *... get me a milky coffee with sugar.* |

## How it works

### a Oporto and Rio de Janeiro

English *Oporto* is, in fact, the Portuguese definite article – **o** – and the name of the Portuguese city – **Porto** – put together into one word. Indeed, the definite article is used with the name of a number of cities.

| | |
|---|---|
| **Queria um bilhete para o Porto.** | *I would like a ticket to Oporto.* |
| **Queria duas passagens para o Rio.** | *I would like two fares to Rio.* |

This tendency applies to the name of countries and place-names where the name (or part of it) is recognizable as a common noun with an existence of its own.

| | |
|---|---|
| **Queria três para a Madeira.** | *I would like three (tickets) to Madeira.* |

(**porto, rio, madeira**, *port, river, wood,* respectively)

## b 'A / an'

For the indefinite article, in English we have *a* (or *an*), but in Portuguese we have **um** (m.) or **uma** (f.), as it agrees with the noun (masculine or feminine).

**um homem** *a man*       **uma saída** *an exit*

Also **uns** or **umas**, which translates *some / any* in the sense of *a certain number* or *a certain quantity*, and *a certain* (= *specific*).

**uns amigos, umas amigas**   *some / a few friends*

## c Numbers 1 to 10

| | | | | |
|---|---|---|---|---|
| **1** um / uma | **3** três | **5** cinco | **7** sete | **9** nove |
| **2** dois / duas | **4** quatro | **6** seis | **8** oito | **10** dez |

Note the following:

▶ there is a masculine and a feminine form for *one* and *two*: **um / uma** and **dois / duas**.
**um** bilhete *one ticket*       **duas** passagens *two fares*

▶ **um / uma** can translate both the indefinite article (*a* or *an*) and the numeral *one*.
**um** bilhete *a ticket*       **um** bilhete *one ticket*

## Insight

*a ticket – a fare*
**um bilhete – uma passagem**
*one ticket – one fare*
**um bilhete – uma passagem**

*two tickets – two fares*
**dois bilhetes – duas passagens**
*three tickets – three fares*
**três bilhetes – três passagens**

### d Plurals

A few words (nouns and adjectives) end in -s in the singular and sound like a plural. They do not change.

**cais; cais** *quay* **simples; simples** *simple, single*

In the sequence noun + **de** + noun or other word, only the first element takes a plural ending.

**bilhete de passagem; bilhetes de passagem** *travel ticket; travel tickets*
**fim de semana; fins de semana** *weekend; weekends*

### e Verbs: the three conjugations

**-ar, -er, -ir**
All Portuguese verbs have one of the three infinitive endings above, with the exception of the verb **pôr** *(to put)* and its compounds, e.g., **compor** *(to compose)*, **supor** *(to assume)*. You do not need to use the accent (^) with the compounds.

Some verbs have anomalous forms, but most fall into one of three conjugation patterns according to their infinitive endings. Below are three regular verbs which will give you the model endings for the three conjugations throughout this course:

|  | **Infinitive** |  |
|---|---|---|
| comp**rar** *(to buy)* | vend**er** *(to sell)* | part**ir** *(to leave)* |
|  | **Past participle** |  |
| comp**rado** *(bought)* | vend**ido** *(sold)* | part**ido** *(left)* |

e.g.   $\boxed{\text{Vendido}}$   for a   $\boxed{\textit{Sold}}$   notice

For verbs with anomalous forms see the **Verb guide** at the back of the book. Always check a new verb against these notes.

**Infinitives** are often used in public notices and instructions as well as in a variety of other messages directed at the general public.

Some examples:

On a door:

**Empurrar** (lit. *to push*) for *Push* or **Puxar** (lit. *to pull*) for *Pull*.

On a machine dispensing travel tickets, chocolates or drinks:

**Colocar as moedas** *place the coins.*

**Introduzir as moedas** (lit. *to introduce + the coins*) for *Insert the coins.*

On a cash dispenser / cashpoint:

**Introduzir o cartão** for *Insert your card.*

**Digitar o número** for *Key in your number.*

On a food packet:

**Consumir antes de** (lit. *to consume + before + of*) meaning *Use by* followed by a date.

In a telephone booth, depending on the country you are in:

**Introduzir o cartão** *Insert the telephone credit card* or

**Depositar uma ou mais fichas** (lit. *to deposit…*) for *Insert one or more phone tokens.*

On a mobile phone:

**Ler** (lit. *to read*), **Enviar** (lit. *to send*), for, respectively, *Read and Send a text message.*

Facing your aircraft seat:

**Não fumar** (lit. not to smoke) and **Apertar cintos** (lit. to fasten belts), for, respectively, *No smoking* and *Fasten your seatbelt.*

Note that there are two ways of wording, say, a *No smoking* sign: **Não fumar**, presented as an instruction, and **É proibido fumar**, presented as a prohibition. Past participles are also often used, as, e.g., **proibido** in **É proibido fumar.**

## Insight

*What to do or… not*
Empurr**ar** ↔ Pux**ar**
Apert**ar** cintos
Não fum**ar**
É proibido fum**ar**
É favor esper**ar** aqui

---

## Exercises

### 3.3

Work out what the following public notices and signs mean. You saw 1–3 on different doors; 4–5 at the railway station; 6–7 as you were travelling along the road; 8 in a restaurant; and 9 above a litter-bin in a public park.

In order to best work out their meaning, convert the past participles into their infinitives (e.g., **fechado > fechar**). When you have done so, look up the obtained word in the vocabulary at the end of the book.

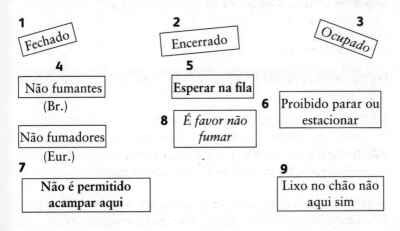

**1**
Fechado

**2**
Encerrado

**3**
Ocupado

**4**
Não fumantes
(Br.)

Não fumadores
(Eur.)

**5**
Esperar na fila

**8**
*É favor não fumar*

**6**
Proibido parar ou estacionar

**7**
Não é permitido acampar aqui

**9**
Lixo no chão não aqui sim

**3.4**

You will hear a number of people asking for various things.

**3.4.1** Number the boxes in the order of what you hear. The first one you hear has been done for you.

| i | um mapa *a map* | |
|---|---|---|
| ii | dois cafés *two coffees* | 1 |
| iii | quatro sandes (Eur.) / sanduíches *four sandwiches* | |
| iv | papel de carta e uma caneta *writing paper and a pen* | |
| v | um penso adesivo (Eur.) / esparadrapo (Br.) *a sticking plaster* | |
| vi | alguma coisa para dor de cabeça *something for a headache* | |
| vii | alguma coisa para indigestão *something for indigestion* | |
| viii | alguma coisa para queimadura de *sol something for sunburn* | |

**3.4.2** Listen again to the different requests and write them down. Then take these people's place and ask for the same things as they did.

**3.5**

You will hear different people buying train, coach, ferry and air tickets.

**3.5.1** Complete and tick the boxes according to how many tickets they want and whether these are single or return fares. The first line has been done for you.

|       | Quantos bilhetes? (Eur.)/ Quantas passagens? (Br.) | Para onde?     | Ida/ Simples | Ida e volta |
| ----- | -------------------------------------------------- | -------------- | ------------ | ----------- |
| i     | *três*                                             | Faro           | ✓            |             |
| ii    |                                                    | Porto          |              |             |
| iii   |                                                    | Cacilhas       |              |             |
| iv    |                                                    | Estoril        |              |             |
| v     |                                                    | Manaus         |              |             |
| vi    |                                                    | Belo Horizonte |              |             |
| vii   |                                                    | Rio            |              |             |
| viii  |                                                    | Salvador       |              |             |

**3.5.2** Listen again to the recording and repeat what you hear.

**3.5.3** Now buy these tickets:

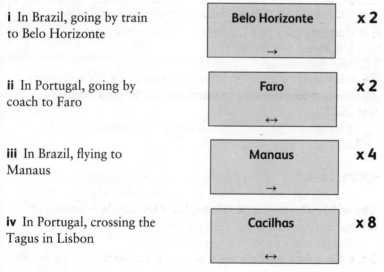

**i** In Brazil, going by train to Belo Horizonte

Belo Horizonte → x 2

**ii** In Portugal, going by coach to Faro

Faro ↔ x 2

**iii** In Brazil, flying to Manaus

Manaus → x 4

**iv** In Portugal, crossing the Tagus in Lisbon

Cacilhas ↔ x 8

## 3.6

**3.6.1** Rearrange the words below so as to ask whether:

**i** you can have the telephone directory – (a) **lista dos telefones**
Pode / a lista / me / dos telefones? / dar

**ii** you can be put through – **ligar** – to 'this number'– **este número**
Pode / para / este número? / me / ligar

◀)) CD1, TR 17

**3.6.2** Listen to the two voices on your recording and find out:

**i** the telephone booth – (a) **cabine** – you are being directed to for your call – (a) **chamada** – at the post office.

**ii** the cashdesk – (a) **caixa** – you are being directed to when cashing traveller's cheques – (os) **cheques de viagem** – at the bank.

---

## Summary

**1** Por favor, um (bilhete) / uma (passagem) para *(your destination)*.
Um mapa, por favor.

**2** Ida – Ida e volta

**3** Sim – Não

**4** Para o Hotel Sol-Mar / o aeroporto / a estação / o hospital, por favor.

**5** Empurrar – Puxar – Apertar cintos – Não fumar

**6** Fechado – Ocupado
É proibido fumar

**7** Queria três / quatro / cinco para (*your destination*).
Queria um café / mapa / ir para o Hotel Sol-Mar.

**8** Pode me dar um café / mapa?
Importa-se de me dar um café / mapa?
Faça o favor de me dar um café / mapa.

**9** Pode me chamar um táxi?
Importa-se de me chamar um táxi?
Faça o favor de me chamar um táxi

**10** Pode falar mais devagar / repetir?
Importa-se de falar mais devagar / repetir?
Faça o favor de falar mais devagar / repetir.

# 4

# Um quarto simples ou duplo?
A single or double room?

In this unit you will learn how to
- **Book in at a hotel**
- **Find your way around town**
- **Locate shops and services**

**Na estação** *In the station*

Maria goes to the information desk to look for a hotel.

CD1, TR 18

| | |
|---|---|
| **Maria** | Por favor, pode me dizer onde fica o hotel mais próximo? |
| **Empregado** | O hotel mais próximo fica na primeira rua à esquerda a seguir à estação. É o Hotel Central. |
| **Maria** | É longe? |
| **Empregado** | Não, não é. Fica perto, a uns dez minutos a pé. |
| **Maria** | Muito obrigada. Bom dia. |
| **Empregado** | Não tem de quê. Bom dia. |

QUICK VOCAB

**fica** *is, (it) is (alternative to* **é** *for location)*
**o hotel mais próximo** *the nearest hotel (lit. the hotel most near)*
**(a) primeira rua** *first street*
**é longe?** *is (it) far?*
**não, não é** *no, (it) is not*
**perto** *near, nearby*
**a uns dez minutos** *about ten minutes (lit. at some ten minutes)*

**a pé** *on foot, walking*
**não tem de quê** *(alt. to **de nada**)*

### Na recepção do Hotel Central *In the reception of the Hotel Central*

Maria is at the reception desk at the Hotel Central asking for a room.

CD1, TR 19

| | |
|---|---|
| **Maria** | Tem quartos vagos? Queria um quarto simples, para uma noite. |
| **Empregada** | *(checking)* Um momento. Vago somente quarto duplo, com cama dupla. |
| **Maria** | Duplo… Pode me mostrar o quarto? |
| **Empregada** | Claro! Fica lá em cima no segundo andar. A escada é à direita e o elevador é a seguir. Com licença… *(stepping in front of Maria to lead the way).* |
| **Maria** | *(after viewing the room)* Está bem. Fico com o quarto. *(back in reception)* |
| **Empregada** | Tem um documento de identidade? *(Maria produces her passport.)* Faça o favor de assinar. *(Maria signs the registration form.)* Obrigado. Aqui está a chave do quarto. |

**QUICK VOCAB**

**(a) recepção** or **receção** *reception*
**tem…?** *have (you), has (it)?*
**(o) quarto vago** *vacant room*
**simples, duplo** *single, double*
**um momento** *just a moment (please)*
**(a) cama dupla** *double bed*
**mostrar** *(to) show*
**claro** *of course*
**(o) segundo andar** *second floor*
**a escada** *the stairs, staircase*
**o elevador** *the lift*
**com licença** *excuse me*
**está bem** *it's all right, Ok*
**fico com** *I'll have* (lit. *(I) have*)

**um documento de identidade** *an identification document*
**assinar** *to sign*
**aqui está** *here (it) is*
**a chave** *the key*

## Exercises

### 4.1 Certo ou errado? *Right or wrong?*

|   | C | E |
|---|---|---|
| **1** O hotel é longe. | ☐ | ☐ |
| **2** O hotel tem um quarto vago. | ☐ | ☐ |
| **3** O quarto tem cama dupla. | ☐ | ☐ |

### 4.2 Perguntas e respostas *Questions and answers*

**1** Onde fica o hotel?
    **a** Na primeira à direita a seguir à estação.
    **b** Na primeira à esquerda a seguir à estação.

**2** Onde fica o quarto duplo?
    **a** Lá em baixo (Eur.)/embaixo (Br.).
    **b** Lá em cima no primeiro andar.
    **c** Lá em cima no segundo andar.

**3** Onde é o elevador?
    **a** Longe da escada. **b** Perto da escada.

## How to pronounce it

🔊 **CD1, TR 20**

Below are some sounds for you to pronounce after the speaker on the recording. They are diphthongs, in other words, sounds such as in the English word *coin* where you begin with one vowel (*o*) but move towards another (*i*).

| | | |
|---|---|---|
| **-ai-:** mais. | **-au-:** automóvel. | **-ei-:** direita; chuveiro. |
| **-eu-:** meu; museu. | **-oi-:** dois; noite. | **-ou-:** ou. |
| | **-ui-:** muito. | |

In 'praia' the diphthong -ai- is followed by the usual ending -a.

Note that there are vowel sequences which are not diphthongs. Instead each vowel is pronounced separately. Practise the following:

**dia** (=di+a); **boa** (=bo+a); **duas** (=du+as); **saída** (sa+í+da) (in saída the accent over the i is used to 'undo' the diphthong -ai-).

## Expressions
### Somewhere to stay

There is a wide range of options as regards where to stay. These include *hotel* (**o hotel**), *boarding house* (**a pensão**), *motel* (**o motel**), *inn* (**a pousada** or **a estalagem** or **a albergaria**), *youth hostel* or *students' hostel* (**o albergue da juventude** or **o lar de estudantes**), *camping / caravanning complex* (**o parque de campismo** (Eur.) or **a aldeia de campistas** (Eur.) or **o camping** (Br.)). Or you may opt for a small holiday house advertised under names such as **a vila** or **o chalé**.

You may wish to have a *double room* (**um quarto duplo** or **um quarto de casal**) with *double bed* (**com cama dupla** or **com cama de casal**) or *twin beds* (**com duas camas** or **com camas individuais**). You may want instead a single room (**um quarto simples** or **um quarto individual** or **um quarto de solteiro** or **um quarto para uma pessoa**). In some cases, **o quarto** may not be expected to include a private bathroom, but **o apartamento**, or *a suite,* will. By **apartamento** / *suite* a wide meaning is covered which can range from a hotel room with en-suite bathroom and, in some cases, a kitchenette (**uma pequena cozinha**) to a bedsitter or small flat.

To ask for private bathroom facilities, you can just say **com banho**. If you wish to be more specific, say **com chuveiro** or **com duche / ducha** (Br.) to ask for *a shower,* and **com banheira** to ask for a bathtub. **A casa de banho** (Eur.) / **o banheiro** (Br.) is the *bathroom*. This name is also used euphemistically as an alternative word to **o sanitário** when referring to the *toilet,* a term equally used as **o toilete** (Eur.) or **o toalete** (Br.). 'Facilities for the disabled' finds its translation in **(as) instalações** or **(as) facilidades para deficientes físicos**.

**A diária** is the daily cost of your stay at a hotel. Options usually available include bed and breakfast – **dormida e pequeno-almoço** (Eur.) / **pernoite e café da manhã** (Br.) – half-board – **meia pensão** – and *full-board* – **pensão completa**.

## Insight
**Onde fica o hotel mais próximo?**
**Onde fica a pousada mais próxima?**

------------------------

**É perto?**
**É longe?**

## Cultural information
**a Queria...** *I'd like...* **Pode...** *Can you...* **Faça o favor de...** *Would you please...*

You have come across these three different approaches to asking for something. Although often they are interchangeable, they also play specific roles. The following guidelines will help you select which to use:

**Queria...** (*I would like...*), puts the focus on you, the person who is making the request.

*(Contd)*

**Queria um quarto duplo.**    *I would like a double room.*

**Pode... ?** (*Can you... ?*), **Faça o favor de...** and **Importa-se de...** (*Would you please... / Would you kindly... / Could you please...*) put the focus on the person who is being asked to help. **Pode... ?** (*Can you... ?*) is better reserved for cases when you are enquiring about possibility rather than willingness.

| | |
|---|---|
| **Pode me dar um quarto duplo?** | *May I have a double room? (Can you give me a double room?)* – is better for making an enquiry. (is it possible / available?). |
| **Faça o favor de me dar um quarto duplo.** | *May I have a double room? (Would you kindly give me a double room?)* – is better for making a request. |
| **Importa-se de me dar um quarto duplo?** | *May I have a double room? (Would you kindly give me a double room?)* – is better for making a request. |

## Insight

**Pode me dar um quarto individual?**

----------

**Faça o favor de me dar um quarto individual.**
**Importa-se de me dar um um quarto individual?**

**b Com licença** *With (your) permission*

**Com licença** means, literally, *with (your) permission*. Use this expression when in English you would say *Excuse me* to accompany an action, for example, when you need someone to step back for you to get through the door or a queue of people or when you are trying to get out of a crowded train or bus.

## How it works

**a Quarto vago; bom dia** *Room empty; good morning*

**Word order**
Noun + adjective is the usual word-order.

**quarto vago**
*room    vacant*

*vacant room*

This applies to adjectives and adjective-like words such as past participles used adjectivally, as in the following 'no entry' sign:

**entrada proibida** *no entry* (lit. *entry prohibited*)

However, adjective + noun is the word-order when the adjective, or adjective-like word, is used in a less literal and/or more emotive sense.

**pequeno-almoço** (Eur.) i.e., *small lunch, for breakfast*

**bom dia!** *good morning!*

The latter word-order also applies for ordinal numbers.

**segundo andar** *second floor*; **primeira rua** *first road, street*

**Agreement**
Adjectives, adjective-like words and ordinals must agree with their noun in both gender (masculine or feminine) and number (singular or plural).

| | |
|---|---|
| *Fem. pl.* entrad**as** proibid**as** | *Masc. sing.* pequen**o**-almoç**o** (Eur.) |
| *Fem. sing.* primeir**a** ru**a** | segund**o** andar |
| *Masc. pl.* quart**os** vag**os** | b**om** dia |

### b 'Not' and 'no'

To make the verb negative, i.e., 'not', say **não** before the verb.

O hotel **não** é longe.　　　*The hotel is not far.*

Note that **não** can translate both *no* and *not*.

**Não,** o hotel **não** é longe.　　*No, the hotel is not far.*

More than one element of negation can be present in the same sentence. This is the practice when **nada** (*nothing*), **nenhum** (*none*) or **ninguém** (*no one*) comes after the verb. For example, you use a double negative when you tell the customs officer that you have nothing to declare: **Não** tenho **nada** a declarar.

### c 'Ping-pong' replies

**Sim** translates *yes*. However, in a yes reply, the main verb of the question tends to be bounced back instead. This is known as the reiterative reply. **Sim** may follow, or precede, the reiteration but is often omitted.

Question: **É** longe?　　　　　　　　　　*Is it far?*
Reply: **É.**　*or*　**É,** sim.　*or*　Sim, **é.**　　*Yes, it is.*

In a *no* reply, there is a tendency to add the verb, in the negative.

Question: **É** longe?                 *Is it far?*
Reply:    **Não, não é.**              *No, it isn't.*

**d É – fica – está:** *How to say 'is'*

Use é, *(it) is,* for location of non-movables.

O hotel **é** na primeira rua à      *The hotel is in the first road on*
  esquerda.                          *the left.*

Use **está**, *(it) is*, for something that can change easily as is the case
with the location of movables.

Aqui **está** a chave.               *Here is the key (your key).*

**Fica** can be used as an alternative to **é** above:

O hotel **fica** na primeira rua à   *The hotel is in the first road on the*
  esquerda.                          *left.*

The plural of **é, fica** and **está** is, respectively, **são, ficam** and **estão.**

Os hotéis **são / ficam** na         *The hotels are in the first road on*
  primeira rua à direita.            *the right.*
Aqui **estão** as chaves.            *Here are the keys (your keys).*

**Fico com** is used to say that you accept something (an object).

**Fico com** o quarto.               *I'll have / take the room.*

**e Whose is it?**

In English we use *your* more often than Portuguese speakers use its counterpart **seu** (m.) or **sua** (f.).

Aqui está **a** chave.　　　　*Here is your key. (lit., the key)*

Another difference is that in Portuguese the definite article (**o/a**) can be used with *your* and the other possessives: **o seu – a sua** (*your*); **o meu – a minha** (*my*). However, in Brazil it is often omitted in the spoken language.

| | |
|---|---|
| **a minha** mala *or* **minha mala** | *my suitcase* |
| **a sua** mala *or* **sua** mala | *your suitcase* |
| *but* | |
| **a** mala **dele** (= de + ele) | *his suitcase (lit. the suitcase + of + he)* |
| **a** mala **dela** (= de + ela) | *her suitcase (lit. the suitcase + of + she)* |

---

**Insight**

Onde **está** a chave do meu quarto?
Onde **estão** as malas dele?

------------

Onde **é / fica** o meu quarto?
Onde **são / ficam** as lojas mais próximas?

---

## Exercises

**4.3**

◀ **CD1, TR 21**

You will hear some people asking for hotel accommodation.

**4.3.1** Listen to what each one would like and tick the row of pictures it matches. The first one you will hear has been entered for you.

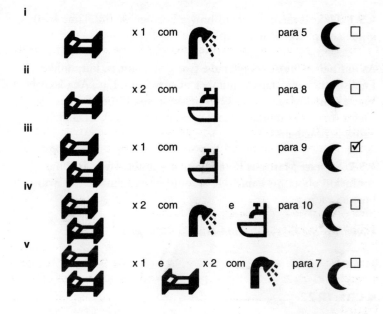

**i** ▢ x 1 com 🚿 para 5 🌙 □

**ii** x 2 com 🚰 para 8 🌙 □

**iii** x 1 com 🚰 para 9 🌙 ☑

**iv** x 2 com 🚿 e 🚰 para 10 🌙 □

**v** x 1 e 🛏 x 2 com 🚿 para 7 🌙 □

**4.3.2** Write down what the five people have said, and read aloud what you have written.

### 4.4

Say that you would like the following:

**a** One single room, with shower, for one night.
**b** A double room, with bathtub, for two nights.
**c** One double room and one single room, with shower and bathtub, for seven nights.
**d** A double room, with shower, for five nights. Add that you would like two beds.

### 4.5 O nome *Your name*

**(o) nome de batismo** *Christian name* or
**(o) nome próprio** (Eur.) **/ (o) prenome** (Br.) *first name, given name*
**(o) nome de família** *family name* or
**(o) apelido** (Eur.) **/ (o) sobrenome** (Br.) *surname*

**4.5.1** Make a mental note of how a Portuguese full name – (o) **nome completo** – is made up.

As in English, most people have two given names, but, unlike English, they may have a number of surnames. E.g., Ana Isabel Vieira Gama Magalhães – given names: Ana Isabel. Surnames: Vieira (from her mother), Gama (from her father), Magalhães (from her husband).

**4.5.2** Stewart Martin is booking in at a hotel. There is some confusion about his name. How could he explain the following in Portuguese?

*Stewart is the first name and Martin is the surname.*

### 4.6

◆) **CD1, TR 22**

You will hear people requesting and giving directions in town.

**4.6.1** Study the map. Then listen to the different people asking the way on your recording. Put a number against the place each one wants to go to.

**(a) estrada** *open road*
**(o) supermercado** *supermarket*
**(as) bombas de gasolina** *petrol pumps*
or
**(o) posto de gasolina** *petrol station*
**(o) restaurante** *restaurant*
**(a) igreja** *church*
**(o) museu** *museum*
**(o) (centro de) turismo** *tourist office*
**(a) paragem de autocarros** (Eur.) /
**(a) parada de ônibus** or **(o) ponto de ônibus** (Br.) *bus stop*
**(a) passagem subterrânea** *subway* (lit. *underground passage*)
**(a) praia** *beach*

**4.6.2** Listen again, repeating each question after the speaker.

**4.6.3** Miguel is equally trying to find his way through town. He is standing where the cross is, facing Rua da República. Below are the directions Miguel has been given.

Write Miguel's question for each direction received, starting with **Por favor, pode me dizer onde...** Then read them aloud.

**atrás (de)** *behind*
**ao lado (de)** *beside*
**no fim (de)** *at the end*
**em frente a = em frente de**

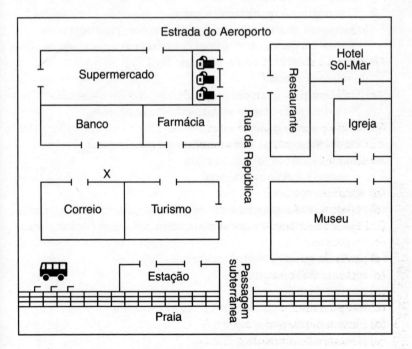

i   É a estrada à esquerda, no fim da Rua da República.
ii  Fica lá em baixo (Eur.) / lá embaixo (Br.), à direita, no fim da Rua da República.

**iii** É à direita, no fim da Rua da República, a seguir à estação.
**iv** Fica em frente do turismo. A entrada é em frente à igreja.
**v** Fica na rua atrás, à esquerda, a seguir ao banco.
**vi** É atrás do correio, ao lado da estação.
**vii** São na Rua da República, à esquerda, a seguir à farmácia e em frente ao restaurante.
**viii** Fica numa rua atrás da igreja.

---

## Summary

**1** Onde fica o hotel mais próximo / o Hotel Sol-Mar?
Fica perto? – É longe?
**2** Tem quartos / apartamentos vagos?
Queria um quarto individual, com chuveiro, para uma noite.
Queria um quarto duplo, com chuveiro, para cinco noites.
**3** o nome próprio (Eu.) / o prenome (Br.)
o nome de família
**4** Onde é o meu quarto?
No primeiro / segundo andar, à direita / esquerda.
**5** Onde é o meu quarto?
Onde está a minha mala / a chave do meu quarto?
**6** (o) meu quarto / (a) minha mala
o quarto / a mala dele – dela
**7** Com licença
**8** Onde é / fica o restaurante mais próximo / a praia mais próxima?
Onde são / ficam os restaurantes mais próximos / as lojas mais próximas?
**9** atrás da igreja
ao lado do supermercado
no fim da rua
na primeira / segunda rua à direita / esquerda
**10** Tem um quarto duplo?
Queria um quarto duplo.
Pode me dar um quarto duplo?
Importa-se de me dar um quarto duplo?
Faça o favor de me dar um quarto duplo.

# 5

**Tem pão e leite?**

Do you stock bread and milk?

In this unit you will learn how to
- **Ask for what you want in a shop**
- **Ask whether what you want is available**
- **Book in at a caravan or camping site**

**Numa loja** *In a shop*

At a convenience store Sandra is asking the sales assistant whether what she is looking for is available.

| | |
|---|---|
| **Sandra** | Por favor, tem pão e leite? |
| **Vendedor** | O pão e o leite estão à esquerda a seguir às frutas. *(Sandra takes her shopping to the checkout.)* |
| **Vendedor** | Uma garrafa de leite, dois pães, meia dúzia de ovos, três maçãs e quatro bananas. Mais alguma coisa? |
| **Sandra** | Queria, sim, mas provavelmente não tem. Queria um guarda-chuva. |
| **Vendedor** | Não, nesta loja não. Mas pode encontrar guarda-chuvas numa das lojas mais perto da cidade. Não ficam longe. |

CD1, TR 23

**estão** *are, (they) are*
**(a) fruta** *fruit*
**uma garrafa de leite** *a/one bottle of milk*

**dois pães** two loaves of bread
**meia dúzia** half a dozen
**(o) ovo** egg
**(a) maçã** apple
**(a) banana** banana
**mais alguma coisa?** anything else? (lit. more + some + thing)
**mas** but
**provavelmente** probably
**(o) guarda-chuva** umbrella
**nesta (= em + esta)** in this
**encontrar** to find
**numa (= em + uma)** in one

## No turismo In the tourist office

Mário is finding out whether the campsite he has been
recommended has a space for his large caravan and family tent.

| Empregada | Este está quase cheio. Não tem vagas para veículos grandes ou barracas, somente para automóveis e tendas. Há outro aqui perto, com vagas, mas não tem piscina. |
|---|---|
| Mário | Não tem importância. Queria uma reserva. (*before leaving*) Desculpe, pode me fazer o favor de indicar o caminho? |
| Empregada | Continuando nesta estrada e virando à direita no segundo semáforo, fica à esquerda. Fica a uns dez minutos daqui, de carro, claro. |

**este** this, this one
**quase cheio** nearly full
**(a) vaga** vacancy
or
**(o) espaço** space
**(o) veículo grande** large vehicle
**(a) barraca** tent, frame tent
**(o) automóvel** automobile, car

**(a) tenda** *tent, ridge or bell tent*
**há...** *there is...*
**outro** *other, another one*
**aqui perto** *nearby (lit. here + near)*
**(a) piscina** *swimming pool*
**não tem importância** *it doesn't matter (lit. not + has + importance)*
**indicar o caminho** *to direct*
**(o) caminho** *way, route*
**continuando** *continuing*
**virando** *turning*
**(o) semáforo** *traffic lights*
**daqui (= de + aqui)** *from here*
**de carro** *by car*

## Exercises

### 5.1 Certo ou errado? *Right or wrong?*

|  | C | E |
|---|---|---|
| **1** Na loja há pão. | ☐ | ☐ |
| **2** O primeiro parque de campismo (Eur.) / camping (Br.) está cheio. | ☐ | ☐ |
| **3** O segundo parque de campismo (Eur.) / camping (Br.) tem piscina. | ☐ | ☐ |

### 5.2 Perguntas e respostas *Questions and answers*

**1** Loja: Tem pão e leite?
  **a** Não, tem somente frutas. **b** Tem, tem pão e leite.

**2** Primeiro parque de campismo (Eur.) / camping (Br.): Tem vagas?
  **a** Não, não tem vagas. **b** Tem, para automóveis e tendas.

**3** Segundo parque de campismo (Eur.) / camping (Br.): Onde fica?
  **a** Fica perto do segundo semáforo.
  **b** Fica nesta estrada, a dez minutos daqui, a pé.

## How to pronounce it

◄❯ CD1, TR 25

Below there are some singular-to-plural sound changes for you to practise following the speaker on the recording. See also the section on plurals in Unit 2 and later in the present unit.

-l to -is:
   hospital → hospitais; hotel → hotéis; automóvel → automóveis; lençol → lençóis.

-o- (say English *o* in *note*) to -o- (say English *o* in *jolly*):
   ovo → ovos; novo → novos; almoço → almoços.

-ão to -ões (revise what you learned about -ão and -ões in Unit 2):
   estação → estações; informação → informações.

-ão to -ães (say *ey* in *they* but through your nose):
   pão → pães.

Note that -ão, -ões and -ães are all nasal diphthongs (revise what you learned about diphthongs in Unit 4).

## Expressions
**a Tem...?** *Do you have...?*

We have been using different ways of asking for something when you can expect it to be available – **queria...**; **faça o favor de me dar...**

If, however, you don't know whether what you want is available, then use one of the following approaches:

**tem...?** *have you got?*
**há...?** *is / are there...?*

which you can precede with **por favor, faz favor** or **desculpe**.

| | |
|---|---|
| **Por favor, tem pão e leite?** | *Excuse me, please, do you stock bread and milk?* |

Similarly,

| | |
|---|---|
| **Faz favor (Eur.), tem vagas?** | *(any hotel rooms / any campsite spaces available?)* |
| **Desculpe, tem sacos de dormir?** | *(sleeping bags?)* |
| **Por favor, tem uma mesa vaga?** | *(a table free?)* |
| **Faz favor, há lojas aqui perto?** or **... perto daqui?** | *(any shops nearby?)* |
| **Por favor, há água potável por aqui?** | *(drinking water hereabouts?)* |

Although **há...? / há...**, (*is there...? / there is...*) is used on both sides of the Atlantic, some Brazilians also use **tem...?** for *have you got...?* in the sense of *has one got...? / is there...?*. Therefore, the question **Tem pão e leite?** may receive the reply **Tenho** (*Yes, (I) have*); or the reply **Temos**, *Yes, (we) have*; or the reply **Tem**, meaning both *Yes, (you) have / one has* and *there is / are*.

Another special use of **tem** can be found, this time on both sides of the Atlantic, where **tem** is used to express a relationship that in English is expressed with *your* when something is being handed over.

| | |
|---|---|
| **Aqui tem o recibo.** | *Here is your receipt. (lit. here (you) have the receipt)* |
| **Aqui tem a chave.** | *Here is your key. (lit. here (you) have the key)* |

This is an alternative to

| | |
|---|---|
| **Aqui está o recibo.** | *Here is your receipt. (lit. here is the receipt)* |
| **Aqui está a chave.** | *Here is your key. (lit. here is the key)* |
| | *(Contd)* |

### b Motor caravans and towed caravans

**Um carro de moradia** (*caravan*, lit. *a home car*) can be motorized (**motorizado**) or towed by vehicle (**rebocado por automóvel**). Therefore, *a motor caravan* is **um carro de moradia motorizado**, whilst *a towed caravan* is **um carro de moradia rebocado**. Anything being towed is known as **um reboque**. You will also come across other names, depending on which side of the Atlantic you are. On the American side, **o trailer**, on the European side, **a caravana** or **a rulote** are synonymous with **o carro de moradia rebocado**. You may also come across **o carro-cama**, a shorter term for **o carro de moradia motorizado**.

| | |
|---|---|
| **Tem vagas?** | *Have you got spaces?* |
| **Tem vaga para um trailer, isto é, carro de moradia rebocado, e uma barraca?** | *Have you got space for a 'trailer', I mean, a towed caravan, and a tent?* |

## Insight
**Tem / Há vagas?**
**Aqui tem / está o recibo.**

## Cultural information
**Sorry...**
'Sorry to disappoint you' is often conveyed by tone of voice and facial expression, rather than verbally.

**Não, nesta loja não. Mas pode encontrar guarda-chuvas ...**
*No, not in this shop. But you can find an umbrella...*

Empathy with the disappointed customer can also be expressed verbally, with **lamento**.

**Não, lamento, nesta loja não. Mas pode encontrar guarda-chuvas ...** *No, sorry, not in this shop. But you can find an umbrella...*

# How it works

### a Verbs: the three conjugations

**Present participle / Gerund** (the *-ing* form)
compr**ando** (*buying*) vend**endo** (*selling*) part**indo** (*leaving*)

Vir**ando** à direita no primeiro       *Turning right at the first set of*
semáforo, o hotel fica à esquerda.       *lights, the hotel is on the left.*

### b Contracted words

The following prepositions contract and combine with a following
definite article (*the*) or indefinite article (*a/an*):

| | | | | |
|---|---|---|---|---|
| por + o | → pelo | por + a | → pela | *by / for the* |
| de + um | → dum | de + uma | → duma | *of / from a* |
| em + um | → num | em + uma | → numa | *in / on a* |

O trânsito é **pela** esquerda       *Does one drive on the left or on the*
  ou **pela** direita?                       *right? (*lit.*, Is the traffic by the left*
                                                 *or by the right?)*
Há lojas **numa** rua aqui perto.     *There are shops in a street nearby.*

Note the following:

▶ In **pela esquerda / direita**, the word for hand (**a mão**) is omitted
   but implied. This is also the case with **à direita / esquerda**:

   **pela direita = por + a (+ mão) direita**
   **à direita = a + a (+ mão) direita**

▶ There is a general preference for **de um / de uma** although the
   following form also occurs: **dum / duma** (sometimes spelt
   **d'um / d'uma**).

A loja fica perto **de uma** igreja.       *The shop is near a church.*

Prepositions can also contract and combine with a number of other words, as, for example:

| | | |
|---|---|---|
| de + este → deste | de + esta → desta | *of / from this* |
| em + este → neste | em + esta → nesta | *in / on this* |
| em + outro → noutro | em + outra → noutra | *in / on other* |
| de + aqui → daqui | | *from here* |
| de + ele, eles → dele, deles | | *his, their/theirs* |
| de + ela, elas → dela, delas | | *her/hers, their/ theirs* |

| | |
|---|---|
| A loja fica **nesta** estrada, a cinco minutos **daqui**, de carro. | *The shop is on this road, five minutes from here, by car.* |
| A mala **dele** está aqui. | *His suitcase is here.* |
| Aquelas malas são **delas**. | *Those suitcases are theirs.* |

## Insight

pel**o** – pel**a**
num – num**a**
dest**e** – dest**a**
noutr**o** – noutr**a**
del**es** – del**as**
daqui

### c Plurals

Words (nouns and adjectives) ending:

| | | |
|---|---|---|
| **-el (–)** | *substitute* | **-eis** |
| **-el (+)** | | **-éis** |
| **-il (–)** | | **-eis** | *(+) stressed* |
| **-il (+)** | | **-is** | *(–) unstressed* |
| **-ol (–)** | | **-ois** |
| **-ol (+)** | | **-óis** |
| **-ul** | | **-uis** |

automóvel (*automobile*), automóveis (*automobiles*); hotel (*hotel*), hotéis (*hotels*); fácil (*easy*), fáceis (*easy*); gentil (*courteous*), gentis (*courteous*); álcool (*alcohol*), álcoois (*alcohols*); lençol (*sheet, bed sheet*), lençóis (*sheets, bed sheets*); azul (*blue*), azuis (*blue*)

There are three different plural forms for words ending in -ão:

| Some just add -s | Some change to -ões | Some change to -ães |
|---|---|---|
| mão (*hand*) | estação (*station*) | pão (*bread, loaf*) |
| mãos (*hands*) | estações (*stations*) | pães (*loaves*) |

Similarly,

cidadão → cidadãos, (*citizen(s)*); botão → botões (*button(s)*) edredão → edredões (Eur.) (*eiderdown(s) bed quilt(s)*); cão → cães (*dog(s)*).

Words in -ês lose the accent in the plural:

mês (*month*); meses (*months*)
português (*Portuguese*); portugueses (*Portuguese*)

A number of masculine words which have a closed -o- in the stressed root syllable open this vowel in the plural in addition to adding -s.

ovo (*egg*), ovos (*eggs*)
novo (*new, young*), novos (*new, young*)
posto (*post/mail, service station*), postos (*post/mail, service stations*)
porto (*port, harbour*), portos (*ports, harbours*)

In compound words (verb / etc. + noun), only the noun takes a plural ending:

> guarda-chuva, guarda-chuvas (*umbrella(s)*, from **guardar**, *to guard*); guarda-sol, guarda-sóis (*parasol, sunshade*).

But some already end in -s in the singular:

> saca-rolhas, saca-rolhas (*corkscrew*, from **sacar**, *to take / pull out*).

In compound words (adjective / ordinal + noun), both elements take a plural ending:

> pequeno-almoço (Eur.) (*breakfast*), pequenos-almoços (*breakfasts*) (*); sexta-feira (*Friday*), sextas-feiras (*Fridays*).

(*) Lit. *small lunch* – (o) **almoço**, *lunch*

---

## Insight

| | |
|---|---|
| guarda-**sol** | guarda-**sóis** |
| saca-rolhas | saca-rolhas |
| ---------- | |
| sext**a**-feir**a** | sext**as**-feir**as** |

---

## Exercises

### 5.3

You have entered a food store to look for some provisions.

**5.3.1** Bread and milk are items you cannot find. Ask whether they are available, starting with **Desculpe, tem…**

**5.3.2** They are available, and there is fruit too. Say you would like the following, starting with **Queria…**

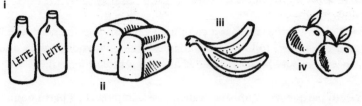

**5.4**

You will hear some people talking about campsites.

🔊 **CD1, TR 26**

**5.4.1** Campo-Mar is publicizing its facilities. Study their advertisement and listen to its radio version on your recording. Use the vocabulary at the end of the book for any words you may not know.

Write the answers in Portuguese:

 **i** current opening days (it's winter): _____
 **ii** summer opening days: _____
 **iii** distance to the nearest beach: _____
 **iv** distance to the nearest town: _____

**5.4.2** Ask whether there is a camping / caravanning site near where you are, with the following facilities. Write down your enquiry and then read it out aloud (number **i** has been written for you):

Há um parque de campismo (Eur.) / um camping (Br.) perto daqui com piscina, secador de cabelo e restaurante?

◀) **CD1, TR 27**

**5.4.3** Four people are looking for somewhere to stay. Listen to them and tick what they need a space for. Then write down all they said.

| | ![carro de moradia motorizado] carro de moradia motorizado | ![carro de moradia rebocado] carro de moradia rebocado | ![reboque pequeno] reboque pequeno | ![barraca] barraca | ![tenda] tenda |
|---|---|---|---|---|---|
| **i** | | | | | |
| **ii** | | | | | |
| **iii** | | | | | |
| **iv** | | | | | |

**5.4.4** Ask whether there is a space for you. Write down your enquiry and then read it out aloud (number **i** has been written for you):

Tem vaga para um carro-cama, isto é, carro de moradia motorizado, e uma barraca?

**5.5**

🔊 **CD1, TR 28**

Study the pictures below, listen to your recording and complete the speech bubbles. Say them yourself aloud.

**5.6**

You are trying to work out how to pay for making phone calls.

**5.6.1** Rearrange the following words so as to say that you would like to make a reversed charge call (**uma chamada a cobrar**) to Canada.

Queria / uma / a cobrar / para o Canadá. / chamada / fazer

**5.6.2** Rearrange the words below so as to ask whether the following is available:

  **A**  In Portugal
     **i**  phone cards (**o cartão credifone**)
       Tem / credifone / cartões / ?
    **ii**  mobile phones (**o telemóvel**)
       telemóveis / ? / Tem

  **B**  In Brazil
     **i**  phone cards (**o cartão de telefone**)
       Tem / de / ? / telefone / cartões
    **ii**  cellphones (**o celular**)
       celulares / ? / Tem

**5.7**

◆) **CD1, TR 29**

You have overheard someone asking for the cost of one hour on the Internet:

Por favor, quanto custa uma hora na Internet?

Now rearrange the words below so as to ask for half an hour on the Internet.

Por favor, / na Internet? / meia hora / custa / quanto

## Summary

**1** Tem pão e leite?
Tem vaga para um veículo grande?
Tem espaço para duas tendas?

**2** Tem sacos de dormir / chuveiro frio e quente / secador de cabelo / sala de televisão?

**3** Há sacos de dormir / secador de cabelo / piscina aqui perto / uma mesa vaga para quatro pessoas?

**4** Queria um saco de dormir / dois guarda-sóis / três pães / meia dúzia de ovos.

**5** Tem um saca-rolhas?
Sim, tenho.
Tem guarda-sóis / sacos de dormir / mesas vagas / espaço para mais tendas?
Não, não tenho.
Lamento, não tenho.

**6** Mas pode encontrar guarda-sóis nas lojas mais perto da cidade.
Mas pode encontrar uma mesa vaga noutro restaurante perto daqui.
Mas pode encontrar espaço para duas tendas noutro parque de campismo (Eur.) / camping (Br.).

**7** O outro parque de campismo (Eur.) / camping (Br.) fica nesta estrada, a dez minutos daqui, de carro.

**8** Continuando nesta rua, o restaurante fica a cinco minutos a pé.
Virando à direita no primeiro semáforo, o outro parque de campismo (Eur.) / camping (Br.) fica à esquerda.

**9** Quanto custa?
Quanto custa uma hora na Internet / uma garrafa de leite?

**10** Aqui tem a garrafa de leite / o recibo.
Aqui está a garrafa de leite / o recibo.

# 6

**Tudo bem**
All is well

In this revision unit there is more practice on how to
- **Speak to the people you meet on arrival**
- **Work out your route and use different forms of transport**
- **Get what you need and the accommodation you like**

**6.1**

◀) **CD1, TR 30**

You have been attending Portuguese classes, and your teacher has given you a language self-help kit that you can use to overcome any communication difficulties you may experience initially.

**6.1.1** Study what she has written on the board and listen to the new words being pronounced for you. Tick each word as you hear it.

| Faça o favor de | falar | mais devagar |
|---|---|---|
| | repetir *repeat, say it again* | mais alto *louder* |
| | escrever aqui *write down* (lit., *write here*) | quanto é *how much it is* |
| | | o nome *the name* |
| | | o endereço *the address* |
| | | o número do telefone *the telephone number* |
| | | essa palavra *that word...* |
| | | essas palavras *those words...* |
| | | (*... that you have said*) |

| | me mostrar<br>*show me* | no dicionário<br>*in the*<br>*dictionary* | essa(s) palavra(s)<br>*the word(s) you*<br>*have just said* |
| | | no mapa<br>*on the map* | onde fica *where it is*<br>onde estou *where*<br>*I am* |
| | | as horas *the time (... on your watch)* | |

**6.1.2** Listen again and say the new words.

**6.1.3** Follow the example you already know – **Faça o favor de falar mais devagar** – and combine words from the different columns so as to say the following (write it down):

Could you please / Would you kindly...

  **i** say it again, more slowly
 **ii** write down how much it is.
**iii** write down the name, address and telephone number.
 **iv** write down what you have just said.
  **v** show me that word in the dictionary.
 **vi** show me on the map where it is.
**vii** show me on the map where I am.
**viii** show me the time (... on your watch).

**6.1.4** Say aloud what you have written.

   **6.2**

◀) **CD1, TR 31**

When going through Customs, you want to say that you have nothing to declare, but the words have got jumbled up. Listen to the officer's question and rearrange your words so as to give your reply.

   – Tem alguma coisa a declarar?
   – Não / não / a / tenho / , / declarar / . / nada

**6.3**

◄ CD1, TR 32

You are producing some personal documents you have been asked for, first at the passport control, then at the car hire.

**6.3.1** Fill in the gaps with words from the box, listen to the recording and play your part in the mini-dialogues.

> (o) meu     (a) minha

## A In Portugal

**i** No controle de passaporte

– O seu passaporte, por favor.

– Aqui está _____ passaporte.

**ii** No aluguer de carros/automóveis

– A sua carta de condução, por favor.

– Aqui está _____ carta de condução.

## B In Brazil

**iii** No controle de passaporte

– Seu passaporte, por favor.

– Aqui está _____ passaporte.

**iv** No aluguel de carros/automóveis

– Sua carteira de motorista, por favor.

– Aqui está _____ carteira de motorista.

**6.3.2** Listen again to what you are being asked. This time reply with **Aqui tem...**

**6.4**

◄ CD1, TR 33

Study the following words you may need when you hire a car.

**(a) lista dos modeles e preços**     *model and price list*
**pagando** ... *paying...*
| **por dia** *per day*
| **por semana** *per week*
| **por quilómetro** (Eur.) / *per kilometre travelled*

| | |
|---|---|
| **(o) seguro contra todos os riscos** | *comprehensive insurance* |
| **(a) caução** | *guarantee deposit* |
| **com / sem motorista** | *with / without a driver* |
| **(os) documentos do carro** | *car documents* |
| **(o) recibo** | *receipt* |

**6.4.1** Listen how the people on your recording are going about hiring a car, and tick each new word above as you hear it.

**6.4.2** Listen again to what they say, write it down and read aloud what you have written.

**6.4.3** It's your turn to choose a car.

Make your enquiry, asking:
  **i** to be shown the model and price table (**Pode...**)
  **ii** how much it is per day (**Quanto...**)
  **iii** how much is the insurance and the guarantee deposit.

Make your decision, saying:
  **iv** you would like this car, paying per day (**Queria...**)
  **v** you would like the car for two days and no driver.

Ask for:
  **i** a receipt (**Pode...**)
  **ii** the car documents

### 6.5

Read the signs on the petrol and other fuel pumps, work out their meaning and match each sign with the English version below.

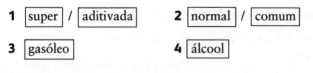

**1** super / aditivada   **2** normal / comum

**3** gasóleo   **4** álcool

**a** standard grade   **b** top grade
**c** alcohol fuel   **d** diesel fuel

**6.6**

● CD1, TR 34

You are going to help four different people who have got lost in town.

**6.6.1** Study the signposted directions.

**(a) câmara municipal** (Eur.) **/ (a) prefeitura** (Br.) *town hall*
**(a) polícia** *police*
**(o) centro de saúde** *health centre*
**(os) bombeiros** *fire services*

**6.6.2** Listen to your recording and reply to each question using a complete sentence.

Example:
**1**
A polícia fica
à esquerda

**6.7**

● CD1, TR 35

Four people are trying to find out what platform their train leaves from. Two are travelling in Portugal and two are travelling in Brazil.

**(o) comboio** (Eur.) **/ (o) trem** (Br.) *train*
**(a) plataforma / (o) cais** (Eur.) *platform*

Note: 'plataforma' is used both in Portugal and Brazil for a train platform; 'cais' is for a quay but in Portugal it is also used for a train platform.

**6.7.1** First, look at the destination boards, study the questions and replies below, and fill in the gaps as appropriate.

**PORTUGAL**

| Porto |
|---|
| 3 |

| Braga |
|---|
| 1 |

**BRASIL**

| Rio |
|---|
| 5 |

| Campinas |
|---|
| 2 |

   **i**  – De que cais parte o comboio para o Porto?
       – Do cais _____ .
  **ii**  – De que _____ parte o comboio para Braga?
       – Do cais número _____ .
 **iii**  – De que _____ parte o trem para o Rio?
       – Da plataforma _____.
  **iv**  – De que plataforma parte _____ para Campinas?
       – Da segunda _____.

**6.7.2** Now you are ready to help the four travellers. Listen to their questions on your recording and give them the right information. Read it aloud.

**6.7.3** Finally, take their place and ask the questions yourself (**De que...?**).

   **6.8**

◀) **CD1, TR 36**

On your recording, some people are asking for specific features they would like in their hotel accommodation.

**6.8.1** Number each feature being asked for as you hear it.

| i | (a) varanda or (a) sacada balcony | |
|---|---|---|
| ii | (a) vista para o mar sea view (view on to the sea) | |
| iii | (o) ar condicionado air conditioning | |
| iii | (o) aparelho de televisão television set | |
| iv | (o) barulho noise | |

**6.8.2** Write down everything each person says and read it aloud.

**6.8.3** Check that the accommodation you are being offered has got the following: (**Tem...**)

 i air conditioning; ii television set; iii balcony and sea view.

**6.8.4** Say you would like (**Queria...**) a room with no noise.

**6.9**

◄) CD1, TR 37

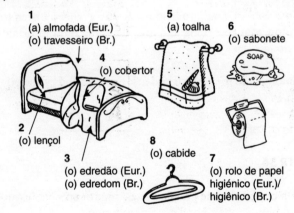

**1**
(a) almofada (Eur.)
(o) travesseiro (Br.)

**4**
(o) cobertor

**2**
(o) lençol

**3**
(o) edredão (Eur.)
(o) edredom (Br.)

**5**
(a) toalha

**6**
(o) sabonete

SOAP

**8**
(o) cabide

**7**
(o) rolo de papel
higiénico (Eur.)/
higiênico (Br.)

**6.9.1 mais um / uma** one more...

Ask whether you can be brought one more of each item in the picture.

Examples:

> Por favor, pode me trazer mais uma almofada (Eur.)?
> Por favor, pode me trazer mais um travesseiro (Br.)?

Listen to the above examples on your recording. Then continue on your own.

**6.9.2 mais dois / duas** *two more...*

Ask whether you can be brought two more of each.

**6.9.3** Write a note to leave in your room asking for four extra hangers and two extra blankets. Start with **Por favor** and don't forget to finish with a thank you.

**6.10**

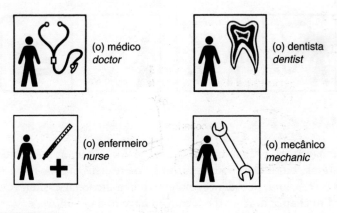

(o) médico *doctor*

(o) dentista *dentist*

(o) enfermeiro *nurse*

(o) mecânico *mechanic*

◀) **CD1, TR 38**

**6.10.1 Há ... perto daqui?** *Is there a ... near here?*

Listen to your recording and **a** enter **Há** or **Não, não há** on the line above the following pictures, depending on whether there is, or not, one nearby; **b** then write down what you heard and say it aloud.

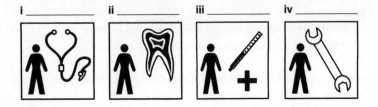

i _____  ii _____  iii _____  iv _____

🔊 **CD1, TR 39**

**6.10.2 Pode chamar um … para mim?** or **Pode me chamar um…?**
*Could you call a … for me?*

Ask whether the following can be sent for, for you. Write down
your questions and then read them aloud. The first one is on the
recording.

i            ii            iii            iv

**6.11**

You have tried to look up a word in the vocabulary at the end of
the book, but it does not appear to be there. This may be because
it is a verb, and, in order to find a verb in a dictionary, often you
need to change it, from the form you have to its infinitive, e.g.,
from *is* to *(to) be*.

In the left-hand column, there are a number of verb forms you have
come across. Work out their respective infinitives and enter them
in the right-hand column. Remember that they will have to end
in **-ar**, **-er** or **-ir**. Some irregular and other examples have been
done for you.

| Word as you have seen it | Word as a dictionary entry |
|---|---|
| desculpe | a |
| é, são | b ser |
| está, estão, estou | c estar |
| faça, faz | d |
| fica, ficam, fico | e |
| há | f haver |
| parte | g |
| pode | h |
| queria | i querer |
| tem, temos, tenho | j ter |

When you have completed this exercise, look up the obtained
words (infinitives) in the Portuguese–English vocabulary at the
end of the book.

### 6.12

This is the shopping list
(**a lista de compras**)
that you have written
and taken with you
to the local store.
Read it out loud.
Start with

> *pão x 3*
> *maçã 1/2 dúzia*
> *leite*
> *1 garrafa pequena*
> *água*
> *1 garrafa grande*

**Por favor, queria ...**

### 6.13

◀) **CD1, TR 40**

You are having Internet problems.

**6.13.1** Rearrange the words below so as to ask someone to help
you out.

Por favor, / ajudar? / me / pode

**6.13.2** Everything comes up in Portuguese. Rearrange the words below so as to ask whether the settings can be changed to English.

Por favor, / para inglês? / mudar / pode / a língua

**6.13.3** Combine the words in the box below so as to express the following difficulties.

(If you need to, look the words up in the vocabulary lists at the end of the book.)

**6.13.3.1** I can't log on.
**6.13.3.2** I can't get access to my e-mail.
**6.13.3.3** I can't get access to this site (showing the web address).

| | |
|---|---|
| Não consigo | entrar. |
| I can't | acesso a este sítio. |
| | acesso ao meu email. |

**6.14**

◄୬ CD1, TR 41

On the left are the courtesy words you have learned. On the right are their respective replies.

| Pode me fazer um favor? | Claro!<br>Com certeza /<br>Pois não (Br.) | *Certainly* |
|---|---|---|
| Perdão<br>Desculpe | Não tem<br>  importância<br>Não faz mal (Eur.)<br>Não foi nada /<br>Tudo bem | *It's all right* |
| Com licença | Por favor<br>Faz / faça favor<br>  (Eur.)<br>Pois não (Br.) | *Please do* |

| Obrigado / obrigada<br>Muito obrigado/a<br>Agradecido / agradecida<br>Muito agradecido/a | De nada<br>Não tem de quê<br><br>Eu é que agradeço | *Not at all*<br><br><br>*It's I who must<br>thank you* |
| --- | --- | --- |

**6.14.1** Listen to the new words on your recording.

**6.14.2** Practise saying aloud the different courtesy expressions and the appropriate response to each one.

### 6.15

Follow the clues and complete the courtesy crossword puzzle.
Number 4 across and number 2 down have been done for you.

#### Palavras cruzadas

Horizontais:
**1** - Perdão
**2** - Por favor
**3** - Não tem importância
**4** - Não tem de quê
**5** - Obrigada
**6** - De nada

Verticais:
**1** - Muito obrigado
**2** - Eu é que agradeço
**3** - Muito obrigada
**4** - Com licença

## Summary

**1** Tem alguma coisa a declarar? – Não, não tenho nada a declarar. – Sim, tenho. Aqui está.

**2** De que plataforma parte o comboio (Eur.) / trem (Br.) para (your destination)?
Onde há um comboio (Eur.) / trem (Br.) para (your destination)?

**3** O apartamento tem vista para o mar? – O quarto tem ar condicionado?

**4** Queria mais um cobertor / uma toalha / dois cabides / uma garrafa grande de água.
Pode me trazer mais um saco de dormir / duas toalhas / uma garrafa de vinho?

**5** Queria um carro para dois dias.
Quanto é por dia / semana?

**6** Aqui está / tem o meu passaporte. – Aqui está / tem a minha carta de condução (Eur.) / carteira de motorista (Br.).

**7** Onde há gasolina super / aditivada?
Há um dentista perto daqui?
Onde fica / é a polícia? – Onde ficam / são os bombeiros?

**8** Pode me ajudar / fazer um favor? – Não consigo encontrar o hotel / as maçãs / essa palavra no dicionário.

**9** Pode / Importa-se de falar mais devagar / escrever aqui o endereço?
Pode / Importa-se de chamar um táxi / médico / mecânico para mim?

**10** Faça o favor de me mostrar no mapa onde fica o hotel.
Perdão / Desculpe → Não tem importância. / Tudo bem.
Com licença → Por favor.
(Muito) obrigado – obrigada → De nada.
(Muito) agradecido – agradecida → Eu é que agradeço.

# 7

# Você está de férias?
## Are you on holiday?

In this unit you will learn how to
- *Introduce a friend or relation*
- *Say where you are from and talk about yourself*
- *Find out about others*

**Na rua** *In the street*

Portuguese João is introduced to Brazilian Celso by a mutual friend, Tânia.

| | |
|---|---|
| **Tânia** | *(apresentando João a Celso)* Este é meu amigo João. |
| **Celso** | *(apertando a mão)* Muito prazer. |
| **João** | O prazer é todo meu. |
| **Celso** | Você está de férias? |
| **João** | Infelizmente não estou de férias, mas o trabalho também é bom. |
| **Celso** | Está sozinho? |
| **João** | Estou. |
| **Celso** | Num hotel? |
| **João** | Sim, num hotel. |
| **Celso** | Então pode vir jantar em nossa casa, talvez amanhã. |
| **João** | Muito obrigado. |

◉ CD1, TR 42

**apresentando** *introducing*
**(o) amigo** *friend*
**apertando a mão** *shaking hands*
**o prazer é todo meu** *the pleasure is all mine*
**você** *you*
**de férias** *on holiday*
**infelizmente** *unfortunately*
**(o) trabalho** *work*
**também** *also, too*
**sozinho** *by oneself*
**então** *then*
**vir jantar** *come to dinner* (lit. *come to dine*)
**em nossa casa** or **na nossa casa** *with us at home* (lit. *in our house*)
**talvez** *perhaps*
**amanhã** *tomorrow*

### Num café *In a café*

Two students who have joined the same course exchange information about themselves.

| | |
|---|---|
| **Lino** | Desculpe, mas você… de onde é? |
| **Rita** | Eu sou de Lisboa. E você, de onde é? |
| **Lino** | Eu sou de São Paulo, mas moro no Rio de Janeiro há muito tempo. Você é de Lisboa, mas agora onde mora? |
| **Rita** | Moro aqui. |
| **Lino** | Com quem? |
| **Rita** | Com uma irmã. |
| **Lino** | Então você é solteira, não é? |
| **Rita** | Não sou casada, mas estou noiva. O nome dele é Luís. |

**de onde é?** *where are (you) from?*
**eu sou de …** *I am from …*
**há muito tempo** *since long* (lit. *there is much time*)
**moro, mora** *(I) live, (you) live*
**agora** *now*
**com quem?** *with whom?*

**(a) irmã** *sister*
**solteira, casada** *single, married*
**não é?** *aren't you? (lit. isn't it?)*
**noiva** *engaged*
**dele (= de + ele)** *his (lit. of him)*

---

## Exercises

### 7.1 Certo ou errado? *Right or wrong?*

|   | C | E |
|---|---|---|
| **1** João está de férias. | ☐ | ☐ |
| **2** João está sozinho. | ☐ | ☐ |
| **3** Rita não é de Lisboa. | ☐ | ☐ |

### 7.2 Perguntas e respostas *Questions and answers*

**1** Rita mora sozinha ou não mora sozinha?
  **a** Mora sozinha.     **b** Não mora sozinha.

**2** Lino é de onde? E onde mora?
  **a** É do Rio de Janeiro mas mora em São Paulo.
  **b** É de São Paulo mas mora no Rio de Janeiro.

**3** Rita é casada ou solteira?
  **a** É solteira.     **b** É casada.     **c** Está noiva.

---

## How to pronounce it

🔊 **CD1, TR 44**

The letter sequence **qu** can be pronounced in more than one way.
Practise after the voice on the recording.

**qu** before **a** or **o** sounds like English *kw*: **qua**rto; **qua**tro; **qua**nto; **quo**ta (*quota, share*).

**qu** before **e** or **i** sounds like *k*: **que**ria; **que**m; a**qui**; **qui**nze (*fifteen*) but, in some cases,

**qu** before **e** or **i** sounds like *kw*, as in the word for *fifty*: cin**que**nta

The end sound in el<u>e</u> / el<u>a</u>, *he / she*, influences the quality of the first sound. Follow the voice on the recording.

ele (say *e* in *they* but without the final glide)

ela (say *e* in *tell*)

Similarly,

dele-dela;

este-esta (*this, this one*); esse-essa (*that, that one*);

aquele-aquela (also *that, that one*)

····················································································

## Expressions

**Este – esse – aquele:** *Saying 'this' and 'that'*

In English, *this*, or *this one*, and *that*, or *that one*, establish a distinction between what or who is near you and what or who is away from you. Portuguese **este**, **esse** and **aquele** establish a further distinction as follows:

▸ **este** is near you or near you and the person / people you are talking to;

▸ **esse** is away from you but near the person / people you are talking to;

▸ **aquele** is away from both you and the person / people you are talking to.

**esta**, **essa** and **aquela** are the respective feminine forms.

| | |
|---|---|
| **Este** é (o) Pedro, **esse** é (o) Paulo e **aquela** é (a) Maria. | *This is Peter, that is Paul and that one (over there) is Mary.* |

(For **o/a** please refer to Unit 7:HIWc.)
Please note that the distinction between **este/esta** and **esse/essa** is not made by everyone in Brazil.

## Cultural information
**a Muito prazer** *With pleasure*

When introducing someone, say **este é (o) meu amigo João / esposo** or **marido** (*husband*) / **pai** (*father*) or **esta é (a) minha amiga Joana / esposa** or **mulher** (*wife*) / **mãe** (*mother*). Or simply point to the person you are introducing and say **(o) meu amigo João** / etc. Brazilians often leave out **o/a**.

**Muito prazer** is the abridged version of **muito prazer em conhecê-lo** or **muito prazer em conhecê-la**, *delighted to meet you*, when you are talking, respectively, to a man or to a lady. Sometimes you may find that the abridged version is further reduced to **prazer**. This doesn't mean that you are not 'delighted' but is just a relaxed way of speaking. However, **muito prazer** or **igualmente** are the usual responses. If you wish to be very polite, then you can also say **o prazer é meu** or **o prazer é todo meu**, *the pleasure is (all) mine.*

## Insight
**Aquela** é a minha amiga.
**Aquele** é o meu amigo.

----------

**Esta / Essa** é a minha amiga.
Muito prazer em conhecê-la.
**Este / Esse** é o meu amigo.
Muito prazer em conhecê-lo.

### b Information about yourself
Both in a social situation and for official purposes, you may want to provide information about yourself. You may

*(Contd)*

also wish to find out about other people. Below are some questions and answers that will help you fit in with the way people interact in a Portuguese-speaking society.

**Nome** *Your name*

> **Qual é o seu nome?** (Eur.) / **Qual é seu nome?** (Br.)

has the following alternatives:

> **Como é o seu nome?** (Eur.) / **Como é seu nome?** (Br.)
> (lit. *how is your name?*)
> **Como se chama você?** (Eur.) / **Como você se chama?** (Br.)
> (lit. *how do you call yourself?*)
> or, equally on both sides of the Atlantic,
> **Como se chama?**
> (lit. *how do you call yourself?*)

As for the reply:

> **O meu nome é…** (Eur.) / **Meu nome é…** (Br.)

has the following alternative:

> **Eu chamo-me…** (Eur.) / **Eu me chamo…** (Br.) (lit. *I call myself*)

To reciprocate the question, instead of

> **E o seu?**

on both sides of the Atlantic you can equally ask

| | |
|---|---|
| **E você, como se chama?** | *asking anyone* |
| **E o senhor, como se chama?** | *asking a man* |
| **E a senhora, como se chama?** | *asking a woman* |

The two last versions are more polite.

## Insight

> (O) meu nome é (_your name_)
>
> **or**
>
> Eu chamo-me (_your name_) (Eur.) / Eu me chamo
> (_your name_) (Br.)

---

**Local de nascimento** _Place of birth;_ **Nacionalidade** _Nationality_

**De onde é você?** (Eur.) or **De onde você é?** (Br.)

The word '**você**' is more likely to be used by a Brazilian
speaker and omitted by a Portuguese speaker: **De onde é?**

Reply:   **Eu sou de Portugal.**
         **Eu sou do Rio, no Brasil.**
         **Eu sou da Inglaterra.**     _from England_
         **Eu sou dos Estados Unidos.**   _from the United States_

Reciprocating:

         **E você, de onde é?**
         **E o senhor / a senhora, de onde é?**

Also:    Are you...
         **Você é português? / Você é portuguesa? ...**
           _Portuguese?_
         **O senhor é brasileiro? / A senhora é brasileira?**
         _... Brazilian?_

         **O senhor é inglês? / A senhora é inglesa? ...** _English?_
         **O senhor é americano? / A senhora é americana? ...**
         _American?_

Reply:   **Sou, sim.**
         **Não, não sou. Eu sou australiano / australiana.**
         _Australian_

                                               _(Contd)_

**Profissão** *Profession;* **Ocupação** *Occupation*

**Qual é a sua profissão?** (Eur.) / **Qual é sua profissão?** (Br.)

or

| | |
|---|---|
| **O que faz?** | *What do you do (for a living)?* |
| **Eu sou ...** | *I am a / an ...* |
| **estudante** | *student* |
| **professor / professora** | *teacher* |
| **engenheiro / engenheira** | *engineer* |
| **homem / mulher de negócios //** **empresário / empresária** (Br.) | *businessman / woman* |
| **dona de casa** | *housewife* |
| **aposentado/aposentada //** **reformado/reformada** (Eur.) | *retired (from employment)* |

**Estado civil** *Marital status*

| | |
|---|---|
| **Você é solteiro?** | |
| **A senhora é casada?** | |
| **A senhora está noiva?** | |
| **Eu sou viúvo / viúva** | *a widower / widow* |
| **Eu sou divorciado / divorciada** | *divorced* |

**Idade** *Age*

**Quantos anos tem você?** (Eur.) / **Quantos anos você tem?** (Br.)

*How old are you? (lit. How many years have you got? i.e., have you completed?)*

| | |
|---|---|
| **Eu tenho vinte e cinco anos.** | *I am twenty-five years old.* |

*(lit. I have i.e., have completed twenty-five years.)*

**Filhos** *Children*

| | |
|---|---|
| **Você tem filhos?** | *Have you got any children?* |
| **Eu tenho dois filhos.** | *I have two children.* |
| **Eu tenho um filho e uma filha.** | *a son and a daughter.* |
| **Eu não tenho filhos.** | *no children.* |
| **Eu tenho um neto e uma neta.** | *a grandson and a granddaughter.* |

## Insight

**Eu sou de / do / da** (*your place of origin*)
**Eu sou** (*your nationality*)
**Eu sou** (*what you do for a job / your occupation*) (lit. *what you are…*)
**Eu sou** (*your marital status*)

----------

**Eu tenho** (*your years of age*)
**Eu tenho** (*number of children*)

**Endereço ou morada** *Address*

**Onde mora você?** (Eur.) or **Onde você mora?** (Br.)
**Onde mora a senhora?** or **Onde a senhora mora?**
**Eu moro na Inglaterra.**
**Eu moro em Portugal.**
**Eu moro no Brasil, no Rio.**
**Qual é o seu endereço?** (Eur.) / **Qual é seu endereço?** (Br.)
**Como é o seu endereço?** (Eur.) / **Como é seu endereço?** (Br.)
**Qual é (o) seu número de telefone?** / **Qual é o número do seu telefone?**

**Estada ou estadia** *Your visit*

| | |
|---|---|
| **Quanto tempo (você) vai ficar?** | *How long are you going to stay?* |

*(Contd)*

| | |
|---|---|
| **Eu vou ficar um mês.** | *I am going to stay for one month.* |
| **Onde vai ficar?** | *Where are you staying?* |
| **Onde está?** | *Where are you staying (now)?* |
| **Com amigos.** | *With friends.* |
| **No Hotel Central.** | |
| **Estou aqui de férias** | *... on holiday* |
| **em negócios** (Eur.) **/ a** | *... on business* |
| **negócios** (Br.) | |

---

## How it works

**a** I, you, s/he...

With verbs, the subject pronoun (*I, you, s/he*, etc.) is optional. In fact it is often omitted where the verb ending itself shows whether it is *I, you*, etc.

⬜ Mor**o** em Lisboa.　　　　　**I** *live in Lisbon.*

However, use the pronoun with the verb where it could otherwise be ambiguous, or for emphasis.

**Eu** é que agrade**ç**o.　　　　　*It's **I** who must thank you.*

| | |
|---|---|
| **eu** | *I* |
| **você** | *you (both m. and f.)* |
| **o senhor / a senhora** | *you (m.) / you (f.) [polite]* |
| **tu** | *you (both m. and f.) [for close friends]* |
| **ele / ela** | *he / she / it* |
| **nós** | *we* |
| **vocês** | *you (both m. and f. plural)* |
| **os senhores / as senhoras** | *you (m. pl.) / you (f. pl.) [polite]* |
| **eles / elas** | *they* |

Note that 'os senhores' can be m. and f. together. See Unit 10:HIWd.

## Insight

(**Eu**) sou do Brasil.
(**Eu**) moro em Portugal.
(**Eu**) tenho trinta anos.
**Eu** é que agradeço.

..........

**Você / O senhor** é do Brasil?
**Ele** é do Brasil?
**Você / O senhor** mora em Portugal?
**Ele** mora em Portugal?
**Você / O senhor** tem trinta anos?
**Ele** tem trinta anos?
**Você / O senhor** é que agradece?
**Ele** é que agradece?

### b Numbers 11 to 100

| | | | |
|---|---|---|---|
| 11 | onze | 21 | vinte e um/uma |
| 12 | doze | 22 | vinte e dois/duas |
| 13 | treze | 30 | trinta |
| 14 | catorze | 40 | quarenta |
| 15 | quinze | 50 | cinquenta |
| 16 | dezasseis (Eur.) dezesseis (Br.) | 60 | sessenta |
| 17 | dezassete (Eur.) dezessete (Br.) | 70 | setenta |
| 18 | dezoito | 80 | oitenta |
| 19 | dezanove (Eur.) dezenove (Br.) | 90 | noventa |
| 20 | vinte | 100 | cem |

### c João *or* o João?

The use of the definite article (**o / a**) with the name of a person is optional and is more widely heard on the eastern side of the Atlantic rather than in Brazil.

Este é **o João**    *or*    Este é **João**        *This is John.*

However, it is not used in a vocative, i.e., when calling someone.

**João!**    *John! (come here)*

### d A civil servant and a vegetarian

Unlike English practice, the Portuguese indefinite article (**um /
uma**) is not used before a noun denoting profession or occupation,
affiliation, marital status or origin.

| | |
|---|---|
| Sou funcionário público | *I am a civil servant* |
| vegetariano | *vegetarian* |
| católico | *Catholic* |

> **Insight**
> Ele é **professor.**
> Elas são **médicas.**
> (Eu) sou **vegetariano.**
> (Nós) somos **católicos.**

## Exercises

**7.3**

Fill in the missing words in what Joana is saying to Paulo.

Paulo! Este é _____, _____
Rosa e _____ Mariana.

Nuno    Joana    Paulo    Rosa    Mariana

**7.4**

◀) **CD1, TR 45**

José, Glória, Osvaldo and Amélia are explaining where they come from and talking about themselves.

**7.4.1** Study the picture on the following page, listen to your recording and complete the table below writing in Portuguese the correct information about each individual. The first answer has been done for you.

| Name | S/he comes from... | Age and occupation | Married? children? |
|---|---|---|---|
| **i** José | *Faro, Algarve* | *22 anos, estudante* | *solteiro, não tem filhos* |
| **ii** Glória | | | |
| **iii** Osvaldo | | | |
| **iv** Amélia | | | |

**7.4.2** Listen again to what they say and transcribe their words. Then act out each one's role by reading aloud what you wrote.

**7.5**

Matthew has to provide some information about himself. Help him out and answer the following questions on his behalf.

– Por favor, o senhor é americano?
– *(say No, I am not, I am English)*
– Como se chama e de onde é na Inglaterra?
– *(say My name is Matthew Smith. I come from Manchester)*
– Quanto tempo vai ficar aqui e com quem?
*(Contd)*

– (say *I am on my own and I am going to stay for eight days, on holiday*)
– Faça o favor de me mostrar um documento de identidade com o seu endereço de Manchester.
– (say *There you are showing your driving licence*)

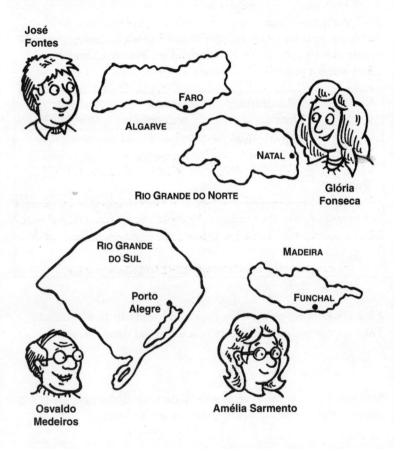

José Fontes

FARO

ALGARVE

NATAL

RIO GRANDE DO NORTE

Glória Fonseca

RIO GRANDE DO SUL

Porto Alegre

MADEIRA

FUNCHAL

Osvaldo Medeiros

Amélia Sarmento

## Summary

**1** Este é (*your male friend or relation*)
Esta é (*your female friend or relation*)
Muito prazer em conhecê-lo.
Muito prazer em conhecê-la.
Igualmente.

**2** Eu chamo-me (*your name*) (Eur.) / Eu me chamo (*your name*)
(Br.) – E você / o senhor – a senhora, como se chama?

**3** E você? [general] – E o senhor – a senhora? [courteous]

**4** Eu sou de / do / da (*your place of origin*). E você, de onde é?
Eu sou brasileira. E você, é americano?

**5** Eu tenho trinta e seis anos. E você?

**6** Eu sou solteiro. E você, é casada?

**7** Eu tenho um filho e uma filha. E você?

**8** Eu sou (*what you do for a job / your occupation*). E você,
o que faz?

**9** Eu estou aqui de férias. – Estou no Hotel Central. – Estou aqui
sozinho / com uma amiga. – Vou ficar duas semanas. – E você?

**10** Eu moro em / no / na (*your place of residence*). E você, onde
mora?
(O) meu número de telefone é (*your telephone number*).
E o seu?

# Quando começa a excursão?
## When does the tour start?

In this unit you will learn how to
- *Talk about time and the days of the week*
- *Find out when a service is available*
- *Identify a person you are going to meet for the first time*

**Numa agência de viagens** *In a travel agency*

Susana is in a travel agency enquiring about local tours.

CD1, TR 46

| | |
|---|---|
| **Susana** | Queria ver a lista das excursões nesta região. |
| **Empregado** | Algum local em particular? |
| **Susana** | Não, queria conhecer a região em geral. |
| **Empregado** | Então recomendo a excursão de dois dias. A próxima é na quarta-feira, partindo de manhã. Ficamos uma noite num hotel e regressamos quinta à tarde. |
| **Susana** | E a que horas começa a excursão na quarta-feira? |
| **Empregado** | Vamos partir às nove. A senhora quer fazer reserva? Hoje ainda tem lugar, mas amanhã talvez não. |

**ver** *to see*
**(a) excursão** *excursion, tour*
**(a) região** *region*

**em particular** *in particular*
**em geral** *in general*
**recomendo** *I would recommend* (lit. *(I) recommend*)
**(a) quarta-feira** *Wednesday*
**de manhã** *in the morning*
**ficamos** *(we) stay*
**regressamos** *(we) return*
**(a) quinta(-feira)** *Thursday*
**à tarde** *in the afternoon / evening*
**a que horas..?** *at what time…?*
**começa** *starts*
**às nove (horas)** *at nine (o'clock)*
**a senhora quer...?** *do you want...?*
**ainda tem lugar** *(you) still have a seat*

### Falando com um amigo *Chatting to a friend*

Dulce is in charge of collecting David from the coach station and is trying to find out what he looks like.

| | |
|---|---|
| **Dulce** | Pode me descrever a aparência física dele? Preciso saber como ele é. |
| **Sílvio** | Para quê? |
| **Dulce** | Ele vai chegar hoje à noite. Tenho que ir buscá-lo à estação. |
| **Sílvio** | A que estação? |
| **Dulce** | À rodoviária. Não sei como vou reconhecê-lo. Não sei se ele é gordo ou magro, alto ou baixo... |
| **Sílvio** | Oh! Não tem problema. Ele nem é gordo nem é magro, nem é alto nem é baixo. |
| **Dulce** | Mas que grande ajuda! Muito obrigada. |

**descrever** *to describe*
**aparência física** *physical appearance*
**preciso (de) saber** *(I) need* (lit. *of*) *(to) know*
**como ele é** *what he looks* (lit. *is*) *like*
**ele vai chegar** *he is going to arrive*
**à noite** *at night / in the evening*

> **tenho que** *(I) have got to*
> **ir, vou** *to go, (I) go / am going*
> **buscá-lo** *to fetch him*
> **(a) rodoviária** *coach (station)*
> **não sei como** *(I) don't know how*
> **reconhecê-lo** or **identificá-lo** *to identify him*
> **se** *whether, if*
> **gordo – magro** *fat – thin*
> **alto – baixo** *tall – short*
> **oh! não tem / há problema** *oh! ((you) have / there is) no problem*
> **que grande ajuda!** *what a great help!*

## Exercises

### 8.1 Certo ou errado? *Right or wrong?*

|   |   | C | E |
|---|---|---|---|
| **1** | Susana quer conhecer a região. | ☐ | ☐ |
| **2** | Susana ainda tem lugar na excursão. | ☐ | ☐ |
| **3** | David vai chegar amanhã à noite. | ☐ | ☐ |
| **4** | Sílvio vai buscar David à estação rodoviária. | ☐ | ☐ |

### 8.2 Perguntas e respostas *Questions and answers*

**1** Excursão para Susana: Quando é a partida? e o regresso?

  **a** A partida é quinta-feira de manhã e o regresso quinta-feira à noite.

  **b** A partida é quarta-feira de manhã e o regresso quinta-feira à tarde.

  **c** A partida é quarta-feira à tarde e o regresso quarta-feira à noite.

**2** David: Qual é a aparência física dele?

  **a** Ele nem é gordo nem é magro mas é alto.

  **b** Ele nem é alto nem baixo mas é magro.

  **c** Ele não é alto mas não é baixo, não é gordo mas não é magro.

# How to pronounce it

🔊 **CD1, TR 48**

Sounds spelt **s** or **z** can change depending on their position in the word and within the sentence. Practise the following after the speaker on the recording.

s-    at the beginning of a word (like English *s* in *so*): sol; sou; saber; senhora.

-s-   between vowels (like *z* in *zebra*): casa; brasileiro.

-s    at the end of a word and often at the end of a syllable
      in Portugal (like *sh* in *push*): horas; português; ficamos; lista.
      in most of Brazil (like *s* in *us*): horas; português; ficamos; lista.

but

      when the next word starts with a vowel, a fast speaker, on either side of the Atlantic, will change the final -s into a *z* for *zebra*:

às <u>o</u>ito horas; vamos <u>a</u>manhã às <u>o</u>ito horas.

→          →          →

z     sounds like *z* in *zebra* in general: zero (*nought*)

-z    at the end of a word
      in Portugal (like *sh* in *push*) : talvez; feliz (*happy*),
      in most of Brazil (like *s* in *pleasure*): talvez; feliz.
      but like *z* for *zebra* when the next word starts with a vowel:
      talve<u>z</u> amanhã (*perhaps tomorrow*); feli<u>z</u> <u>a</u>no (*happy year*).

→                              →

····································································································

## Expressions
### a Days of the week

**Que dia da semana é hoje?** *What day of the week is it today?*

(Contd)

**É...** *It is...*
**domingo** *Sunday*
**segunda-feira** *Monday*
**terça-feira** *Tuesday*

**quarta-feira** *Wednesday*
**quinta-feira** *Thursday*
**sexta-feira** *Friday*
**sábado** *Saturday*

The days of the week are feminine except for the weekend days which are masculine; and so is **(o) feriado**, *public holiday*. In the compound word, **-feira** is often dropped and the first part is represented as **2ª, 3ª, 4ª, 5ª** or **6ª**.

For something that happens regularly, you can say: **às segundas**, or, **à segunda, aos fins de semana**, or, **ao fim de semana, todos os fins de semana, todos os anos**, and so on.

A excursão é **às quartas-feiras**. *The tour is on Wednesdays.*

A excursão é **às quartas**.

## Insight
Hoje é **terça-feira**.
Hoje é **3ª-feira**.
Hoje é **terça**.

### b Telling the time

For *What time is it?* say **Que horas são?** lit. *What hours are (they)?*

Look at the clock faces for the answers:

**É uma (hora)**    **São duas (horas)**

98

São seis (horas)

São doze (horas)
É meio-dia
É meia-noite

 É uma (hora) e cinco (minutos)

É uma (hora) e quinze (minutos)
É uma (hora) e um quarto

 É uma (hora) e trinta (minutos)
É uma (hora) e meia

É uma (hora) e quarenta e cinco (minutos)
São duas (horas) menos quinze (minutos)
São duas (horas) menos um quarto

São quinze (minutos) para as duas (horas)
É um quarto para as duas (horas)
Faltam quinze (minutos) para as duas (horas)
Falta um quarto para as duas (horas)

For the hour, remember to use **é** for **meio-dia, meia-noite** and one (**é uma hora**) but **são** for the others (**são onze horas**). In the 24-hr clock reading, time past and time to the hour are expressed as hour + minutes or quarters (**são onze horas e trinta e cinco minutos**). In the more colloquial 12-hr reading, time past the hour finds expression in the same way (**são onze e vinte e cinco**). For time to the hour the **para** and the **menos** versions

*(Contd)*

are both widely heard (**são vinte e cinco para a meia-noite** or **é meia-noite menos vinte e cinco**). Finally, on the dot has its Portuguese equivalent in **em ponto** – É uma (hora) em ponto.

### c Parts of the day

When using the 12-hr clock you can add **da manhã, da tarde** or **da noite** (**nove horas da noite** = 9 p.m.). If you wish to refer to the different parts of the day with no mention of time, say:

| | |
|---|---|
| **de manhã** | *in the morning* |
| **à tarde** or **de tarde** | *in the afternoon / early evening* |
| **à noite** | *in the late evening / at night* |

| | |
|---|---|
| **A partida é na quarta-feira de manhã.** | *The departure is on Wednesday a.m.* |
| **De manhã como cereais com leite.** | *In the morning I eat cereals with milk.* |

**De noite** is better reserved for *at night* in the sense of *during the night*.

| | |
|---|---|
| Está escuro **de noite**. | *It is dark at night.* |

**Hoje de manhã** means *this morning*, **hoje de tarde** means *this afternoon* (or *early evening*) and **hoje à noite** means *tonight* (or *late evening*). However, **esta manhã, esta tarde** and **esta noite** are equally used.

For *see you tomorrow* say **até amanhã** (lit. *until tomorrow*) and for *see you tomorrow morning* **até amanhã de manhã**. For *see you on Monday* say **até segunda(-feira)** and so on.

### Insight
É uma (hora).
**São** quatro e um quarto.
**São** quatro e meia.

Até amanhã **de manhã**.
Até sexta-feira, **às nove da noite**.

## Cultural information
**Agências, centros e estações** *Agencies, centres and stations*

Sometimes what you see on notice boards and paperwork is a bit different from what people will say in casual speech where a simplified version is used.

The word **agência** is used for a *services office* – **a agência de viagens, a agência dos correios**. Concerning the latter, **o posto dos correios** is also used. **O turismo** is an abridged version of **o centro / a agência de turismo** or **o centro / a agência de informações turísticas**. **A estação** is used for both coach station and railway station. The full name for the former is **a estação rodoviária** and for the latter **a estação ferroviária / a estação dos caminhos de ferro** (Eur.).

## How it works

**a Verbs: the three conjugations – present indicative**

|  | *I buy, etc* | *I sell, etc.* | *I leave, etc.* |
|---|---|---|---|
| *S1* eu | comp**ro** | vend**o** | part**o** |
| *S2* você, o sr / a sra<br>tu | comp**ra**<br>comp**ras** | vend**e**<br>vend**es** | part**e**<br>part**es** |
| *S3* ele / ela | comp**ra** | vend**e** | part**e** |
| *P1* nós | comp**ramos** | vend**emos** | part**imos** |
| *P2* vocês, os sres / as sras | comp**ram** | vend**em** | part**em** |
| *P3* eles / elas | comp**ram** | vend**em** | part**em** |

The three *S* (for singular) boxes are for just one person – *I*, *you* (*one*), *he* / *she* / *it*. The three *P* boxes are for their respective plurals – *we*, *you* (*more than one*), *they*.

With exception of the **tu** endings (**-as, -es, -es**), *S2* and *S3* are the same (**-a, -e, -e**). *P2* and *P3* are also the same (**-am, -em, -em**). They will be grouped together in further tables for verb tenses you will come across.

**Use the present tense for:**
▶ a description of something or someone
A saída fica em frente. *The exit is straight ahead.* (verb fic**ar**, with ending **-a** as for comprar *S3*)
▶ a description of a situation as it is now
Mor**o** no Rio. *I live in Rio.* (mor**ar**)
▶ a habitual action or event
Normalmente, as lojas abr**em** às 9h. *Usually, shops open at 9 a.m.* (abr**ir**)
▶ a constant fact
Gost**o** de música. *I like music.* (gost**ar**)
▶ an accepted truth
As pessoas que viv**em** num clima frio vest**em** roupa quente. *People who live in a cold climate wear warm clothes.* (viv**er**, vest**ir**)
▶ a factual statement about a future occurrence
Part**imos** amanhã. *We are leaving tomorrow.* (part**ir**)
▶ something started sometime in the past and not yet completed
Estud**o** Português há um mês. *I have been studying Portuguese for one month.* (estud**ar**)

### b You

The tendency to omit the subject pronoun (*I*, *you s/he*, etc.), which you learned in Unit 7, is not affected much by the fact that the verb ending can be the same for *you* and *s/he* and for *you* (more than one) and *they*. The situational context is likely to make the meaning clear. If someone looks at you and asks **Fala Português?**, it should be obvious that this means *Do you speak Portuguese?* not *Does s/he speak Portuguese?*

However, if you want to use a word for *you* which should you choose?
**Você** fala Inglês? or **O senhor** fala Inglês? or **Tu** falas Inglês?

### Você
Use **você** in general and when talking to friends.

### O senhor / a senhora
Use **o sr / a sra** with strangers you want to be particularly courteous to.

> ## Insight
> (Você) **fala** Inglês?
> (O senhor – A senhora) **fala** Inglês?
> (Tu) **falas** Inglês?

### Tu
Here we have to make a distinction. In most of Brazil subject pronoun **tu** is not used but the corresponding object pronoun **te** is. We shall come back to this in later units.

Other than in most of Brazil, **tu** is used by those who grow up together or who have become very close later in life. Native speakers use this form to address children. Children use this form amongst themselves through their school days and beyond. In many families children use this form to address their parents, and most adults use it for someone they have become intimate with. Remember to use the different verb form! In Brazil these areas of meaning are covered by **você**.

Also please note the following:
▶ **vocês** is plural to both **você** and **tu**.

**Vocês** falam Português? *Do you* (more than one) *speak Portuguese?*

▶ o senhor / a senhora and os senhores / as senhoras are nouns used as pronouns for you.

O senhor fala Português? Do you speak Portuguese? (lit., *does the gentleman speak Portuguese?*)

▶ vós is an alternative to vocês and os senhores / as senhoras. It has not been mentioned before because it has fallen into disuse in most of the Portuguese-speaking world. However, you can find its verb forms, in brackets, in the tables at the end of the book.

### c Para mim e para você *For me and for you*

You came across **um táxi para mim**, *a taxi for me*, in Units 3 and 6. To say *a taxi for you* you have more than one option.

| | |
|---|---|
| um táxi para você | general approach |
| um táxi para o senhor / a senhora | when you want to be particularly courteous |
| um táxi para ti | when you use subject pronoun 'tu' and, in Brazil, also when you use subject pronoun 'você', for a more casual tone |

## d Ordinal numbers

| | | | |
|---|---|---|---|
| 1°/1ª | primeiro/a | 20°/20ª | vigésimo/a |
| 2°/2ª | segundo/a | 30°/30ª | trigésimo/a |
| 3°/3ª | terceiro/a | 40°/40ª | quadragésimo/a |
| 4°/4ª | quarto/a | 50°/50ª | quinquagésimo/a |
| 5°/5ª | quinto/a | 60°/60ª | sexagésimo/a |
| 6°/6ª | sexto/a | 70°/70ª | septuagésimo/a (Eur.) |
| 7°/7ª | sétimo/a | | setuagésimo (Br.) |
| 8°/8ª | oitavo/a | 80°/80ª | octogésimo/a |
| 9°/9ª | nono/a | 90°/90ª | nonagésimo/a |
| 10°/10ª | décimo/a | 100°/100ª | centésimo/a |
| 11°/11ª | décimo/a primeiro/a | | |

**as duas primeiras ruas à direita**   *the first two roads on the right*
**o vigésimo primeiro andar**   *the twenty-first floor*

Note that the ordinals are used for the days of the week from Monday to Friday, but **terça** not **terceira** is used for Tuesday: **terça-feira**.

---

## Exercises

### 8.3

Put the days of the week in the right order, starting with Sunday.

**8.4**

**A que horas... ?** *At what time...?*
**À uma hora.** *At one o'clock.*
**Ao meio-dia.** *At midday.*
**A um quarto para as cinco.** *At a quarter to five.*

**8.4.1** Fill in with the correct form of the verb.

  **i** Outside a shop with a **Fechado** sign on the door
    A que horas _____ esta loja? (verb abrir)
  **ii** In a restaurant
    A que horas _____ o restaurante? (fechar)
 **iii** In a hotel
    A que horas _____ o almoço? (começar)
  **iv** At a coach station in Brazil
    A que horas _____ o próximo ônibus (Br.) para o Rio?
    (partir)
  **v** At a railway station in Brazil
    A que horas _____ o próximo trem (Br.) de São Paulo?
    (chegar)
  **vi** At a coach station in Portugal
    A que horas _____ o próximo autocarro (Eur.) para Faro?
    (partir)
 **vii** At a railway station in Portugal
    A que horas _____ o próximo comboio (Eur.) de Coimbra?
    (chegar)
**viii** At a bus stop in Portugal
    A que horas _____ o próximo autocarro (Eur.) para o
    centro? (passar)

**8.4.2** Look at the times and answer the questions above, using the
12-hr clock. The first one has been done for you.

**i** Às nove da manhã.

| i | ii | iii | iv |
|---|---|---|---|
| 9h00 | 24h00 | 12h00 | 14h15 |
| **v** | **vi** | **vii** | **viii** |
| 22h30 | 13h00 | 10h20 | 15h45 |

**8.5**

◀) **CD1, TR 49**

Six people are describing their physical appearance.

**8.5.1** Study the vocabulary lists below. They contain words you will hear in the descriptions of what people look like. Listen to your recording and tick each word as you hear it.

**(o) cabelo** *hair*

| | |
|---|---|
| **louro** or **loiro** *blond* | **liso** *straight* |
| **castanho** *brown* | **ondulado** *wavy* |
| **ruivo** *red* | **frisado** or **crespo** *curly* |
| **preto** *black* | **curto** *short* |
| **grisalho** *grey* | **comprido** *long* |

QUICK VOCAB

**(os) olhos** *eyes*

| | |
|---|---|
| **azuis** *blue* | **castanhos** *brown* |
| **verdes** *green* | **pretos** *black* |

QV

**(a) pele** *skin*
**clara** *light* **morena** *dark*

QV

**8.5.2** Write down what the six people on the recording said about themselves.

**8.5.3** Sérgio is describing Linda:

Ela tem
cabelo preto,
liso e comprido,
tem olhos pretos
e pele muito clara.

  **i** How would he describe the following people:
 **ii** Jane (*long, very straight, blond hair + blue eyes + light skin*)
**iii** Henry (*short, grey, wavy hair + black eyes + very dark skin*)
 **iv** James (*very short, brown, curly hair + brown eyes + dark skin*)
  **v** Claire (*very long, red, wavy hair + green eyes + light skin*)

---

## Summary

**1** Que dia da semana é hoje? – É sábado / domingo / segunda (-feira).

**2** Que horas são? – É uma (hora). – São duas (horas) e cinco (minutos).

**3** Em que dia é a excursão? – Quando abre esta loja? – A que horas fecha o restaurante?

**4** (no) domingo / sábado – (na) segunda(-feira) / terça(-feira) – de manhã – à / de tarde – à noite

**5** à uma (hora). – às três (horas) e dez (minutos).

**6** Qual é o nome dele-dela? – Qual é a aparência física dele-dela?

**7** Ele-ela é baixo-baixa. – Ele-ela nem é gordo-a nem é magro-a.

**8** Ele-ela tem pele clara / morena. – Ele-ela tem cabelo preto / louro // liso / frisado // comprido / curto. – Ele-ela tem olhos castanhos / pretos / azuis.

**9** – Você fala Inglês? – O senhor – A senhora fala Inglês? – Ela-ele fala Português? – Há quanto tempo vocês estudam Inglês? – Há quanto tempo os senhores estudam Inglês? – Há quanto tempo eles-elas estudam Português?

**10** Até amanhã às nove da noite. – Até terça(-feira) à tarde.

# 9

# Vou encontrar-me com ela amanhã
## I am going to meet her tomorrow

In this unit you will learn how to
- *Say what you are going to do*
- *Describe people's clothes as a form of identification*
- *Follow the route described to you*

**Falando com um colega** *Chatting to a colleague*

Zaida is asking her colleague Abel about his reunion with an old friend.

CD1, TR 50

| | |
|---|---|
| **Zaida** | Então quando vai chegar a sua amiga? |
| **Abel** | Amanhã. Vou encontrar-me com ela ao meio-dia. |
| **Zaida** | Oh! E onde vai ser o encontro? |
| **Abel** | Na estação. |
| **Zaida** | Muito bem! Ainda se lembra como ela é? Como vai reconhecê-la? |
| **Abel** | Lembro. E tenho aqui a carta em que ela descreve como está agora e o que vai vestir para a viagem. *(lendo)* "Estou um pouco mais gorda e agora uso o cabelo comprido. Vou estar vestida de saia branca e casaco azul claro. Vai ser fácil reconhecer-me." |

**vou encontrar-me com** *I am going to meet*
**vai ser** *is going to be*
**muito bem!** *well done!* (lit. *very well*)
**ainda se lembra…?** *do / can (you) still remember…?*
**a carta** *the letter*
**em que** *in which*
**descreve** *describes*
**vai vestir** *(she) is going to wear*
**lendo** *reading*
**um pouco** *a little*
**uso** *(I) wear*
**vou estar vestida de** *(I) am going to be dressed in*
**(a) saia branca** *white skirt*
**(o) casaco azul claro** *light blue jacket*

**Na rua** *In the street*

Eduardo is looking for Hotel Baía and seeks help from a passer-by.

| Eduardo | Por favor, pode me dizer como se vai para o Hotel Baía? |
|---------|--------------------------------------------------------|
| Transeunte | É um pouco longe. O senhor vira à esquerda ali naquela esquina, depois segue em frente e toma … a quinta ou sexta rua à direita. É a Rua Augusta. O hotel fica à esquerda, no primeiro quarteirão, antes de um semáforo. |
| Eduardo | Então, naquela esquina viro à esquerda, depois sigo em frente e tomo a Rua Augusta, que é a quinta ou sexta à direita. É isso? |
| Transeunte | É isso mesmo. |

**como se vai…?** *how does one get to …?*
**ali** *over there*
**naquela (= em+aquela)** *at that*
**(a) esquina** *corner*
**o sr vira, segue, toma** *you turn, go, take*
**viro, sigo, tomo** *(I) turn, go, take*
**depois** *next, afterwards*

**(o) quarteirão** *block*
**antes de** *before*
**(o) semáforo** *traffic lights*
**isso mesmo** *that's it, exactly that*

---

## Exercises

### 9.1 Certo ou errado? *Right or wrong?*

| | C | E |
|---|---|---|
| **1** A amiga da Zaida vai chegar amanhã. | ☐ | ☐ |
| **2** Abel não vai poder reconhecer a sua amiga. | ☐ | ☐ |
| **3** Eduardo pergunta como se vai para o Hotel Baía. | ☐ | ☐ |

### 9.2 Perguntas e respostas *Questions and answers*

**1** Como está a amiga que vai chegar amanhã?
   **a** Está um pouco mais gorda e com o cabelo comprido.
   **b** Está mais gorda e com o cabelo um pouco mais curto.

**2** Como vai estar vestida a amiga do Abel?
   **a** De saia e casaco brancos **b** De saia e casaco azuis
   **c** De saia branca e casaco azul claro.

**3** Como se vai para o Hotel Baía?
   **a** Vira-se à esquerda naquela esquina, depois segue-se em
   frente e toma-se a quinta ou sexta rua à esquerda.
   **b** Naquela esquina vira-se à esquerda, depois segue-se em
   frente e toma-se a quinta ou sexta rua à direita.

---

## How to pronounce it

🔊 **CD1, TR 52**

The spellings **gu** and **g** can alternate within the same verb. Practise
after the voice on the recording the different values of **g** and words
with **gu**.

**g**      sounds like the first *g* in *garage* in general: che**g**ar; a**g**ora; **g**ordo but like the second g in garage before **e** or **i**: lon**ge**; **ge**ral; re**gi**ão.

**gu**      sounds a bit like like *gu* in *arguing* – á**gu**a, **gu**arda-sol – except before **e** or **i** where it 'preserves' the first *g* sound in *garage*: se**gui**r (*to follow/go*). For example, in forms of the verb se**gu**ir, note that for **você** or **ele** you say se**gue** but for **eu** you say si**go**. However, in some cases, the **u** is pronounced: não a**gu**ento (*I can't stand it*).

The different sounds represented by **x** have a lot to do with the different origins the respective words have. Practise the following after the voice on the recording.

**x**      sounds like *sh* in *show* at the beginning of a word and in some cases between vowels: **X**avier; **x**arope (*cough syrup*); **x**ícara (*cup*); pu**x**ar.

**x**      sounds like *s* in *so* between two vowels: pró**x**imo; má**x**imo (*maximum*); trou**x**e (*brought*).

**x**      sounds like *z* in *zebra* where **ex** comes before a vowel: e**x**ame (*exam*); e**x**emplo (*example*); e**x**austo (*exhausted*).

**x**      sounds like *ks* in *taxi* in some words: tá**x**i; fi**x**ar (*to fix, set*); se**x**o (*sex*).

**x**      before a consonant sounds like *sh* for *show* in Portugal but like *s* for *so* in most of Brazil: se**x**ta-feira.

## Expressions
### a Colours

Below you have the names for the colours. Some are different from what you have learned for physical appearance, e.g., **grisalho** for *grey* when applied to hair but not for *grey* in general. The word **castanho** in Brazil translates *brown* for hair and in Portugal for hair and in general.

**branco/a** *white*
**preto/a** *black*

**vermelho/a – encarnado/a** (Eur.) *red*
**amarelo/a** *yellow*
**verde** *green*
**azul** *blue*
**cinzento/a** (Eur.) – **cinza** (Br.) *grey*
**castanho/a** (Eur.) – **marrom** (Br.) *brown*
**cor de rosa** *pink*
**cor de laranja** *orange*

To say that a colour is light or dark, add **claro** or **escuro**: **azul escuro**.

Colour names agree – **o(s)** or **a(s)** endings – with what they describe, but there is no m./f. change of ending in **verde** and **azul**. Also there is no change in expressions such as **cor de rosa**, (lit. *colour of the rose*), **cor de laranja** (*colour of the orange*), **cor de cinza** (*ash colour*) or their shortened versions, **rosa, laranja**, and **cinza**.

### b Clothes

In general the same names are used on both sides of the Atlantic:

**a saia; a blusa,** *blouse*; **o vestido,** *dress*; **a camisa,** *shirt*; **a camiseta** or **a t-shirt**. There are, however, some distinctions to be made.

For anything that comes in pairs, for example shoes, the Portuguese will more often use the plural and the Brazilians the singular, but you can use either: **os sapatos / o sapato**. Similarly, for trousers, you may hear **as calças** or **a calça**. This also explains the following: **os jeans = as calças de ganga** (Eur.) but **o jeans = a calça de zuarte** or **brim** (Br.).

**O casaco** means basically *coat* or *jacket*, but the range of meaning covered is not quite the same in Portugal and in

*(Contd)*

Brazil. If you are referring to the jacket in a suit, for a man or a lady, use **o casaco** in Portugal. In Brazil, it will be **o paletó** for a man and **a jaqueta** for a lady. For a casual jacket such as denim wear, you can say **o blusão** on both sides of the Atlantic.

For a man's suit, in Portugal say **o fato** (= **casaco** + **calças**) and in Brazil say **o terno** (= **paletó** + **calça**). For a lady's suit, you can simply say **saia e casaco** (Eur.) / **saia e jaqueta** (Br.). A tracksuit is **o fato de treino** (Eur.) / **o training** (Br.).

## Insight

Ela tem uma **mala azul**.
Você tem um **guarda-chuva laranja?**
Eu vou estar vestido de **camisa branca e calça(s) preta(s)**.

**c Como se vai para…?** *How do you get to…?*

In previous units you were given street directions as locations, with **fica / ficam** or **é / são** – e.g., **O hotel fica na segunda rua à esquerda** – and you also learned how to ask to be shown on the map the place you want to go to – **faça o favor de me mostrar no mapa onde fica …** – and the place where you are – **… onde estou.** Now you can also ask **como se vai para…?** or **por onde se vai para…?**

> **Por favor, como se vai para o Hotel Baía?** or
> **Por favor, por onde se vai para o Hotel Baía?**
> *Which way does one / do you go to get to the Hotel Baía?*

For possible answers when the route is described to you, you will need the following verb forms:

|  | **vai** *go* | **segue** *go, carry on* | **continua** *carry on* | **vira** *turn* | **toma** *take* |
|---|---|---|---|---|---|
| *from* | **ir** | **seguir** | **continuar** | **virar** | **tomar** |

Landmarks are given depending on what stands out as a good reference point, e.g., **o semáforo** or **o sinal de trânsito** (*the traffic signal*). Also, geometric expressions for road layout are used, such as **paralela** (*parallel*), **perpendicular** (*at a right angle*), **transversal** (*cutting across*), e.g., **na segunda transversal**, *at the 2nd cutting across*.

**d Até** *As far as, until*

**Até**, meaning *as far as*, is another useful word when it comes to describing a route. (In Portugal **até a** is often preferred to just **até**.)

A senhora segue em frente **até a**o segundo semáforo (Eur.)
A senhora segue em frente **até** o segundo semáforo (Br.)
   *You carry on as far as the second set of traffic lights.*

**Até** is also used for time, with the meaning of *until, till*. It is so in expressions you have learned such as:

**até** amanhã; **até** segunda-feira; **até** a próxima.

In Portugal this last expression tends to be pronounced with an open sound, so as to signal the contraction of preposition and article (**à = a**, preposition + **a**, article). The word for time, occasion (**a vez**) is implied – **até à próxima vez**, *see you again* (lit. *until (the) next time*).

## Insight

Por favor, como **se vai** para a praia?

----------

**(Você / O senhor) vai** pela rua paralela a esta,
**vira** à esquerda no semáforo,
na segunda transversal, **segue** à direita,
e **continua** mais uns cinco minutos até chegar lá.

*or*

**Vai-se** pela rua paralela a esta, **vira-se** à esquerda ...

## How it works

### a Reflexive verbs

Sometimes the action of a verb is done to the subject of that verb. In Portuguese this is often shown with a reflexive construction, in other words, the subject and the object are the same. Below you have the present tense of the verb **lavar** (*to wash*) employed reflexively, i.e., *to wash oneself*.

| | |
|---|---|
| eu | lavo-**me** |
| tu | lavas-**te** |
| você, o sr / a sra | |
| ele / ela | *lava*-**se** |
| nós | lavamo-**nos***  |
| vocês, os sres / as sras | |
| eles / elas | lavam-**se** |

*Note the omission of **-s** at the end of **lavamos**.

Reflexive pronouns (**me, te, se...**) are attached to the end of the verb by a hyphen or are placed before the verb and no hyphen is used.

> Lava-**se** às sete horas. *(He) has a wash at 7 a.m.*
> Ele **se** lava às sete horas. (Br.) *He has a wash at 7 a.m.*
>     (In both cases, lit. *he washes himself at 7 a.m.*)

In Brazil there is a strong tendency to place the reflexive pronoun before the verb. In order to avoid starting a sentence with a reflexive pronoun, you can begin with e.g., **ele, nós**, etc.:

> **Ele se** lava às sete horas. **Nós nos** lavamos às sete horas. (Br.)

Both in Brazil and elsewhere, the reflexive pronoun precedes the verb in the following cases:

**a** Negative sentence:
**Não** se lava às sete horas. *He doesn't have a wash at 7 a.m.*

**b** Question introduced by a question word or phrase:
**Quando** se lava? *When does he have a wash?*
**A que hora**s se lava? *At what time does he have a wash?* but
Lava-se às sete horas? (Eur.) *Does he have a wash at 7 a.m.?*

**c** Sentence introduced by a short adverb or adverbial phrase:
**Já** se lavou.   *He has already had a wash.*

**d** A subordinate clause introduced by a conjunction (e.g., *I think that...*) or a relative pronoun (e.g., *the person who...*):

| | |
|---|---|
| Penso **que** se lava às sete horas. | *I think that he has a wash at 7 a.m.* |
| Ele é a pessoa **que** se lava às sete horas. | *He is the person who has a wash at 7 a.m.* |

This still stands if a subject (**ele** or other) is being used:

**Ele** não se lava às sete horas.
Penso que **ele** se lava às sete horas.

---

## Insight

A que horas eles **se lavam?**
Eles **lavam-se** às oito horas.
Eles não **se lavam** às oito horas.
Penso que eles **se lavam** às nove horas.

---

Also note the following:

**a** Portuguese employs the reflexive construction in a variety of cases where English finds a different kind of rendering:

▶ To do with the 'self'

Como (você) **se** chama?   *How do you call yourself? or What is your name?*

| | |
|---|---|
| Lavo-**me** e visto-**me** às sete. | *I have a wash and get dressed at 7 a.m.* |
| Ainda **se** lembra como ela é? | *Do you still remember what she looks like?* |

▶ Reciprocal action

| | |
|---|---|
| A que horas **nos** encontramos amanhã | *At what time are we meeting tomorrow?* |

▶ You..., One...

| | |
|---|---|
| Por onde **se** vai para o Hotel Baía? | *Which way does one / do you go to get to Hotel Baía?* |
| Como **se** escreve esse endereço? | *How does one / do you spell that address?* |
| Aqui não **se** fuma. | *Here one doesn't smoke, meaning No smoking* |

b  In a question-answer situation, the reflexive can be dropped:

– E ainda **se** lembra como ela é?
– Lembro.

### b Verbs: the three conjugations – colloquial future

Future action or state is often expressed by using the present tense of
the verb **ir**, *to go*, plus the infinitive of the verb you want to express.

**Vamos** part**ir** amanhã. *We are going to leave tomorrow.*

|  |  | *I am going to...* | *buy* | *sell* | *leave* |
|---|---|---|---|---|---|
| eu | **vou** | compr**ar** | vend**er** | part**ir** |
| tu | **vais** | | | |
| você, o sr / a sra ele / ela | **vai** | | | |
| nós | **vamos** | | | |
| vocês, os sres / as sras eles / elas | **vão** | | | |

(Note that the verb **ir** is irregular.)

In Unit 8 you learned that you could simply use the present tense for the future. How does this compare with the 'colloquial future'?

The former is a mere factual reference to an expected future action or event, the latter implies an element of determination or certainty.

Part**imos** amanhã.　　　　　*We are leaving tomorrow.*
 (That is what is likely to happen)
**Vamos** part**ir** amanhã.　　　*We are going to leave tomorrow.*
 (That is our intention)
**Vou** est**ar** vestida de　　　*I am going to be dressed in a*
casaco azul.　　　　　　　*blue jacket.*
 (You can rely on it to identify me)

Note: the **vou** + infinitive sequence is not normally used with the verb **ir** itself. Therefore,

**Vou** para o Porto na 2ª-feira.　　*I am going to Oporto on Monday.* or
　　　　　　　　　　　　*I am going to go to Oporto on Monday.*

Tone of voice can be used to convey determination or certainty.

## Exercises

### 9.3

Tricia would like to go to the swimming pool and has asked

**Por onde se vai para a piscina?**

**9.3.1** Fill in the gaps in the route she has been told, choosing the words you need from the list below.

**toma – vira – segue**
**transversal – perpendicular**

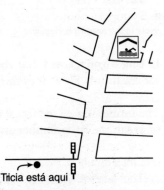

Naquela esquina ali com o semáforo,
você _____ à esquerda, depois
_____ em frente, na terceira
_____ vira à direita e depois
_____ a primeira rua à esquerda.
A piscina é aí, à esquerda.

Tricia está aqui

**9.3.2** What could you have said instead of **você...** to add a touch of extra politeness?

### 9.4

◀) CD1, TR 53

Four people are talking about their clothes.

**9.4.1** Listen to your recording and match up the pictures with the description of what each individual is going to wear. Tick each item as you hear it.

**9.4.2** Listen to the recording again and write out a full description of what each person is going to wear.

**9.4.3** How would they have said that, for travelling, this is the kind of clothes they usually wear? The first one is done for you:

**Para viajar normalmente visto terno (ou um terno).**

**9.4.4** Out of the four individuals describing their clothes, which two come from Brazil?

**9.4.5** You want to point out some people in a crowd. Complete the following sentences in Portuguese so as to explain who they are by reference to what they are wearing.

 **i** É aquela senhora de (<u>pink blouse + green skirt</u>)
**ii** É aquele senhor de (<u>white shirt + brown trousers</u>)

fato (Eur.) / terno (Br.)
[castanho (Eur.) / marrom (Br.) claro]

blusa [vermelho]

saia e casaco (Eur.) /
saia e jaqueta (Br.)
[cinzento (Eur.) / cinza (Br.)]

camiseta
[branco]
casaco
[laranja escuro]

calça(s)
[verde]

blusão [preto]

camisa
[amarelo]

calça(s) de ganga (Eur.) /
zuarte (Br.) [azul]

**9.5**

The list of participants in a guided tour cannot be found and the guide is trying to sort out who is who. The questions, answers and statements below come from the group. Complete them, putting the jumbled-up words in the correct order.

1 O senhor, por favor, como (<u>chama / se</u>)?
2 Eu? (<u>Chamo / Valdemar Nascimento / me / -</u>).
3 Por favor! Esta é a pessoa que (<u>se / Mauro de Sá / chama</u>).
4 Aquele senhor? Eu penso que (<u>chama / Fernando Camargo / se / ele</u>).
5 Desculpe a pergunta, a senhora (<u>- / se / Flávia Couto / chama</u>)?
6 Não, (<u>Flávia Couto / . / me / Chamo / chamo / me / não / - / Rute Bento</u>).

---

## Summary

1 Vou partir amanhã. – Parto amanhã. – Vamos para o Rio (na) quinta(-feira).
2 Vou encontrar-me / me encontrar com eles ao meio-dia. – Vamos para a praia de tarde.
3 Vou comprar bananas. – Vou vestir-me / me vestir. – Vou estar vestido-a de casaco verde.
4 Ele-ela tem uma mala vermelha. – Ele-ela tem um guarda-sol laranja. – Ele-ela tem um casaco verde claro e calça(s) preta(s).
5 É aquela senhora de vestido rosa. – É aquele senhor de camisa branca.
6 A senhora que se chama Eloisa é aquela que está vestida de saia comprida vermelha.
7 Onde nos encontramos esta noite? – No restaurante.
8 Não me lembro onde fica o restaurante. – Como se escreve o nome da rua?
9 Por favor, como se vai para a piscina / o supermercado mais perto? – Vai(-se) por / pelo / pela….
10 Vai-se por esta rua. – Você / o senhor - a senhora vai por esta rua. – (Você) vai por aquela estrada ali. – Toma a terceira à direita. – Segue pela estrada perpendicular a essa. – Vira à esquerda na segunda transversal.

# 10

# Ontem fui de carro
## Yesterday I went by car

In this unit you will learn how to
- *Describe your daily routine or someone else's*
- *Talk about the months, seasons and the weather*
- *Talk about something you did or what happened in the past*

**Falando acerca do seu dia-a-dia** *Talking about one's daily routine*

Alexandra is trying to find out about Reinaldo's daily routine.

| | |
|---|---|
| **Reinaldo** | Levanto-me cedo, às sete e meia da manhã, e saio de casa às oito e meia. À noite volto para casa tarde, às nove, e deito-me pelas dez e meia. |
| **Alexandra** | E no fim de semana? |
| **Reinaldo** | Deito-me mais tarde. |
| **Alexandra** | Então levanta-se também mais tarde? |
| **Reinaldo** | Depende. Levanto-me mais tarde, quando faz mau tempo. Quando faz bom tempo, levanto-me às sete e meia como de costume mas para ir à praia. Gosto de chegar lá muito cedo. |

*CD1, TR 54*

**levanto-me** *(I) get up*
**cedo – tarde** *early – late*
**saio de casa** *(I) leave home*
**volto para casa** *(I) return home*
**deito-me** *(I) go to bed*
**mais tarde** *later*
**depende** *(it) depends*
**faz mau tempo** *the weather is bad* (lit. *(it) makes bad weather)*
**faz bom tempo** *the weather is fine*
**como de costume** *as usual* (lit. *like of habit)*
**no fim de semana = ao fim / aos fins de semana**

### Falando de como vai para o trabalho *Talking about how one gets to work*

Nazaré is explaining to Marcos how she goes to work.

| | |
|---|---|
| **Marcos** | Onde é que você trabalha? |
| **Nazaré** | Trabalho numa loja relativamente perto da minha casa. |
| **Marcos** | E como vai para o trabalho? |
| **Nazaré** | Normalmente vou a pé. |
| **Marcos** | E quanto tempo leva? |
| **Nazaré** | Levo meia hora. Mas às vezes, quando me levanto mais tarde ou faz mau tempo, vou de carro. Por exemplo ontem fui de carro. Levei mais ou menos dez minutos. |

**é que** *filler words,* lit. *(it) is that*
**trabalho** *(I) work*
**relativamente** *relatively*
**vou a pé** *(I) walk, (I) go on foot*
**quanto tempo leva?** *how long does it take you?* (lit. *how much time (it) takes? / (you) use up?)*
**às vezes** *sometimes* (lit. *at times)*
**por exemplo** *for instance*
**ontem** *yesterday*
**fui de carro** *(I) went by car*
**levei** *it took me* (lit. *(I) took / used up)*
**mais ou menos dez minutos = uns dez minutos**

## Exercises

### 10.1 Certo ou errado? *Right or wrong?*

|   | C | E |
|---|---|---|
| **1** Reinaldo sai de casa às 8h30. | ☐ | ☐ |
| **2** O Reinaldo volta para casa às 22h30. | ☐ | ☐ |
| **3** Sabemos que a Nazaré gosta de ir à praia. | ☐ | ☐ |

### 10.2 Perguntas e respostas *Questions and answers*

**1** Reinaldo: Quando é que ele se levanta às 7h30?
   **a** De 2ª a 6ª feira.
   **b** Ao fim de semana quando faz bom tempo.
   **c** De 2ª a 6ª feira e nos fins de semana em que faz bom tempo.

**2** Nazaré: Onde é que fica a loja em que ela trabalha?
   **a** A 15 minutos da casa dela, de carro.
   **b** A 30 minutos da casa dela, a pé.

**3** Nazaré: Ontem como é que ela foi para o trabalho?
   **a** Foi a pé e levou uma meia hora.
   **b** Foi a pé e levou uma hora e meia.
   **c** Foi de carro e levou uns 10 minutos.

## How to pronounce it

🔊 **CD1, TR 56**

You may wish to get your accent right for the side of the Atlantic where you are intending to speak the Portuguese you are learning.

In Units 8 and 9 you learned the *so*-versus-*push*-or-*show* sound differences. Now please also note that a large number of Brazilians pronounce the t and the d, particularly before spelling e or i, as, respectively, [tj] and [dj], a bit like the *ch* in *cheese* and the *j* in *jar*. The final -e then sounds like *i* in *cigarette*. Listen to the recording and practise the following examples which will be pronounced for you first by a Brazilian voice and then by a Portuguese voice:

dia; tarde; noite; universidade (*university*); tive (*I had*).

## Expressions
### a Months and dates

**Que data é hoje?** *What is the date today?*

| | |
|---|---|
| **janeiro** *January* | **julho** *July* |
| **fevereiro** *February* | **agosto** *August* |
| **março** *March* | **setembro** *September* |
| **abril** *April* | **outubro** *October* |
| **maio** *May* | **novembro** *November* |
| **junho** *June* | **dezembro** *December* |

Unlike English, days of the month are expressed in cardinals but **primeiro** can be used for the first day of the month.

no dia **um** de novembro or no **primeiro** de novembro
(**um** – cardinal) (**primeiro** – ordinal)

Also unlike English, years are not read in hundreds.

2999 = **dois mil, novecentos e noventa e nove,** *twenty-nine ninety-nine.*

| | |
|---|---|
| Hoje é **cinco de agosto.** | *Today it is the fifth of August.* |
| Pedro Álvares Cabral avistou o Brasil no dia **vinte e dois de abril de 1500 (mil e quinhentos).** | *Pedro Álvares Cabral sighted Brazil on the twenty-second April 1500 (fifteen hundred).* |

**b Seasons**

**As quatro estações do ano** *The four seasons*

(a) **primavera** *spring*          (o) **outono** *autumn*
(o) **verão** *summer*              (o) **inverno** *winter*

> Em dezembro é **inverno**          *In December it is winter*
> em Portugal mas **verão** na       *in Portugal but summer*
> maior parte do Brasil.             *in most of Brazil.*

(Please remember that winter in the Northern hemisphere
coincides with summer in the Southern hemisphere.)

**c Weather**

Study the following ways of expressing the weather.

| | | |
|---|---|---|
| **1** Está | nublado | *It is cloudy* |
| | quente | *hot* |
| | frio | *cold* |
| **2** Faz | frio | *It is cold* |
| | calor | *hot* |
| | sol | *sunny* |
| | vento | *windy* |
| **3** Há | nevoeiro | *It is foggy* |
| | neblina | *misty* |
| | geada | *frosty* |
| | gelo | *icy* |
| **4** Chove | | *It rains (usually)* |
| Neva | | *snows* |

*(Contd)*

Some tips to help you describe the weather correctly:

**1** Use **está** (verb **estar**) with an adjective (e.g., **quente**) or with a past participle (e.g., **nublado**).

**2** Use **faz** (**fazer**) with a noun (e.g., **sol**). Note that **frio** can be both an adjective (**um dia frio** = *a cold day*) and a noun (**o frio** *the cold*). As a result it fits into both categories (1) and (2) above and can be used with both verb **estar** and verb **fazer**. By analogy, the verb **estar** is also used with **calor** (*heat*) as an alternative to **quente** (**está calor** = **está quente**).

**3** Use preferably **há** (**haver**) with a noun for something that looks dense or static (e.g., **nevoeiro**, fog).

**4** Use a verb expressing the weather condition – **chove** (**chover**), **neva** (**nevar**) – for forms of precipitation, i.e., rain, snow, etc., seen to be falling. However, frost or ice on the ground is better expressed with **haver** – **há geada / gelo**.

The notion of movement that may be behind the preference for a conjugated verb for rain, etc. can be extended to **vento**, wind, with the verb **ventar**, as is the case in Brazil (**está ventando**, the wind is blowing – see continuous present and past, in Unit 15).

## Insight
**Hoje está quente e nublado.**

----------

**Aqui chove muito no outono.**

----------

**Lá faz muito frio e neva no inverno.**

----------

**Gosto de estar na praia quando faz calor.**

# Cultural information
## Children and adults

The English word *child* (and its plural *children*) finds a Portuguese translation in **criança/s**, in contrast with **adulto/s** (*adult/s*). The word **criança** is grammatically feminine even when applied to a male child; **adulto** is masculine even when applied to a female adult. There is also the word **menino / menina** which translates litte boy / girl. Note the way a parent may refer to his / her young children depending on whether s/he is talking about his / her family or buying tickets for them:

**Tenho dois filhos, um menino de quatro anos e uma menina de dois anos.**

or

**Tenho duas crianças, um menino de quatro anos e uma menina de dois anos.**

but

**Três, por favor, para um adulto e duas crianças.**

Particularly the feminine **menina** can assume a courteous form of address.

**O leite é para a menina.** *The milk is for the little girl (the young lady).*

Also, **moço** (Br.) or **rapaz** can translate *young man, lad.*

**Tenho dois filhos, dois rapazes.** *I have two sons, two lads.*

The feminine of **rapaz, rapariga,** is better not used in Brazil, where it has acquired pejorative overtones. The safe alternative is **moça.**

## Insight

**Eles levam os filhos à praia quando o tempo está bom.**

-------------

**As crianças têm umas grandes férias de verão.**

-------------

**Os filhos deles, Marta e Tiago, já são adultos.**

---

## How it works

### a Questions

You have come across two different types of question.

**a** Questions which are like a statement, with the same word-order. The only change is an inquisitive rising intonation.

> Você está de férias. *You are on holiday.* (statement)
> Você está de férias? *Are you on holiday?* (question)

**b** Questions which start with a question-word (**onde, quando, como, qual,** etc.), in which case the subject (e.g., *you*) may come before or after the verb.

> **Onde** você trabalha?       *Where do you work?*
> subject **(você)** + *verb* **(trabalha)**
> **Onde** trabalha você?       *Where do you work?*
> verb **(trabalha)** + *subject* **(você)**

Subject + verb is more widely heard on the American side of the Atlantic and verb + subject on the European side.

Please note that in both question type **a** and **b** the subject can also be omitted, as you learned in Unit 7, and therefore you are also likely to hear the following versions:

**a** **Está de férias.** (statement) **Está de férias?** (question)
**b** **Onde trabalha.** (statement) **Onde trabalha?** (question)

> **b É que** *It is … that*

These are merely filler words, meaning literally *(it) is + that*.

> Eu **é que** agradeço. *It is I who must thank you.*

On both sides of the Atlantic, **é que** helps to fix the word-order in a subject + verb sequence. This means that with **é que** you will fit in with your question word-order wherever you speak Portuguese.

**Onde é que** você trabalha?

Note also that the subject can be omitted. **Onde é que** trabalha?

**Insight**
> Como **você vai** para o trabalho?
> Como **vai você** para o trabalho?
> Como **é que você vai** para o trabalho?
> Como **vai** para o trabalho?
> Como **é que vai** para o trabalho?

**c Gender**

How to change masculine to feminine:

**1** Words ending in **-o** (masc.) (but not **-ão**) substitute **-a** (fem.)
amigo / amiga *friend* (*male / female*)

**2** Words ending in **-or** or **-ês** (masc.) add **a** (fem.)
senhor / senhora *gentleman* / *lady*
inglês / inglesa (no accent ^ in the feminine) *English man / woman*

**3** Words ending in **-eu** (masc.) in general substitute **-eia** (fem.).
europeu / europeia *European*

**4** Words ending in -e or -a do not change.

estudante *student (male / female)*
dentista *dentist (male / female)*

**5** A few words in -ão (masc.) drop the final -o (for the fem.).

irmão / irmã *brother / sister*

**6** ô changes to ó.

avô / avó *grand father/mother*

**7** A different word is used.

pai / mãe *father / mother*

Adjectives, past participles used as adjectives, and ordinals follow the above rules according to the noun to which they refer.

**o** senh**or** ingl**ês** / **a** senh**ora** ingl**esa** *the English gentleman / lady*
obrigad**o** / obrigad**a** *thank you (said by male / female)*
n**a** primeir**a** ru**a** *in the first street*

Note the irregular formation of the following adjectives for *good* and *bad*.

**bom** tempo (masc.) *good/fine weather*; **boa** tarde (fem.) *good afternoon*
**mau** tempo (masc.) *bad weather*; **má** notícia (fem.) *bad news*

### d Plurals

A masculine plural noun may include both genders.

os amigos *male friends* but also *male + female friends*
os pais *fathers*, i.e. *male parents*, but also *father + mother*
os filhos *male children* but also *male + female children*

Exception: os avós *grandparents (male + female grandparents)*

Note that the word **parente** does not translate the English word parent but means 'relative'.

Um tio é um parente. *An uncle is a relation.*

A masculine plural adjective or past participle is required where nouns of both genders are to be covered.

**O** filho e **a** filh**a** casad**os**. *The married son and daughter.*

### e Verbs: the three conjugations – preterite indicative

|  | I bought<br>I have bought | I sold<br>I have sold | I left<br>I have left |
|---|---|---|---|
| eu | compr**ei** | vend**i** | part**i** |
| tu | compr**aste** | vend**este** | part**iste** |
| você, o sr / a sra<br>ele / ela | compr**ou** | vend**eu** | part**iu** |
| nós | compr**amos** (*) | vend**emos** | part**imos** |
| vocês, os sres / as<br>sras eles / elas | compr**aram** | vend**eram** | part**iram** |

(*) **compramos** or **comprámos** – the use of the accent is optional.

### Use the preterite for...

▶ an action / event (or a series of actions / events) which was completed at some definite time in the past

Cheg**uei** ontem.          *I arrived yesterday.* (cheg**ar**)

No domingo passado **fui** de carro.    *Last Sunday I went by car.* (**ir**)

▶ an action / event (or a series of actions / events) which has been completed at some indefinite time in the past, including recent past

Cheg**uei**.          I have arrived. (cheg**ar**)

Sa**í** de casa.          I have left home. (sa**ir**)

(Check **chegar** (-**gar** verb), **ir** and **sair** in the VG at the end of the book.)

---

## Exercises

### 10.3

Complete the sentence below by putting the weather and season pictures into words.

Onde eles moram...

**10.4**

🔊 CD1, TR 57

**(a) terra** *land, native country*

On your recording you will find some people talking about what the months are like in their own and someone else's country.

**10.4.1** From what they say, enter month(s) and weather in the grid below. The first one has been done for you.

no mês /
nos meses de...                                     normalmente...

| | | | |
|---|---|---|---|
| **i** | Na minha terra | maio | bom tempo |
| **ii** | Na terra do meu marido | | |
| **iii** | Na terra da minha esposa | | |
| **iv** | Na terra dos meus avós | | |
| **v** | Aquele rapaz é de uma terra onde | | |
| **vi** | Estas crianças são de uma terra onde | | |

**10.4.2** Listen again and make a written note of all that they say.

**10.4.3** Can you describe that summer holiday when the weather went terribly wrong? (Look up verbs **estar**, **fazer** and **haver** in the table of irregular verbs at the end of the book.)

*The weather was bad. It was cold, it was windy, it rained,*
*it was foggy and the sun didn't come out.*

**10.5**

In the pictures below you can see Tony's normal daily routine and
how it changed yesterday.

Normalmente

| 7h00 | 8h00 | 20h30 | 23h00 |

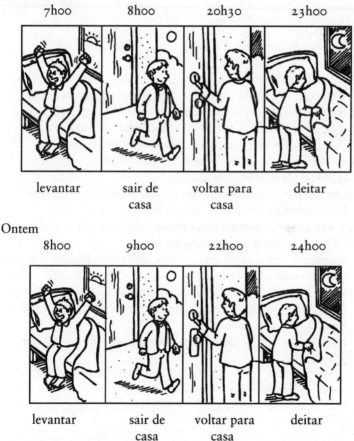

| levantar | sair de casa | voltar para casa | deitar |

Ontem

| 8h00 | 9h00 | 22h00 | 24h00 |

| levantar | sair de casa | voltar para casa | deitar |

**10.5.1** Help Tony explain his daily routine.
Start with **Normalmente eu...**

**10.5.2** Now help him describe how things were different yesterday. Start with **Ontem eu…**

**10.5.3** How would his mother describe his daily routine? Start with **Normalmente ele…**

**10.5.4** How would she describe yesterday's changed routine? Start with **Ontem ele…**

---

## Summary

1 Normalmente, eu levanto-me às seis (horas), tomo o pequeno almoço (Eur.) / café da manhã (Br.) e saio de casa cedo; vou para o trabalho / a universidade, onde tomo alguma coisa pela uma (hora) e meia e fico lá de tarde; volto para casa às sete (horas) e deito-me uma ou duas horas depois do jantar.

2 Ontem, eu levantei-me às seis (horas). – Ontem, eles levantaram-se às seis (horas).

3 Ontem, eu fui para o trabalho às oito da manhã. – Ontem, nós fomos para o trabalho às oito da manhã.

4 Normalmente, quando é que chove e neva na terra deles? – Chove no outono e neva no inverno.

5 Na minha terra, agora está quente, mas esteve frio em março e choveu muito em abril.

6 Quando o tempo está bom, levo as crianças à praia. – Quando faz muito calor, fico na praia somente uma ou duas horas de manhã.

7 Venho para este hotel todos os anos em setembro. – Cheguei 6ª feira dia 12.

8 Normalmente, vou a casa dos meus pais todos os fins de semana, mas este fim de semana não fui.

9 No verão, vou à praia todos os fins de semana, mas no fim de semana passado não fui.

10 No verão, eles vão à praia todos os fins de semana, mas no fim de semana passado não foram.

# 11

## Lugares e pessoas
### Places and people

In this revision unit there is more practice on how to
- *Move around and meet people*
- *Talk about times, dates and weather*
- *Talk about the past and what is expected to happen in the future*

**11.1**

◀) **CD2, TR 1**

You are intending to travel around the country and want to know which direction you have to take for the different places you would like to visit.

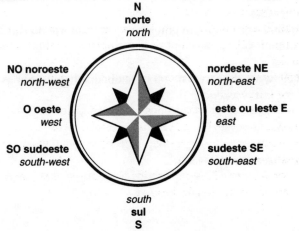

**11.1.1** Study the above compass rose – **a rosa dos ventos** – and listen to your recording. Place a number, from 1 to 9, against each cardinal point as you hear it.

**11.1.2** Check that you have understood everything the speakers on the recording have said. Write it down.

### 11.2

**(os) graus centígrados** *degrees centigrade*

a temperatura está alta = está quente
a temperatura está baixa = está frio

**11.2.1** Find a combination for the half-sentences below that will suit the weather forecast shown on the map of Portugal for the coming weekend.

No próximo fim de semana...

| | | | |
|---|---|---|---|
| **i** | vai fazer sol | **a** | no Porto |
| **ii** | vai fazer vento / vai ventar (Br.) | **b** | em Lisboa |
| **iii** | vai chover | **c** | nordeste-sudoeste |
| **iv** | vai estar muito nublado | **d** | a sul do Rio Tejo |
| **v** | vão estar vinte e seis graus centígrados | **e** | a norte do Rio Douro |
| **vi** | vão estar vinte e quatro graus centígrados | **f** | a norte do Rio Tejo |

**11.2.2** Re-write the forecast you have obtained above but as a report for last weekend.

Start with:

**No fim de semana passado...**

**11.2.3** Answer the following questions, giving full answers:

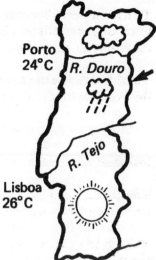

i Fez mais calor no Porto ou em Lisboa?

ii A temperatura esteve mais baixa em Lisboa ou no Porto?

iii Fez bom tempo no Norte ou no Sul?

iv Como é que esteve o tempo a norte do Rio Douro?

v Fez vento / ventou (Br.) de nordeste?

vi Onde é que choveu?

**11.3**

You may be travelling both in Portugal and Brazil.

**11.3.1**

**(a) poltrona** *luxury seat*

Below is a ticket bought at a coach station in Brazil. Fill in the gaps in the dialogue between the lady traveller and the ticket clerk.

## BILHETE PASSAGEM RODOVIÁRIO

| SEGURO FACULTATIVO | | LEI FEDERAL |
|---|---|---|
| **DE** MARINGÁ | **PARA** CURITIBA | **BILHETE Nº** 7500364 |
| **DATA EMBARQUE** 15 / 10 | **HORÁRIO** 22:45 | **POLTRONA** 15 |
| **TIPO ÔNIBUS** EXECUTIVO | **PLATAFORMA** 01 | **DATA EMISSÃO** 14/10 |

ônibus (Br.) = autocarro (Eur.)    plataforma = cais (Eur.)

– Queria fazer uma reserva para Curitiba para amanhã à noite.
– À noite tem o Executivo.
– A que _____ parte?
– Às _____ e quarenta e cinco.
– Está bem. Queria 'não fumante', somente ida.
– O ônibus é todo _____. É proibido _____.
– Certo.
– Aqui está a passagem da senhora. Poltrona _____ no
   Executivo das dez e _____ amanhã
   _____. O _____ sai da primeira plataforma.

## 11.3.2

(a) linha (Eur.) = (o) cais (Eur.) = (a) plataforma

**(o) lugar, lugar sentado** *seat*
**junto à janela** *by the window*
**(a) carruagem** *train carriage*

Below is a ticket bought at a railway station in Portugal. Fill in the gaps in the dialogue between the lady traveller and the ticket clerk.

```
            TIPO DE COMBOIO – IC
RESERVA    01.02              Nº 16 50050
                  BILHETE
   1 LUGAR SENTADO       NÃO FUMADOR
       COIMBRA - B  →  LISBOA - S.A.
PARTIDA   02.02       10:25        LINHA 2
    CARR.   021      JANELA 22
```

comboio (Eur.) = trem (Br.)     fumador (Eur.) = fumante (Br.)

B – B station, as opposed to A station in the city centre, Coimbra.

S.A. – Santa Apolónia, Lisbon railway station serving the north.

- Queria fazer uma reserva para Lisboa para amanhã de manhã.
- De manhã tem o Intercidades.
- _____ parte?
- Às dez e _____.
- Está bem.
- 'Fumador' ou _____ ?
- 'Não fumador', somente ida.
- Quer lugar junto à janela?
- _____, sim. Obrigada.
- Aqui está o bilhete da senhora. Lugar _____ e dois na
  carruagem vinte e _____ do Intercidades das _____ e vinte
  e cinco amanhã _____. O _____ sai da linha
  número dois.

**11.4**

◄» CD2, TR 2

**Como é que se escreve?** *How do you spell it?*
**A de África...** *A for (lit. of) Africa...*

QV

**11.4.1** Practise saying the Portuguese names for the letters after
the voice on the recording. You will hear the alphabet twice, in a
Portuguese and in a Brazilian voice.

A, B, C, D, E, F, G, H, I, J, L, M, N, O, P, Q, R, S, T, U, V, X, Z

K, W, Y: These letters are found in some place names, words of
foreign origin and international abbreviations.

**11.4.2** Take Peter Ralph's place in the dialogue below and carry
on, using the words in the box (these are words you already know).

- Como é que o senhor se chama?
- Peter Ralph.
- Peter... (escrevendo) E o outro nome,
  como é que se escreve?
- Escreve-se com R de rua...

| | |
|---|---|
| praia | |
| | longe |
| homem | |
| | água |

**11.5**

◆ CD2, TR 3

**11.5.1 Onde é que você mora?**
  **i** Can you ask this question using **o senhor** for you?
  **ii** Can you now ask the same question but using **tu** for *you*. Remember to change the verb ending too.

**11.5.2** Look at the three street names and also at the three front door numbers.

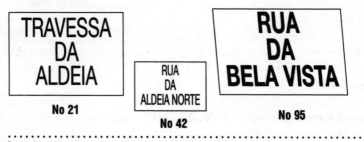

TRAVESSA DA ALDEIA
No 21

RUA DA ALDEIA NORTE
No 42

RUA DA BELA VISTA
No 95

a travessa = a rua pequena transversal

  **i** Listen to the two people on the recording who are saying where they live and tick their road name and door number.
  **ii** Play the role of the person who lives at the third address and say where you live.

**11.6**

◆ CD2, TR 4

On your recording you will hear a lady talking to a taxi driver.

This is the piece of paper she is showing him.

> Rua do Atlântico, n° 100

**11.6.1**

  **i**  Listen to what she says and rearrange the words below so as to match her own words.

        Pode / levar / para / me / ? / endereço / este

  **ii**  What did she ask?

 **iii**  Now, without showing the written note to the taxi driver,

      **a**  enquire whether he can take you to that address:
          **Pode...**

      **b**  request to be taken to that address:
          **Faça o favor de...**

**11.7**

Three different people are looking for the public gardens Antero de Quental in the centre of Ponta Delgada in the Azores (**os Açores**). They have asked:

**Por onde se vai para o Jardim Antero de Quental?**

**11.7.1** Match the three sets of directions below with the three spots on the map where the question was asked – A, B, C.

i   Esta rua é perpendicular à rua do jardim. Segue-se em frente até chegar lá.

ii  Toma-se a primeira rua à direita, depois vira-se à esquerda e continua-se nessa rua. O jardim fica em frente.

iii Vai-se em frente. Na primeira transversal vira-se à esquerda. O jardim fica nessa rua, mas antes de chegar lá tem-se que passar duas ruas à direita.

**11.7.2** These directions were given using **se** just like the question. What changes do you have to make to use **você** instead? Reword the three directions.

**11.7.3** If you wish to be more courteous, what can you replace **você** with?

### 11.8

**(os) calções de banho** (Eur.) **/ a tanga** (Eur.) **(o) calção de banho** (Br.) **/ a sunga** (Br.) *male beachwear, bathing trunks*
**(o) fato de banho** (Eur.) **/ (o) maiô** (Br.) *bathing costume, bathing suit*
**(o) biquíni** *bikini*

[rosa]          [laranja]

**11.8.1** Listen to the following mini-dialogues on your recording and write down the replies given to these questions.

**i** – Qual é a sua filha? **ii** – Qual é a sua irmã? **iii** – Qual é o seu pai?

**11.8.2**

◄ **CD2, TR 6**

**em pé** or **de pé** *standing* (lit. *on one's feet*)
**deitado/a** *lying down* (lit. *laid*)
**sentado/a** *sitting* (lit. *seated*)

Listen to the second set of mini-dialogues and write down the replies.

**i** – Qual é a sua neta? **ii** – Qual é a sua mãe? **iii** – Qual é o seu avô?

**11.8.3** Following the above models, describe your:

**i** female friend (red bikini; very brown; standing)
**ii** male friend (green trunks; black hair; lying down)

**11.9**

Chamo-me Álvaro Maia. Sou de Maputo, em Moçambique. Tenho dezoito anos e sou estudante. Moro aqui na África do

Sul há dois anos, com os meus pais, a minha irmã e o meu irmão.
Os meus pais são portugueses e o negócio do meu pai tem uma
agência grande no norte de Portugal. Vamos para lá no próximo
ano e eu vou estudar na Universidade do Porto. Quero ser médico.

**11.9.1** *What? Where? Where from? Where to? With whom?*
*How long?*

Based on what Álvaro has said about himself and his family, what
replies would he give to the following questions?

   **i**  Como é que você se chama?
  **ii**  De onde é que você é?
 **iii**  Quantos anos é que você tem?
 **iv**  Onde é que você mora?
   **v**  Há quanto tempo é que mora aqui?
 **vi**  Quando é que vai sair daqui?
 **vii**  Com quem é que você mora?
**viii**  Qual é que é a terra dos seus pais?
 **ix**  Para onde é que você vai no próximo ano?
   **x**  O que é que você quer ser profissionalmente?
 **xi**  Em que universidade é que você vai estudar?

**11.9.2** Você or tu?

You are interviewing Álvaro for a school magazine in Portugal.
Ask the same questions as above but with **tu** instead of **você**.
Remember to change the verb endings accordingly.

The first question has been done for you: **Como é que tu te chamas?**

(Before answering question viii, study the contents of Unit 20:HIWc.)

   **11.10**

🔊 **CD2, TR 7**

You may wish to send a Christmas card or express your good
wishes verbally. Study the contents of the chart below and say

the right words for each occasion after the speaker on the recording.

| Natal *Christmas* | Feliz Natal |
|---|---|
| Ano Novo *New Year* | Feliz Ano Novo / Próspero Ano Novo / Boas entradas |
| Páscoa *Easter* | Feliz Páscoa or Páscoa Feliz |
| Aniversário *Birthday* | Feliz aniversário / Parabéns |
| Casamento *Wedding* | Parabéns / Felicidades |
| Aniversário de casamento *Wedding anniversary* | Parabéns / Felicidades |
| Nascimento *Newborn baby* | Parabéns / Felicidades |
| Falecimento *Bereavement* | Sentidos pêsames |
| Sucesso, êxito *Success, any happy event* | Parabéns / Felicidades |

**11.11**

A birthday card for someone who is sixty years old reads:

**Parabéns no seu sexagésimo aniversário. Muitas felicidades.**

Re-write the birthday card for someone who is twenty-five years old.

Note: You can say **Parabéns no seu aniversário** (*on your birthday*) or **Parabéns pelo seu aniversário** (*for your birthday*), for **Parabéns** contains both the notion of 'good wishes' and 'congratulations'.

**11.12**

Add your good wishes for the New Year to this Christmas card.

# Feliz Natal

## Summary

1 Há quanto tempo é que você mora aqui? – Onde é que morou antes? – Para onde é que vai morar no próximo ano?

2 Essa cidade, onde fica / é? – Fica / é no Norte / Sul / Este / Oeste.

3 Como é que se escreve o nome? – P de Portugal, A de Algarve...

4 Queria um bilhete (Eur.) / uma passagem (Br.) para esta cidade, para amanhã à noite no autocarro (Eur.) / ônibus (Br.) das 10h30, junto à janela. De que linha (Eur.) / plataforma (Br.) sai?

5 Por favor, pode me levar para este endereço? – Pode me levar para a Avenida Oceano, número 204, por favor?

6 No mês passado, a temperatura esteve alta / baixa. – Hoje faz sol mas está nublado. – Amanhã vai fazer calor, 30 graus (centígrados). – Amanhã vai estar um bom dia de praia.

7 Por onde se vai para a praia / o aquário / o jardim zoológico? – Você / o senhor – a senhora segue por esta rua, vira à esquerda e tem que passar duas ruas à direita.

8 Qual é o seu filho / pai / irmão / neto / avô? – Qual é a sua filha / mãe / irmã / neta / avó?

9 O meu marido é aquele senhor de tanga (Eur.) / sunga (Br.) azul. – A minha esposa é aquela senhora de biquíni verde claro.

10 As minhas netas são aquelas meninas que estão sentadas. – O meu filho é aquele menino de cabelo castanho que está em pé. – A minha filha é aquela menina de cabelo louro comprido que está deitada.

# 12

**Siga em frente**
Go straight on

In this unit you will learn how to
- *Receive and give directions and instructions*
- *Be specific about what you want in a shop*
- *Talk about weights, measures and quantities*

**Na rua** *In the street*

Daniela stops two passers-by to ask the way to the local grocer's.

| | |
|---|---|
| **Daniela** | Por favor, onde é a mercearia? |
| **1° Transeunte** | Não sei. Eu não sou daqui. Desculpe. |
| **Daniela** | Não tem importância. Obrigada. |
| | ———————— |
| **Daniela** | Por favor, sabe me dizer onde é a mercearia? |
| **2° Transeunte** | Sei, sim. É perto. Siga em frente e no segundo semáforo vire à esquerda. A mercearia fica à direita. |

**a mercearia** *the grocer's shop*
**sabe me dizer…?** *can you tell me…? (lit. do you know to tell me…?)*
**siga** *go*
**vire** *turn*

**Na mercearia** *In the grocer's shop*

The sales assistant at the grocer's serves Daniela and a second customer.

CD2, TR 9

| | |
|---|---|
| **Daniela** | Queria meio quilo de queijo. |
| **Vendedor** | Qual prefere? |
| **Daniela** | Prefiro esse à sua direita. |
| **Vendedor** | Aqui tem o meio quilo de queijo. Mais alguma coisa? |
| **Daniela** | Não. Só isso. Quanto custa? |

| | |
|---|---|
| **2ª Freguesa** | Queria meia dúzia de ovos, duzentos gramas daquele queijo (*apontando*), uma garrafa de litro de água mineral e salsicha em lata … uma daquelas latas na segunda prateleira a contar de cima. E por favor dê-me um saco. (*pegando no saco com as compras*) Obrigada. Quanto é tudo? |

**QUICK VOCAB**

**meio quilo de queijo** *1/2 kilo of cheese*
**prefere** *(you) prefer*
**prefiro** *(I) prefer*
**só = somente**
**só isso** *that's all* (lit. *only that*)
**quanto custa? = quanto é?**
**duzentos gramas** *200 grams*
**daquele (= de+aquele) queijo** *of* (lit. *from*) *that cheese*
**apontando** *pointing*
**(a) garrafa de litro** *1 litre bottle*
**(a) água mineral** *mineral water*
**(a) salsicha em lata** *canned sausage*
**uma daquelas (=de+aquelas)**
**latas** *one out of those tins, cans*
**(a) prateleira** *shelf*
**a contar de cima** *counting from the top* (lit. *at + to count + from*)
**dê-me um saco** *give me a carrier bag*
**pegando no saco** *picking up the bag*

**as compras** *the shopping*
**quanto é tudo?** *how much does it come to? (lit. how much is (it) all?)*

## Exercises

### 12.1 Perguntas e respostas *Questions and answers*

1  Quem sabe onde é que a mercearia é?
   **a**  O primeiro transeunte.    **b** O segundo transeunte.

2  Por onde é que Daniela vai para a mercearia?
   **a**  Ela segue em frente e vira à esquerda no segundo semáforo.
   **b**  Ela segue em frente e vira à direita no segundo semáforo

3  Qual é o queijo que a Daniela prefere?
   **a**  Ela prefere o queijo que está à direita dela.
   **b**  Ela prefere o queijo que está à direita do vendedor.

4  Quantas coisas é que a segunda freguesa quer comprar?
   **a**  Quatro: ovos, queijo, água e salsicha em lata.
   **b**  Cinco: ovos, queijo, água, salsichas e uma lata de outra coisa.

5  Onde é que está a lata que a segunda freguesa quer comprar?
   **a**  Na quarta prateleira a contar de baixo.
   **b**  Na segunda prateleira a contar da esquerda.
   **c**  Na segunda prateleira a contar de cima.

........................................................................................

## Expressions
### a  Being served

Someone entering a shop may be welcomed with a question
like **Em que posso ajudar?** or **Como posso ajudar?**, *How can
I help?* Alternatively, you may hear expressions of welcome
such as **Faz favor** or **Faça favor**, mainly in Portugal, and **Pois
não**, mainly in Brazil. These are polite phrases in an implicit
*(Contd)*

invitation to the potential customer to express his / her request and are usually given a question-like intonation.

**I would like…**

As you have learned and practised in earlier units, you can say the polite **Queria…** , *I'd like* , but you can equally say **Quero…** , *I want…*

Also revise what you learned in Unit 5 about **tem…?** and **há…?** and on how to find out whether what you want is available.

**Qual prefere?** *Which do you prefer?*

Use **prefiro…** to express your preference, but if you don't mind one way or the other, say **Tanto faz.**

**Prefiro esse à sua direita.** *I prefer that one on your right.*

## Insight
**Tem / Há laranjas?**
**(Eu) queria fruta.**
**(Eu) quero três pães.**
**(Eu) prefiro um queijo grande.**

### 'How much more?'… *or* 'less'?

**Muito mais** (*much more*), **muito menos** (*much less*), **um pouco mais** (*a little bit more*), **mais um-uma** (*one more*).

**Um pouco menos, por favor.** *A little less, please.*

### 'Enough' *and* 'too much'

**Bastante** (*enough*) is often used hyperbolically for *rather a lot*. **Muito** (*a lot*) is often used euphemistically for *too much*.

| | |
|---|---|
| **É bastante caro.** | *It is rather expensive.* |
| **É muito caro!** | *It is too expensive!* |

But *enough* and *too much*, when controlling someone's actions, find a rendering in, respectively, **chega** and **é demais**.

| | |
|---|---|
| **Chega.** | *It's enough (stop there).* |
| **É demais**. | *It's too much (go back, take away a bit).* |

**Is this all right? OK?**

**Está bem** or **certo** will translate *all right* to express agreement.

**Mais alguma coisa?** *Anything more?*

If you don't want anything else, you can say **Não**, and add one of the following: **só isso**, *that's it*, or **nada mais**, *nothing else*, or **é tudo**, *that's all*.

**Something to carry your shopping in**

For a carrier bag ask for **um saco** or in Brazil also **uma sacola**.

**'How much is it?'** *and* **'How much does it come to?'**

Just ask, respectively, **quanto é?** or **quanto custa?** and **quanto é / custa tudo?** or **quanto é / custa ao todo?**

## Insight

**Mais ↔ Menos**
**Um pouco mais ↔ menos**
**Muito mais ↔ menos**
**Mais ↔ Menos um-uma**

----------

**Chega.**
**Está bem / certo.**
**Só isso / É tudo.**

----------

**Quanto é / custa?**

### b Weights and quantities

The litre (**o litro**) is used for fluids and the kilogram
(**o quilograma** or **o quilo**) for weights.

| | |
|---|---|
| **um litro de** | *a litre of* |
| **meio litro de** | *half a litre of* |
| **um quarto de litro de** | *a quarter litre of* |
| **um quilo (= quilograma) de** | *a kilogram of* |
| **meio quilo de** | *half a kilogram of* |
| **Queria uma garrafa de litro de água.** | *I would like a one litre bottle of water.* |
| **Queria uvas, isto é, meio quilo de uvas.** | *I would like grapes, I mean, half a kilo of grapes.* |

For smaller weights refer to grams (**os gramas**). *Ham* –
**o fiambre** (Eur.) / **o presunto (cozido)** (Br.) – can also be
bought by the slice – **a fatia**. Items such as eggs are usually
bought by the dozen (**a dúzia**). For approximate weight or
quantity use **mais ou menos** (*more or less*).

**Queria meio quilo de maçãs, mais ou menos 100 gramas de
queijo, dez fatias de fiambre** (Eur.) / **presunto** (Br.), **uma dúzia
e meia de ovos e uma garrafa de meio litro de água.**

### c Bottles, cartons, jars, tins / cans, boxes and tubes

For beverages, **a garrafa** translates *bottle*; otherwise there is
**o frasco** or **o vidro** (Br.). The word *jar* can be translated with
**o boião** (Eur.) / **o vidro** (Br.), but for a yoghurt ask for **um
copo de iogurte** (Eur.) / **um pote de iogurte** (Br.). Other types
of container and package include **o tubo**, *tube*, **a caixa**, *box*,
e **o pacote**, *packet* or *paper carton*. Finally, when in doubt,
you can use the generic term, **uma embalagem**, packaging.
Together with your tinned hot-dog sausages (**salsicha em
lata**), you may also wish to buy some extras:

> **Queria um pacote de manteiga** (*butter*), **um tubo de mostarda** (*mustard*), **um frasco de molho de tomate** (*tomato ketchup*) **e duas latas de cerveja** (*beer*).

## Insight

| | |
|---|---|
| (Eu) queria | **um litro** de leite. |
| (Eu) quero | **um quilo** de maçãs. |
| | **meia dúzia** de ovos. |
| | **uma garrafa** de vinho. |
| | **um pacote** de açúcar. |

**d  Isto – isso – aquilo** *Saying 'this one' and 'that one'*

Revise what you learned in Unit 7 about **este, esse, aquele** and their respective feminine forms. There is also another set of three related words: **isto** (*this thing here*); **isso** (*that thing there by you*); **aquilo** (*that thing over there away from both me and you*).

**Queria isto, isso e aquilo.** *I would like this one, that one and that one over there.*

All these three sets of forms serve to point out something or someone. You will learn details of how they function later in this unit.

## How it works

### a Verbs: the three conjugations – imperative or command forms

| *buy!* | *sell!* | *leave!* | |
|---|---|---|---|
| compr**a** | vend**e** | part**e** | *one person (i)* |
| compr**e** | vend**a** | part**a** | *one person (ii)* |
| compr**em** | ven**dam** | part**am** | *more than one person (iii)* |

When talking to:

**i** a person you would address with **tu**; **ii** a person you would address with **você** or **o sr / a sra**; **iii** more than one person in i or ii.

*Keep your voice down!:*
Fala mais baixo! **i**; Fale mais baixo! **ii**; Falem mais baixo! **iii**.

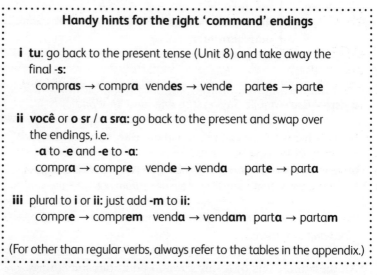

### Handy hints for the right 'command' endings

**i tu**: go back to the present tense (Unit 8) and take away the final **-s**:
   compr**as** → compr**a**   vend**es** → vend**e**   part**es** → part**e**

**ii você** or **o sr / a sra**: go back to the present and swap over the endings, i.e.
   **-a** to **-e** and **-e** to **-a**:
   compr**a** → compr**e**   vend**e** → vend**a**   part**e** → part**a**

**iii** plural to **i** or **ii**: just add **-m** to **ii**:
   compr**e** → compr**em**   vend**a** → vend**am**   part**a** → part**am**

(For other than regular verbs, always refer to the tables in the appendix.)

#### b Command forms and their alternatives

In Unit 3 you learned that public instructions are often given in the infinitive. You can also use the infinitive as the basis for different ways of telling someone verbally to do or not to do something.

For an instruction or invitation:

| EMPURRAR |          on a door

You are standing by the door and are asked to push it open.

Faça o favor de **empurrar**          or
Queira **empurrar**

Similarly, when being offered a seat you may hear

Faça o favor de **sentar**-se          or
Queira **sentar**-se          and also
O sr / a sra quer **sentar**-se?          or
Você quer **sentar**-se?

The last two examples, though presented as a question in the present tense, are in fact an invitation. This format is used on both sides of the Atlantic, but the practice is further extended in Brazil where, depending on tone of voice, it can equally be used for a command – *Will you sit down?*

For a prohibition:

NÃO FUMAR          on the wall

You haven't noticed the *No smoking sign* and have lit a cigarette. You may be told

É favor não **fumar**          or
Faça o favor de não **fumar**

You may also be reminded that this is a no-smoking area by means of a statement in the present, e.g, Aqui não **se fuma**, *here one doesn't smoke*, as shown in Unit 9, or, back to the infinitive you learned in Unit 3, Aqui é proibido **fumar**.

In the examples above, if a direct command form had been used, this would have been, respectively,

**Empurre**          Sent**e**-se          Não fum**e**

to which an expression such as **por favor** could be added for politeness.

**Empurre, por favor**          Sent**e**-se, **por favor**          **Por favor** Não fum**e**

The degree of politeness or assertiveness will vary with the tone of voice in which these words are said.

Both the infinitive and the command forms are used in public instructions, but the latter, being a more direct approach, tends to be given preference where the need is felt for a more forceful message, for example, where failing to observe the instruction may result in danger for yourself or others.

**Pare Olhe Escute**     *Stop Look Listen (at a level crossing)*

> **Insight**
> **Empurrar**
> Queira **empurrar**
> Faça o favor de **empurrar**
> Quer **empurrar?**
> **Empurre**

### c Numbers 101 to 1,000

| | |
|---|---|
| 101 cento e um/uma | 500 quinhentos/-as |
| 102 cento e dois/duas | 600 seiscentos/-as |
| 121 cento e vinte e um/uma | 700 setecentos/-as |
| 200 duzentos/-as | 800 oitocentos/-as |
| 300 trezentos/-as | 900 novecentos/-as |
| 400 quatrocentos/-as | 1.000 mil |

cento e vinte e cinco gramas (o grama)
cento e oitenta e duas pessoas
duzentas pessoas
mil pessoas

### d Isto – este – esta: *Saying 'this'*

Despite its ending **-o, isto** is not masculine but neuter. It is for something (or someone) you have identified as being present but you don't know much about. Once you do, then it changes to **este** or **esta**, i.e., acquires a gender. The same happens with **isso** – **esse** – **essa** and **aquilo** – **aquele** – **aquela**.

| | |
|---|---|
| – O que é **aquilo?** | *What is that* (neuter) *over there?* |
| – É uma lata de cerveja. | *It is a can of beer.* |
| – Ah! **aquela** lata de cerveja… | *Ah! that* (fem.) *can of beer over there…* |

Also, **isto** – **isso** – **aquilo** is always singular, but the other forms can be plural, if you find out that there is more than one can of beer…

– Ah! **aquelas** latas de cerveja…     *Ah! those cans of beer over there…*

Finally, **isto** – **isso** – **aquilo** is always on its own, but the other forms can be on their own or accompany a noun.

| | |
|---|---|
| **aquelas** | (on its own) |
| **aquelas** latas | (with a noun) |

........................................................................................
## Insight
    **isto, isso, aquilo**
    **este, esse, aquele**
    **estes, esses, aqueles**
    **esta, essa, aquela**
    **estas, essas, aquelas**
........................................................................................

---

## Exercises

### 12.2

Ranging from a parking ticket to a cup of coffee, what you want may come out of a vending machine.

**12.2.1** Study the information given on the coffee dispensing machine.

**pressionar a tecla** *to press the key*
**onde diz** *where it says*
**retirar o troco** *to take out the change*

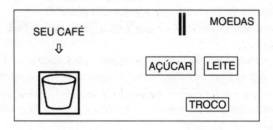

◀) **CD2, TR 10**

**12.2.2** Carla would like a cup of coffee with milk and no sugar. She is having trouble in operating the automatic dispenser and seeks help.

  **i** Listen to the recording and read what she asks and what she is told. This is both on the recording and transcribed below.
     – Desculpe, o que tenho que fazer para comprar café com leite e sem açúcar?
     – A senhora tem que introduzir as moedas, pressionar a tecla onde diz LEITE, esperar um pouco e depois retirar o troco e o café.
  **ii** Give similar instructions but for a black coffee with sugar. (Note that the instructions are given in the infinitive.)

**12.2.3** Carla tries but to no avail. She seeks help again, from someone else.

  **i** Listen and read what she is told this time.
     – A senhora introduz as moedas, pressiona a tecla onde diz LEITE, espera um pouco e depois retira o troco e o café.
  **ii** Explain how to operate the machine in a similar way but for a black coffee with sugar.
     (Note that the different steps are described in the present.)

**12.2.4** Still no good. Carla seeks help for the third time.

 **i** Listen and read how she is told to solve the problem.
  – Introduza as moedas, pressione a tecla onde diz LEITE, espere
  um pouco e depois retire o troco e o café.
 **ii** Can you now give similar instructions but for a black coffee
  with sugar.
  (Note that command forms are being used.)

**12.2.5** Despite all the effort, the machine won't dispense any coffee.

Conclusion:

  A máquina está avariada.
  A máquina está com defeito (Br.) *or* a máquina está
  desarranjada (Br.).
  What does this mean?

### 12.3

Check that you remember how to say the following in Portuguese
for when you are shopping for food over the counter:

**1** I would like…                **5** It's all right.
**2** How much is it?            **6** That's all, thank you.
**3** I would rather have…      **7** How much does it come to?
**4** A bit more / less, please.   **8** Can you give me a carrier bag?

### 12.4

You are in the grocer's shop. Some of the items you want are near
you or near both you and the assistant (*location 1*); others are
relatively distant from you but near the assistant (*loc. 2*); others are
distinctively away from both you and the assistant (*loc. 3*).

Re-write the following sentences completing them with one of the three choices in brackets:

**Queria...**

|      |                                                                                          | loc. |
| ---- | ---------------------------------------------------------------------------------------- | ---- |
| **i**   | _____ que está à sua frente. (isto / isso / aquilo)                                | 2    |
| **ii**  | _____ lata de cerveja. (esta / essa / aquela)                                      | 1    |
| **iii** | quatro fatias _____ fiambre (Eur.) / presunto (Br.) (deste / desse / daquele)      | 3    |
| **iv**  | mais ou menos meio quilo _____ maçãs. (destas / dessas / daquelas)                 | 1    |
| **v**   | uma garrafa de vinho, uma _____ de litro. (destas / dessas / daquelas)             | 2    |
| **vi**  | 250 g _____ queijo, o terceiro a contar da esquerda. (deste / desse / daquele)     | 3    |

### 12.5

These are instructions on the escalator at an underground train station.

**manter-se** to stand / stay still / keep
**caminhar** to walk, move forward

> MANTENHA-SE À DIREITA
> CAMINHE PELA ESQUERDA

**12.5.1** What does it say?

**12.5.2** Advise a group who are with you. Start with: **Na escada rolante...** *On the escalator...* Complete the sentence by reading out the notice but remember to make the verb endings plural.

**12.5.3** Give this set of instructions to someone you use **tu** with. The first verb has been done for you: **mantém-te...** Now complete the sentence.

---

## Summary

1 Empurrar / Empurre.
Puxar / Puxe.
2 Na escada rolante, mantenha-se à direita e caminhe pela esquerda.
3 Para comprar café, coloque as moedas, pressione a tecla, espere um pouco e depois retire o café e o troco.
4 Vá por esta rua, tome a terceira à direita, siga pela rua perpendicular a essa, vire à esquerda na segunda transversal e continue mais uns cinco minutos.
5 (Eu) queria uvas. – Quero um pão grande. – Prefiro dois queijos pequenos.
6 (Eu) queria dois pacotes de litro de leite. – Quero um quilo de uvas / 250 gramas de queijo / meia dúzia de ovos / três garrafas de litro de vinho.
7 Prefiro isto / este pacote / tubo. – Prefiro isso / essa garrafa / embalagem. – Prefiro aquilo / aquela caixa, na terceira prateleira a contar de baixo.
8 Quero mais um / dois. – Quero (um pouco) mais / menos. – Chega. – Nada mais / é tudo / só isso.
9 Quanto é / custa? – Quanto é / custa tudo?
10 Pode me dar um saco / uma sacola (Br.)?

# 13

## Quando estará pronto?
## When will it be ready?

In this unit you will learn how to
- *Deal with currency including large figures*
- *Explain what you want as an alternative to*
- *Self-service*
- *Find different ways of expressing yourself about the future*

**Numa agência dos correios** *In a post office*

Débora is with Alexandre at the post office and wants to buy some stamps.

CD2, TR 11

| | |
|---|---|
| **Débora** | Não tenho trocado para a venda automática de selos. Você tem? |
| **Alexandre** | Não, só tenho notas. A máquina não troca notas? |
| **Débora** | Não, esta não. Apenas aceita moedas. Não faz mal. Posso comprar os selos no balcão. |
| | |
| **Débora** | (*falando para o empregado do balcão*) Queria selos para enviar postais para o estrangeiro, por via aérea. São dois, um postal para a Europa e um para os Estados Unidos da América. Quanto é tudo? |

**(o) (dinheiro) trocado** *small change*
**(a) venda automática** *vending machine* (lit. *automatized sale*)

**(o) selo** stamp
**(a) nota** paper money, note
**trocar** to change
**apenas = só, somente**
**aceita** accepts
**não faz mal** never mind (lit. (it) does not do harm)
**posso** (I) can
**no / ao balcão** at the counter
**(o) postal** postcard
**(o) estrangeiro** abroad
**por via aérea** by air mail

### Num posto de abastecimento At a filling station

Carolina is at a filling station and wonders whether someone could check the tyre pressures for her.

| | |
|---|---|
| **Carolina** | Bom dia. É só autosserviço ou pode verificar a pressão dos pneus? |
| **Empregado** | Posso. Não há problema. A senhora pode deixar o carro que eu dou uma olhada nos pneus. Quer mais alguma coisa? |
| **Carolina** | Não, muito obrigada, é tudo. Quando estará pronto? |
| **Empregado** | Isso é rápido. Vai estar pronto daqui a dez minutos, mais ou menos. Enquanto espera, a senhora pode tomar um cafezinho. O bar é ali à esquerda. |

**(o) autosserviço** self-service
**verificar** to check
**a pressão dos pneus** the tyre pressure
**deixar** to leave (something)
**dou** (I) give
**uma olhada/olhadela** (Eur.) a look
**pronto** ready
**rápido** quick
**daqui (= de + aqui)** from now
**enquanto** while

**tomar** *to have (drink)*
**(o) cafezinho** *small black coffee*
**bar** *bar*

---

## Exercises

### 13.1 Perguntas e respostas *Questions and answers*

1 Quem não tem dinheiro trocado para a venda automática de selos?
 **a** Débora. **b** Alexandre.
 **c** Débora e Alexandre.

2 Para onde é que a Débora quer comprar selos?
 **a** Para a Europa.
 **b** Para os Estados Unidos da América.
 **c** Para os EUA e a Europa.

3 O empregado pode verificar a pressão dos pneus?
 **a** Não, não pode. É só autosserviço.
 **b** Pode e vai verificar a pressão dos pneus.

4 Quando é que o carro estará pronto?
 **a** Hoje. **b** Hoje à noite. **c** Amanhã de manhã.

5 A Carolina quer mais alguma coisa?
 **a** Não, não quer.
 **b** Quer, quer também gasolina.
 **c** Quer, quer tomar um cafezinho.

## Expressions
### a Self-service and automation

A vending machine can be simply referred to as **a venda automática de selos / bilhetes /** etc. and you don't

166

normally say the whole name which is **a máquina de venda automática de...** You may need to get change (**trocar dinheiro**) for these and other coin-operated machines.

| | |
|---|---|
| **Onde posso trocar dinheiro para ...** | *Where can I get change for ...* |
| **... a venda automática de selos?** | *... the stamp vending machine?* |
| **... esta máquina?** | *... this machine?* |

Also, you may prefer personal service where self-service is available. You can start with **Pode...** or **Não se importa de...** , lit. *you don't mind...?*

| | |
|---|---|
| **Pode ... / Não se importa de ...** | |
| **... verificar a pressão dos pneus?** | *... check the tyre pressure?* |
| **... pôr gasolina no carro?** | *... put petrol in the car?* |
| **... encher? (o tanque)** | *... fill it up? (the fuel tank)* |

**b 'Here' or 'there' – 'now' or 'then'**

| **isto** | **isso** | **aquilo** | a |
|---|---|---|---|
| ↓ | ↓ | ↓↓ | parallel |
| **aqui = cá** | **aí** | **ali lá** | concept |
| (*here*) | (*there*) | (*there*) | |

There is no significant difference in meaning between **aqui** and **cá**; **ali** is nearer than **lá**; and **aí** is near the person/people you are talking to.

Also, **isso** is what is near your interlocutor (**aí**) and / or in his / her thoughts or words:

**É isso mesmo** *It's exactly that (i.e., what you have said)*
**Isso é rápido** *That won't take a minute (i.e., what you have mentioned)*

(Contd)

This means that **isso / esse / essa** can sometimes correspond to an English rendering where *your* or *you* is used.

| | |
|---|---|
| **Isso é boa ideia** | *That is a good idea* |
| | or |
| | *Your idea is good* |
| | *You have had a good idea* |
| **Esse chapéu é bonito** | *Your hat looks nice* |

Furthermore, **aqui, aí, ali** and **lá** can be applied to time.

| | |
|---|---|
| **Daqui (= de + aqui) a dez minutos** | *In ten minutes from now* |
| **Daqui (= de + aqui) a uma semana** | *In a week's time* |

## Insight

| | |
|---|---|
| Pode | **lavar** o carro? |
| Não se importa de | **pôr** gasolina no carro? |
| | me **dar** aquilo que está ali na prateleira? |
| | **ter** o carro pronto daqui a meia hora? |

## How it works

### a Verbs: the three conjugations – future indicative

| I shall... | buy | sell | leave |
|---|---|---|---|
| eu | compra**rei** | vende**rei** | parti**rei** |
| tu | compra**rás** | vende**rás** | parti**rás** |
| você, o sr / a sra ele / ela | compra**rá** | vende**rá** | parti**rá** |
| nós | compra**remos** | vende**remos** | parti**remos** |
| vocês, os sres / as sras eles / elas | compra**rão** | vende**rão** | parti**rão** |

The simple future (future indicative) is formed by attaching the endings -**ei**, -**ás**, -**á**, -**emos**, -**ão** to the infinitive of the verb. There are three exceptions – **dizer**, **fazer**, **trazer** – where the endings are added to shortened forms of the infinitive: **dir**ei etc., **far**ei etc., **trar**ei etc.

........................................................................

**Handy hints**

Have you noticed that the endings for the simple future are basically the same as the present tense of the verb **haver**?

| -ei | -ás | -á | -emos | -ão |
|-----|-----|----|-------|-----|
| hei | hás | há | havemos | hão |

........................................................................

### b Verbs: the three conjugations – emphatic future

This is formed by the present tense of the verb **haver**, *to exist / there to be*, plus **de** plus the infinitive of the verb you want to express.

| I will / am to... | | buy | sell | leave |
|-------------------|--------------|---------|--------|--------|
| eu | **hei de** | comprar | vender | partir |
| tu | **hás de** | | | |
| você, or sr / a sra ele / ela | **há de** | | | |
| nós | **havemos de** | | | |
| vocês, os sres / as sras eles / elas | **hão de** | | | |

(Note that **haver** is an irregular verb.)

### c Comparing the 'futures'

**Simple future**
▶ in formal writing or speech as well as colloquially where futurity is the dominant notion:

Part**iremos** amanhã. *We shall leave tomorrow.*

▶ where uncertainty is expressed:

**Não sei** se part**iremos amanhã.** *I don't know whether we shall leave tomorrow.*

**Emphatic future**

to express firm determination about a future action or firm conviction about a future event:

**Havemos** de part**ir** amanhã.     *We will leave / are to leave tomorrow.*

**Colloquial future**

(Revise what you learned in Unit 9.)

Just imagine the following different outlooks on tomorrow's weather coming from three people who are planning to spend the day on the beach:

A – Não sei se f**ará** sol amanhã. (simple future)
B – **Vai** faz**er** sol amanhã. (colloquial future)
C – **Há de** faz**er** sol amanhã. (emphatic future)

Speaker A is wondering whether the sun will come out; but speaker B knows that the weather forecast is for a sunny day; and speaker C trusts that the weather won't let them down.

**Note:**

The simple future can also be used as a courteous way of expressing someone's obligation.

O senhor dev**erá** reservar lugar.     *You are advised to book a seat. (you should really do it)*

The emphatic future can correspond to English *What shall I / we do?*

Que **havemos de** faz**er?**     *What shall we do?*
Não sei o que **hei de** faz**er.**     *I don't know what to do.*

**d Diminutives and augmentatives**

Diminutives and augmentatives are usually treated as single nouns and take plural ending -s.

**(o) cafezinho** (from **café**) *small coffee, for small cup of coffee*
**um cafezinho – dois cafezinhos (uma bica – duas bicas (Eur.))**

**(a) florzinha** (from **flor**) *little flower*
**uma florzinha – duas florzinhas**

**(o) casarão** (from **casa**) *big house*
**um casarão – dois casarões**

Exception:

**(o) pãozinho** (from **pão**) *bread roll*, i.e., *small loaf*
**um pãozinho – dois pãezinhos** (from **pães**). See Plurals in Unit 5.

**e Numbers from 1,000 and notes on numbers**

| 1.001 | mil e um / uma |
| 1.022 | mil e vinte e dois / duas |
| 2.000 | dois / duas mil |
| 100.000 | cem mil |

| 1.000.000 | um milhão |
| 2.000.000 | dois milhões |

**Notes:**

▶ e is used between digits in general, except after thousands when the hundreds are followed by tens or units; and so on.
**vinte e um / uma** (*21*); **mil e duzentos** (*1,200*); **mil, duzentos/ -as e vinte** (*1,220*); **um milhão, duzentos / -as mil e sessenta e cinco** (*1,200,065*).

▶ **cem**, for 100, becomes **cento** when a number from 1 to 99 follows.
**cem pessoas** (*100 people*); **cento e vinte pessoas** (*120 people*)

▶ where the number follows a noun, the masculine is used, as it agrees with the word (**o**) **número**, expressed or understood.
(a) **porta número** vinte e **um** *door number 21*
(b) **carruagem** vinte e **dois** *carriage 22*

▶ the use of the comma – (a) **vírgula** – and dot is the reverse of English practice.
1 001,5 – **mil e um vírgula cinco** (*1,001.5 – one thousand and one point 5*)
For the thousands, etc. instead of using a dot you can leave a space.
1 001,5 – **mil e um vírgula cinco** (*1,001.5 – one thousand and one point 5*)

---

**Insight**

mil e um
dois mil e trinta e um
duas mil e trinta e uma
duzentas mil e cinquenta e quatro
dois milhões, cem mil e quinhentos

---

## Exercises

### 13.2

◀) **CD2, TR 13**

For centuries the word **escudo** was used in Portugal in connection with money and became the unit of currency, but the **euro** (€) is now in use.

**o euro (€)** *euro*
**o real (R$)** *Brazilian currency*

QV

**13.2.1** Some digits are missing in the following grid. Listen to your recording and fill in the gaps.

|     |   |   |   |   |   |   |   |   |   |   |
|-----|---|---|---|---|---|---|---|---|---|---|
| **i**   |   |   |   |   |   | 9 | . | 8 | o |   |
| **ii**  |   |   |   |   | 4 |   | . | 5 |   | o |
| **iii** |   |   |   | 7 |   | o | . | 1 | 2 |   |
| **iv**  | 1 |   | . | 6 | 3 |   | . | 7 |   | 1 |
| **v**   |   | 8 | . |   | o | 7 | . |   | o | 6 |
| **vi**  | 9 |   | . | 3 |   | o | . | 8 |   |   |

**13.2.2** Listen to the recording again and write down what the speakers said.

**13.2.3** Can you put into words the prices shown on these labels?

The first one has been done for you.

**i** Quarenta e dois reais e meio.

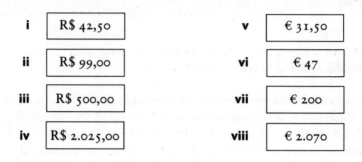

| | |
|---|---|
| **i** R$ 42,50 | **v** € 31,50 |
| **ii** R$ 99,00 | **vi** € 47 |
| **iii** R$ 500,00 | **vii** € 200 |
| **iv** R$ 2.025,00 | **viii** € 2.070 |

**13.3**

Carlos has taken some friends to a café in Portugal. They are Portuguese Gabriela, Jorge and Judite and Brazilian Fábio and Eliana.

**13.3.1** See below how Carlos went about finding out what each one wanted.

| | |
|---|---|
| **Carlos** | Então o que é que vocês querem? |
| **Eliana** | Queria uma água mineral e um iogurte de banana. |
| **Fábio** | Por favor um café sem leite e com açúcar e um sanduíche (Br.) de presunto (Br.). |
| **Jorge** | Eu queria um café com leite e sem açúcar e uma sandes (Eur.) de fiambre (Eur.). |
| **Gabriela** | Queria uma cerveja e uma sandes (Eur.) de queijo. |
| **Judite** | Eu não quero nada, obrigada. |

**13.3.2** Take Carlos's place and make a list for the waiter (a Portuguese waiter), including a beer and a ham sandwich for yourself.

**13.3.3** The group are invited to place their order.

**13.3.4** Put the following words in the right order so as to ask whether you will have to wait a long time:

Teremos / muito / ? / que / tempo / esperar

**13.3.5** When the waiter comes with the order there is some confusion over who has ordered what. Explain that the mineral water and yoghurt are for the lady in the red T-shirt, and the white coffee and one of the ham sandwiches for the gentleman in the green shirt.

**13.3.6** It is time to pay. Put the following words in the right order to ask for the bill (**a conta**):

A / por / . / favor / , / conta

**13.3.7** Put the following words in the right order so as to tell the waiter he can keep the change (**o troco**):

Pode / o / ficar / . / troco / com

**13.4**

**incomodar** *to disturb, inconvenience*
**arrumar** *to tidy up*

On the next page is a card you found in your hotel room and you can hang on the door handle. On one side it has a 'do not disturb' message, on the other a message asking your chambermaid to tidy up your room.

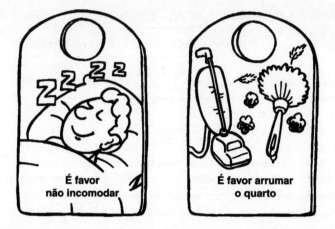

É favor
não incomodar

É favor arrumar
o quarto

**13.4.1** Someone has not noticed the sign hanging on your door and is making considerable noise in the corridor.

  **i** Use the words on the card so as to ask verbally not to be disturbed.

  **ii** Can you also ask not to be disturbed using the verb as a command instead? Add **por favor**.

**13.4.2** You have turned over the card on your door handle and the other message is now showing. As you leave your room you meet the chambermaid in the corridor.

  **i** Starting with **Já pode...** and using words from the card, tell her that now the room is available to be done. Add **por favor**.

  **ii** Re-arrange these words to ask her when the room will be ready:

    Quando / é / ? / quarto / pronto / o / que / estará

### 13.5

This is the laundry form for nightwear and underwear that Craig and Barbara Howell had in their hotel room in Brazil.

| LAVAGEM DE ROUPA – LAUNDRY SERVICE | | |
|---|---|---|
| Quarto 405 | Nome Howell | Data 6 de fev. |
| Quant.<br>Qty | Roupa de noite e de baixo<br>Night and underwear | Total (R$) |
| 1 | Pijama – pyjamas | |
| 1 | Camisola – nightdress | |
| 2 | Roupão – dressing gown | |
| | Camiseta interior – vest | |
| 4 | Cueca – underpants | |
| 4 | Calcinha – panties | |
| 2 | Sutiã– bra | |
| | Combinação – slip | |
| | Meia – sock, stocking | |

Quant. = Quantidade

camisola (Br.) = camisa de noite (Eur.)

camiseta interior (Br.) = camisola interior (Eur.)

**13.5.1** Read the form and the items they have entered. The Howells haven't brought many clothes with them, and Barbara added a note asking whether all the washing could be done before Wednesday. Read her note.

> Será possível ter tudo pronto antes de 4ª-feira? Obrigada
>
> B. Howell

**13.5.2** If Barbara had wanted only the dressing gowns (**os roupões**), not everything, ready before Thursday, not Wednesday, what would she have written instead?

## Summary

1 Onde posso trocar dinheiro para a venda automática de café? – Por favor, pode trocar-me / me trocar dinheiro para esta máquina?

2 Duzentos – duzentas
Dois mil – duas mil
Três mil e dois – três mil e duas

3 Custa dois mil e quarenta e dois reais. – Vai custar mais de um milhão de euros. – Provavelmente custará mil e dois reais.

4 Pode verificar a pressão dos pneus? – Pode ter tudo pronto daqui a dez minutos?

5 Não se importa de encher o tanque? – Não se importa de me trazer um cafezinho?

6 É isso mesmo. – Isso é rápido?

7 Teremos que esperar muito? – Isso quando estará pronto?

8 Já pode arrumar o quarto. – Já pode trazer a conta. – Já pode levar a roupa para lavar.

9 Partirei amanhã. – Iremos para o Rio (na) quinta(-feira). – Havemos de ir para o Rio (na) quinta(-feira).

10 Amanhã vou sair de casa cedo. – Amanhã sairei de casa cedo. – Não sei se amanhã sairei de casa cedo. – Amanhã hei de sair de casa cedo.

# 14

# Eu costumava calçar 43
# I used to wear shoe size 43

In this unit you will learn how to
- *Make comparisons and choices*
- *Talk about what something is made of, design and pattern*
- *Find different ways of expressing yourself about the past*

**Numa sapataria** *In a shoe shop*

Ricardo has entered a shoe shop and is interested in some footwear which is on display.

| | |
|---|---|
| **Ricardo** | Queria um par destes sapatos e um destas sandálias, número 43. |
| **Vendedor** | O senhor quer sentar-se e esperar um momento? |
| | ———————— |
| **Vendedor** | (*trazendo os dois pares*) Queira experimentar por favor. |
| **Ricardo** | (*experimentando um sapato e uma sandália*) Desculpe. Eu costumava calçar número 43, mas esta sandália está um pouco folgada e este sapato está muito apertado. Por favor traga-me outros iguais a estes mas a sandália no número abaixo e o sapato em dois números acima. |

◆》 CD2, TR 14

**um par** *a pair*
**(a) sandália** *sandal*
**experimentar** *to try on*
**eu costumava calçar** *I used to wear (footwear)*
**um pouco folgada** *a bit loose*
**muito apertado** *very tight*
**iguais a estes** *like these*
**no número abaixo** *in the next size down* (lit. *in one number below*)
**em dois números acima** *in two sizes up* (lit. *in two numbers above*)

**Numa loja de modas** *In a fashion shop*

Marlene is in a fashion shop looking for some clothes.

CD2, TR 15

| | |
|---|---|
| **Marlene** | Queria um conjunto de saia e blusa. |
| **Vendedora** | Temos vários. A senhora pode ver aqueles ali (*acompanhando a cliente*). O seu tamanho é 40 ou 42? |
| **Marlene** | 42. |
| **Vendedora** | (*mostrando um conjunto*) Gosta deste? |
| **Marlene** | Gosto, mas preferia uma blusa com manga comprida e em roxo. |
| **Vendedora** | Em roxo não temos mas (*mostrando outro conjunto*) temos este aqui com blusa em rosa escuro e com manga comprida. Fica-lhe bem. |
| **Marlene** | Sim… talvez este. Posso provar? |
| **Vendedora** | Claro, as cabines de provas são ali à esquerda. |
| **Marlene** | (*voltando da cabine*) O conjunto assenta bem. Vou levá-lo. |

**um conjunto** *an outfit*
**vários** *several*
**acompanhando** *going with*
**(o) tamanho** *size*
**a cliente = a freguesa**
**gosta deste (= de+este)?** *do you like this one?*
**(a) manga** *sleeve*
**roxo** *purple*
**fica-lhe bem** *it suits you*

**provar = experimentar**
**(as) cabines de provas** *fitting rooms*
**assenta / serve** (Br.) **bem** *is a good fit*
**vou levá-lo** *I'll have it (lit. I am going to take it)*

---

# Exercises

## 14.1 Perguntas e respostas *Questions and answers*

**1** O que é que o Ricardo quer comprar?
**a** Dois pares de sapatos. **b** Dois pares de sandálias.
**c** Um par de sandálias e um de sapatos.

**2** Quais são os números que assentarão bem?
**i** Sandália: **a** 44. **b** 45. **c** 42. **ii** Sapato: **a** 44. **b** 45. **c** 42.

**3** Que tamanho é que Marlene veste?
**a** 40. **b** 40 ou 42. **c** 42.

**4** O que é que ela quer comprar?
**a** Um conjunto com blusa de manga curta.
**b** Um conjunto com blusa de manga comprida.

**5** De que cor é a blusa do conjunto que ela vai levar?
**a** Roxa. **b** Rosa escuro. **c** Rosa claro.

....................................................................................

# Expressions
## a Accessories

In addition to clothes you may also wish to buy some accessories such as: **a gravata**, *tie*; **o lenço (de pescoço)**, *scarf (square)*; **o cachecol**, *scarf (long)*; **o cinto**, *belt*; **o chapéu**, *hat*; **o boné**, *cap*; **a luva**, *glove*; **a bolsa / a mala de mão** (Eur.), *handbag*. (Note that **mala** or **mala de viagem** translates *suitcase*.)

**um par de luvas** *a pair of gloves*; **um chapéu de praia** *a beach hat*
*(Contd)*

**b What is it made of?**

In order to ask this question, say **de que é feito?**

| | |
|---|---|
| **Isto aqui, de que é feito?** | *This here, what is it made of?* |
| **De que são feitas aquelas gravatas que estão ali?** | *What are those ties over there made of?* |

The reply may come as: **de algodão**, *cotton*; **linho**, *linen*; **lã**, *wool*; **seda**, *silk*; **couro**, *leather*; **pelica**, *kid*; **fibra sintética**, *man-made fibre*.

| | |
|---|---|
| **Esta blusa é (feita) de seda.** | *This blouse is made of silk.* |
| **Aquelas blusas são (feitas) de algodão.** | *Those blouses are made of cotton.* |

---

**Insight**

**(Eu) queria um lenço de seda.**

----------

**A mala dele é de couro.**

---

**c Design and pattern**

You may like something plain – **liso** – or not. Here are some alternatives you can ask for: **listrado/a** or **às riscas / com riscas** (Eur.), *striped*; **xadrez**, *checked*; **estampado/a**, *with a printed pattern*.

| | |
|---|---|
| **uma camisa xadrez** | *a checked shirt* |
| **uma blusa em rosa, lisa** | *a pink blouse, plain* |
| **um vestido em tecido estampado** | *a dress in a material with a printed pattern* |
| **uma gravata listrada / às riscas** (Eur.) **em azul escuro e branco** | *a striped tie in dark blue and white* |

## How it works

### a Comparatives

| i mais | | (do) que |
|---|---|---|
| ii menos | .... | |
| iii tão | | como / quanto |

**i** mais... do que *-er than, more... than*
Peter é **mais** alto **do que** Mary. or
Peter é **mais** alto **que** Mary.
Peter fala Português **mais** fluentemente **(do) que** Mary.
Peter tem **mais** bagagem **(do) que** Mary.
Peter tem **mais** malas **(do) que** Mary.

**ii** menos... do que *less... than, fewer... than, not so... as, not so much/many... as*
Peter é **menos** alto **(do) que** Mary.
Peter fala Português **menos** fluentemente **(do) que** Mary.
Peter tem **menos** bagagem **(do) que** Mary.
Peter tem **menos** malas **(do) que** Mary.

Note that in both **i** and **ii** above **do** in **do que** is often omitted.

**iii** tão... como... or tão ... quanto ... *as... as, so... as*
There is a preference for the former on the European side of the Atlantic and for the latter in Brazil.
Peter é **tão** alto **quanto** Mary. = Peter é **tão** alto **como** Mary.
Peter não é **tão** alto **quanto** Mary. = Peter não é **tão** alto **como** Mary.
Peter fala Português **tão** fluentemente **quanto** Mary.
Peter fala Português **tão** fluentemente **como** Mary.

Similarly,

**tanto / tanta / tantos / tantas... como** or
**tanto / tanta / tantos / tantas... quanto**
*as/so much and as/so many... as*
Peter tem **tanta** bagagem **quanto** Mary.
= Peter tem **tanta** bagagem **como** Mary.
Peter tem **tantas** malas **quanto** Mary.
= Peter tem **tantas** malas **como** Mary.

## Insight

| (Eu) queria | **mais** | escuro. |
| Prefiro | | claro. |
| | | curto. |
| | | comprido. |
| | **maior** (do) que este. | |
| | **maior** / no número **acima** / no tamanho **acima**. | |

### b Verbs: the three conjugations – imperfect indicative

| *I was...* | *buying* | *selling* | *leaving* |
| *I used to...* | *buy* | *sell* | *leave* |

| | | | |
|---|---|---|---|
| eu | compr**ava** | vend**ia** | part**ia** |
| tu | compr**avas** | vend**ias** | part**ias** |
| você, o sr / a sra | compr**ava** | | |
| ele / ela | | vend**ia** | part**ia** |
| nós | compr**ávamos** | vend**íamos** | part**íamos** |
| vocês, os sres / as sras | compr**avam** | vend**iam** | part**iam** |
| eles / elas | | | |

The imperfect is formed with the above endings and is regular even for irregular verbs except in the case of **ser, ter, vir** and

**pôr**, as well as their compounds e.g. **conter** (*to contain*), **supor** (*to assume*).

## Use for...

**1** A continuous state or condition, action or event, in the past:

| Est**ava** / faz**ia** calor. | *It was hot.* |
| Eu l**ia** o jornal. | *I was reading the newspaper.* |

**2** A habitual action or event, in the past

| Eu l**ia** o jornal regularmente. | *I used to / would read the newspaper regularly.* |
| Eu tom**ava** chá todas as manhãs. | *I used to / would have tea every morning.* |

or imperfect of **costumar** + infinitive:

| Eu costum**ava** ler o jornal regularmente. | *I used to / would read the newspaper regularly.* |

**3** For politeness, often when asking for something:

| Quer**ia** um pão. | *I wanted a loaf of bread.* |
| Meaning: | *I would like a loaf of bread.* |
| Prefer**ia** uma blusa em roxo. | *I preferred a blouse in purple.* |
| Meaning: | *I would prefer a blouse in purple.* |

## c Queria or eu queria?

In the imperfect indicative, verb endings **-ava** and **-ia** are the same for **eu**, **você**, etc. As a result, the speaker may opt to use the subject pronoun – **eu**, **você**, etc. – in order to avoid ambiguity.

**Eu queria** um pão.    *I would like a loaf of bread (it's me who wants a loaf of bread, not him).*

When you ask the shopkeeper for a loaf of bread, it's likely to be obvious that it is your request, not someone else's, and you don't really need to say 'eu'. (Revise what you learned in Unit 7 about omitting a subject pronoun.) Using the subject pronoun where it is not needed can be a way of stressing what you are saying.

**Eu queria** um café com leite.    *As for me, I would like a coffee with milk.*

## d Comparing the 'pasts'

How does the imperfect compare with the preterite you learned in Unit 10? In a nutshell, use the imperfect for a 'close-up' of something in the past and the preterite for something finished with.

### Imperfect
for something (state / condition / action / event) going on in the past:

**Estava calor. Eu lia o jornal.**

### Imperfect + imperfect
for something going on in the past at the same time as something else:

**Eu lia o jornal enquanto ela estudava.**
*I was reading the newspaper while she was studying.*

**eu lia o jornal**
|————————————————————————|

**ela estudava**
|————————————————————————|

**Quando eu era criança, passava muito tempo na praia.**
*When I was a child, I used to spend a lot of time on the beach.*

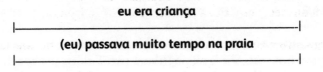

**eu era criança**

|————————————————————————————|

**(eu) passava muito tempo na praia**

|————————————————————————————|

**Preterite + imperfect**
for something that happened when something else was going on in the past:

**Quando cheguei, estava calor.**    *When I arrived, it was hot.*

**Cheguei**
↓
**estava calor**

|————————————————————————————|

**Preterite**
for something that happened in the past when you look at it as a whole:

**Cheguei na quarta-feira passada.**    *I arrived last Wednesday.*
**Li o jornal esta manhã.**    *I read the newspaper this morning.*

**Insight**

**Comprei** uma garrafa de água e depois **fui** para a praia.

----------

Quando **comprei** uma garrafa de água, **estava** calor.

----------

(Eu) **comprava** uma garrafa de água e depois **ia** para a praia.
(Eu) **costumava** comprar uma garrafa de água e depois **ir** para a praia.

## Exercises

### 14.2

Missanga is a young lady from Angola who spent some time in Portugal last year. She is talking about two T-shirts she bought from different places where she stayed for a while.

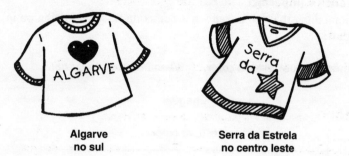

Algarve
no sul

Serra da Estrela
no centro leste

◀) CD2, TR 16

**14.2.1** Listen to your recording and tick each T-shirt as you hear it being mentioned.

**14.2.2** Listen again and write down all you hear.

**14.2.3** In what two ways does Missanga talk about that time in the past? Why?

**14.2.4** Missanga is now talking about her visit to Portugal globally rather than taking you through different stages in her stay. Listen to her next two sentences and rearrange the words below to match what she says.

Estive / ano / . / lá / passado / no

Fui / voltei /. / março / maio / em / em / dois / e / depois / , /meses

**14.2.5** The two sentences above (in 14.2.4) are Missanga's reply to a question she has been asked.

  **i** For the question, listen to the recording and unscramble the following words.
    Quando / você / lá / é / esteve / que / ?

  **ii** Can you reword this question for a friend who would address Missanga with **tu** instead of **você**?

### 14.3

Patrícia wants to buy a dress but cannot find one that will fit her.

**14.3.1** This is what she says to the shop assistant:

Este vestido está muito comprido. Tem outro mais curto do que este?

Carry on on her behalf:

  **i** dress too short; a longer one (**curto; comprido**).
  **ii** dress too tight; a wider one (**apertado; folgado**).

**14.3.2** Now she says:

Este vestido está muito curto. Tem outro menos curto do que este?

Carry on:

  **i** dress too long; not so long.
  **ii** dress too wide; not so wide.

### 14.4

Jason is trying to buy a pair of boots – **a(s) bota(s)** – and tells the shop assistant his shoe size in his country.

**14.4.1** Put the following sentences in the right sequence for his dialogue with the shop assistant.

**a** – Talvez o número acima, o 45.
**b** – No meu país calço n° 9 mas aqui não sei que número é.
**c** – Então quer experimentar o n° 44?
**d** – (*experimentando o n° 43*) Esta bota está muito apertada.
**e** – (*experimentando o n° 45*) Esta está bem, obrigado. Levo este par.
**f** – (*experimentando o n° 44*) Esta está menos apertada do que a 43, mas está um pouco apertada.
**g** – Nove... isso será número 43 ou 44. Eu trago três botas, uma em 43, uma em 44 e uma em 45.

**14.4.2** Re-write the dialogue for Sarah. She wants training shoes – o(s) ténis (Eur.) / o(s) tênis (Br.). At home her size is 5 and the shop assistant suggests 37, 38 and 39 to choose from.

**14.4.3** Later on Sarah tells a friend how she tried on different sizes until she found some trainers that fitted her. This is what she said. Fill in the gaps with the correct form of the verb **estar**.

O número 37 _____ muito apertado. O 38 _____ menos apertado que o 37, mas ainda _____ um pouco apertado. Finalmente, o 39 _____ bem. Comprei o 39.

### 14.5

You are shopping for clothes, footwear and accessories and you are particular about material, pattern and colour.

**14.5.1** What you are buying

> uma camisa
> uns sapatos
> um vestido
> uma gravata
> uma saia

Ask for:
**i** shirt; **ii** shoes; **iii** dress; **iv** tie; **v** skirt.

The first one has been done for you.
**i** Por favor, queria uma camisa.

**14.5.2** Material

```
de…
algodão
pelica
linho
seda
fibra sintética
```

Add the material you would like:

**i** cotton; **ii** kid; **iii** linen; **iv** silk; **v** man-made fibre.
**i** Por favor, queria uma camisa de algodão.

**14.5.3** Pattern

```
lisa
lisos
estampado
listrada / às riscas (Eur.)
xadrez
```

Add the pattern you would like:

**i** plain; **ii** plain; **iii** printed; **iv** striped; **v** checked.
**i** Por favor, queria uma camisa de algodão, lisa.

**14.5.4** Colour

```
em…
branco
azul escuro
amarelo e verde
preto e vermelho
duas ou três cores diferentes
```

Add your choice of colour:

**i** white; **ii** dark blue; **iii** yellow and green; **iv** black and red; **v** two or three different colours.
**i** Por favor, queria uma camisa de algodão, lisa, em branco.

**14.5.5** Your shopping has impressed your friends and they have some questions for you.

  **i** You are asked:
   Quando é que você comprou esses sapatos?
   Say:
   *I bought these shoes last week.*
 **ii** You are asked:
   Quando é que você comprou essa camisa e essa gravata?
   Say:
   *I bought this shirt last Monday and this tie last Wednesday.*
**iii** Make the necessary alterations to change the questions in
   (i) and (ii) from **você** to **tu**.

---

## Summary

 **1** (Eu) queria um par de sapatos de pelica. – (Eu) queria uns
  sapatos de pelica.
 **2** Isto aqui, de que é feito? – Esta camisa é (feita) de algodão?
 **3** Pode trazer-me / me trazer outra camisa. (Eu) preferia de
  algodão.
  Importa-se de me trazer uma gravata de seda. (Eu) preferia.
 **4** A camisa dele é listrada, em branco e azul escuro. – A blusa
  dela é estampada, em três cores diferentes. – A minha saia é
  lisa; é toda vermelha.
 **5** Este vestido está (muito) folgado / apertado. – Estas sandálias
  estão (muito) folgadas / apertadas.
 **6** mais escuro / claro / curto / comprido – no número / tamanho
  abaixo / acima

**7** Esta saia está comprida (para mim). – Esta saia é mais comprida (do) que aquela. – Esta saia é tão comprida como / quanto aquela.

**8** Esse casaco tem mais botões (do) que aquele. – Esse casaco tem menos botões (do) que aquele. – Esse casaco tem tantos botões como / quanto aquele.

**9** Hoje faz / está tanto calor como ontem. – Hoje estão tantos graus centígrados como / quanto ontem.

**10** Ontem de manhã comprei uma garrafa de água e depois fui para a praia. – Quando estava calor, eu comprava uma garrafa de água. – Quando estava calor, eu costumava comprar uma garrafa de água. – Quando comprei a garrafa de água, estava muito calor.

# 15

..................................................................

# Fazendo isto e aquilo
## Doing this and that

In this unit you will learn how to
- *Meet someone socially*
- *Fit in with local life and times*
- *Talk about what is happening and express the idea of progression*

**Combinando um encontro** *Arranging a meeting*

Marta and Tiago are arranging to go horse riding together.

**♦ CD2, TR 17**

| | |
|---|---|
| **Marta** | Você ainda quer ir andar a cavalo esta semana? |
| **Tiago** | Quero. Quando e onde é que nós nos encontramos? |
| **Marta** | Quando, talvez 6ª.-feira. |
| **Tiago** | Ou sábado de manhã? |
| **Marta** | Pode ser sábado de manhã. Eu não me importo. |
| **Tiago** | E onde? Eu escolhi o dia, você escolha o lugar e a hora. |
| **Marta** | No correio, às 9 e meia. |
| **Tiago** | Dentro ou fora? |
| **Marta** | Dentro, junto das máquinas de venda automática. |
| **Tiago** | Sábado, às 9 e 30, junto das máquinas dentro do correio. |
| **Marta** | Combinado. Até sábado. |

**andar a cavalo** *to ride a horse*
**eu não me importo** *I don't mind* (conceding)
**eu escolhi** *I have chosen*
**você escolha** *you choose*
**dentro ou fora** *inside or outside*
**junto de = junto a** *by, close to*
**combinado** *agreed*

## Tomando alguma coisa *Having a drink*

Artur and Lúcia have arranged to meet at the café for a snack and a chat.

| | |
|---|---|
| **Lúcia** | *(chegando)* Como vai? |
| **Artur** | *(sentado a uma mesa)* Bem, obrigado, e você? |
| **Lúcia** | Tudo bem. Desculpe se estou um pouco atrasada. Tive que fazer umas compras antes de vir. |
| **Artur** | Não, não está. Eu é que cheguei muito cedo. Enquanto estava sozinho, pensei em perguntar se você queria ir ao cinema. |
| **Lúcia** | Quero, sim. Ainda temos bastante tempo antes da segunda matiné. |
| **Artur** | Temos. E agora, o que é que havemos de pedir? |
| **Lúcia** | Para mim, um sorvete misto e depois um chá. E para você? |
| **Artur** | Uma água mineral com gás e uma porção de batatas fritas. |

**como vai? = como está?** *how are you? how are you keeping?*
**atrasada** *late*
**fazer umas compras** *to do some shopping*
**pensei em** *I thought about*
**(o) cinema** *cinema*
**(a) matiné** *afternoon session* (French 'matinée')
**pedir** *to ask for, order*
**para mim** *for me*
**um sorvete misto** *an ice cream in assorted flavours*
**com gás** *fizzy*
**uma porção** *a portion*
**(as) batatas fritas** *chips*

# Exercises

## 15.1 Perguntas e respostas *Questions and answers*

**1** Em que dia é que Marta e Tiago se vão encontrar?
 **a** Na sexta-feira. **b** No sábado. **c** No domingo.

**2** A que horas?
 **a** Às oito e meia. **b** Às nove. **c** Às nove e meia.

**3** Onde?
 **a** Fora do correio. **b** Dentro do correio.

**4** Quem está atrasado?
 **a** Artur. **b** Lúcia. **c** Ninguém.

**5** O que é que Artur e Lúcia vão pedir?
 **a** Uma água mineral sem gás, meia porção de batatas fritas, um sorvete de chocolate e um chá.
 **b** Uma água mineral com gás, uma porção de batatas fritas, um sorvete misto e um chá.

**6** O que é que eles vão fazer depois?
 **a** Vão para a praia. **b** Vão para o cinema. **c** Vão fazer compras.

## Expressions

**a De carro, a cavalo** *By car, on horseback*

For travelling, we have been using the phrase **de** + means of transport: **de** carro; **de** táxi; **de** autocarro (Eur.) / ônibus (Br.); **de** comboio (Eur.) / trem (Br.).

Similarly,
**de** metro (Eur.) / metrô (Br.) (*by underground train*); **de** elétrico (Eur.) / bonde (Br.) (*by tram*); **de** barco (*by boat*); **de** navio (*by ship*); **de** avião (*by aeroplane*); **de** moto, i.e., motocicleta

(*on a motorbike*); **de** bicicleta (*on a bicycle*); **de** boleia (Eur.) / carona (Br.) (*hitchhiking, getting a lift*).

| In Portugal: | In Brazil: |
|---|---|
| – Onde é que você foi ontem? | – Onde é que você foi ontem? |
| – A Braga. | – A Brasília. |
| – E como é que você foi? | – E como é que você foi? |
| – De carro. | – De avião. |

We have also been using the phrase **a pé** (*on foot*) for walking – **andar a pé** meaning lit. *to go / move along on foot*. Similarly, **andar a cavalo** or **ir a cavalo** is used for *to ride a horse*, where **a cavalo** corresponds to *on horseback*.

## Insight

| Onde Quando | **nos encontramos?** |
|---|---|

----------

| **Você quer ir** | ao cinema? à praia? |
|---|---|

----------

| **Vamos** | a pé? de carro? de táxi? a cavalo? |
|---|---|

**b 'Late', 'early', 'slow' and 'fast'**
For *late*, use **atrasado/a** for a person and **tarde** for an action or event. For *early*, use **adiantado / adiantada** for a person and **cedo** for an action or event.

| **Desculpe se estou um pouco atrasada.** | *Sorry if I am a little late.* |
|---|---|
| **Eu é que cheguei muito cedo.** | *It's I who arrived too early.* |
| | *(Contd)* |

You may also hear **atrasado** or **adiantado** in connection with an action, in which case what is being described is the person involved, not the action.

**Eu é que cheguei muito adiantado.**   *It's I who arrived too early.*

For clock reading, use **adiantado** for *fast* and **atrasado** for *slow*.

| | |
|---|---|
| **– Que horas são no seu relógio?** | *What is the time by (lit. on) your watch?* |
| **– Uma e dez.** | *Ten past one.* |
| **– Está adiantado. É uma em ponto.** | *It is running fast. It is one on the dot.* |

What about having the right time and arriving on time?

For clock reading, use **certo**, and for an action or event, use **na hora** or **a tempo** or **a horas**.

| | |
|---|---|
| **Este relógio está certo.** | *This watch / clock is right, i.e., telling the right time.* |
| **Cheguei na hora.** or **Cheguei a tempo.** | *I have arrived on time.* |

## Cultural information

a **Como vai?** *How are you?*

When you greet someone you already know, you may wish to say more than a simple hello.

For *How are you?* or *How are you keeping?* use **Como está?** and **Como vai?** The latter is general practice in Brazil but can also be used anywhere else. Another alternative is **Como passa?**

If you are talking to more than one person, then ask **Como estão / vão / passam?**

Although the expected reply may be *Well, thank you*, you may hear *Awful* instead. Usually they don't mean it!

Possible replies, ranging from good to bad, will be: **Ótimo** (*splendid*); **Muito bem** (*very well*); **Tudo bem** (*everything fine*); **Bem** (*well*); **Mais ou menos** (*so so*); **Não muito bem** (*not too well*); **Mal / Ruim** (Br.) // **Muito mal** (*not well // rather unwell*); **Terrível** (*awful*).

To enquire about a third person, say: **Como está / vai / vai passando…**

– Como vai?
– Eu vou bem. E você, tudo bem?

----------

– Olá! bom dia. Como está e como vai a sua mãe?
– Vamos bem, obrigada.

**b Passe bem** *Take care*

When parting, you can add **Passe bem** or **Fique bem** (*take care*, lit. *be well*) to what you learned in Unit 1. If it is more than one person, then say **Passem bem** or **Fiquem bem**.

To send regards to someone, you can say **Cumprimentos meus para…** For children, say **Beijos para as / nas** (Br.) **crianças**.

– Até depois do Natal. Passe bem. Cumprimentos meus para a sua esposa e beijos para as crianças.
– *See you after Christmas. Take care. My regards to your wife and kisses for the children.*

(For the use of the possessive – **seu / sua**, etc. – with or without the article – **o / a** – please refer to 4:HIWe and 20:HIWf.)

## How it works

### a Verbs: the three conjugations – continuous present and past

| I am... | | buying | selling | leaving |
|---------|---|--------|---------|---------|
| eu etc. | **estou** etc. | a compr**ar** (Eur.) compr**ando** (Br.) | a vend**er** (Eur.) vend**endo** (Br.) | a part**ir** (Eur.) part**indo** (Br.) |

| I was... | | buying | selling | leaving |
|----------|---|--------|---------|---------|
| eu etc. | **estava** etc. | a compr**ar** (Eur.) compr**ando** (Br.) | a vend**er** (Eur.) vend**endo** (Br.) | a part**ir** (Eur.) part**indo** (Br.) |

These are colloquial alternatives to the present indicative (Unit 8) and the imperfect indicative (Unit 14), in some cases.

**The continuous present** is formed with the present indicative of **estar** followed by i **a** + infinitive of the verb you want to express (Eur.); ii the gerund (*-ing* form) of the verb you want to express (Br.).

The **continuous past** is formed with the imperfect indicative of **estar** followed by **i** a + infinitive of the verb you want to express (Eur.); **ii** the gerund (*-ing* form) of the verb you want to express (Br.).

The continuous forms are more exact for the unfolding of an action or event which is happening now or was happening some time ago.

> Eu **estou a ler** a lição 15 neste momento (Eur.).
> / Eu **estou lendo** a lição 15 neste momento (Br.).
> *I am reading lesson 15 at this moment.*
> Eu **estava a ler** o jornal quando ele chegou (Eur.).
> / Eu **estava lendo** o jornal quando ele chegou (Br.)
> *I was reading the newspaper when he arrived.*

Instead of the verb **estar** (**eu estou**, etc. and **eu estava**, etc.) you are likely to also hear the verb andar (**eu ando**, etc. and **eu andava**, etc.). Preference is given to the latter where the notion of 'lately' is involved.

> Eu **ando a** estudar muito (Eur.). / Eu **ando** estud**ando** muito (Br.).
> *I have been studying hard lately.*

**Ir** is another verb you are likely to hear as an auxiliary for the continuous present and the continuous past (**eu vou**, etc. and **eu ia**, etc.). In this case there is no difference between European and Brazilian Portuguese.

| | *I am / was…* | *buying* | *selling* | *leaving* |
|---|---|---|---|---|
| eu, etc. | **vou / ia,** etc. | compr**ando** | vend**endo** | part**indo** |

> – Como **vai**?      *How are you keeping?*
> – Eu **vou indo** bem. E você?      *I am keeping well. And you?*

The verb **ir** option can emphasize progression.

> **Vou indo** um pouco melhor.      *I am getting a little better (after an illness).*
> **Vou fazendo** progressos.      *I am making progress (in my studies).*

### b Passive voice

The Portuguese passive voice is formed as follows:

> verb **ser** + past participle of the verb you want to use
> **Cadeiras de rodas são transportadas gratuitamente**
> *Wheelchairs are carried free of charge*

The past participle (**transportadas**) agrees in gender (feminine or masculine) and number (singular or plural) with the subject of the sentence (**cadeiras de rodas**).

As in English, the agent – who does the action – may or may not be expressed. When expressed, it is introduced by preposition **por**:

> **Cadeiras de rodas são transportadas gratuitamente pelo pessoal da empresa (por+ o)**
>
> *Wheelchairs are carried free of charge by the airline's staff*

However, in some cases the English passive voice finds a Portuguese translation in the reflexive construction you learned in Unit 9.

| | |
|---|---|
| Como **se escreve** isso? | *How is that spelled?* |
| **Fala-se** inglês. | *English (is) spoken.* |
| **Vendem-se** selos postais aqui. | *Postage stamps are sold here.* |
| **Aceitam-se** cheques. | *Cheques are accepted.* |
| **Aceitam-se** cartões de crédito. | *Credit cards are accepted.* |

### c Half a...

Have you noticed that English *a* is left out in the translation of *half a*...: meia hora; meia dúzia; meio quilo; meia porção?

| | |
|---|---|
| Temos que esperar **meia hora**. | *We have to wait half an hour.* |
| Queria **meia dúzia de** pãezinhos. | *I would like half a dozen bread rolls.* |
| Queria **meio quilo** de laranjas. | *I would like half a kilo of oranges.* |

| | |
|---|---|
| Traga-me **meia garrafa** de vinho. | *Bring me half a bottle of wine.* |
| Traga-me **meia porção** de batatas fritas. | *Bring me half a portion of chips.* |

## Insight

A bagagem **está a ser** (Eur.) / **sendo** (Br.) **transportada** no tapete rolante.

A minha mala **está a aparecer** (Eur.) / **aparecendo** (Br.) no tapete rolante.

**Estamos a chegar** (Eur.) / **chegando** (Br.) na hora.

**Estávamos a pedir** (Eur.) / **pedindo** (Br.) meia garrafa de vinho.

**Vou fazendo** progressos no meu estudo de Português.

---

## Exercises

### 15.2

**15.2.1** Look at the picture and answer the following questions about Sally:

  i  Ela vai de carro?
 ii  Como é que ela vai?

**15.2.2** Use the words in brackets to say the following in Portuguese, on Sally's behalf:

  i  *I like horse riding.*
    (Gosto / a / andar / cavalo / . / de)
 ii  *I go horse riding every Saturday.*
    (Ando / sábados / todos / cavalo / a / os / .)
iii  *I went horse riding last Saturday.*
    (Andei / cavalo / sábado / . / a / no / passado)

**15.2.3** Fill in the gaps in what Sally says next in Portuguese.

Eu encontrei o Raul quando _____ (I was horse riding) _____
_____ no sábado passado. Ele também ___ (was riding
a horse) _____.

**15.2.4** What did she say? What happened when?

### 15.3 Você fala Português muito bem *Your Portuguese is very good*

**amável** *kind*
**fazer erros** *to make mistakes*
**corrigir** *to correct*
**aprender** *to learn*
**conseguir** *to manage*

**15.3.1** Put the following sentences in a different order so as to
make a dialogue.

**a** – Você fala Português muito bem.
**b** – Há dois meses.
**c** – Está. Há quanto tempo aprende Português?
**d** – Estudando um pouco todos os dias.
**e** – Há só dois meses!? Como consegue aprender tão rapidamente?
**f** – Obrigado. Você é muito amável. Eu ainda faço muitos erros.
  Corrija-me, está bem?

**15.3.2** Rewrite the dialogue for two people who address each other
with **tu**.

(For verb **corrigir** check orthography-changing verbs in VG.)

### 15.4

**15.4.1** Read the following question and reply which took place at a
shop with this notice in the window:

– Aceitam este cartão de crédito?
– Aceitamos.

What did these two people say?

**15.4.2**

**pagar a** or **em** or **com dinheiro** *to pay cash*

In the same shop, other people are trying to find out how they can pay for their shopping. Write down the reply that is likely to be given to each question.

  **i** – Aceitam este cheque? (**aceitar**)
 **ii** – Posso pagar com este cheque? (**poder**)
**iii** – Tenho que pagar a dinheiro? (**ter que**)

**15.5**

◄》 **CD2, TR 19**

**15.5.1** Study the notice boards.

**15.5.2** Answer the following questions, in Portuguese. Give full answers.

   **i** – A que horas é que o clube abre?
  **ii** – A que horas é que o jantar começa?
 **iii** – Até que horas é que o museu está aberto?
 **iv** – Quando é que a primeira matiné começa?
  **v** – Em que dia da semana há futebol?
 **vi** – A piscina está aberta à noite?
**vii** – A partir de que horas é que a piscina está aberta?
**viii** – A que horas é que a biblioteca fecha?
 **ix** – Posso estudar na biblioteca de manhã?
  **x** – A farmácia está fechada às dez horas da noite?
 **xi** – Qual é o horário de atendimento do médico de clínica geral?
**xii** – Vou pôr uns postais no correio antes das vinte horas. Ainda vou a tempo para a terceira tiragem (Eur.) / coleta (Br.)?

**15.5.3** Listen to your recording. You will hear four people, each one asking a question about local facilities. Find the answers on the notice boards. Give informative but brief answers.

**15.5.4** Listen again to the four people on the recording and write down what they said.

**15.5.5** Can you say the following in Portuguese:

  **i**   At what time does the restaurant open?
 **ii**   At what time does the evening performance start?
**iii**   Up to what time is the chemist's open tonight?
 **iv**   At what time does the museum close?

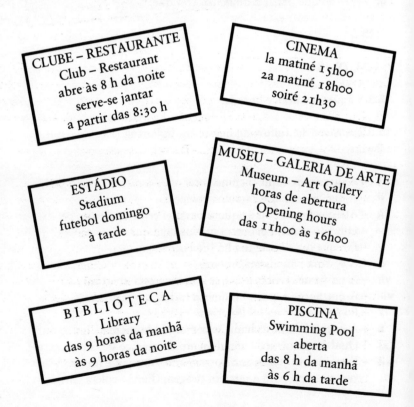

CLUBE – RESTAURANTE
Club – Restaurant
abre às 8 h da noite
serve-se jantar
a partir das 8:30 h

CINEMA
1a matiné 15h00
2a matiné 18h00
soiré 21h30

ESTÁDIO
Stadium
futebol domingo
à tarde

MUSEU – GALERIA DE ARTE
Museum – Art Gallery
horas de abertura
Opening hours
das 11h00 às 16h00

BIBLIOTECA
Library
das 9 horas da manhã
às 9 horas da noite

PISCINA
Swimming Pool
aberta
das 8 h da manhã
às 6 h da tarde

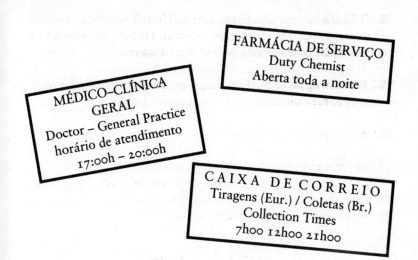

MÉDICO–CLÍNICA GERAL
Doctor – General Practice
horário de atendimento
17:00h – 20:00h

FARMÁCIA DE SERVIÇO
Duty Chemist
Aberta toda a noite

CAIXA DE CORREIO
Tiragens (Eur.) / Coletas (Br.)
Collection Times
7h00 12h00 21h00

## Summary

**1** Quando e onde nos encontramos? – Esta tarde, na biblioteca. Está bem? – Está. Combinado.

**2** Desculpem, se estou atrasada. – Desculpe, se estamos atrasados.

**3** Vocês querem ir ao cinema / ao clube / à piscina / à praia? – Querem ir a pé / de carro / a cavalo?

**4** Como se paga aqui? O que aceitam, cheques, cartões de crédito? Ou é só em dinheiro? – Aqui a que horas são as tiragens (Eur.) / coletas (Br.) de correio?

**5** Como vai / vai passando (você / o sr – a sra)? – Como vão / vão passando (vocês / os sres – as sras)? – Como vai / vai passando (sua esposa)? – Como vão / vão passando (seus pais)?

**6** Bem. – Não muito bem. – Vou indo um pouco melhor.

**7** Passe / Passem bem. – Fique / Fiquem bem.

**8** Cumprimentos meus para sua esposa. – Beijos para as crianças.

**9** Eu vi a Lena quando estava a jantar (Eur.) / jantando (Br.) no restaurante. – Ela também estava a jantar (Eur.) / jantando (Br.) lá. – Também vi o Zé. Ele chegou quando eu e a Lena estávamos a jantar (Eur.) / jantando (Br.).

**10** Ando a aprender (Eur.) / aprendendo (Br.) Português. Estudo duas horas todos os dias. – Vou fazendo progressos.

# 16

## Ontem, hoje e amanhã
### Yesterday, today and tomorrow

In this revision unit you will learn how to
- *Check your restaurant bill*
- *Order a hotel breakfast in bed*
- *Discuss alternative means of transport*
- *Enjoy a sunny day on the beach*
- *And enlarge on what you have learned so far*

This is a major revision unit that will take you through the different topic areas you have been studying. You will be given extra practice on what you have learned about expressing yourself in the present, past and future and you will be using the language structures you already know in a variety of new ways.

### 16.1

The words on the right mean the opposite of the words on the left, but they are in a different order. Can you pair up each word on the left with its opposite on the right? One has been done for you.

| | | | |
|---|---|---|---|
| **1** | antes | **a** | tarde |
| **2** | cedo | **b** | depois |
| **3** | adiantado | **c** | amanhã |
| **4** | ontem | **d** | atrasado |
| **5** | na 2ª.-feira passada | **e** | no próximo ano *or* no ano que vem |
| **6** | no ano passado | **f** | no próximo mês *or* no mês que vem |
| **7** | no mês passado | **g** | na próxima 2ª-feira *or* na 2ª-feira que vem |

**SÁBADO**

**Trabalhar**

This diary note is our starting point. But will working on Saturdays mean the same to everyone?

Aline, Guilherme, Ester and Rafael work in the same shop. Rearrange the words in brackets and find out how they view their Saturday work.

**1** *Sexta-feira*. Aline always goes in Saturdays and she is referring to tomorrow's work factually, just as what is expected to happen.
(Amanhã / , / , / sábado /. / trabalho)

**2** *Sexta-feira*. Guilherme doesn't always work on a Saturday. But he has committed himself to doing so tomorrow.
(Amanhã /. / trabalhar / vou)

**3** *Sexta-feira*. Ester does not know yet for certain whether she will be working tomorrow, but she is likely to.
(Provavelmente /. / amanhã / trabalharei)

**4** *Sexta-feira*. Rafael has always been reluctant about working on a Saturday, but he has made a new resolution and is determined to put it to practice tomorrow.
(Amanhã /. / de / trabalhar / hei)

**5** *Sábado*. Aline is working when Hugo phones inviting her to take a break. Aline feels she can't now.
(Agora /. / não / posso / Estou /. / trabalhar / a) (Eur.)
(Agora /. / não / posso / Estou /. / trabalhando) (Br.)

**6** *Domingo*. Aline is explaining to a friend that she worked yesterday, Saturday.
(Trabalhei / , / ontem /. / sábado)

**7** *Domingo.* Aline is telling her friend about Hugo's phone call yesterday when she was working.

(Hugo / telefonou / eu / a / . / quando / trabalhar / ontem / estava) (Eur.)

(Hugo / telefonou / eu / . / quando / trabalhando / ontem / estava) (Br.)

**8** *Umas semanas depois.* Aline is now going out with Hugo. She has given up working on Saturdays.

(Eu / aos / , / agora / não / trabalhava / sábados / mas / . / trabalho)

*or*

(Eu / aos / , / costumava / agora / não / trabalhar / sábados / . / mas / trabalho)

### 16.3

Your watch may be right or not, you may be on time... or not.

Gonçalo's watch and Bernardo's are not showing the same time.

o relógio do Gonçalo

o relógio do Bernardo

The 'speaking clock' – **a informação horária** – tells us that the following is the right time:

> vinte horas e quarenta e cinco minutos

**16.3.1** Give brief answers in Portuguese to the following questions:

**i** O relógio do Gonçalo está certo, atrasado ou adiantado?
**ii** O relógio do Bernardo está certo, atrasado ou adiantado?

**16.3.2** Gonçalo and Bernardo had arranged to meet at a café halfway between where each one lives. Leaving home at the same time should result in arriving at the same time. They both set off at 8.30 p.m. by their respective watches. Who is likely to have thought the following on arrival:

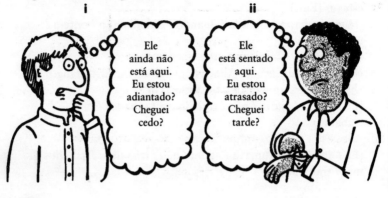

**i**

Ele ainda não está aqui. Eu estou adiantado? Cheguei cedo?

**ii**

Ele está sentado aqui. Eu estou atrasado? Cheguei tarde?

**16.4**

You don't want wrong figures in your bill, particularly if it adds up to more than expected.

You are paying for cakes (**bolos**), drinks (**bebidas**) and your bill includes 10% service (**dez por cento de serviço**), but there is a problem, the bill is wrong (**errada**).

**uma conta errada**

| Bolos | 1 600 |
| Bebidas | 1 760 |
| | 3 360 |
| Serviço 10% | 336 |
| Total | 3 796 |

**uma conta certa**

| Bolos | 1 600 |
| Bebidas | 1 760 |
| | 3 360 |
| Serviço 10% | 336 |
| Total | 3 696 |

**16.4.1** To argue your point over the wrong bill enter the missing words in the gaps below.

Importa-se de verificar esta conta. A conta está errada. Três mil, _____ e sessenta de bolos e

bebidas mais _____

e seis de serviço não são _____
e seis. São _____ e seis.

**16.4.2**

> $2 + 3 = 5$
> dois mais três igual a cinco
> *or*
> dois mais três são cinco

Still about the mistake on the bill, say this in Portuguese:

$$3 + 3 = 6, \text{not} = 7$$

**16.5**

Júlio is trying to concentrate and get on with his work but his colleagues are being somewhat noisy. Rearrange the words in brackets and find out how he starts by being very polite and ends up turning a bit dictatorial.

**1** In a very polite tone, Júlio asks his colleagues to keep their voices down.
(Façam / baixo / mais / . / o / favor / de / falar)

**2** They do but soon appear to forget and the noise comes back. Júlio asks again, still very politely.
(Por / , / falar / baixo / favor / . / queiram / mais)

**3** They oblige, but it's not long before they forget once more. Júlio places his request a third time.
(Querem / mais / , / por / falar / baixo/ ? / favor)

**4** There is silence for a few moments but peace and quiet does not last long. Júlio is beginning to lose his patience and politeness is no longer a priority. He shouts:
(Falem / ! / baixo / mais)

**16.6**

**carregue** (Eur.) = **aperte** (Br.) = **pressione**

**16.6.1** Look at the photographs below. They were taken in Portugal. Photo (A) shows an instruction notice on a train, by the door, photo (B) shows an instruction notice by a pedestrian crossing.

   **i** What 'command' word is shared by both instructions?
   **ii** What does the writing in A say?
   **iii** What does the writing in B say?
   **iv** Rewrite the two instructions – A and B – using the infinitive you first learned in Unit 3.

(Check orthography-changing verbs, VG.)

A                                    B

🔊 **CD2, TR 20**

**16.6.2** Listen to your recording. You will hear people trying to help someone who does not appear to have noticed the instructions for the train door. Advice comes in five different ways. Write them down.

**16.6.3** Continue listening. You will hear five different pieces of advice on the pedestrian crossing. Write them down.

**16.6.4** Refer to the photos again.

**a** Rewrite notice A for Brazil, using the 'command' form.
**b** Rewrite notice B for Brazil, using the 'command' form.

**16.6.5** Rewrite the two instructions – (A) and (B) – for Brazil, using the infinitive.

**16.6.6** Listen to what comes next on your recording. Write down the new five pieces of advice on the train door.

🔊 **CD2, TR 21**

**16.6.7** Listen further. Write down the new five pieces of advice on the pedestrian crossing.

### 16.7

Joyce is explaining how she always (**sempre**) goes to the language school (**colégio**).

**16.7.1** Look at the picture of Joyce going to school and fill in her missing words in the dialogue.

– Como é que você vai para as aulas de Português?
– Vou _____.
– Normalmente ou sempre?
– Sempre. O colégio fica muito perto de minha casa.

**16.7.2** Talking about the previous day, how would she describe how she went to school. Start with **Ontem...**

**16.7.3** And what would she say about tomorrow: **Amanhã...**

**16.7.4** How would you have asked the first question above if you were addressing her as **tu** instead of **você**?

### 16.8

QV **(o) horário** or **(a) tabela de horário** (Br.) *timetable*

a camioneta (para passageiros) (Eur.) = o autocarro (interurbano)
(Eur.) = o ônibus (interurbano) (Br.)

Pode me dar o horário dos autocarros? (Eur.)
Pode me dar o horário das camionetas? (Eur.)
Pode me dar a tabela de horário dos ônibus? (Br.)

Following the above models, ask for the timetable for the
trains:

**a** in Portugal             **b** in Brazil

### 16.9

**(o) voo** *flight*
**sem escala** *non-stop*
**fazer escala em** *to call at*

◀)) **CD2, TR 22**

**16.9.1** Brazilian Antônio is in Lisboa enquiring about his flight
back home to Brasília. Listen to your recording and write down
both what he asks and the information he is given.

**16.9.2** Portuguese António is in Brasília enquiring about his flight
back home to Lisboa. Listen to your recording and write both
question and answer.

### 16.10

**direto** *direct*
**(o) transbordo** *passenger transfer*

In Portugal

– O comboio das 15.25
para o Porto é direto ou
tem transbordo?
– É direto.

PARTIDA

PORTO (CAMPANHÃ)\*
GUARDA – TOMAR
DIR\*\* 15h25

*\*Campanhã – railway station in Porto*

*\*\*DIR = direto*

**1** Taking the above mini-dialogue as a model and referring to the picture, give a question and answer for:

**i** Tomar.　　**ii** Guarda.

**2** What word would you have said in Brazil instead of **comboio**?

### 16.11

When talking about coach and train stations, some people prefer using colloquial alternatives to **a estação rodoviária** and **a estação ferroviária / dos caminhos de ferro** (Eur.). These alternatives are in the column on the right. Can you match the words on the left with their synonyms on the right?

**1** estação rodoviária
**2** estação dos caminhos de ferro (Eur.)
**3** estação ferroviária

**a** estação dos comboios (Eur.)
**b** estação dos autocarros (Eur.)
**c** estação dos trens (Br.)
**d** estação das camionetas (Eur.)
**e** estação dos ônibus (Br.)

**16.12**

◀) CD2, TR 23

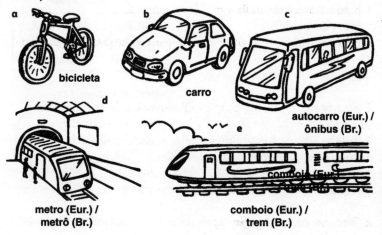

a bicicleta

b carro

c autocarro (Eur.) / ônibus (Br.)

d metro (Eur.) / metrô (Br.)

e comboio (Eur.) / trem (Br.)

**16.12.1** On your recording you will hear six people talking about how they travel, where they travel to and how long it takes them.

**16.12.2**

**a** Listen to what they say and enter the information they give in the grid below. One has been done for you.

|   | where to? | how? | how long? |
|---|-----------|------|-----------|
| 1 |           |      |           |
| 2 |           |      |           |
| 3 |           |      |           |
| 4 |           |      |           |
| 5 |           |      |           |
| 6 | praia     | bicicleta | + / − 5 minutos |

**b** Listen again to what they said and write down all you hear.

**16.12.3** Refer to the pictures and use the combinations below so as to compare how you usually go to work now and how you used to go to work over a period of time in the past. The first one has been done for you.

**i** b mas a. **ii** c mas d. **iii** e mas b. **iv** c mas a.

**i** Agora normalmente vou de carro mas costumava ir de bicicleta.

### 16.13

Point out the following people in a crowd by describing their physical appearance / clothes / where they are / what they are doing:

**1** Four-year-old Mariazinha **Aquela menina ...**
(*long, blond hair + red and white dress*)

**2** Teenage Bruno **Aquele rapaz ...**
(*standing by the coffee vending machine*)

**3** Adult Cecília **Aquela ...**
(*black bikini + talking + by the yellow car*)

**4** Adult Rúben **Aquele ...**
(*short black hair + striped shirt + sitting down + reading the paper*)

### 16.14

◄» **CD2, TR 24**

You are in Portugal booking in at a hotel for a group.

**16.14.1** Try this for a tongue twister:

Quero quatro quartos no quarto andar para quatro noites.

## 16.14.2

**QV** **o andar térreo / o rés-do-chão** (Eur.) *ground floor*
**a cave** (Eur.) / **o subsolo** (Br.), **o porão** (Br.) *basement*

| | |
|---|---|
| 4 | ☐ |
| 3 | ☐ |
| 2 | ☐ |
| 1 | ☐ |
| r/c | ☐ |
| c/v | ☐ |

You are inside the hotel lift going down. You are standing by the operating buttons and ask the other three guests joining you **Para que andar?** Listen to your recording and make a note of the floor where each one wants to get out.

**16.14.3** When you come back to the hotel you want to ask for your room key you had handed in: **Por favor, pode me dar...** Complete the sentence and say your room number:

**i** the easy way (4-3-9). **ii** the not-so-easy way (*four hundred...*).

## 16.15

Below is your hotel breakfast order form, in Portugal.

**16.15.1** You would like breakfast in bed between 8 and 8.30 a.m. and you have decided on toast, jam, butter, orange juice, coffee, milk, boiled egg and bacon. Complete the form accordingly. Also, use the space provided and enter your three special requirements: hard-boiled egg (**ovo bem cozido**), skimmed milk (**leite magro** (Eur.) / **leite desnatado** (Br.)) and wholemeal bread (**pão integral**).

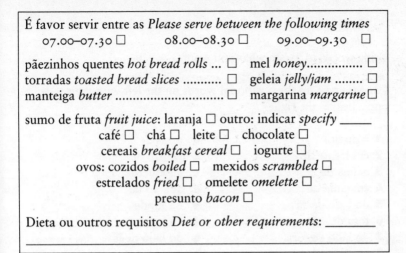

<br>

É favor servir entre as *Please serve between the following times*
07.00–07.30 ☐        08.00–08.30 ☐        09.00–09.30 ☐

pãezinhos quentes *hot bread rolls* ... ☐      mel *honey*............... ☐
torradas *toasted bread slices* ........... ☐      geleia *jelly/jam* ........ ☐
manteiga *butter* .............................. ☐      margarina *margarine* ☐

sumo de fruta *fruit juice*: laranja ☐ outro: indicar *specify* ____
                café ☐    chá ☐    leite ☐    chocolate ☐
                cereais *breakfast cereal* ☐    iogurte ☐
        ovos: cozidos *boiled* ☐    mexidos *scrambled* ☐
            estrelados *fried* ☐    omelete *omelette* ☐
                        presunto *bacon* ☐

Dieta ou outros requisitos *Diet or other requirements*: _____

**ovo estrelado** (Eur.) = **ovo frito** (Br.)
**sumo** (Eur.) = **suco** (Br.) **presunto** (Eur.) = **bacon** (Br.)

**16.15.2** The breakfast order form is on a long rectangular card with a large circular perforation at the top and says: **Antes de se deitar, queira pendurar na maçaneta exterior da porta.** Can you work out what this message means?

**16.15.3** When you wake up at 8 o'clock the following morning you realize that the form is still lying on your bedside table. You phone reception to explain what happened and place the order verbally.

**esquecer-se (de)** is the opposite of **lembrar-se (de)**

Fill in the gaps in your dialogue with the receptionist.

– Bom dia. Esqueci-me de pendurar na maçaneta da porta o cartão
  para pedir o ____*(breakfast)*____. Ainda posso pedir?
– Pode, sim. O que deseja?
– Queria __*(boiled egg, toast, bacon, butter, jam, orange juice,*
  *coffee and milk)*.
– Prefere o ovo bem ou mal cozido?
– __*(well done)*. E só mais duas coisas, desculpe. Prefiro _*(skimmed*
  *milk, wholemeal bread)*. Terei que _____ muito tempo?
– Não, meia hora mais ou menos.

**16.16**

Using words to locate what you want...

Can you pair up the positional words on the left with their opposites on the right?

| | | | |
|---|---|---|---|
| **1** | à direita | **a** | atrás de |
| **2** | em frente de | **b** | dentro de |
| **3** | acima de | **c** | à esquerda |
| **4** | em cima de | **d** | abaixo de |
| **5** | do lado de cá | **e** | no fundo |
| **6** | fora de | **f** | ao fundo |
| **7** | do lado de fora | **g** | do lado de lá |
| **8** | em volta de | **h** | no lado interior de |
| **9** | à superfície | **i** | a contar de baixo |
| **10** | em primeiro plano | **j** | do lado de dentro |
| **11** | no lado exterior de | **k** | de baixo para cima |
| **12** | de cima para baixo | **l** | o último a contar de cima |
| **13** | a contar de cima | **m** | no meio de *or* no centro de |
| **14** | o primeiro a contar de cima | **n** | em baixo de (Eur.) / embaixo de (Br.) |

**16.17**

QUICK VOCAB

**no canto** *in the corner*
**na parede** *on the wall*
**no chão** *on the floor*
**no teto** *on the ceiling*
**nas traseiras** (Eur.) **/ nos fundos** (Br.) *in the back (of house)*
**no balcão** *on the counter*
**na montra** (Eur.) **/ na vitrine** (Br.) *in the shop window*

no lado exterior = no lado de fora
ao lado de = junto de
de um e do outro lado de = em ambos os lados de

**16.17.1** Read the following description of a shop. Then check your comprehension of the text by answering the questions in English.

> No lado exterior da loja vê-se a palavra ALIMENTAÇÃO na parede,
> acima da porta, que fica ao lado da montra (Eur.) / vitrine (Br.).
> Dentro da loja, há, no centro, um balcão. Na parede atrás do
> balcão há três prateleiras. Nas paredes de um e do outro lado do
> balcão há prateleiras, do chão até ao (Eur) / o (Br) teto. Abaixo da
> montra há uma prateleira. No canto direito ao fundo há uma porta
> para as traseiras (Eur.) / os fundos (Br.) da loja.

**i** What can you read above the front door as you approach the
shop?

**ii** As you approach the shop, what can you see next to the door?

**iii** Where exactly inside the shop is the counter?

**iv** What can you see on the wall behind the counter and the walls
either side of it?

**v** What is there in the right corner, at the far end of the shop?

**16.17.2** Four different customers (*A*, *B*, *C* and *D*) enter the shop.
They all want boxes of chocolates.

**i** Read their words to find out who wants which box.

*A*: Queria a caixa grande que está em cima do balcão.

*B*: Quero a segunda caixa a contar da esquerda na prateleira
abaixo da montra (Eur.) / vitrine (Br.).

*C*: Queria a caixa grande que está entre as duas caixas pequenas na
prateleira do meio atrás do balcão.

*D*: Prefiro uma das caixas pequenas que estão em volta da caixa
grande, na prateleira dentro do balcão.

**ii** Answer the following questions, using full sentences in Portuguese:

**a** Onde é que está a caixa que *A* quer?

**b** A caixa que *B* quer está perto ou longe da montra (Eur.) /
vitrine (Br.)?

**c** A caixa que *D* quer está fora ou dentro do balcão?

**d** Qual é a pessoa que prefere uma das caixas pequenas em volta
da caixa grande?

**e** Quem quer uma caixa que está na segunda prateleira a contar de
baixo, atrás do balcão?

**16.18**

Browsing and buying

**16.18.1** In a shop, you want to explain that you are just looking. Do so by using the verbs in brackets and filling the gaps with the correct words.

Estou só _____ (**ver**) (Eur.) / Estou só _____ (**olhar**) (Br.)

**16.18.2** You are having difficulty in finding the right shop. Fill the gaps in the following sentence with the correct form of the words in brackets, so as to ask where you can find a shop that sells / may sell parasols.

Onde _____ (**poder, encontrar**) uma loja que (**vender, guarda-sol**) _____.

(For verb **vender** see both Unit 8: HIWa and Unit 17: HIWa.) (If you need to, see VG for verb **poder** and Unit 5: HIWc for **guarda-sol**.)

**16.18.3** You are about to complete a purchase but you are asked to produce a voucher as proof of payment before your shopping can be handed over to you (**o talão** (Eur.) / **o comprovante** (Br.)). This is what the shop assistant says:

Por favor, quer pagar ali na caixa? Depois traga-me o talão. (Eur.)
Por favor, quer pagar ali na caixa? Depois traga-me o comprovante. (Br.)
What must you do?

**16.19**

**(a) maré** *tide*
**(a) maré alta** or **preia-mar** (Eur.)/**preamar** (Br.) *high tide*
**(a) maré baixa** or **baixa-mar** *low tide*

High and low tide are going to reach their peaks at these times.

| | marés |
|---|---|
| preia-mar | 02.50 e 15.15 |
| baixa-mar | 08.43 e 20.55 |

**16.19.1** Answer the following questions, using the 24-hr clock reading.

  **i** A que horas termina a maré baixa de manhã?
 **ii** A que horas termina a maré baixa à noite?
**iii** A que horas termina a maré alta à noite?
 **iv** A que horas termina a maré alta à tarde?

**terminar** means the opposite of **começar**

**16.19.2** What is the answer to the following questions:

 **i** Ao meio-dia a maré estará mais alta do que está agora? (agora são 10 horas da manhã)
**ii** Às seis horas da tarde a maré estará mais baixa do que está agora? (agora são 4 horas da tarde)

**16.20**

**a cadeira de praia**
*beach chair*

**o guarda-sol**
*beach parasol, sunshade*

**16.20.1** Can you ask for the beach chair and parasol hire? Start with

**Pode me dizer onde ...**

**16.20.2** Unscramble the following sentences to say that you would like to hire:

**i** two beach chairs for one day.
  (Queria / alugar / cadeiras / . / dia / por / de / duas / um / praia)
**ii** a parasol for half a day.
  (Queria / dia / meio / um / alugar / . / guarda-sol / por)

**16.20.3** Ask how much it is:

**i** for the beach chairs for one day; **ii** for the parasol for half a day.

---

## Summary

**1** Pode trazer-me / me trazer o pequeno-almoço (Eur.) / café da manhã (Br.) ao quarto, no quinto andar?
  Queria um ovo bem cozido, dois pãezinhos quentes, manteiga, fruta e café com leite.
**2** Queria alugar um guarda-sol e uma cadeira de praia por um dia.
  Hoje a que horas é a maré alta?
**3** Cedo ou tarde?
  No ano passado ou no ano que vem?
  Do lado de cá ou do lado de lá?
  Certo ou errado?
**4** Esta conta está errada.
  Cinco e cinco são dez, não doze.
**5** Pagar na caixa.
  Pague na caixa.
  Tem que pagar na caixa.
  Quer pagar na caixa?
  Queira pagar na caixa.
  Faça o favor de pagar na caixa.

**6** Importa-se de levar o recibo àquela senhora de cabelo louro comprido e biquíni preto que está sentada a ler (Eur.) / lendo um jornal.

**7**

**7.1** No ano passado eu tinha um trabalho que ficava longe de casa; costumava ir de carro.

**7.2** Agora estou a trabalhar (Eur.) / trabalhando (Br.) perto de casa. Normalmente vou para o trabalho a pé.

**7.3** Ontem fui de carro porque estava atrasada.

**7.4** Amanhã vou a pé; vou sair de casa mais cedo. Na sexta-feira provavelmente irei de carro. Na próxima semana hei de ir sempre a pé ou de bicicleta.

# 17

# Espero que a consulta seja hoje
## I hope you can book me in for today

In this unit you will learn how to
- *Cope in the event of illness or injury*
- *Distinguish between a wish, an invitation, a suggestion and an order*
- *Use a new way of expressing yourself about something in the future*

**Marcando consulta pelo telefone** *Arranging an appointment by telephone*

Leonor is phoning for an urgent medical appointment.

**CD2, TR 25**

| | |
|---|---|
| **Leonor** | Eu queria marcar consulta para hoje. |
| **Empregada** | Por quê hoje? |
| **Leonor** | Porque não me sinto nada bem. É urgente. Agradeço que a consulta seja hoje, mesmo que seja tarde. |
| **Empregada** | Então... às 20 horas e 30. |

**QV**

**por quê? / porquê** (Eur.) *why?*
**porque** *because*
**não me sinto nada bem** *I don't feel at all well*

**seja** *may be, could be*
**agradeço que a consulta seja hoje** *I'd appreciate it if the appointment could be today* (lit. *I thank that...*)
**mesmo que** *even if*

### No consultório do médico e depois na farmácia
*In the doctor's surgery and then in the chemist's*

Leonor is now at the doctor's surgery explaining her problem.

CD2, TR 26

| | |
|---|---|
| **Leonor** | Tenho uma dor forte no estômago. |
| **Médico** | É a primeira vez que tem essa dor? |
| **Leonor** | Não, a primeira vez foi há um ano. Estive no hospital. |
| **Médico** | Foi operada? |
| **Leonor** | Não, não fui. |
| **Médico** | Por favor, dispa-se e deite-se para ser examinada. *(examinando Leonor)* Dói aqui? |
| **Leonor** | Ai! Dói, sim. |
| **Médico** | *(escrevendo a receita)* Deve tomar este medicamento de 4 em 4 horas. Se não se sentir melhor dentro de dois dias, marque consulta novamente. *(despedindo-se)* Estimo as suas melhoras. |
| **Leonor** | Para quando é que pode aviar esta receita? |
| **Farmacêutico** | Isso é rápido. O medicamento vai estar pronto daqui a um quarto de hora o mais tardar. |

QUICK VOCAB

**uma dor forte no estômago** *a sharp / strong pain in my stomach*
**(a) vez** *time, occasion*
**há um ano** *one year ago*
**foi operada?** *were you operated on?*
**dispa-se** *get undressed*
**deite-se** *lie down*
**dói aqui?** *does it hurt here?*

**ai!** *(exclamation of pain)*
**(a) receita** *prescription*
**deve tomar** *you must take*
**de 4 em 4 horas** *every 4 hours*
**se não se sentir melhor** *if you don't feel better*
**marque** *book*
**despedindo-se** *saying good-bye / parting words*
**aviar esta receita** *to make up this prescription*
**o mais tardar** *at the latest*

---

## Exercises

### 17.1 Perguntas e respostas *Questions and answers*

**1** Leonor quer falar com o médico. Por quê? / Porquê? (Eur.)
  **a** Porque não foi operada.
  **b** Porque toma um medicamento.
  **c** Porque tem uma dor no estômago.

**2** Quando é que a Leonor esteve no hospital?
  **a** Há seis meses.    **b** Há um ano.    **c** Há um mês.

**3** Quantas vezes por dia é que a Leonor deve tomar o medicamento?
  **a** Duas vezes.    **b** Seis vezes.    **c** Quatro vezes.

**4** Que mais é que a Leonor deve fazer?
  **a** Marcar consulta o mais tardar daqui a dois dias.
  **b** Marcar consulta se não se sentir melhor dentro de dois dias.

**5** Quando é que o medicamento estará pronto?
  **a** Dentro de 10 minutos.    **b** Daqui a 15 minutos ou menos.

## Expressions

### a Vez *Time, occasion*

You will come across the word **vez** and its plural **vezes** meaning *time(s)*, *occasion(s)*, *turn(s)*, depending on the context.

| | | alternatives |
|---|---|---|
| quantas **vezes?** | *how many times?* | |
| | *how often?* | |
| duas **vezes** | *twice, two times* | |
| às **vezes** | *sometimes* | **ocasionalmente** |
| muitas **vezes** | *often* | **frequentemente** |
| poucas **vezes** | *seldom* | **raramente** |
| outra **vez** | *again* | **novamente** |

Also, you wait your turn (**a sua vez**) in the doctor's or the dentist's waiting room. In the supermarket, you help yourself to a 'your turn' ticket instead of queuing up for the delicatessen counter; your ticket shows the words **sua vez** and a number.

### b Economizing on words

Small words such as the articles – **o** (*the*), **um** (*a / an*) – and others are sometimes dispensed with in everyday speech and writing, particularly in brief messages.

**Faz / Faça ☐ favor de...** *for* Faz / Faça o favor de... *please...*
**Queria fazer ☐ reserva.** *for* Queria fazer uma reserva.
　　　　　　　　　　　　　　　　　　　*...a reservation.*
**Queria marcar ☐ consulta.** for Queria marcar uma consulta.
　　　　　　　　　　　　　　　　　*...a medical appointment.*
**Apertar ☐ cintos,** the lit-up *Fasten your seatbelt sign facing your plane seat.*

*(Contd)*

### c Clothes, shoes, hats on and off

Study the following Portuguese renderings:

| vestir-se despir-se | vestir despir | o casaco, etc. | *it will cover your body* |
| calçar-se descalçar-se | calçar descalçar | o sapato, a luva, etc. | *you slip it on your feet or hands* |
| | pôr tirar | o chapéu, o cachecol, o cinto, etc. | *you put it on your head, etc.* |

Note that **pôr / tirar** are often used as an alterantive to **vestir / despir** and **calçar / descalçar,** but the reverse does not always apply.

**Quer tirar o (seu) casaco?**  *Do you want to take your coat off?*
or
**Quer despir o (seu) casaco?**  *Do you want to take your coat off?*
but
**Quer tirar o (seu) chapéu?**  *Do you want to take your hat off?*

### d Emergency treatment and 'emergency' words

The following are usual ways of signposting a hospital accident department and a first-aid post.

EMERGÊNCIA                PRONTO-SOCORRO

Also note the following 'emergency' words: **Cuidado!** (Watch out!); **É perigoso!** (It's dangerous!); **Há /Tem perigo** (There is danger!); **Fogo!** (Fire!); **Depressa!** (Hurry!); **Socorro!** (Help!).

## Insight

**Socorro!**
**Cuidado!**

----------

Pode me **levar para o hospital.**
**Depressa,** por favor.

## Cultural information

When you make a telephone call, you are likely to hear one of the following responses:

**a** the number, e.g., *104 99 23 56*
**um zero quatro, nove nove, dois três, cinco seis** (Eur.) /
**meia** (Br.).

In Brazil there is the general practice of saying **meia** (from **meia dúzia**) instead of **seis** when you give a number digit by digit.

**b** the name of the subscriber
**Consultório do doutor Armando Gonçalves.**

**c** hello!
  **i** **Está?** (Eur.) or **Está lá?** (Eur.) (lit. *are you / is anyone there?*)
  **ii** **Alô?** (Br.)

To announce yourself, say:

  **Fala...** You can also say **Daqui fala...** (Eur.) / **Aqui fala...** (Br.)
  **Fala Henrique Bernardes**

To express the intention of your call, you can start with:

**Queria...** (*I would like...*) or **Posso...** (*May I...*)

*(Contd)*

| Queria marcar consulta | I *would like to book an appointment* (e.g. for a medical appointment) |
| Queria marcar hora para... | I *would like to book an appointment for...* (e.g., with the hairdresser) |

(See Unit 17:Eb, above.)

---

## How it works

**a  Verbs: the three conjugations – present subjunctive**

| I may... | buy | sell | leave |
|---|---|---|---|
| eu | compre | venda | parta |
| tu | compres | vendas | partas |
| você, o sr / a sra ele / ela | compre | venda | parta |
| nós | compremos | vendamos | partamos |
| vocês, os sres / as sras | | | |
| eles / elas | comprem | vendam | partam |

The present subjunctive of regular verbs and the majority of irregular verbs is formed by dropping the final -o of the first person singular (the verb form for **eu,** *I*) of the present indicative (see Unit 8) and adding the endings highlighted in the above box.

**Use for...**
   **1** The expression of a wish or hope.
   Espero que a consulta **seja** hoje. *I hope that the appointment is today.*
   Estimo que (você / a senhora) **melhore** rapidamente *I wish you a speedy recovery*
   (*often abridged to* Estimo as suas melhoras / rápidas melhoras *or simply* Melhoras!)

   **2** The expression of sorrow or sympathy.
   Sinto muito que ela est**eja** doente. *I am very sorry that she is ill.*

   **3** An action or event regarded as a possibility.
   Ela talvez tom**e** uma bebida quente. *She may perhaps have a hot drink.*

   **4** After a statement that implies influence upon other people or things.
   A hospedeira (Eur.) / aeromoça (Br.) pede ao passageiro que apert**e** o cinto de segurança. *The stewardess asks the passenger to fasten his safety belt.*
   Peço a / à (Eur.) Maria que compr**e** o jornal. *I ask Mary to buy the paper.*

Peço a / à (Eur.) Maria que faça o favor de comprar o jornal.
*I ask Mary to be so kind as to buy the paper.*

(Note the different sentence construction in English – *to buy / to be*.)

**b  A wish, a hope... and a 'polite imperative'**

wish → hope → expectation

The command forms borrowed from the present subjunctive are a wish made expectation. They are often referred to as the 'polite' command, or imperative, forms.

**Compre** o jornal. *Buy the paper.*

Unless tone of voice indicates otherwise, this does not bear the harshness of tone the English translation may suggest, bearing in mind the inbuilt uncertainty of the subjunctive forms.

**c  Command form 'let's go'!**

The verb endings for **nós** (*we*) – **-emos, -amos** – render English *let's*.

compr**emos** / vend**amos** / part**amos** *let's buy / sell / leave*

These days this format is used mainly for verb **ir.**

**Vamos!** *Let's go!*

**d  Don't**

For a command in the negative – *don't...* – just use **não** before the verb (see Unit 12).

**Não** compre isso. *Don't buy that.*  **Não** fume. *Don't smoke.*

In this case, the command for the **tu** approach borrows from the present subjunctive just like the others.

**Não** compr**es** isso. *Don't buy that.* **Não** fum**es**. *Don't smoke.*

## e Verbs: the three conjugations – future subjunctive

| (If / when) | I buy | I sell | I leave |
|---|---|---|---|
| eu | compr**ar** | vend**er** | part**ir** |
| tu | compr**ares** | vend**eres** | part**ires** |
| você, o sr / a sra<br>ele / ela | compr**ar** | vend**er** | part**ir** |
| nós | compr**armos** | vend**ermos** | part**irmos** |
| vocês, os sres / as sras<br>eles / elas | compr**arem** | vend**erem** | part**irem** |

The future subjunctive is formed by dropping the final **-ram** of the third person plural (for **eles/elas**, *they*) of the preterite (see Unit 10) and by adding -r, -res, -r, -rmos, -rem.

## Use for...

An action or event the realization of which will determine the viability or purposefulness of another action or event.

Quando cheg**arem** lá, atravessem. *When you get there, cross over.* (they must get 'there', before crossing)

Pode me dizer por favor quando cheg**armos** lá. *Can you please tell me when we get there? (the bus-stop where you want to get off)*

Se qu**iser,** podemos / poderemos ir ao cinema amanhã. *If you wish, we can / shall be able to go to the cinema tomorrow.*

The future subjunctive can be used for a very elegant way of saying please: **se fizer favor**. This expression is sometimes simplified to **se faz favor** which you learned in Unit 2.

Note the use of, respectively, the present and the future subjunctive with the meaning of *Bless you!* and *God bless!*
- ▶ As a warm wish for someone's well-being or as a warm expression of gratitude, *Bless you!* finds a translation in **Bem haja!** (addressing one person) and **Bem hajam!** (addressing more than one) – verb **haver**.
- ▶ *Good night, God bless!* Calling upon divine protection in the hours of darkness finds a different rendering, i.e., **Boa noite! Até amanhã, se Deus quiser**. Literally **se Deus quiser** means *if God so wishes* – verb **querer** – and, to some extent, corresponds to English *God willing*.

## f  Irregular comparatives

Some adjectives and adverbs have irregular comparatives.

| | |
|---|---|
| **bom** (*good*), **bem** (*well*) | **melhor** (*better*) |
| **mau, ruim** (*bad*), **mal** (*badly, poorly*) | **pior** (*worse*) |
| **grande** (*big, large*) | **maior** (*bigger*) |

| | |
|---|---|
| **pequeno** (*small*) | **menor** (*smaller*) |
| **muito** (*much*) | **mais** (*more*) |
| **pouco** (*little*) | **menos** (*less*) |

However, sometimes both regular and irregular forms coexist.
It is so with **mais pequeno** which is often preferred to **menor** in
Portugal.

**Insight**

> **Pode sair** de casa quando **estiver** melhor.
>
> ----------
>
> Quando **chegarmos** ao hospital, por favor **informe** o meu
> marido.

---

## Exercises

### 17.2

The person in **A** is being invited to sit down – **Quer sentar-se?** – ,
the person in **B** to lie down – **Quer deitar-se?** –, and the person in
C to stand up – **Quer levantar-se?**

**17.2.1** Ask the following:

  **i** the person in (D) to lie down;
 **ii** the person in (C) to get up and sit down;
**iii** the person in (B) to stand up.

**17.2.2** Starting with **Faça favor de...** ask the following:

  **i** the person in (A) to take position (B);
  **ii** the person in (B) to take position (C);
  **iii** the person in (C) to take position (D).

**17.2.3** Ask the same as in **17.2.2** above but starting with **Queira...** .

**17.2.4** Ask the same as in **17.2.2** above but using the command form.

**17.2.5** Ask the same again in the command form but talking to more than one person. (i) **Sentem-se.** Carry on.

**17.2.6** Ask the same again in the command form but talking to a person you would use **tu** with. (i) **Senta-te.** Carry on.

**17.2.7** Ask the same yet again in the command form but talking to more than one person you would individually use **tu** with.

### 17.3

Starting with **Queira...** ask someone to take off his/her:

**i** coat   **ii** boots   **iii** hat

### 17.4 Dores *Aches and pains*

**17.4.1** Put together the broken-up sentences in the box below so as to complain of the following:

  **i** a very bad sore throat since last Sunday.
  **ii** an aching tooth for the past two days.
  **iii** a severe earache in your right ear since last night.
  **iv** a slight pain 'here' since last Wednesday.

| Dói-me | muito<br>um pouco | a garganta<br>um dente<br>o ouvido direito<br>aqui | há dois dias<br>desde ontem à noite<br>domingo passado<br>4ª.-feira passada |
|---|---|---|---|

**17.4.2 i** The doctor is waiting for you to remove your clothes so you can be examined. To say you have done so insert the correct form of the verb:

Já me _____ . (**despir**)

**ii** Now unscramble the following sentence to say the same in a different way

Já / a / . / tirei / roupa

**17.4.3** Can you tell how often the following medicines must be taken?

**i** de 6 em 6 horas     **ii** 2 vezes por dia     **iii** dia sim dia não

**17.5**

Read the health information card completed by Kelly, who has a heart complaint and is allergic to penicillin. She has also entered her GP's name and phone number and that of her next of kin to be contacted in case of accident.

On Kelly's behalf, write the answers to the following questions.

| | |
|---|---|
| **1** É doente?<br>**2** De que sofre?<br>**3** É alérgica a algum medicamento?<br>**4** Tomou alguma vacina recentemente?<br>**5** Em caso de acidente, quem devo avisar? Qual é o número do telefone? | MÉDICO ASSISTENTE *dr. Rui Vasco*<br><br>TEL.: 4571096<br><br>VACINA _____ EM __ /__ / __<br>VACINA _____ EM __ /__ / __<br><br>EM CASO DE ACIDENTE, POR FAVOR AVISAR *meu marido, Óscar Campos*<br>TEL.: 4381022 OUTRA INFORMAÇÃO<br>*sofro do coração; sou alérgica a penicilina.* |

**17.6**

◀) CD2, TR 27

Listen to your recording and you will hear seven people saying 'emergency' words. Write them down, and say them aloud.

**17.7**

**(o) passeio** (Eur.) **/ (a) calçada** (Br.) *pavement*
**(a) berma (Eur.) / (o) acostamento** (Br.) *hard shoulder*

**17.7.1** You are in Portugal and see this poster by a school promoting road and traffic awareness in children. The child is being addressed in the **tu** verb form (revise the 'command forms' in Unit 12).

Caminha
pelo
lado direito
do passeio
ou da berma

  **i** What is the written instruction that accompanies the picture?
 **ii** Rewrite it for an adult pedestrian.

**17.7.2** Nearby there is more written advice. It reads:

| |
|---|
| Para atravessar |
| Para no passeio |
| Olha primeiro para a esquerda e depois para a direita para ver se vem algum carro |
| Se não vier nenhum, atravessa, olhando novamente para a esquerda até ao meio da rua e depois para a direita |

Note: **Para** in 'Para atravessar' means *to*. The first **a** sounds like *a* in *among*. **Para** in 'Para no passeio' means *stop*. The first **a** sounds like *a* in *car*. A pitfall for foreign language learners!

  **i** What do these instructions say? (Note that **vier** comes from **vir**)
  **ii** Rewrite them for an adult pedestrian.

**17.7.3** Rewrite for Brazilian readers the instructions in i 17.7.1 and ii 17.7.2 above.

---

## Summary

  **1** Fala (*your name*)
    (Eu) queria marcar consulta para hoje.
    Espero que a consulta seja hoje.
  **2** Cuidado! Perigo! Depressa! Socorro!
  **3** Pode levar-me / me levar para o hospital.
  **4** Não me sinto bem.
    Dói-me a garganta / este ouvido / aqui.
    Dói muito / pouco.
  **5** Dói há dois dias / desde esta manhã.
    Dói às vezes / muitas vezes / sempre.

**6** Sofro do coração.

Sou alérgica a penicilina.

**7** Faça (o) favor de descalçar o sapato.

Dispa o casaco.

Deite-se.

Já pode levantar-se.

**8** Tome este medicamento de 6 em 6 horas / 2 vezes por dia.

Marque outra consulta, se não estiver melhor.

**9** Espero que tenham tempo para tomar um cafezinho.

Façam (o) favor de se sentarem.

Queiram sentar-se.

Querem sentar-se.

Sentem-se.

**10** Quando chegarmos ao hospital, por favor informe o meu marido.

Se na próxima semana não estiver melhor, vou marcar outra consulta.

Quando estiver melhor, vou à praia.

Cuidado! Olhem primeiro. Atravessem a rua só se não vierem carros.

# 18

## Se os acharem, telefonem logo
## If you find them, phone right away

In this unit you will learn how to
- *Report lost property*
- *Cope with road accident and car breakdown*
- *And solve a number of other problems*

**'Perdidos e achados'** *'Lost and found'*

Heloísa is reporting the loss of some valuables.

| | |
|---|---|
| **Heloísa** | Perdi a minha carteira e um saquinho com joias que eu tinha dentro da bolsa. |
| **Empregado** | Sabe onde e quando perdeu essas coisas? |
| **Heloísa** | Não, não sei, mas usei a carteira há umas quatro horas quando fui fazer compras. Creio que não foi roubo. A carteira e o saquinho devem ter caído para fora da bolsa. |
| **Empregado** | E o que tinham dentro? |
| **Heloísa** | A carteira tinha cartões de crédito, notas e moedas e o saquinho tinha um anel de ouro com um brilhante e um pendente de prata em forma de coração *(depois de ter dado o endereço e o número do telefone do hotel)*. Se os acharem, telefonem-me logo para o hotel, por favor. |

**perdidos e achados** *lost and found (items)*
**perder – achar** *to lose – to find*
**(a) carteira** *wallet / purse*
**(o) saquinho** *small bag*
**(as) joias** *items of jewellery*
**(o) roubo** *theft*
**(o) anel de ouro** *gold ring*
**(o) brilhante** *diamond*
**em forma de coração** *heart-shaped*
**(o) pendente / pingente** (Br.) *pendant*

## Numa garagem *In a garage*

Teresa has taken her car to a garage for some repair work.

| Teresa | Queria mandar consertar o carro. Está amolgado na frente e riscado no lado. Além disso, às vezes não pega. Eu tenho muita pressa, preciso muito do carro. Para quando é que pode consertá-lo? |
| --- | --- |
| Mecânico | O carro não pega... Depende da causa. Se o problema não for grande, estará pronto daqui a dois dias, incluindo pintura. |
| Teresa | Obrigada. Pode também verificar o óleo, encher o lavador de para-brisa e completar o tanque. |
| Mecânico | Estará tudo em ordem quando a senhora vier, mas é melhor telefonar primeiro. |

**mandar consertar** *to have (something) repaired*
**amolgado, riscado** *dented, scratched*
**além de** *in addition to*
**pegar** *to start (engine)*
**ter pressa** *to be in a hurry*
**(a) pintura** *paintwork*
**encher** *to fill*
**(o) tanque/(o) depósito** (Eur.) *tank*
**(o) lavador de para-brisa/para-brisas** (Eur.) *windscreen bottle*
**completar** *to top up (tank)*

## Exercises

### 18.1 Perguntas e respostas *Questions and answers*

**1** O que estava dentro da carteira que Heloísa perdeu?
   **a** notas e moedas.   **b** dinheiro e bilhetes.
   **c** cartões de crédito, notas e moedas.

**2** Que joias é que Heloísa perdeu?
   **a** Um anel de ouro e um pendente de prata.
   **b** Um anel de prata e um pendente de ouro.

**3** Em que forma era o pendente?
   **a** Em forma de estrela.   **b** Em forma de coração.

**4** O carro da Teresa precisa de ser consertado. Por quê? / Porquê? (Eur.)
   **a** Porque às vezes não pega, está riscado no lado e amolgado na frente.
   **b** Porque está amolgado no lado e riscado na frente e às vezes não pega.

**5** Além do carro consertado, que mais é que a Teresa quer?
   **a** Água no lavador de para-brisa, gasolina no tanque e mais óleo.
   **b** Mais óleo se necessário, o lavador de para-brisa cheio de água e o tanque cheio de gasolina.

## Expressions

   **a Ser** or **estar?** – **estar com** or **ter?** Saying *'to be'* and *'to have'*

As you learned in Unit 4 for **está** and **é**, **estar** (*to be*) is for something that can change easily in contrast with **ser** (*to be*) which is used to identify or characterize something or someone.

*(Contd)*

| **ser** (inherent condition) | **estar** (condition not inherent) |
|---|---|
| **Sou professor.** *I am a teacher.* | **Hoje está quente.** *Today it's hot.* |
| **Ela é bonita.** *She is pretty.* | **Estou cansado.** *I am tired.* |
| **Ele é simpático.** *He is nice.* | **Ele está constipado** (Eur.) / |
| **Eles são ingleses** *They are English*. | **resfriado** (Br.). *He has a cold.* |
| **Sou doente.** *I do not enjoy good health.* | **Estou doente** *I am ill (currently).* |
| **Ele é uma pessoa ansiosa.** | **Ele está ansioso por ver o que está dentro da caixa.** |
| *He is a person of an anxious disposition.* | *He is looking forward / eager to see what is inside the box.* |

**Estar com** or **ter** + noun is used with certain expressions of feeling.

| **Tenho** (lit. *I have*) | **sede / fome.** | *I'm* | thirsty / hungry |
|---|---|---|---|
| | **frio / calor.** | | cold / hot |
| | **pressa.** | | in a hurry |
| **Estou com** (lit. *I am with*) | **febre.** | *I've got* | a fever |
| | **dor de cabeça.** | | a headache |

To express physical pain **dói-me** (lit. *it hurts* me) is, however, of more versatile application.

**Caí. Dói-me aqui... e aqui...** *I fell down. It hurts here... and here...*

**b** How long? / for / ago

Note that **há** can translate all three.

| **Há quanto tempo está aqui?** | *How long have you been here?* (verb in the present) |
|---|---|
| **Estou aqui há duas horas.** | *I have been here for two hours.* (verb in the present) |
| **Cheguei há duas horas.** | *I arrived two hours ago.* (verb in the preterite) |

As an alternative to the last example you can also say

**Cheguei duas horas atrás.**

Note: You may also hear **'Cheguei há duas horas atrás'**, although **'há'** already contains the notion of elapsed time.

Another possibility is the combined use of preposition **a** and **atrás**.

**Isso aconteceu a milhões** *That happened millions of years ago.*
**de anos atrás.**

## Insight

| | |
|---|---|
| Perdi | a minha carteira. |
| | o meu passaporte. |
| Usei | a carteira quando fui fazer compras. |
| | o passaporte quando cheguei há uma semana. |

O carro **está avariado**. Não anda. Foi um acidente há dois dias.
Pode me **consertar** o carro.
Tenho **pressa**.

## How it works

### a Perfect tenses

The Portuguese compound or perfect tenses are formed with the verb **ter** as an auxiliary plus the past participle of the verb you want to express. The latter remains invariable, i.e., does not agree with the subject (in gender or number). The former changes as follows:

Perfect indicative – (**ter** in the present)
Use for a continuous state or for a continuous or frequently repeated action or event, or series of actions or events, occurring within a period of time which has not yet elapsed.

| | |
|---|---|
| O tempo t**em** est**ado** bom. | *The weather has been fine.* |
| Eu **tenho** trabalh**ado** muito ultimamente. | *I have been working hard lately.* |

Pluperfect indicative – (**ter** in the imperfect)
Use for a state which had existed or for an action or event which had been completed before something else happened in the past or before a set time in the past.

| | |
|---|---|
| O tempo t**in**ha est**ado** bom, antes da trovoada. | *The weather had been fine, before the storm.* |
| Eu já **tinha saído** quando ele chegou. | *I had already left when he arrived.* |
| Ele ainda não **tinha** cheg**ado** quando eu saí. | *He had not yet arrived when I left.* |
| Foi a paisagem mais bela que eu já **tinha visto**. | *It was the most beautiful scenery I had ever seen.* |

Meaning the same as the compound pluperfect indicative, there is also a simple, or synthetic, pluperfect indicative.

| | |
|---|---|
| O tempo est**ivera** bom, antes da trovoada. | *The weather had been fine, before the storm.* |
| Foi a paisagem mais bela que eu já **vira**. | *It was the most beautiful scenery I had ever seen.* |

This tense is not used much nowadays other than in literary and formal style, but you will find its endings in the verb tables at the end of the book. In speech it tends to be used only in idiomatic expressions.

**Tom**ara estar de férias.          *I wish I were on holiday.*

The pluperfect (compound or simple) can be said to express the past of the past. The compound format can also be used with other forms of the verb **ter** and express the 'past of the future' as well as other kinds of sequence.

Poderemos falar quando eu t**iver** acab**ado** este trabalho.
  *We shall be able to talk when I have finished this work.*
Espero que você t**enha** consegu**ido** consulta ontem.
  *I hope that you have managed to get an appointment yesterday.*

Note: You may come across the verb **haver** instead of **ter** as the auxiliary in compound or perfect tenses: e.g., Eu já ha**via** sa**í**do quando ele chegou.

### b Reported speech

As in English, when you report what someone has said or what you have thought, you often use a form of the past of the verb you want to express.

Ele disse que **gosta** de música.          *He has said that he likes music.*

but also

Ele disse que **gostava** de música.          *He has said that he liked music.*

and, similarly,

Pensei que ele **ia falar**.          *I thought that he was going
                                        to speak.*

**c Não funciona** or **não está funcionando?** *Saying*
*'it doesn't work'*

There are some cases in which you can use the present (Unit 8) and
the imperfect (Unit 14) but Brazilians tend to prefer the continuous
forms of the verb (Unit 15), particularly for the present, e.g. with
any device that is out of order.

Não **funciona**           *It is not working (lit. it does not work)*
Não **está funcionando** (Br.)   *It is not working*

Of course, you can also say

Não **está a funcionar** (Eur.)   *It is not working*

**d Superlatives**

**i** muito *very*

Peter é **muito** alto.
Peter fala Português **muito** fluentemente.
**muito/muita/muitos/muitas** *much, a lot of*

Peter tem **muita** bagagem.
Peter tem **muitas** malas.

ii   -íssimo/-íssima/-íssimos/-íssimas  *most, extremely; a very large
     quantity/number of;* -issimamente *extremely*

Peter é alt**íssimo**.
Peter tem muit**íssima** bagagem.
Peter tem muit**íssimas** malas.
Peter fala Português fluent**issimamente**.

iii   o mais... *the -est, the most...*

Peter é **o mais** alto (de todos).
Peter fala Português **o mais** fluentemente (de todos).

**a maior quantidade de...** *the most, the largest quantity of*

Peter tem **a maior quantidade de** bagagem (de todos).

**o maior número de...** th*e most, the largest number of*

Peter tem **o maior número de** malas (de todos).

There is also a parallel format for **o menos...** *the least,* but this is
not so widely used.

Joseph é **o menos** alto (de todos).

The irregular superlatives in **iii** above are the same as the irregular
comparatives you learned in Unit 17. For the superlative in **i** and **ii**
above, where no comparison is involved, note the following:

grande            **máximo**
pequeno           **mínimo**
bom; bem          **ótimo; otimamente**
mau, ruim; mal    **péssimo; pessimamente**

**e Mais que or mais de?** *Saying 'more than'*

Use **mais (do) que**, and **menos (do) que**, where the second term of the comparison involves a verb, expressed or implicit (see Unit 14).

Peter é **mais** alto **do que**          *Peter is taller than Mary (is).*
  Mary (é).

Use **mais de**, and **menos de**, before a number or another expression of quantity, where no comparison is implied.

**Mais de** 60 km por hora.          *More than 60 km per hour.*
**Menos de** 60 km por hora.          *Less than 60 km per hour.*

> **Insight**
>
> Nós **íamos** a **pouco mais de** 60 km por hora.
> Penso que **foi** uma infração de trânsito **mínima**.

**f Gender**

In Portuguese there isn't a neuter form as such, but you have come across the masculine ending -o acting as a neuter, e.g. in **isto** (Unit 12).

Also compare the following:

Ess**a** infra**ção** de trânsito é gravíssim**a**.
*That traffic offence is extremely serious.* Feminine endings throughout.

but

É gravíssim**o**. *It is extremely serious.* Ending -o acting as a neuter.

# Exercises

**18.2 Tive um acidente** *I have had a car crash*

🔊 **CD2, TR 30**

**18.2.1**

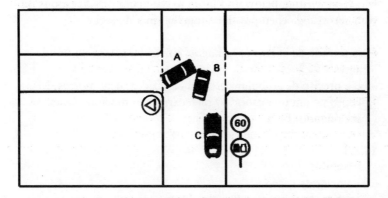

o cruzamento = o ponto de encontro com a estrada transversal

Study the following exchange of words between the two drivers who have had an accident, and find out who was driving which car.

| | |
|---|---|
| **Afonso** | O senhor não parou no cruzamento, infringindo o sinal de obrigação de parar. |
| **Olavo** | O senhor ultrapassou, infringindo o sinal de proibição de ultrapassar. |

### 18.2.2

**(a) ambulância** *ambulance*
**(o) rebocador** or **reboque** *breakdown truck*
**(o) ferido** *injured person*
**(o) morto** *dead person*

Afonso phones the rescue service for help. Study Afonso's words which are written below and listen to the operator's questions on your recording. Then put them together in a dialogue.

– Na estrada de Sagres para Lagos, a mais ou menos 10 km de Sagres.
– Não preciso de ambulância. Não há feridos, nem mortos. Mas preciso de um rebocador. O meu carro não funciona / está funcionando (Br.).

### 18.2.3

**(a) velocidade** *speed*
**(o) quilómetro** (Eur) **/ quilômetro** (Br.) *kilometre*

When the police arrive...

Match the official's questions with Afonso's replies:

**1** O senhor ultrapassou?  **a** Vi...
**2** A que velocidade ia?  **b** Hum... ultrapassei.
**3** Não viu o outro carro?  **c** Hum... a 60 km por hora.

### 18.2.4

**parecer que** *to appear to, look as if*
**avançar** *to move forwards*
**bater em** *to hit (collide)*

Write a report on the accident. It is Afonso's version of the story.

Fill in the gaps with the appropriate forms of the verbs in brackets.

Eu _____ (*seguir*) pela estrada a
60 km por hora. Na minha frente _____
(*seguir*) o carro C, muito lentamente. Eu _____
_____ (*ver*) o carro A, que parecia que tinha parado
no cruzamento. Eu _____ (*ultrapassar*)
o carro C, mas o carro A _____
(*avançar*) e _____ (*bater*) no meu.

**18.3**

This is a drink-drive warning sign from Portugal.

**conduzir** (Eur.) = **dirigir** (Br.)

**18.3.1** 'If you drive (any time in
the future) do not drink', says the
safety warning. Starting with **Nunca**
say in Portuguese *I never drink when
I drive.*

**18.3.2** Say the same again but for when you are in Brazil.

### 18.4 Mishaps, complaints and solutions

**18.4.1** Study the following list of mishaps and complaints:

  i  Penso que me roubaram a carteira e o telefone portátil.
     telefone portátil = telemóvel (Eur.) = celular (Br.)
 ii  Perdi o meu passaporte e o visto.
iii  Perdi uma lente de contacto (Eur.) / contato (Br.).
 iv  O quarto é muito barulhento.
  v  O chuveiro não funciona / está funcionando (Br.).

**18.4.2** Can you find below a suggestion or solution for each
mishap or complaint? Match them.

**a**  Há um oculista perto daqui.
**b**  Por favor, pode mandar consertar o chuveiro?
**c**  Então deve informar a polícia.
**d**  Talvez seja melhor pedir para mudar de quarto.
**e**  Pergunte na secção (Eur.) / seção (Br.) de perdidos e achados.

**18.5**

**fugir** *to flee (run or drive away)*

**18.5.1** Emy's pendant may have been stolen. She may have seen the thief running down a nearby road. Help her describe the following in Portuguese:

**i**  pendant: (*made of gold and* ★ *shaped*)
**ii**  the suspect: Ele fugiu pela rua ali à direita. Ele deve ter uns vinte anos, (*black hair / white T-shirt / blue jeans*)

**18.5.2** Ben has been hit by a car and the driver did not stop. Help him describe in Portuguese what he remembers for a police report.

**i**  *car:* Não vi bem o número da placa nem de que marca o carro é. O motorista fugiu. Sei apenas que... (*a dark green car*).
**ii**  *driver:* Não vi bem. Foi tudo muito rápido, mas penso que ele... (*around 40 / short blond hair / yellow shirt*)

**18.6**

Can you match the different words of sympathy with the two pieces of bad news below, according to how serious they are?

**1** Ontem a minha melhor amiga foi atropelada. Está no hospital em observação.

**a** Não se preocupe. Podia ter sido pior.

**2** Caí. Torci o pé direito e hoje não posso nadar. Também feri / machuquei (Br.) a mão esquerda.

**b** Sinto muito. Estimo rápidas melhoras.

### 18.7 A multa *The fine*

In Curitiba, capital city of the State of Paraná, Brazil, the local authorities have issued a leaflet showing the penalties incurred for speeding.

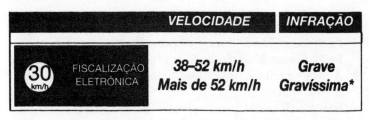

| | VELOCIDADE | INFRAÇÃO |
|---|---|---|
| 30 km/h FISCALIZAÇÃO ELETRÔNICA | **38–52 km/h** **Mais de 52 km/h** | **Grave** **Gravíssima\*** |

*\*Com suspensão da carteira da habilitação por 2 a 7 meses.*

**18.7.1** Study this extract and answer the questions which follow.

eletrônica (Br.) = eletrónica (Eur.)
carteira da habilitação (Br.) = carteira de motorista (Br.) = carta de condução (Eur.)

  i  Numa rua de 30 km por hora, 40 km/h é grave ou gravíssimo?
 ii  A partir de que velocidade é gravíssimo?
iii  Se fizer mais de 52 km/h que outra penalidade terá além da multa?

**18.7.2** The other side of the leaflet shows this picture and text.

CUIDADO COM
O EXCESSO
DE VELOCIDADE.
A PRESSA
E A SEGURANÇA
NUNCA ESTÃO
NA MESMA MÃO.

**i** What does the first sentence say?

**ii** What does the second sentence say? Do you 'get' the pun?

---

## Summary

**1** Perdi a minha carteira / o meu passaporte.
Perdi um pendente (Eur.) / pingente (Br.).
Perdi a carta de condução (Eur.) / carteira de motorista (Br.).

**2** A carteira tinha notas e moedas. Usei a carteira quando fui fazer compras.
Usei o passaporte quando cheguei há uma semana.
O pendente (Eur.) / pingente (Br.) é de ouro, em forma de estrela.

**3** O carro está avariado. Não anda.
Pode me consertar o carro. Tenho pressa.

**4** O carro / esta máquina / o chuveiro não funciona (Eur.) / está funcionando (Br.).
Pode me consertar o carro / esta máquina / o chuveiro.

**5** Tive um acidente.
Preciso de ambulância / rebocador / a polícia.

**6** Eu ia devagar, a 30 km por hora.
Ele ia a velocidade máxima; deve ser uma infração gravíssima.
Foi a velocidade mais alta que eu já tinha visto.

**7** O motorista ultrapassou / bateu no meu carro / não parou.
O motorista fugiu.
Era um carro vermelho escuro.

**8** Penso que me roubaram o telemóvel (Eur.) / celular (Br.).
O homem fugiu.
Ele deve ter uns trinta anos, tinha cabelo louro curto e calça(s) preta(s).

**9** Quando voltei para casa notei que tinha perdido a carteira.
Eu tinha virado à esquerda no semáforo, quando tive o acidente.

**10** Ele disse que me telefona para o hotel, se acharem a carteira.
Ele disse que o carro vai estar pronto daqui a três dias.
Ele disse que o carro ia estar pronto dali a três dias.

# 19

# Gostaria muito de viajar mais
## I'd love to travel more

In this unit you will learn how to
- **Express likes and dislikes**
- **Talk about interests, leisure pursuits and sport**
- **Express a condition, a wish or a hope**

**Falando acerca de lazer e férias** *Talking about leisure and holidays*

Roberto and Natália are talking about leisure and holidays.

| | |
|---|---|
| **Roberto** | O que é que você faz nas horas vagas? |
| **Natália** | Tenho poucas horas vagas, mas, quando posso, sento-me diante do televisor, relaxando. |
| **Roberto** | E quando está de férias, o que faz? Para onde vai? |
| **Natália** | Normalmente não vou longe. Passo o tempo na praia, ao sol. Tomo banho de mar e banho de sol ... e não faço nada. Gostaria muito de viajar mais. Infelizmente agora não posso, mas espero poder num futuro próximo, talvez no ano que vem ou daqui a dois anos. |

◈ CD2, TR 31

QV

**(as) horas vagas** *spare time*
**diante de** *facing*
**relaxando** *relaxing*

**tomar banho de mar** *to bathe, have a swim in the sea*
**tomar (banho de) sol** *to sunbathe*
**(eu) gostaria de** *I should / would like to*
**gostaria muito de** *I'd love to*
**viajar mais** *to do more travelling* (lit. *travel more*)

### Comparando interesses *Comparing interests*

Silvana and Alfredo are comparing their interests and leisure pursuits.

| | |
|---|---|
| **Alfredo** | O que é que você faz no seu tempo livre? |
| **Silvana** | Leio, principalmente romances históricos, e adoro pintar quadros. Aos fins de semana normalmente vou a uma galeria de arte ou visito um museu. Também gosto muito de música, isto é, música clássica, e às vezes vou a um concerto. Também vou ao teatro, uma ou duas vezes por mês. E você? |
| **Alfredo** | Eu não gosto muito de ler mas leio revistas e novelas policiais. Gosto de música popular. Faço natação. Jogo futebol, ocasionalmente, mas tenciono jogar mais vezes. |
| **Silvana** | Eu detesto jogos de bola, principalmente futebol. Nado, mas raramente, e só na piscina; no mar não. Às vezes dou um passeio a pé e uma vez por outra faço uma caminhada. |
| **Alfredo** | Hum... Temos interesses bastante diferentes. |

**(o) tempo livre = (as) horas vagas**
**(o) romance histórico** *historical novel*
**adoro** *I love*
**pintar quadros** *to do painting*
**(a) novela policial** *detective novel*
**uma vez por outra** *once in a while*
**(a) natação** *swimming (sport)*
**jogo futebol** *I play football*
**tenciono** *I intend to*
**eu detesto** *I detest, hate*
**(os) jogos de bola** *ball games*

**dou um passeio a pé** *I go for a stroll*
**(a) caminhada walk (long),** *rambling*

---

## Exercises

### 19.1 Perguntas e respostas *Questions and answers*

**1** Quem tem pouco tempo livre?
   **a** Roberto. **b** Natália. **c** Alfredo. **d** Silvana.

**2** Como é que a Natália passa o dia quando está de férias?
   **a** Toma banho na piscina. **b** Nada no mar.
   **c** Toma banho de mar e sol.

**3** O que é que a Silvana gosta mais de fazer nas horas vagas?
   **a** Pintar quadros. **b** Dar passeios.
   **c** Ler livros e revistas.

**4** O que é que a Silvana detesta mais?
   **a** Futebol. **b** Caminhadas. **c** Jogos de bola.

**5** Quais são os interesses do Alfredo?
   **a** Jogos de bola, caminhadas, natação, e ler romances históricos.
   **b** Ir a concertos e ao teatro, e visitar galerias de arte e museus.
   **c** Futebol, natação, música popular, e ler revistas e novelas policiais.

## Expressions
   **a** *'I love'* and *'I'd love'*

To express a strong wish, say **(eu) gostaria muito de.**
**Eu gostaria muito de viajar mais.** *I'd love to travel more.*

*(Contd)*

For likes and dislikes, use **(eu) gosto** and **(eu) não gosto**.

**Gosto de peras mas não gosto de maçãs.** *I like pears but I don't like apples.*

An emphatic alternative to **(eu) gosto muito de** is found in the verb **adorar** (lit. *to adore*), with **detestar** (*to hate, detest*) as its opposite.

**Adoro jardinagem e detesto cozinhar.** *I love gardening and hate cooking.*
**Adoro viajar. É o melhor dos meus passatempos prediletos.** *I love travelling. It's the best of my favourite pastimes / hobbies.*

**Adoro animais. Tenho um cão / cachorro** (Br.) **e também um gato.** *I love animals. I have a dog and also a cat.*

Otherwise English *'to love'* finds a translation in **amar**.

**Amo (os) meus filhos.**          *I love my children.*

## Insight

| | |
|---|---|
| (Eu) **gosto** (muito) **de** | música. |
| (Eu) **adoro** | teatro. |
| (Eu) **não gosto** (muito) **de** | pintar. |
| (Eu) **detesto** | viajar. |

### b Intentions

**Tencionar** (*to intend*) or **ter a intenção de** (*to have the intention of*) are ways of expressing one's intention.

**Tenciono / tenho a intenção de fazer mais exercício.** *I intend / It's my intention to take more exercise.*

(You are planning to take more exercise.)

Also revise what you have learned about **vou…** (Unit 9) and **hei de…** (Unit 13).

| | |
|---|---|
| **Vou fazer mais exercício.** | *I am going to take more exercise.* |
| **Hei de fazer mais exercício.** | *I will take more exercise.* |

**c Play**

Note that the verb to play finds a Portuguese translation as follows:

**jogar** *(to participate in a game)*

| | |
|---|---|
| **Jogo futebol.** | *I play football.* |

**tocar** *(to perform on a musical instrument)*

| | |
|---|---|
| **Toco piano.** | *I play the piano.* |

**brincar** *(to engage in children's play)*

**Onde há um parque infantil onde as crianças possam brincar?**

*Where is there a children's playground for the children to play?*

**brincar** *(to engage in frivolous play, as, for example, playing with words; hence to joke)*

**Isso não é a sério, você está a brincar** (Eur.) / **está brincando** (Br.).

*You are not being serious, you are joking (kidding).*

**d Passear** and **dar passeios**: *'Walking' and 'going for a walk'*

**Passear** translates *to stroll* but it also translates *to ride* and *to drive*, when this is a leisurely activity. Similarly, **dar um**

*(Contd)*

**passeio** and **dar uma volta** translate *to go for a stroll / ride / drive*. If you want to specify whether you are walking or using a means of transport, then you add **a pé** or **de carro, a cavalo,** or the appropriate term.

**Vou passear / dar um passeio / dar uma volta a pé.** *I am going to go for a stroll.*

**Vou passear / dar um passeio / dar uma volta de carro.** *I am going to go for a drive or ride (for pleasure).*

## Insight

| | |
|---|---|
| O que é que você **faz** | nas horas vagas? |
| | no seu tempo livre? |

**Leio** um livro.
**Jogo** futebol.
**Faço** natação.

| | |
|---|---|
| **Vou** | à praia. |
| | à piscina. |
| | a um concerto. |
| **Dou** passeios | a pé. |
| | a cavalo. |
| | de carro. |

**Sento**-me diante do televisor, relaxando,

mas

**tenciono** fazer mais exercício.

## How it works

### a Verbs: the three conjugations – conditional

| *I might / should…* | *buy* | *sell* | *leave* |
|---|---|---|---|
| eu | compr**aria** | vend**eria** | part**iria** |
| tu | compr**arias** | vend**erias** | part**irias** |
| você, o sr / a sra ele / ela | compr**aria** | vend**eria** | part**iria** |
| nós | compr**aríamos** | vend**eríamos** | part**iríamos** |
| vocês, os sres / as sras eles / elas | compr**ariam** | vend**eriam** | part**iriam** |

The conditional, also known as 'future in the past', is formed by attaching endings **-ia, -ias, -ia, -íamos, -iam** to the infinitive of the verb. As with the simple future (Unit 13), the three exceptions are **dizer, fazer, trazer,** where the endings are added to shortened forms of the infinitive: **diria** etc., **faria** etc., **traria** etc.

> **Handy hints**
>
> Note that these endings are the same as the imperfect indicative of **ir**. (See VG.)

### Use in the following cases

**1** Where a condition is involved and in English you would say *I should, you would,* etc.

Podemos sair, mas eu **gostaria** de, primeiro, ler o jornal.
*We can go out, but I should like to, first, read the paper.*

**2** In reported speech or thought for something that had not happened yet when it was talked / thought about (see also Unit 18).

Pensei que ele **iria** falar. *I thought that he would be speaking.*

Note that in speech the conditional is often replaced with the imperfect indicative (Unit 14).

> Pensei que ele **ia** falar. *I thought that he was going to speak.*
> Pensei em perguntar se você que**reria** (*or* queria) ir ao cinema.
> *I thought of asking whether you would like to go to the cinema.*

### b I would like

**Eu gosto de jogar golfe** means *I like playing golf*, i.e., *I enjoy playing golf*. **Eu gostaria de jogar golfe** translates *I should like to play golf*. It is the expression of a wish rather than a courteous way of asking for something. For this, you find a more appropriate rendering in **Eu queria jogar golfe**. In fact, **queria** is the imperfect indicative you learned in Unit 14 used in place of the conditional. In all these cases you don't normally need to say 'eu' – **gosto / gostaria / queria de jogar golfe** (see '**queria** or **eu queria?**' in Unit 14).

| **Insight** | |
|---|---|
| (Eu) **gostaria de** | pintar. |
| (Eu) **queria** | jogar golfe. |

### c Poderia *and* importaria

Verbs **poder** and **importar-se** are used in the conditional for extra politeness. Although this distinction is not always made, **poder** is a better choice when you are in doubt whether your request can be granted, and **importar-se** when you are just appealing to someone's willingness.

A senhora **poderia** esperar um pouco? *Could you possibly wait for a short while, please?*

A senhora **importar-se-ia de** esperar um pouco? (Eur.) / A senhora **se importaria de** esperar um pouco? (Br.), *Could you possibly wait for a short while, please? (Would you mind at all…?)*

**d Verbs: the three conjugations – imperfect subjunctive**

| I might / should… | buy | sell | leave |
|---|---|---|---|
| eu | comp**r**a**sse** | vend**esse** | part**isse** |
| tu | comp**r**a**sses** | vend**esses** | part**isses** |
| você, o sr / a sra<br>ele / ela | comp**r**a**sse** | vend**esse** | part**isse** |
| nós | comp**rássemos** | vend**êssemos** | part**íssemos** |
| vocês, os sres / as sras<br>eles / elas | comp**r**a**ssem** | vend**essem** | part**issem** |

The imperfect subjunctive is formed by dropping the final **-ram**
of the third person plural (for **eles/elas**, *they*) of the preterite
(see Unit 10) and by adding **-sse, -sses, -sse, -ssemos, -ssem**.

**Compare with the present subjunctive (Unit 17) and use for**

**1** The expression of a wish or hope (like present subjunctive,
note 1) transferred to past time and / or a more remote degree
of probability.
Esperava que a consulta **fosse** hoje. *I hoped / was hoping that
the appointment might be today.*

**2** The expression of sorrow or sympathy (like pres. subj., note 2)
transferred to a past time.
Senti muito que ela esti**vesse** doente. *I was very sorry that
she was ill.*

**3** An action or event regarded as a possibility (like pres. subj.
note 3) but with a greater degree of doubt.
Ela talvez tom**asse** uma bebida quente. *She might perhaps have
a hot drink.*

**4** After a statement that implies influence upon other people or things (like pres. subj., note 4) transferred to a past time.
A hospedeira (Eur.) / aeromoça (Br.) pediu ao passageiro que aper**tasse** o cinto de segurança. *The stewardess asked the passenger to fasten his safety belt.*
Eu pedia a / à (Eur.) Maria que fiz**esse** o favor de comprar o jornal.
*I used to ask Mary to be so kind as to buy the paper.*

### e If

Conditional sentences usually consist of two parts:

a *if*-part and **b** the conclusion (the main clause)

**1** When the *if*-part refers to the present or the past and is not contrary-to-fact, the present indicative is used for both verbs **a + b**.
Normalmente se chove fic**o** em casa, se f**az** bom tempo, d**ou** um passeio.
*Usually if it rains, I stay at home, if the weather is fine, I go for a stroll.*

**2** When the *if*-part expresses an unfulfilled condition, the imperfect subjunctive is used for **a** and the conditional (or the imperfect indicative in its place) for **b**.
Se não chov**esse** / estiv**esse** chovendo (Br.), d**aria** (or d**ava**) um passeio.
*If it were not raining, I would go for a stroll.*

**3** When the *if*-part expresses a condition to be fulfilled in the future, the future subjunctive is used for **a** and an 'indicative' future for **b** (simple / colloquial / emphatic).

*If it rains tomorrow,*

Se chov**er** amanhã, não d**arei** um passeio. *I shall not go for a walk.*
Se chover amanhã, não **vou** d**ar** um passeio. *I am not going to go for a walk.*

Se chover amanhã, não **hei de dar** um passeio. *I will not go for a walk.*

Some people will also use the present indicative instead of the future subjunctive. Se chove amanhã, não **vou dar** um passeio.

## Insight

Esperava que não **chovesse** hoje.

Se não **chovesse, iria / ia** à praia.

| Se não **chover** amanhã, | **irei** | |
| | **vou** | à praia. |
| | **hei de ir** | |

----------

A senhora **poderia** esperar um pouco?

Se a senhora **pudesse** esperar um pouco, eu **acabaria / acabava** isto primeiro.

Se a senhora não se **importasse** de esperar um pouco, eu **acabaria / acabava** isto primeiro.

### f Verb helping verb – I have taken up photography...

You have experienced in this course verbs that sometimes are not used alone but as an auxiliary to other verbs.

E.g., Eu **vou** comprar, *I am going to buy.* (Unit 9); Eu **costumava** ler o jornal regularmente. *I used to read the paper regularly.* (Unit 14).

Note some other such cases which are frequently heard:

**começar a...,** *to begin/start to...*; **deixar de...,** *to stop doing...*; **voltar a,** *to do... again*; **acabar de...,** *to have just done....* They are all followed by the infinitive of the action or state of being that you want to express.

Eu **costumava** gostar de pintar. Mas agora **deixei de** pintar e **vou começar a** fazer fotografia. **Acabo de** me inscrever para um curso de fotografia. Um dia no futuro talvez **volte** a pintar. *I used to like painting. But now I have given up painting and I am going to take up photography. I have just enrolled on a course in photography. Some time in the future I may go back to painting.*

---

## Exercises

### 19.2

| | | |
|---|---|---|
| o golfe — *golf* | a pesca — *fishing* | a mergulho — *scuba diving* |
| o esqui aquático — *water skiing* | o ténis (Eur.) / tênis (Br.) — *tennis* | a vela — *sailing* |
| o surfe — *surfing* | o caça — *shooting* | o hipismo — *horse racing* |

o golfe *golf* o esqui aquático *water skiing* o surfe *surfing* a pesca *fishing* o ténis (Eur.) / tênis (Br.) *tennis* a caça *shooting* o mergulho *scuba diving* a vela *sailing* o hipismo *horse racing*

**19.2.1** Read the following expressed intentions and find the right place for each person.

  **i**   Quero fazer esqui aquático.
 **ii**   Tenciono jogar golfe e fazer caça.
**iii**   Tenho a intenção de fazer surfe e mergulho.
 **iv**   Vou fazer vela e pesca.
  **v**   Hei de jogar ténis (Eur.) / tênis (Br.) e fazer hipismo.

**A**                    **B**

**19.2.2** Unscramble the words in brackets and help Ian talk, in Portuguese, about his keep-fit routine and his favourite sport.

*Every day, I go jogging early in the morning. At the weekend, I practise water skiing, when the weather is fine; and I would practise it more often if I had more time.*

(Todos os dias, / Aos fins de semana, / quando faz / pratico / praticaria / bom tempo; / mais tempo. / faço jogging / cooper (Br.) / de manhã cedo. / mais vezes, / esqui aquático, / e / se / tivesse)

**fazer (o) jogging = fazer (o) cooper** (Br.) **= fazer o trote** (Eur.)

### 19.3

◄))) CD2, TR 33

The following information was issued by the local Tourist Office in Funchal, Madeira.

A Madeira é praticamente uma reserva natural, sendo dois terços do território Área Protegida onde abunda fauna e flora raras.

A Madeira foi sempre reconhecida como um paraíso para passeios a pé. Os passeios podem ser tão suaves ou tão desafiadores como desejar. Os que não querem meter-se em grandes aventuras podem apreciar os belos passeios ao longo das 'levadas'*, que circundam toda a ilha, oferecendo as melhores vistas panorâmicas. Para os mais aventureiros há muitos trilhos, bem assinalados com placas, que levam às montanhas.

Mas a Madeira também oferece uma grande variedade de atividades desportivas. Se gosta de golfe, a ilha tem dois campos para campeonatos. E, é claro que, sendo uma ilha, a Madeira é rica em desportos aquáticos. Além disso, a Madeira está a adquirir uma reputação internacional como um destino de primeira classe para a pesca de alto mar, sendo o local certo para pescar espadim azul com mais de 500 kg. Abundam ainda todas as espécies de atum.

Mas o melhor de tudo é que pode praticar o seu desporto favorito durante todo o ano.

*levadas = pequenos canais de irrigação artificiais

**desporto** (Eur.) = **esporte** (Br.)
**desportivas** (Eur.) = **esportivas** (Br.)
**está a adquirir** (Eur.) = **está adquirindo** (Br.)

**19.3.1** Study the above information on Madeira.

**19.3.2** Keith is contemplating a holiday in Madeira and is enquiring about activities that will suit everyone in the family. Below are his questions. The answers are on your recording. Listen to the answers, match them with the questions, and write the dialogue.

– A Madeira tem plantas raras? E animais?
– Que passeios a pé tem para pessoas que não estão em boa forma?
– Desculpe. Não compreendo. O que significa "levadas"?
– E que passeios tem para os mais aventureiros?
– O que tem para quem joga golfe?
– Pode fazer-se mergulho e vela?
– Só mais uma pergunta. Seria possível fazer pesca de alto mar?

**19.4**

**19.4.1** Look at the sports stadium poster and fill in the gaps in the dialogue.

– Ainda tem lugares nas bancadas _____?
– Não, não tenho. Já não há mais. Só _____.
Então não quero.

> **BANCADAS**
>
> AO SOL                À SOMBRA
> *sun seats*          *shade seats*
>
> esgotado
> sold out

**19.4.2** Answer the following questions:

  **i** Esta pessoa comprou ou não comprou uma entrada?
 **ii** Por quê? / Porquê? (Eur.)
**iii** Esta pessoa teria comprado uma entrada se ainda houvesse lugares à sombra?

**19.5**

**todo (o) mundo = toda a gente**

Answer the questions on the following chat between Portuguese Filipe and Brazilian Estela. Write in Portuguese. The first answer has been done for you.

**1** *É uma pessoa natural do Rio de Janeiro.*

**1** What is a *carioca*?
**2** What event takes place in the whole of Brazil and above all in Rio, three days before Lent?
**3** When do the preparations take place?
**4** What name is given to the samba societies?
**5** Where does everybody dance?
**6** Find the names given to **a** the dancers, **b** the percussion section, and **c** the costumes, in the samba societies parade.

### Carnival

> **Filipe** Então você é carioca, é da capital do Carnaval?
> **Estela** Sim, sou carioca. O Brasil inteiro tem Carnaval, mas o Rio de Janeiro é sem dúvida a capital do Carnaval.
> **Filipe** É verdade que vocês preparam tudo com muita antecedência?
>
> *(Contd)*

| Estela | É. Tem que estar tudo pronto com muita antecedência para os três dias antes da Quaresma. É quando há bailes por toda a parte. Todo mundo vai para a rua. |
|--------|-----|
| Filipe | Mas o ponto mais alto da festa é o desfile, não é? |
| Estela | É, sim, o desfile das escolas de samba. |
| Filipe | E que nome é que vocês dão a esses bailarinos? |
| Estela | São os passistas. E os que tocam o ritmo são a bateria. E as fantasias são as roupas alegóricas. |
| Filipe | E quando é o desfile? |
| Estela | É durante as noites de domingo, segunda e terça. |
| Filipe | Eu gostaria muito de ver o desfile. Se puder, irei assistir no próximo ano. Vou começar a pensar nisso a sério. |

**19.6**

arquibancada = bancada grande
**números pares** *even numbers*
**números ímpares** *odd numbers*

**19.6.1** Your admission ticket for the Rio Carnival parade is number 00303, sector 9 (**o setor**), row C (**a fila**), seat 001 (**o lugar**). Say: É o número ... (in words). Continue on your own.

**19.6.2** You are on the northern side of the boulevard trying to get to your seat. You have asked: **Por onde se vai para este lugar?** And you have been told:

Não é por aqui. Deste lado são números pares. Esse lugar fica numa arquibancada no lado sul, do outro lado da Avenida.

**i** Where are you going wrong? **ii** What have you got to do?

**19.7**

You have been given this transport voucher for your return journey from the Carnival parade to the hotel where you are staying.

```
┌─────────────────────────────────────────────────────┐
│          BILHETE DE TRANSPORTE – RIO CARNAVAL        │
│                                                       │
│     Válido para uma (01) pessoa para transporte do desfile de │
│                                                       │
│            Carnaval para qualquer Hotel.              │
│                                                       │
│   Válido somente para 14/fevereiro, 15/fevereiro e 16/fevereiro │
└─────────────────────────────────────────────────────┘
```

**1** Apologize and say that it looks as if you have lost it.
**2** Say you have found it and hand it over to the driver.

---

## Summary

**1**  (Eu) gosto (muito) de música / esqui aquático.
   (Eu) adoro teatro / passeios a cavalo.
   (Eu) não gosto (muito) de pintar / tocar piano.
   (Eu) detesto viajar / jogar futebol.
**2**  O que é que você faz nas horas vagas?
   O que é que você faz no seu tempo livre?
**3**  Leio um livro.
   Faço natação / mergulho / vela.
   Vou à praia / à piscina / a um concerto.
   Dou passeios a pé / de carro.
   Sento-me diante do televisor, relaxando.
**4**  (Eu) gostaria de pintar / jogar golfe / fazer mergulho.
   (Eu) queria pintar / jogar golfe / fazer mergulho.
**5**  (Eu) gostaria de ir dar uma volta a pé agora, mas não tenho
   tempo.
   (Eu) gostaria de viajar mais, mas não é possível.
   (Eu) gostaria de ver o desfile do Carnaval, mas já não há
   lugares nas bancadas à sombra.
**6**
   **6.1** (Eu) esperava que não chovesse hoje.
   **6.2** Se não chovesse, iria / ia à praia.
   **6.3** Se não chover amanhã, irei à praia.
   **6.4** Se não chover amanhã, vou à praia / hei de ir à praia.

**7** A senhora poderia esperar um pouco?
Se a senhora pudesse esperar um pouco, eu acabaria / acabava isto primeiro.
Se a senhora não se importasse de esperar um pouco,
eu acabaria / acabava isto primeiro.

# 20

## Se fosse uma coisa diferente
If it were something different

In this unit you will learn how to
- *Explore local cuisine and drink*
- *Explain what a place is like and what is special about it*
- *Give detailed information about your home town and area*

### Jantando fora *Eating out*

Marília and Gustavo are dining out in a new restaurant tonight.
Waiter Joaquim is waiting for them to place their order from the
menu card.

● CD2, TR 34

| | |
|---|---|
| **Joaquim** | Os senhores já escolheram? |
| **Gustavo** | Já. Para começar, queremos uma canja e uma sopa de tomate. |
| **Joaquim** | E para depois da entrada, o que vão pedir? Peixe, carne, ave, ou um prato vegetariano? |
| **Marília** | Para mim um prato de peixe, bacalhau Gomes de Sá. |
| **Gustavo** | Para mim bife na brasa. |
| **Joaquim** | Prefere mal ou bem passado? |
| **Gustavo** | Ao ponto. |
| **Joaquim** | E para acompanhar, querem guarnições? |
| **Gustavo** | Traga uma salada mista, porção dupla, para os dois. |
| **Joaquim** | E para beber? |
| **Gustavo** | Uma garrafa do vinho da casa. |
| | *(Contd)* |

| | |
|---|---|
| **Joaquim** | Branco ou tinto? |
| **Gustavo** | É melhor meia garrafa de branco para beber com o peixe e meia de tinto para a carne. |
| *(Depois do prato principal)* | |
| **Joaquim** | Estava tudo bem? |
| **Gustavo** | Estava excelente. |
| **Joaquim** | E o que vão querer para sobremesa? |
| **Gustavo** | Para mim, fruta... Pode ser uma laranja. |
| **Marília** | Ainda não conheço o doce da casa. Eu talvez queira provar, mas primeiro gostaria de saber em que consiste. |
| **Joaquim** | É um doce de ovos. |
| **Marília** | Não... Se fosse uma coisa diferente... Não, não quero. Prefiro um sorvete. Que sabores tem? |
| **Joaquim** | Chocolate, morango... |
| **Marília** | Morango, por favor. *(falando para Gustavo)* Adoro morango. |

**QUICK VOCAB**

**(a) canja** *chicken broth*
**(a) sopa de tomate** *tomato soup*
**(a) entrada** *starter*
**peixe, carne, aves** *fish, meat, poultry*
**prato de peixe** *fish dish*
**(o) bacalhau (à) Gomes de Sá** *dried cod speciality*
**(o) bife na brasa** *charcoal grilled beef steak*
**bem / mal passado** *well done / rare*
**ao ponto** *medium*
**para acompanhar** *to go with*
**(as) guarnições** *accompaniments*
**(a) salada mista** *mixed salad*
**(o) vinho da casa** *the restaurant's wine, house wine*
**branco ou tinto** *white or red*
**(a) sobremesa** *dessert*
**(o) doce** *sweet*
**em que consiste** *what it consists of*
**adoro** *I love*

# Exercises

## 20.1 Perguntas e respostas *Questions and answers*

**(o) empregado (de mesa)** (Eur.) **/ (o) garçom** (Br.) *waiter*

**1** O Gustavo e a Marília já tinham escolhido quando o empregado (Eur.) / garçom (Br.) perguntou o que eles queriam?

   **a** Já.         **b** Ainda não.

**2** O que é que eles escolheram para entrada?

   **a** uma salada e uma sopa.  **b** Canja e sopa de tomate.

**3** Que comida é que eles escolheram para prato principal?

   **a** Um prato de peixe e um vegetariano.
   **b** Dois pratos de carne.
   **c** Um prato de peixe, um de carne e salada mista para dois.

**4** E que bebidas pediram?

   **a** Uma garrafa de vinho tinto.
   **b** Uma garrafa de vinho branco.
   **c** 1/2 garrafa de vinho tinto e 1/2 de branco.

**5** Quais são as sobremesas que eles preferiram?

   **a** Doce da casa e fruta
   **b** Laranja e sorvete de morango.
   **c** Sorvete de chocolate e uma laranja.

........................................................................................

# Expressions

**a Pedir** or **perguntar?**

Note that both **pedir** and **perguntar** translate *to ask*. For the right choice remember the following:

**pedir** = *to ask for, to request*
A cliente **pe diu** o sal e a pimenta.

**perguntar** = *to ask, to enquire*
*The client asked for the salt and pepper.*

*(Contd)*

| O cliente **pediu** um prato de carne. | **The client asked for a meat dish.** |
|---|---|

O empregado (Eur.) / garçom (Br.) **perguntou** se ele queria a carne bem passada. *The waiter asked whether he wanted the meat well done.*

**b Que** *or* **qual?**

As with other words, the interrogative pronoun **que** can be used with or without preceding **o**.

>   **O que** é isto? = **Que** é isto?    *What is this?*

Also note that **qual** (and its plural **quais**) translates *which* and **que** translates *what*, but sometimes it can be the other way round.

>   **Qual** prefere? *Which do you prefer?* which? → **qual/quais**
>   **Que** prato prefere? *Which dish do you prefer?* which
>   (+ noun)? → **que**
>   **(O) que** é bacalhau 'Gomes de Sá'? *What is 'Gomes de Sá' cod?* seeking a definition / description → **(o) que**
>   **Quais** são os pratos de bacalhau que prefere? *What are the cod dishes you prefer?* referring to a choice / selection → **qual/quais**

**c Saber** *and* **poder:** *Saying 'can'*

Both **saber** and **poder** translate *can*, but use **saber** for knowledge or ability and **poder** for possibility or permission.

>   **Sei** cantar mas hoje não posso; perdi a voz. *I can sing but not today; I've lost my voice.*
>   Você **sabe** falar Português? *Can you speak Portuguese?*
>   **Posso** falar agora? *May I speak now?*
>   Eles **souberam** a notícia ontem. *They learned the news yesterday.*
>   Eu não **pude** ir à festa dela. *I didn't manage to go to her party.*

**d** **Saber, conhecer** *and* **encontrar**: *Saying 'know'*

Both **saber** and **conhecer** translate *can*, but note the difference:
  **saber** = *to know, to know a fact, to be informed about*
  **conhecer** = *to know, to be acquainted with*

| | |
|---|---|
| **Você sabe** onde é que essa rua é? | *Do you know where that road is? (have you been told where it is?)* |
| **Você conhece** essa rua? | *Do you know that road? (have you been along it?)* |

Both **conhecer** and **encontrar** translate *to meet*, but note the difference:

**conhecer** = *to meet, to make acquaintance with*
**encontrar** = *to meet, arrange to meet*

Vocês já se **conhecem** ? *Have you ever met?*
Muito prazer em **conhecê**-lo. *Delighted to meet you.*
Quando nos **encontramos** outra vez? *When are we meeting again?*

Also note **encontrar** = **achar**
  Felizmente **encontrei** (= **achei**) os óculos que tinha perdido.
  *Fortunately I have found the spectacles I had lost.*

## Insight

**Sabe me dizer** onde posso **encontrar** comida tipicamente angolana / brasileira / moçambicana / portuguesa / etc.?

----------

**Uma pergunta:** em que consiste este prato?
**Queremos pedir** um prato típico desta terra.

**(O) que é isto?** *(pointing to item on the menu card)*

**e Nascer, viver, morar, morrer / falecer:** *living and dying*
Do not translate literally *I was born* or *someone is dead.*

Remember:

to be born is **nascer**       to die is **morrer** or **falecer**
O meu bisavô **nasceu** há cem anos e **morreu**
   (or **faleceu**) há vinte.
*My great-grandfather was born a hundred years ago and*
   *died twenty years ago.*
O meu tio-avô **morreu** (or **faleceu**). *My great uncle is*
   *dead (has died).*

Also remember:

**viver** means *to live, to be alive*
**morar** means *to live, to be resident*

**Nasci** em São Tomé e Príncipe mas agora **vivo** em Portugal;
**moro** em Lisboa. *I was born in São Tomé e Príncipe but now*
*I live in Portugal; I am resident in Lisbon.*

## Insight

**Nasci em** <u>*(your place of origin)*</u> **e moro em** <u>*(your place of*</u>
<u>*residence)*</u> **em / no / na** <u>*(country)*</u>.

**Felizmente encontrei o mapa que tinha perdido e posso
mostrar onde fica.**

**Você agora já sabe onde moro, mas será ainda melhor
conhecer a terra. Poderá também conhecer a minha família.
Terei muito prazer na sua visita. Poderemos marcar data para
um encontro lá no próximo ano.**

## How it works

### a A mala da senhora *The lady's suitcase*

English possessive case – e.g., *the lady's suitcase* – finds its translation in the following construction:

thing possessed     +        **de**       +    possessor
a mala *the suitcase*     **da** (= **de** + **a**) of the     senhora *lady*

Similarly, os pais **de** (*or* **do**) João, *John's parents*

### b Possessives

**My, mine; our, ours**
Unlike English, the possessive adjective – e.g., *my* – and the possessive pronoun – e.g., *mine* – have one same word – **meu**. This word agrees in number (singular or plural) and gender (masculine or feminine) with the thing possessed: **meu, meus,** (masc. sing. and pl.) and **minha, minhas** (fem. sing. and pl.). (Revise 'Plurals' in Unit 10.)
**(O) meu** casaco e **(as) minhas** malas *my coat and my suitcases*
**O** casaco é **meu** *the coat is mine*
**As** malas são **minhas** *the suitcases are mine*

The same with our and ours: **nosso, nossos** (masc. sing. and pl.) **nossa, nossas** (fem. sing. and pl.).

**(Os) nossos** casacos *our coats*
**A** mala é **nossa** *the suitcase is ours*
**Os** casacos e a mala são **nossos** *the coats and the suitcase are ours*

Note: **o / a / os / as** is used mainly in Portugal.

### c Your, yours

The same applies as above: **seu, seus; sua, suas.**

(**Os**) **seus** casac**os** e (**a**) **sua** mala = **seus** casac**os** e mal**a** *Your coats and suitcase*
**Este** casaco **é seu**? *Is this coat yours?*

For someone you address as **tu**, just change to **teu, teus; tua, tuas**.
(**Os**) **teus** casacos e (**a**) **tua** mala = **teus** casac**os** e mal**a** *Your coats and suitcase*
**Este** casaco é **teu**? *Is this coat yours?*

### d His; her, hers; its; their, theirs

Historically this is **seu, seus; sua, suas** (as above for *your/s*) and is still widely used in written Portuguese, but colloquially (including informal writing) preference is given to the following format:

thing possessed + **de** contracted with **ele/ela/eles/elas** (the possessor)
a mala **dela** (lit. *of her*), *her suitcase*
a mala **deles** (lit. *of they*), *their suitcase*

Note that in this case there is agreement in number and gender with the possessor, not with the thing possessed.

### e A mala da senhora... *with a difference*

The format explained above for *his / her/s* etc. is also sometimes applied to your/s.
a mala **de você** (= (a) **sua** mala) (lit. *of you*), *your suitcase*

or, for a courteous approach (revise what you learned about *you* in Unit 8),
a mala **da senhora** (lit. *of the lady*), *your suitcase*

### f O, a, os, as: *('the') and the possessives*

In general, there is considerable flexibility in the use, or omission, of the definite article (o/a/os/as) with the possessive adjectives **meu, teu, seu,** etc. There are some exceptions, as follows:

Omit

▶ In direct address:
**Minha** amiga, como vai?     *My friend, how are you keeping?*
▶ In Brazil, referring to a relative:
**Meu** pai está em casa.     *My father is at home.*

This can be heard in Portugal too, but not to the same extent.

Always use
▶ For emphasis:
A mala preta é **a minha.** *The black suitcase is mine.*
                          (no one else's)

▶ Where subject and possessor are the same, in which case you
  can actually omit the possessive:
Perdi **o (meu)** passaporte. *I have lost my passport.*
Ontem eu fui **no** carro.     *Yesterday I went in the car (my car).*

---

## Exercises

### 20.2

◀) **CD2, TR 35**

You are in a restaurant waiting for the meal you have ordered.
There are people talking around you. What they say is on your
recording. Listen to it and rearrange the jumbled up words in
brackets so as to match what you hear.

**a ementa** (Eur.) / **o cardápio** (Br.) *menu*

1 (Faz / a ementa / favor, / traga-me / .)
2 (O / favor / cardápio, / por / .)
3 (Queríamos / da porta, / uma mesa / se possível. / para quatro, /
  longe)

**4** (Pode / pão / ? / mais / trazer)
**5** (Queria / um prato / experimentar / desta região / . / típico)

**20.3**

| a caneca | o copo | a chávena (Eur.) | a taça | o cálice |
|---|---|---|---|---|
| *mug/* | *glass/cup* | a xícara (Br.) | *champagne* | *goblet* |
| *tankard* | */tumbler* | *cup* | *glass* | |

**Traga-me um copo de coca, por favor.**
*Please bring me a glass of coke.*

Following the above model, ask for the following:

**1** glass of water     **4** tankard of beer
**2** cup of tea         **5** goblet of port ((o) **porto**)
**3** cup of coffee      **6** glass of champagne ((o) **champanhe**)

### 20.4 Festival da pinga *Rum festival*

**Pinga** is an alternative name Brazilians use for **a cachaça** or
**a aguardente de cana de açúcar**, i.e., a sugar-cane spirit.

> **(a) pinga** (Br.) *sugar-cane spirit* (colloquialism)
> **(a) pinga** (Eur.) *alcoholic beverage* (colloquialism)

The **festival da pinga** is a regular event in the town of **Paraty** –
also spelled **Paratii** or **Parati** – on the Brazilian Atlantic coast,
between Rio and Santos. The town's name comes from the Tupi
Indians who were its first inhabitants.

**20.4.1** A leaflet issued by the local tourist office includes the
programme for the festival and some background information
on the area. Study the following excerpt.

A terra propícia ao cultivo da cana de açúcar e o conhecimento dos produtos de aguardente da região têm sido fatores fundamentais para garantir, durante séculos, a qualidade da pinga produzida em Paraty.

O resultado desta combinação de boa terra para o cultivo e o conhecimento acumulado em séculos de tradição só poderia resultar em pingas artesanais de ótima qualidade. Estão aqui algumas das melhores pingas do Brasil.

**20.4.2**

◀) **CD2, TR 36**

**agosto**

**paraty sempre**

This is on the leaflet's cover page and on your recording. What is the play on words? (If you need help, revise 'You' in Unit 8.)

**20.4.3** Silvestre is planning to go to the festival. Fill in the gaps in what he wants to say.

Vou ao festival da _____ em Paraty. Lá a _____ é propícia ao cultivo da _____ e há _____ que fazem aguardente. Vou beber o que dizem ser uma das _____ do Brasil.

**20.4.4** Unforeseen circumstances prevented Silvestre from going to the festival. Complete the gaps and help him talk about the missed event.

Infelizmente eu não pude ir ao festival. Se _____ ido, teria _____ o que dizem ser uma das _____ do Brasil.

## 20.5 Como é a terra natal do senhor? *What is your homeland like?*

| | | |
|---|---|---|
| (Eu) sou de | uma aldeia / vilarejo (Br.) (*village*) | em Portugal / Moçambique |
| | uma cidade (*town*) | no Brasil / Canadá |
| | | na Inglaterra / Nova Zelândia |

que se chama…

| Fica / é | no | norte<br>sudeste | do país | perto de…<br>perto da fronteira (*border*)<br>com... |
|---|---|---|---|---|

no interior (*inland*)
na costa leste / oeste / norte / sul (*east/west/north/ south coast*)
na margem / foz de um rio (*river bank/mouth*)
numa região montanhosa/plana (*mountainous/plain region*)

| Tem | uma superfície (*area*) de… km² (*square kilometres*)<br>quilómetros (Eur.) / quilômetros (Br.) quadrados<br>uma população (*population*) de… (de) habitantes (*inhabitants*)<br>um clima quente / frio (*hot / cold climate*)<br>indústria de …. (*… industry*) |
|---|---|

With the help of the sentences in the above box, say the following:

My home town ((a) **minha cidade natal**)…

**1** is on a river bank.
**2** is in a mountainous region.
**3** is on the north coast of the country.
**4** has one million inhabitants.

**5** has a cold climate in winter.

**6** has a computer industry. ((o) **computador**)

**20.6**

Some people are explaining where they come from and highlighting a couple of distinctive features in their home town.

Irish Cathy was born in Limerick, a town in southwest Ireland which has several monasteries and has given its name to a famous type of 'lace'.

Study her words below:

**Sou irlandesa. Nasci em Limerick, uma cidade no sudoeste da Irlanda. Limerick tem vários mosteiros e um tipo famoso de renda bordada.**

Following the same sentence pattern, help the following people talk about their home town.

**1** Scottish Stewart: born in Dundee, a town on the east coast of Scotland – large harbour – famous type of cake.
(**escocês – Escócia – um porto grande – bolo**)

**2** Welsh Gareth: born in Caerphilly, a town in south Wales – old castle – famous type of cheese.
(**galês – País de Gales – um castelo antigo – queijo**)

**20.7**

◀) **CD2, TR 37**

You are in a restaurant which specializes in dried cod recipes.

**20.7.1** Study the contents of their list of cod dishes.

---

## PRATOS DE BACALHAU

**À Moda da Casa** ..........................
(Posta de bacalhau cozido, acompanhada de cebola, batata e couve)

**Gomes de Sá** ............................
(Bacalhau desfiado refogado, acompanhado de ovo cozido, batata e azeitonas)

**Tropical** ..............................
(Bacalhau em pedaços frito, acompanhado de cebola, tomate, batata e leite de coco)

---

**20.7.2 Em que consiste?** *What does it consist of?*

Three different customers are unfamiliar with the cuisine jargon on the menu card and have asked the waiter what goes into particular dishes. Listen to the waiter's replies and work out what three questions have been asked.

**20.7.3** Ângela would rather have a dish without tomato. She says: **Preferia um prato que não tivesse tomate.**

Say that you would rather have a dish that does not have:

**i** onion; **ii** egg; **iii** cabbage; **iv** coconut milk.

---

## Summary

**1** Sabe me dizer onde posso encontrar comida tipicamente angolana / brasileira / cabo-verdiana / guineense / moçambicana / portuguesa / são-tomense / timorense?

**2** Queria experimentar um prato típico / um vinho típico desta região.

**3** Uma pergunta: em que consiste este prato?
Queremos pedir um prato típico desta terra.
(O) que é isto? (*pointing to item on the menu card*)
Preferia um prato que não tivesse cebola / ovo / batata / couve.

**4** Sou de uma terra que se chama (*your home town*)
Nasci em (*your place of origin*)) em / no / na (*country*).
Moro em (*your place of residence*) em / no / na (*country*).
Visitei (*place you have been to*) em / no / na (*country*).

**5** Fica / É no norte / sul / este / oeste / nordeste do país.
Fica / É perto da fronteira com (*neighbouring country*).
Fica / É no interior / na costa este / oeste / norte / sul.
Fica / É na margem / foz do rio (*name of river*).
Fica / É numa região montanhosa / plana.

**6** Tem uma superfície de (*area*) km².
Tem uma população de (*number of inhabitants*) habitantes.
Tem um clima quente / frio.
Tem indústria de (*main industry*).

**7** Tem um castelo antigo / um porto grande / um queijo famoso.

**8** Felizmente encontrei o mapa que tinha perdido e posso mostrar onde fica essa terra.

**9** Você agora já sabe onde nasci / moro / onde é essa terra.

**10** Será ainda melhor conhecer a terra.
Poderá também conhecer a minha família.
Terei muito prazer na sua visita.
Poderemos marcar data para um encontro lá no próximo ano.

# 21

## Ao voltarmos, abrirei conta bancária

## On our return, I shall open a bank account

In this unit you will learn how to
- *Open and use a bank account*
- *Accept or decline an invitation to a social event*
- *Talk and write about the place where you are staying*

**No banco, abrindo conta** *At the bank, opening an account*

Alberto Lopes and his family live in England but they may be moving to Portugal. Alberto is at a bank in Lisboa, opening an account.

| | |
|---|---|
| **Alberto** | Eu queria abrir uma conta. Que preciso fazer? |
| **Empregada** | Trouxe algum documento de identidade? Passaporte... bilhete de identidade*? |
| **Alberto** | Trouxe, sim. Aqui tem. |
| **Empregada** | Então é só preencher e assinar o formulário e fazer a assinatura modelo. O senhor deseja apenas conta corrente com depósito à ordem ou quer também depósito a prazo? |

| Alberto | Ambos. Agora eu tenho comigo uns cheques que quero depositar à ordem. No próximo mês virá de Londres uma transferência. É uma quantia elevada. É para ser depositada a prazo. Posteriormente virão transferências menores, mensalmente. Essas são para depositar à ordem. |
|---|---|
| Empregada | Certo, Sr. Lopes, trataremos disso. *(depois de tudo preenchido e assinado)* Pronto. O senhor receberá pelo correio o livro de cheques** e um cartão bancário que pode usar no terminal caixa. Regularmente enviaremos para sua casa o extrato de conta e o aviso de lançamento de juros. |

\* = carteira de identidade (Br.) \*\* = talão de cheques (Br.)

**(o) formulário** *form, questionnaire*
**(a) assinatura modelo** *specimen signature*
**(a) conta corrente** *current account*
**(o) depósito à ordem** *instant access*
**(o) depósito a prazo** *deposit / savings account*
**comigo** *with me, on me*
**(a) transferência** *transfer*
**(a) quantia elevada** *lump sum*
**posteriormente** *at a later date*
**trataremos de** *we will see to*
**(o) livro de cheques** *cheque book*
**(o) cartão bancário** *banker's card*
**(o) terminal caixa** *cashpoint*
**enviaremos** *we will send*
**(o) extrato de conta** *statement*
**(o) aviso de lançamento de juros** *earned-interest advice note*

QUICK VOCAB

# Exercises

## 21.1 Perguntas e respostas *Questions and answers*

**1** O que é que Alberto precisa fazer para abrir conta bancária?
**a** Precisa apresentar o passaporte e preencher os documentos.
**b** Precisa apresentar um documento de identidade, preencher e assinar o formulário e fazer a assinatura modelo.

**2** Que tipo de conta é que ele quer?
**a** Depósito à ordem.
**b** Depósito à ordem e a prazo.
**c** Conta corrente e dois depósitos a prazo.

**3** Em que depósito é que deve ficar o dinheiro?
**a** As transferências de Londres à ordem e os cheques a prazo.
**b** Os cheques à ordem e as transferências de Londres a prazo.
**c** A quantia elevada a prazo, as transferências menores e os cheques à ordem.

**4** O que é que ele vai receber?
**a** O livro de cheques (Eur.) / talão de cheques (Br.), o cartão bancário e regularmente aviso de lançamento de juros.
**b** O livro de cheques (Eur.) / talão de cheques (Br.), o cartão bancário, e regularmente extrato de conta e aviso de lançamento de juros.

## Expressions

**a Ir – vir** and **levar – trazer:** *Coming and going – taking and bringing*

Know whether you are coming or going... **Ir** (*to go*) and **levar** (*to take*) imply motion away from the person who is speaking. **Vir** (*to come*) and **trazer** (*to bring*) imply motion towards the person who is speaking.

– **Venha** cá, por favor. *Come here, please.*
– Já **vou.** *I'm coming. (lit. I'm going)*

But as an expression of your personal hospitality, you can use **vir** to invite someone to your home even if you are not speaking from home.

Você pode **vir** jantar em
nossa casa.

*You can come to dinner at
our house / place.*

Also note the different meanings of **levar**, as follows:

O porteiro do hotel **levou**
a mala para o elevador.
O elevador **levou** pouco
tempo a chegar ao décimo
andar.

*The hotel porter took the
suitcase to the lift.
The lift soon arrived at the
10th floor (lit. took little
time to arrive).*

**b Estar or ficar?** *Subtleties in saying 'to be'*

Use **ficar** in preference to **estar** for the inception of a state or situation.

**Eu estou no Hotel Central.** *I am (staying) at Hotel Central.* but

**Eu fico sempre no Hotel Central, quando venho.** *I always stay at Hotel Central, when I come.*

**Hoje eu estou cansada.** *Today I am (feeling) tired.* but

**Eu fiquei cansada depois daquele trabalho todo.** *I was tired after all that work. (became tired)*

**Eu estou contente.** *I am (feeling) happy.* but

**Eu fiquei contente ao saber a notícia.** *I was happy when I heard the news. (became happy)*

*(Contd)*

**Eu fiquei triste ao saber a notícia.** *I was sad when I heard the news. (became sad)*

In some cases **estar** and **ficar** are interchangeable.

**Quando estará pronto?** *When will it be ready?* or
**Quando ficará pronto?** *When will it be ready? (become ready)*

**c Faltar** *To be missing*

**Faltar** means *to be missing* (in relation to a desired or expected whole or completion).

| | |
|---|---|
| **Falta** alguma coisa? | *Is there anything missing?* |
| **Falta** a minha mala. Não estava no tapete rolante de bagagens. | *My suitcase is missing. It wasn't on the baggage conveyor belt.* |
| **Faltam** cinco minutos para as oito. | *It is five minutes to eight.* |

## How it works

### a Object pronouns

In Unit 7 you learned the personal pronouns subject, i.e., the words for *I, you, s/he,* etc. We have also been using some object pronouns, i.e., the words for *me, you, him / her,* etc.

▶ **me** as direct object
Ele viu-**me**. Ele **me** viu. (Br.) *He saw me.*

▶ **me** as indirect object (the direct object is 'o cheque')
Ele deu-**me** o cheque. Ele **me** deu o cheque. (Br.) *He gave me the cheque.*

▶ **me** with preposition (such as **para**) + object
Ele falou para **mim**. *He spoke to me.*

The following table puts together the different object pronouns and shows how they relate to their subject counterparts.

| subject | object | | |
|---|---|---|---|
| | direct | indirect | with preposition |
| eu | me | me | mim |
| tu | te | te | ti |
| você, o sr /a sra | o, a (*) | lhe | você, o sr / a sra, si |
| ele / ela | o, a (*) | lhe | ele / ela |
| nós | nos | nos | nós |
| vocês, os sres / as sras | os, as vos(**) | lhes, vos(**) | vocês, os sres / as sras, vós(*) |
| eles / elas | os, as | lhes | eles / elas |

(*) See also Unit 22:HIWb and HIWc.

(**) Although subject pronoun 'vós' has fallen into disuse (see 'You' paragraphs in Unit 8), its object form can still be heard.

| | |
|---|---|
| Apanhei-**vos**! | *I have caught you!* |
| Vou mostrar-**vos**. | *I am going to show you.* |

A sentence with an object pronoun – example:

| | |
|---|---|
| Vi-**te**. | *I saw you.* |
| Não **te** vi. | *I didn't see you.* |
| Comprei-**te** um livro. | *I bought you a book.* |
| Não **te** comprei um livro. | *I didn't buy you a book.* |
| Comprei um livro para **ti**. | *I bought a book for you.* |

Note the following:

▶ In order to avoid confusion between second and third person, some speakers will use 'você' and not 'o/a' or 'lhe'. (If you need to, revise 'You' in Units 7 and 8.)

| | |
|---|---|
| **Vi-o.** *or* Vi **você.** | *I saw you.* |
| **Não o** vi. *or* Não vi **você.** | *I didn't see you.* |
| Comprei-**lhe** um livro. *or* | *I bought you a book.* |
| Comprei um livro para **você.** | |
| Não **lhe** comprei um livro. *or* Não comprei um livro para **você.** | *I didn't buy you a book.* |

▶ Brazilians prefer 'você' to 'si'.

| | |
|---|---|
| Comprei um livro para **si.** / Comprei um livro para **você.** (Br.) | *I bought a book for you.* |

▶ With the preposition **com** there are some contracted forms: **comigo, contigo, consigo, connosco** (Eur.) / **conosco** (Br.), **convosco.**

| | |
|---|---|
| Ele veio **comigo.** | *He came with me.* |

**Com você** is an alternative to **consigo**, widely used in Portugal.
**com você** *or* **consigo** (Eur.)    *with you*

▶ When applied to an animal or thing, object pronoun **o/a** translates 'it' and **os/as** 'them'.

| | |
|---|---|
| Onde estão os mapas? | *Where are the maps?* |
| Não sei, não **os** vi. | *I don't know, I haven't seen them.* |

▶ me, te, etc. sometimes do not translate literally into English.

| | |
|---|---|
| Pode chamar um táxi para **mim?** *or* | *Can you call a táxi for me?* |
| Pode **me** chamar um taxi? | *(me + to call)* |

| Penso que roubaram **a minha** carteira. | I think my purse was stolen. (they stole) |
| --- | --- |

*or*

| Penso que **me** roubaram a carteira. | (me + (they) stole) |
| --- | --- |

**b Tu, te, ti, teu...** *You, for you, yours ...*

All these forms belong to the same approach, **tu** as a subject pronoun, **te** and **ti** as object pronouns, **teu** as a possessive. In Brazil in general, both the object pronoun and the possessive are more widely used than **tu,** often in combination with **você.**

**Você** estava no aeroporto? Eu não **te** vi lá.

*Were you at the airport? I didn't see you there.*

**Você** não se importa de me emprestar **os teus** livros? Amanhã eu **te** devolvo tudo.

*You don't mind if I borrow your books (lit. lending me…). Tomorrow I'll give you everything back.*

## Insight

**Ao receber o cartão, deverá assiná-lo.**
**Receberá os extratos de conta que regularmente lhe enviaremos / enviaremos para o senhor.**

**c Verbs: the three conjugations – personal infinitive**

| I may... | buy | sell | leave |
| --- | --- | --- | --- |
| eu | compr**ar** | vend**er** | part**ir** |
| tu | compr**ares** | vend**eres** | part**ires** |
| você, o sr / a sra ele / ela | compr**ar** | vend**er** | part**ir** |
| nós | compr**armos** | vend**ermos** | part**irmos** |
| vocês, os sres / as sras eles / elas | compr**arem** | vend**erem** | part**irem** |

The personal infinitive is an inflected infinitive. It is derived from the 'impersonal' infinitive you learned in Unit 3 and is formed by adding 'personal' endings as shown above. It is regular for all verbs. In verbs that have a regular preterite (Unit 10), the personal infinitive is identical to the future subjunctive (Unit 17), though in form only.

The personal infinitive simplifies grammar inasmuch as it can replace other tenses including the subjunctive tenses, because:

**a** it gives the verb the uncharacteristic quality of an infinitive, which will enable it to assume the meaning required by its context – indicative or subjunctive (present, past or future);

**b** it retains awareness of the person who is the subject of the action or state of being.

In fact, we have been using the personal infinitive throughout this book, right from Unit 3:

Faça o favor de fal**ar** mais devagar.     (i.e., **você** fal**ar**)
Façam o favor de fal**arem** mais devagar.     (i.e., **vocês** fal**arem**)

Note the following:
  ▶ 'Person' is the active element in the personal infinitive. The personal pronoun (expressed or understood) is in the subject form:
  para **(ele)** apertar o cinto     *for him to fasten his belt*
                            (lit. *for he to fasten*)

  ▶ The use of personal endings with the infinitive can range from the need to avoid obscurity to optional emphasis for extra clarity or effect:
  Façam o favor de falar(**em**) mais devagar.
  Façam o favor de apertar(**em**) os cintos.

  **d Subjunctive or infinitive?**

When expressing a wish or hope, use:

▶ the subjunctive, if the subject of the second verb is different from that of the first verb. (Revise Units 17:HIWa and 19:HIWd.)

| Desejo que (você) **faça** boa viagem. | *I wish that you may have a nice journey.* |

▶ the infinitive, if the subject is the same.

| Espero **fazer** boa viagem. | *I hope to have a nice journey (that I may have).* |
| Desejo **comprar** isso hoje. | *I wish to buy that today.* |
| Tomara **estar** de férias. | *I wish I were on holiday.* |

## e Personal infinitive and alternative tenses

In the examples below you can see two different ways of saying the same thing, the first using the personal infinitive, the second using a different tense. It does not matter which you choose.

With a request verb (**pedir** or other), however, the personal infinitive is used only colloquially; not in careful speech or writing.

### Noun clauses

| A hospedeira (Eur.) / aeromoça (Br.) pede ao passageiro | para **apertar** o cinto. |
| | que **aperte** o cinto. |

(compare with present subjunctive, Unit 17)

| A hospedeira (Eur.) / aeromoça (Br.) pediu aos passageiros | para **apertarem** o cinto. |
| | que **apertassem** o cinto. |

(compare with imperfect subjunctive, Unit 19)

| É possível | ela **tomar** uma bebida quente. |
| | que ela **tome** uma bebida quente (cf. pres. subj., Unit 17) |
| | que ela **tomasse** uma bebida quente (cf. imp. subj., Unit 19) |

## Time clauses

Gosto de beber alguma coisa | antes e depois de **comer**.
 | antes e depois que **coma**.
 | (pres. subj.)

*(I like to have something to drink before and after eating.)*

Telefonei para a minha amiga | ao **chegar**.
 | quando **cheguei**. (pret., Unit 10)

*(I phoned my friend when I arrived.)*

Atravessem | ao **chegarem** à esquina.
 | quando **chegarem** à esquina. (future subj., Unit 17)

*(Cross over when you get to the corner.)*

Vamos ficar em casa do João | ao **irmos** ao Porto.
Ficaremos em casa do João | quando **formos** ao Porto.
 | (fut. subj.)

*(We are going to stay / shall stay at John's when we go to Oporto.)*

## Causal clauses and clauses of purpose

Não vamos ao cinema | por **termos jantado** tarde.
 | porque **jantamos** tarde. (preterite)

*(We are not going to the cinema because we had dinner late.)*

Comprei-te / Eu te comprei (Br.) um livro | para o **leres**.
 | para que o **leias**.
 | (pres. subj.)

*(I bought you a book for you to read / so that you may read it.)*

## Conditional and concessional clauses

Vocês engordarão | a **comerem** assim.
 | se **comerem** assim. (fut. subj.)

*(You will put on weight if you eat this much.)*

Eles não engordam | apesar de **comerem** muito.
 | embora **comam** muito. (pres. subj.)

*(They do not put on weight despite eating a lot.)*

## Exercises

**21.2 Um cheque preenchido** *A made-out cheque*

```
BANCO COMERCIAL INTERNACIONAL
Nº Conta   10 99 941        Nº cheque   49 2021

Assinatura                  Pague por este
João Castro                 cheque Euros

à ordem de FERNANDO COSTA          60 000
       MACHADO              Local de emissão
a quantia de  SESSENTA MIL          LISBOA
    EUROS                   Data   4/02/
```

> If you make a mistake, write *Ressalva*, correct and sign again.

Study the above cheque and answer the following questions.

**1** À ordem de quem é que João Castro preencheu este cheque?
**2** Que quantia é que se paga com este cheque?
**3** O cheque está completo ou falta alguma coisa?

### 21.3

You are at the bank. Rearrange the jumbled up words in brackets so as to say the following:

**1** *I would like to cash this cheque.*
(Queria / cheque. / descontar / este)

**2** *Where do you keep the credit slips (paying-in forms)?*
(Onde / as guias / estão / de depósito? / é que)

**3** *Is this the receipt for my deposit?*
(Isto / o recibo / de depósito? / é)

**4** *I would like to see my account balance.*
(Queria / o meu / saldo. / ver)

**5** *How much is the pound today? And how much is the commission?*
(A quanto / a libra / hoje? / está / E quanto / a comissão? / é)

**21.4**

◀) CD2, TR 39

You have seen these signs at the post office.

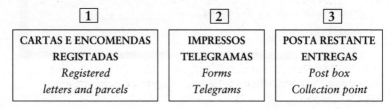

| 1 | 2 | 3 |
|---|---|---|
| **CARTAS E ENCOMENDAS REGISTADAS** *Registered letters and parcels* | **IMPRESSOS TELEGRAMAS** *Forms Telegrams* | **POSTA RESTANTE ENTREGAS** *Post box Collection point* |

**QV** registados (Eur.) = registrados (Br.)

**21.4.1** Listen to the recording and you will hear six people – a to f – at the post office. At which service hatch is each person?

**21.4.2** Write down all that you hear the six people say.

**21.5 Um convite para a festa** *An invitation to the party*

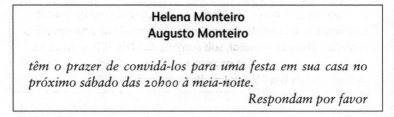

**Helena Monteiro**
**Augusto Monteiro**

*têm o prazer de convidá-los para uma festa em sua casa no próximo sábado das 20h00 à meia-noite.*

*Respondam por favor*

**21.5.1** Study the invitation card which has been sent to Joyce Brown and her friend.

**21.5.2** From the sentences below select and put into the appropriate order those she needs for the following:

> **i** The text of a reply card, accepting;
> **ii** A message to be left on the Monteiros' answering machine. She is declining the invitation.

**a** É com muito prazer que aceitamos.
**b** Estaremos fora do país no sábado. Partimos amanhã.
**c** Lá estaremos no sábado às oito horas. (*or* Aí **estaremos …**)
**d** Agradecemos muito, mas não vamos poder ir.
**e** Fala Joyce Brown acerca do convite para a festa.
**f** Ao regressarmos, telefonaremos para combinar um encontro.

### 21.6 Tower of Belém

This photograph and text are from the admission ticket Phil bought in Portugal when visiting the Tower of Belém just outside Lisbon.

**TORRE DE BELÉM**

**PORTUGAL**

Considerada como 'ex-libris' da arquitetura monumental portuguesa, integrada no conjunto de imóveis que fazem parte do Património Mundial, sob a égide da UNESCO, a Torre de Belém apresenta todas as características individualizantes do estilo Manuelino Português (Séc. XVI).

**património** (Eur.) = **patrimônio** (Br.)
**arquitetónico** (Eur.) = **arquitetônico** (Br.)

**21.6.1** Study the text above as well as the text below.

**(o) imóvel** *building*
**sob a égide** *under the aegis*
**(o) pilar em espiral** *spiral-shaped column*
**(o) cordame** *rigging*
**(a) esfera armilar** *armillary sphere*
**(a) cruz da Ordem de Cristo** *cross, emblem of the Order of Christ*

O estilo manuelino é um estilo ornamental arquitetónico português. Data do fim do século XV e principalmente do século XVI, parte final da época dos descobrimentos marítimos.

Foi de Belém, hoje parte da Grande Lisboa, que partiram muitos navegadores portugueses. Em 1487 Bartolomeu Dias dobra o Cabo das Tormentas, a partir de então denominado Cabo da Boa Esperança. Esperança... de se descobrir o caminho marítimo para a Índia. Esse sonho é realizado por Vasco da Gama em 1498. Os portugueses navegam este e oeste. Em 1500 Álvares Cabral desembarca no Brasil. Os portugueses vão até terras remotas – Timor, Macau, Japão.

Esta época de grandeza para Portugal coincide com o reinado de Dom Manuel I. Daí o nome 'manuelino'. O estilo manuelino é inspirado nos descobrimentos marítimos. Inclui pilares em espiral e, entre vários outros elementos, cordame, esferas armilares e a cruz da Ordem de Cristo, a mesma cruz que se vê nas velas das caravelas.

**21.6.2** Answer, in Portuguese, the questions on both texts.

1 What building is said to be an emblem (ex-libris) of Portuguese historical architecture?
2 This is a World Heritage listed building. What is the international organization involved?
3 What is the Manueline style?

**4** What name was given to the Cape of Torments after having been rounded by Bartolomeu Dias?

**5** The Portuguese travelled both East and West. When did Vasco da Gama arrive in India and Álvares Cabral in Brazil?

**6** List three features characteristic of the Manueline style.

### 21.7

Alda comes from Cape Verde and is on her first visit to Portugal. She has been on the triangular tour of Lisboa, Sintra and Estoril.

**21.7.1** Study what she wrote on the card she sent home.

*Olá, Lúcio!*

*Tudo bem? Aqui faz bom tempo, a comida é boa e eu estou bem. Ontem fui na excursão do triângulo turístico que inclui visita a Lisboa, Sintra e Estoril. Sendo a capital do país, Lisboa tem muita coisa para ver. Em Sintra adorei os palácios. No Estoril tomei banho na praia.*
*Um beijo da Alda*

**21.7.2** On Phil's behalf, write a similar postcard to Georgina, but describe his visit to the Tower of Belém instead: **Ontem fui visitar a...** Say that the tower dates from the 16th century and has all the characteristics that define the Manueline style. Explain what this style is and mention four of its distinctive features.

---

## Summary

**1**

**1.1** (Eu) queria abrir uma conta. Que preciso fazer?
Trouxe um documento de identidade.

**1.2** Quero um depósito à ordem e um depósito a prazo.

**1.3** Virá uma quantia elevada para ficar no depósito a prazo.

**2**

**2.1** O cartão bancário em breve estará / ficará pronto.

**2.2** Ao receber o cartão, deverá assiná-lo.

**2.3** Receberá os extratos de conta que regularmente lhe enviaremos / enviaremos para o senhor. Irão pelo correio.

**3**

**3.1** À ordem de quem devo preencher este cheque?

**3.2** Queria descontar este cheque.

**4**

**4.1** Fiquei muito contente com o seu convite para a festa. É com muito prazer que aceito. Lá / Aí estarei.

**4.2** Agradeço muito, mas não vou poder ir. Estarei fora do país.

**5**

**5.1** Ontem visitei a Torre de Belém / um palácio / a capital do país. Hoje fui numa excursão.

**5.2** Aqui faz bom tempo, e fui à praia. Aqui a comida é boa / diferente. Há / Tem muita coisa para ver.

**5.3** Adorei o palácio que vi / a praia onde fui.

# 22

**Tenciono visitar esse país**

I'm intending to visit your country

In this revision unit you will learn more about
- *Services, from hairdressing to e-mail*
- *Sightseeing and getting to know the country*
- *Expressing yourself both verbally and in writing*

This is the first of the four final revision units where you will
further consolidate the language structures you learned throughout
this course and you will expand your Portuguese vocabulary in a
number of ways.

---

## Exercises

**22.1 No cabeleireiro** *At the hairdresser's*

**22.1.1** Study how Sibélia and Romeu go about their visit to the
hairdresser's, on both sides of the Atlantic.

**cortar (o) cabelo** *a haircut (lit. to cut (the) hair)*
**fazer as unhas** *to do one's nails*
**lavar a cabeça** *to wash one's hair (head)*
**atender** *to see to, serve*
**(a) franja** *fringe*
**(o) verniz** (Eur.) **/ esmalte** (Br.) *nail polish*

QUICK VOCAB

**incolor** *colourless*
**atendê-lo** *serve you*
**bem curto** *quite short*
**penteado** *combed, 'swept'*
**penteado para o lado direito / esquerdo** *swept right / left*
**penteado para trás** *swept back*

## No cabeleireiro de senhoras

| | |
|---|---|
| **Sibélia** | Queria cortar o cabelo. Queria também fazer as unhas. Pode atender-me agora ou preciso marcar hora? |
| **Empregada** | É melhor marcar hora. Quer hoje à tarde às três e meia? |
| **Sibélia** | Está bem. |
| | ———————— |
| **Sibélia** | Boa tarde, eu tenho hora marcada para as três e meia para cortar cabelo, e unhas também. |
| **Empregada** | A senhora pode vir, eu vou lhe lavar a cabeça. (*lavando o cabelo de Sibélia*) A água está bem assim ou está quente demais? |
| | ———————— |
| **Cabeleireira** | Como é que a senhora quer o cabelo? |
| **Sibélia** | Eu quero franja, e dos lados e atrás quero cortar só um pouco. |
| | ———————— |
| **Manicura** | De que cor é que a senhora quer o verniz (Eur.) / esmalte (Br.)? |
| **Sibélia** | Prefiro incolor. |

## No cabeleireiro de homens or barbeiro

| | |
|---|---|
| **Empregada** | Tem hora marcada? |
| **Romeu** | Não, não tenho. |
| **Empregada** | Então faça favor de esperar um pouco. Vamos atendê-lo daqui a dez minutos. |
| | ———————— |

| Cabeleireiro | Como é que o senhor quer o cabelo? |
| --- | --- |
| Romeu | Bem curto dos lados e atrás e penteado para o lado esquerdo. |

**22.1.2** Listen to your recording and you will hear four different people at the hairdresser's. What are they being asked and how do they reply?

**22.1.3** Can you ask for your hair to be done as follows:
  **i** quite short
  **ii** a bit off the sides and back
  **iii** swept back
  **iv** swept right

### 22.2

**retirar** *to pick up*
**(o) auscultador** (Eur.)**/ fone** (Br.) *receiver*
**(o) gancho** *hook*
**aguardar** *to wait for*
**(o) sinal de discar** *dialling tone*
**discar / digitar** *to dial*
**(o) sinal de tocar** *ringing tone*

QUICK VOCAB

**22.2.1** Julie is having problems in making a phone call and someone is trying to help by describing what must be done:

Você tem de* retirar o auscultador (Eur.) / fone (Br.) do gancho e aguardar o sinal de discar; discar primeiro estes números e depois o número do telefone desejado; e aguardar o sinal de tocar.

*ter de = ter que

**22.2.2** Describe again what she must do, but in the following way:

Você retira o auscultador (Eur.) / fone (Br.) do gancho... *Carry on.*

**22.2.3** This time use the 'command' form:

(for verb 'discar' see 'orthography-changing verbs' in VG at the end of the book)

Retire o auscultador (Eur.) / phone (Br.) do gancho... *Carry on.*

### 22.3

**(o) indicativo** (Eur.) **/ código** (Br.) *(phone) code*
**(o) sinal de ocupado** *engaged tone*
**a ligação foi cortada** *it has been cut off*

**22.3.1** Brian wants to ask what the area code is for the phone call he needs to make. Unscramble his words for him:

**A** In Portugal: Qual / o indicativo (Eur.) / ? / é / da região
**B** In Brazil: Qual / o código (Br.) / ? / é / da região

**22.3.2** Now he cannot get through. He wants to ask whether the tone he hears means that the line is engaged. Help him:

Este sinal / ocupado / ? / quer dizer*

**22.3.3** Now help him say 'I think it has been cut off':

Penso / foi /. / que / cortada / a ligação

*quer dizer = significa

......................................................................................

## Expressions
### Looking forward to

To express excitement over something in the future, you need expressions such as **estar ansioso/a** or **não poder esperar / mal poder esperar**.

| | |
|---|---|
| **Estou desejoso de / por ir de férias.** | *I am looking forward to going on holiday.* |
| **Estou ansioso por ir de férias. Não posso esperar.** | *I am looking forward to going on holiday. I can't wait.* |
| **Eles vão chegar amanhã. Não posso esperar por vê-los.** | *They are arriving tomorrow. I can't wait to see them.* |
| **Ela vai telefonar hoje. Mal posso esperar por falar com ela.** | *She is going to phone today. I can hardly wait to talk to her.* |

For 'I look forward to hearing from you', in letter writing, you need verb **aguardar**.

| | |
|---|---|
| **Aguardo as suas notícias.** | *I look forward to hearing from you.* |
| **Fico aguardando resposta.** | *I look forward to your reply.* |

## Cultural information
### a Postcards, letters and parcels

As in English, for informal correspondence, some people simply write the addressee's first and last name plus his / her address.

### Addressee

In formal writing as well as for a more courteous approach in general, use the following for, respectively, a male and female adult addressee:

**Exmo(\*) Sr / Exma(\*) Sra** (Eur.) **// Ilmo(\*\*) Sr / Ilma(\*\*) Sra** (Br.)

> **Exmo Sr. David Almeida** *Mr David Almeida*
> **Ilma Sra Irene Almeida** *Ms / Miss / Mrs Irene Almeida*
> (\*) (= **Excelentíssimo / Excelentíssima**)
> (\*\*) (= **Ilustríssimo / Ilustríssima**)

In business and commercial letters, **Ilmos Sres** corresponds to English *Messrs.* on both sides of the Atlantic.

*(Contd)*

## Address

You are likely to see more than one set of numbers in the address you are given.

*Road and building*

The front door number (after the road) + floor + some additional information (for a private apartment or a business office sharing a section of a floor).

**Rua Duque de Palmela, 37, 2° esq.**

This is the apartment / office *on the left hand side* section of the *2nd floor at number 37*, Duque de Palmela *Road*.

(**dto** abbreviates **direito; fte, frente; esq, esquerdo; tras, traseira; ctro, centro**)

In large apartment blocks you may see the abbreviation **apto,** for **apartamento,** followed by the respective number.

*Town and part of the country*

This will be preceded by *the postcode* (**o código postal,** or **CEP**). In Brazil, also remember to enter the abbreviation for the state:

| | |
|---|---|
| 1250-093 Lisboa | 01417-020 – São Paulo – SP |
| **Portugal** | **Brasil** |

### b Letter writing

Below is a list of salutations – the words you open your letter with such as *Dear...* – and their matching valedictions – the words you close your letter with such as *Yours...* – before signing.

**Form of greeting** *(from informal to formal)*

**a** For a very close friend: **Querido / Querida** + *first name*

**b** For a friend or acquaintance:
**Caro / Cara or Prezado / Prezada** + *first name* or, not so informal, **Caro / Cara** or **Prezado / Prezada** + **Sr / Sra** + surname

**c Caro Senhor / Cara Senhora** or **Prezado Senhor / Prezada Senhora** *Dear Sir / Madam*

**d Exmo Senhor / Exma Senhora** (Eur.) // **Ilmo Senhor / Ilma Senhora** (Br.) *Dear Sir / Madam*
or **Exmos\* Senhores** (Eur.) // **Ilmos\*\* Senhores** (Br.) *Dear Sirs*
\*= Excelentissimos \*\*= Ilustrissimos

**Form of ending** *(from informal to formal)*

**a Um beijo** (*kiss*) or **beijinhos** (lit. *little kisses*) or **Um abraço** (*embrace, hug*) where in English you would have written *Love.*
Also **Saudades** (*missing you*).

**b Um abraço** and/or **Saudades** or, not so informal,
**Saudações** or **Cumprimentos**

**c Saudações** or **Cumprimentos** or, a bit more formal,
**Cordialmente**

**d Subscrevo-me de V. Exa\* / de Vs. Exas\* atenciosamente** or just **Atenciosamente**
   or **De Vs. Sras.\*\* atenciosamente / Atenciosamente**
   (*commercial*)
\* = Vossa/s Excelência/s      \*\* = Vossas Senhorias

## How it works

**a Me, te, etc.**: *Where do they go?*

There is a certain amount of flexibility as to the position of the object pronouns in the sentence. Word-order follows the same fundamental rules you learned in Unit 9 for the reflexives. In fact, the reflexive pronouns themselves are a type of personal object pronoun.

The general tendency is to bring the object pronouns to the first part of the sentence or clause. **Pode me dizer onde é a saída?** *(Can you tell me where the exit is?)* is more widely heard than **Pode dizer-me onde é a saída?**

Similarly,

**Pode me fazer um favor?** instead of **Pode fazer-me um favor?** *(Can you do me a favour?)*

**Pode me dar alguma coisa para dor de cabeça?** instead of **Pode dar-me alguma coisa para dor de cabeça?** *(Can you give me something for a headache?)*

This 'pull' towards the beginning of a sentence or clause is stronger in Brazil. This is linked to the fact that Brazilians give a stronger pronunciation to final **e**, such as in **me** and **te**. If the object pronoun is more audible then it can stand better on its own at the beginning of what you want to say. As with the reflexives, a careful speaker will not make **me, te,** etc. the very first word in the sentence, but in colloquial speech, e.g., for *Give me that*, **Me dê isso** is often heard in Brazil in preference to **Dê-me isso.**

**b Object pronouns go missing!**

You have come across instances in which the object pronoun

**o / a / os / as** appears to 'have gone missing'. Particularly in speech, this pronoun tends to be omitted wherever context provides enough information.

Aqui tem. *for* Aqui **a** tem (a: a chave do quarto). *Here you are (your room key)*
Eu talvez prove. *for* Eu talvez **o** prove. (o: o doce da casa) *I may try it (the restaurant's speciality dessert)*

### c -no, -na *and* -lo, -la

When expressed, **o / a / os / as** become **no / na / nos / nas** after a verbal form ending in a nasal sound such as **m, ão, õe, ões**.

| lavaram-**nos** | *they washed them* (e.g., **os carros**, *the cars*) |
| dão-**nas** | *they give them* (e.g., **as flores**, *the flowers*) |
| põe(s)-**nas** | *she puts / you put them* (e.g., **na jarra**, *in the vase*) |

When expressed, **o / a / os / as** become **lo / la / los / las** after a verbal form ending in **r, s** or **z**, in which case these final letters are dropped.

**comprá-los** (= comprar + os) *to buy them*
**vendê-los** (= vender + os) *to sell them*
**parti-lo** (= partir + o) *to break it* (e.g., **o copo**, *drinking glass*)

(Note the addition of an accent in the infinitive of **-ar** and **-er** verbs.)

Hence,

Muito prazer em **conhecê-lo** *Delighted to meet you.* (... *a man*)
Muito prazer em **conhecê-la** *Delighted to meet you.* (... *a woman*)

This construction can be avoided by changing the word order.

Tive muito prazer em **o conhecer.** *It has been a pleasure to meet you.*

Also,

**comprá-lo-á** (i.e., comprará + o) *s/he will buy it*
**comprá-la-ia** (i.e., compraria + a) *s/he would buy it*

Brazilians avoid the intercalated pronoun by changing the word order.

**o comprará** *s/he will buy it*
**o compraria** *s/he would buy it*

Hence,

A senhora **importar-se-ia** de esperar um pouco? (Eur.) / A senhora **se importaria** de esperar um pouco? (Br.), *Could you possibly wait for a short while, please? (Would you mind at all…?)*

### d Tu and você *verb endings*

As first mentioned in Unit 8, in most of Brazil personal pronoun **tu** is not used. Preference is given to **você** and its respective verb endings (see Unit 8 and entries for 'the three conjugations'). However, in some cases Brazilians use **tu** verb endings without the subject pronoun.

Olha!      *Look!*
Me **dá** isso. *or* **Dá** isso para mim.      *Give me that.*

Furthermore, there are regional variations. Some Brazilians use **tu** subject pronoun with the verb endings for **você**.

Onde é que **tu vai** (instead of **vais**)?      *Where are you going?*

---

## Exercises

### 22.4 Trem do Corcovado *Corcovado Mountain Railway*

Study the following leaflet issued by the Brazilian organization that runs the cog-railway service to the top of the Corcovado mountain.

At the top of this rocky peak stands the statue of Christ the Redeemer overlooking the city of Rio de Janeiro.

O trenzinho do Corcovado é um passeio obrigatório para o turista que vem ao Rio de Janeiro e quer conhecer o Cristo Redentor, o principal ponto turístico da Cidade Maravilhosa. Mais de 250 mil pessoas por ano fazem esse passeio inesquecível.

Na viagem, o passageiro aprecia uma das mais lindas paisagens do Rio. Mas a vista é apenas uma das atrações: passear no trem é fazer uma viagem pela história do Brasil.

**22.4.1** Answer in Portuguese the following questions on the text:

**i**  What does 'trenzinho' mean?
**ii**  What is the main tourist spot in Rio?
**iii**  What attraction is there in addition to enjoying a beautiful view?

**22.4.2** Using form of greeting and ending a you learned earlier in this unit, write a holiday postcard to your friend Simão saying the following:

*The weather is fine, food good, and you are well. Yesterday you went to the Corcovado by cog-railway. This tourist spot is visited by more than 250 thousand people each year. On the journey you enjoy (the passenger enjoys) a beautiful view.*

**22.5 O endereço do e-mail** *The e-mail address*

Graham is asking Marisa how to say in Portuguese the @ in an e-mail address.

| Graham | Como é que se diz '@' em Português? |
| --- | --- |
| Marisa | 'Arroba'. |

Fill in the gaps in his next question.

| Graham | Como é que _____ 'dot' em _____ ? |
| --- | --- |
| Marisa | 'Ponto'. |

### 22.6 Pedindo informação por escrito *Writing for information*

Tenciono | visitar Portugal / o Brasil em março do ano que vem
| passar duas semanas nesse país, do dia ... ao dia ...
Estou especialmente interessado/a | no norte do país
| num hotel perto de uma praia
Peço que | faça(m) o favor | de | me enviar(em)...
| tenha(m) a gentileza* | | me dizer(em)...
| | | informar(em)...
.... lista dos hotéis / transportes públicos na região
.... folhetos de informação acerca da região
Fico aguardando resposta e desde já agradeço.

*a gentileza = *kindness*

**22.6.1** Select and combine words and phrases from the above box as the basis for an e-mail or letter to a tourist office in a Portuguese-speaking country, asking for the following:

**i** list of hotels in the area
(one week in the country / interested in a hotel near a beach / list of hotels, please / looking forward to their reply and thank you)

**ii** list of campsites in the area
(two months / facilities for children / looking forward to their reply and thank you)

**iii** list of youth hostels in the area
(one month / facilities for physically impaired / tourist
information leaflet / looking forward to their reply and
thank you)

**22.6.2** What would you be using for **i** form of greeting and **ii** form
of ending in these e-mails or letters?

---

## Summary

**1** (Eu) queria cortar o cabelo / fazer as unhas.
Pode atender-me / me atender agora?
**2** Quero o cabelo curto / comprido dos lados / atrás.
Prefiro o cabelo penteado para o lado esquerdo / direito.
**3** Prefiro verniz (Eur.) / esmalte (Br.) incolor / vermelho.
**4** Este sinal quer dizer / significa 'ocupado'?
Penso que a ligação foi cortada.
Você tem de / que aguardar o sinal de digitar.
Digite primeiro estes números e depois o número do telefone
desejado.
Aguarde o sinal de tocar.
**5** Como é que se diz 'dot' em Português? 'Ponto'.
'@' é 'arroba' em Português.
**6** **6.1** Querido João – Querida Joana – Um beijo / abraço
**6.2** Caro João – Cara Joana – Cumprimentos
**6.3** Caro Senhor – Cara Senhora – Cordialmente
**7** Ontem fui ao Corcovado, de trenzinho.
Este é o principal ponto turístico da cidade.
Há / Tem uma linda vista.
**8** Tenciono visitar Portugal / o Brasil em março / junho do ano
que vem.
Estou especialmente interessado no norte / sul do país.
Peço que façam o favor de me enviarem a lista dos hotéis.
Peço que façam a gentileza de me informarem dos
transportes públicos na região.
Fico aguardando resposta e desde já agradeço.

# 23

# Tomara que eles telefonem
## I wish they would phone

In this revision unit you will learn about
* **Replying to an advertisement**
* **Writing your CV and applying for a job**
* **Looking for property on the market, to let or for sale**

## Exercises

### 23.1 Um emprego *A job*

**23.1.1** Study the advertisement for the post of translator and interpreter.

> ### Tradutor/a – Intérprete
>
> Pretendemos candidato/a com o seguinte perfil:
> * diploma profissional
> * bom domínio do Inglês falado e escrito
> * bons conhecimentos de informática
> * elevado grau de autonomia e professionalismo
>
> Oferecemos:
> * flexibilidade horária
> * bom ambiente de trabalho
> * remuneração adequada ao exercício da função

> Os interessados deverão enviar, num prazo máximo de 5 dias úteis após publicação, carta de candidatura, manuscrita, C.V. e fotografia tipo passe para o n° 201955 deste Jornal.

**23.1.2** Kevin is applying for the post. What form will he be using for the verbs in brackets in the draft for his letter of application below?

Em resposta ao anúncio n° 201955 desse Jornal, venho apresentar a minha candidatura ao cargo de tradutor e intérprete. Eu (*reunir*) todos os requisitos enumerados, e, embora tenha aprendido Português como língua estrangeira, (*possuir*) um excelente domínio do idioma, falado e escrito.
Juntamente envio (Eur.) / estou enviando (Br.) o meu currículo e fotografia tipo passe, como pretendido. Fico aguardando resposta com grande interesse e espero que (*poder*) conceder-me uma entrevista.

**23.1.3** What would Kevin say at the interview concerning his profile as a candidate if asked about the following:

 **i** professional qualifications;
 **ii** competence in information technology;
 **iii** his level of self-management and professionalism.

### 23.2 Caso seja devolvido ao remetente *If it is returned to sender*

A letter you had posted was sent back to you. On the back you found the following:

> Caso não seja entregue ao destinatário, é favor assinalar a razão com "x":
> ☒ endereço insuficiente
> ☐ desconhecido

What is the reason why your letter wasn't delivered to its addressee?

### 23.3 O currículo ou o 'curriculum vitae' CV

Ana Magalhães (whom you first heard about in Unit 4) completed her general education at Colégio Bom Sucesso and has a degree in Medicine from the Portuguese University of Coimbra. Ana has not done any postgraduate studies or published any work. Currently she works as a general practitioner at Clínica Boa Saúde. She is a member of the Associação dos Médicos.

**23.3.1** Study Ana's CV below.

---

Curriculum Vitae

**1** Informação geral
  **1.1** Nome completo *Ana Isabel Vieira Gama Magalhães*
  **1.2** Nome do pai *José Luís Cabral Gama*
     Nome da mãe *Maria Feliciana Miranda Vieira Gama*
  **1.3** Data de nascimento *29 de Março de 1973*
  **1.4** Naturalidade *Guimarães*
  **1.5** Nacionalidade *Portuguesa*
  **1.6** Estado civil *Casada*
  **1.7** Endereço residencial *Faro*
  **1.8** Documento de identidade *BI 8170771*

**2** Formação educacional
  **2.1** Geral *Colégio Bom Sucesso*
  **2.2** Superior *Licenciatura em Medicina, Coimbra*
  **2.3** Pós-graduação ————

**3** Carreira profissional
  **3.1** Emprego atual *Clínica Boa Saúde*
  **3.2** Empregos anteriores *Hospital Santa Maria, Lisboa*

**4** Informação suplementar
  **4.1** Sociedades culturais *Associação dos Médicos*
  **4.2** Trabalhos publicados ————

---

**23.3.2** What would Ana's answers be to the following questions? (Give brief answers.)

   **i** Onde é que a senhora nasceu?
   **ii** Qual é o seu nome de solteira?
   **iii** A senhora é professora?
   **iv** Onde se formou?
   **v** Fez estudos de pós-graduação?
   **vi** Atualmente trabalha num hospital?

## Expressions

   **a I think, in my opinion...**

**Pensar**, *to think*, and **achar**, *to find*, can both be used to express one's opinion, with basically the same meaning.

   **Penso / Acho** que ele tem razão.      *I think that he is right.*

For an alternative with less conviction, use **parecer** or **na minha opinião**.

   **Parece-me que ele tem razão.**   *It seems to me that he is right.*
   **Na minha opinião, ele tem razão.**   *In my opinion, he is right.*

Also note that *I think so* and *I don't think so* are rendered by **penso que sim** and **penso que não**.

**b I am sure...** *I am right... all right?*

Use **ter a certeza** (Eur.) / **ter certeza** (Br.) for *to be sure* and **ter razão** for *to be right* (to have made the right judgement).

   **Tem a certeza?** (Eur.) /        *Are you sure?*
     **Tem certeza?** (Br.)
   **Tenho a certeza** (Eur.) **de**      *I am sure I am right.*
     **que tenho razão.**

*(Contd)*

**Tenho certeza** (Br.) **de que**    *I am sure I am right.*
   **tenho razão.**
**Você não tem razão.**      *You are wrong.*

You can also use **estar certo** (*to be certain*) for *to be sure*.

Ela **não está certa** de que   *She is not sure that he will/may*
   ele chegue hoje.          *arrive today.*

In addition, **certo** is used to seek, or give, assent.

### (está certo = está bem)

| – Está bem? | – Certo? | *– Is it all right / OK?* |
| – Está. | – Certo. | *–Yes / OK.* |

Another way of requesting assent is the question-tag **não é?** (*isn't it?*). Unlike English, this does not change with the verb in the sentence.

– Você vai à festa, **não é?**   *You are going to the*
                            *party, aren't you?*
– **É.**                       *Yes, I am.*

– Você gosta de música, **não é?**   *You like music, don't you?*
– **É.**                       *Yes, I do.*

## How it works

**a A – de – em – para – por:** *Saying 'for' and more…*

Make the right choices!

▶ **Para** points towards a specific purpose or goal (including time or place)

Levantar **para** abrir.     *Lift to open (lit. for + to open)*
A cerveja é **para** mim.   *The beer is for me.*

▶ **Para** *versus* **por:**

**Para** translates English *for* where the latter means movement towards.

| | |
|---|---|
| Ele partiu **para** África. | *He set out for Africa.* |

**Por** is wider in its meaning while **para** is more specific inasmuch as it points towards a specific purpose or goal.

| | |
|---|---|
| Tem um quarto **para** duas pessoas? | *Have you got a room for two?* |
| Quanto custa **por** noite? | *How much does it cost for a night (per night)?* |

For length of time you can just leave *for* out.

| | |
|---|---|
| Vou ficar aqui (**por**) dois meses. | *I am going to stay here for two months.* |

▶ **Para** *versus* **de:**

| | |
|---|---|
| um copo **de** vinho | *a glass of wine* |

This will mean, depending on context, *a glass measure of wine* or *a glass meant to contain wine*. Should there be ambiguity, the latter meaning can be expressed by the alternative

| | |
|---|---|
| um copo **para** vinho | *a wine glass* |

▶ **A** can **i** be static or **ii** imply movement towards something or someone.

| | |
|---|---|
| **i** Quem está **à** (= a + a) porta? | *Who is at the door?* |
| **ii** Vou **ao** clube. | *I am going to the club.* |

▶ **A** *versus* **para:**

With verbs of motion, both **a** and **para** frequently translate English *to*, but there is a difference.

| Ele vai **a** África. | He is going to Africa. (only temporarily) |
| Ele vai **para** África. | He is going to Africa. (to settle there) |
| Eu vou **a** casa. | I am going home. (only in and out) |
| Eu vou **para** casa. | I am going home. (staying in... for the night) |
| Aonde é que você vai? / **Para** onde é que você vai? | Where are you going? |

▶ **A** *and* **em:**

**Em** is used for a position of rest or for movement into or on to something.

> Meti a máquina fotográfica **na** (= em + a) mala, que estava **no** (= em + o) **balcão da Alfândega.** *I put the camera into the case, which was on the Customs desk.*

Brazilians use **em** with verbs of arrival.

> Cheguei **em** casa. (Br.) Otherwise
> Cheguei **a** casa. *I arrived home.*

### b Logo – já – até já – ainda não – já não – não mais – alguma vez

Both **logo** and **já** refer to time but they don't always have the same English translation. **Logo** can be an alternative to **imediatamente** (*right away*), **em breve** (*soon*) or **mais tarde** (*later*).

> Ele telefonou **logo.** *He phoned right away.*
> Até **logo.** *See you later.*

**Já** can refer to a point in time either in the immediate future or in the past, translating *now / straight away*, *already* or *ever*. It varies with its context.

Verb in the present:

**Já** pode telefonar.    *You can phone now.*
Volto **já.**    *I'm coming back in a moment.*
**Já** está!    *It's done. (already done)*

Verb in the preterite:

Foi a melhor festa de aniversário    *It was my best birthday party*
   que eu **já** tive.    *ever. (the best I ever had)*
Ele é o rapaz mais simpatico    *He is the nicest boy I ever met.*
   que eu **já** conheci.
**Já** foi (alguma vez) ao    *Have you (ever) been to the*
   Algarve?    *Algarve?*
Reply: Sim, **já.** *Yes, I have.* or Não, **ainda não.** *No, not yet.*

As an alternative to **já**, **alguma vez** can translate *ever*.

Este é o mais belo palácio    *This is the most beautiful*
   **alguma vez** construído.    *palace ever built.*

*or*

Este é o mais belo palácio que **já** foi construído.

**Até** and **já** combine as a parting expression when an immediate
return is to be expected.

Até **já**    *See you in a few minutes.*

**Ainda** can also translate *still* (verb in the present):

**Ainda** mora em Edimburgo?    *Do you still live in Edinburgh?*
Reply: **Ainda.** *Yes.* or **Já não**    *I no longer live there.*
   (moro) / **Não moro mais** (Br.).

# Exercises

### 23.4 Um ramo de flores e... a aliança de casamento
*A bunch of flowers and... the wedding ring*

This is Geraldo's horoscope for next week.

> Faça um esforço. Instale um sorriso nessa cara sofrida.
> A sua vida vai mudar completamente. É tempo de amar e
> ser amado. O futuro é hoje e a hora é agora.

Taking the horoscope seriously, select the two best pieces of advice
to give Geraldo:

1 Eu penso que já é tempo de você deixar de ser solteiro e fazer
  planos para o casamento.
2 Eu acho que um ramo de flores está certo, mas ainda é muito
  cedo para pensar na aliança.
3 Casar... Se você não tem a certeza (Eur.) / certeza (Br.),
  o melhor é esperar.
4 Na minha opinião, você deve perguntar muito em breve se ela
  quer ir escolher a aliança.

### 23.5 A viagem de lua-de-mel *The honeymoon trip*

Help Bill and Mel write an e-mail or letter booking a hotel
apartment for their honeymoon. This is their first draft.
Complete their unfinished sentences for them.

Tencionamos visitar esse país (*June this coming year*). Precisamos
de um apartamento (*for a couple*). Preferíamos (*the first week of
the month*).
Se o hotel não tiver vagas (*on those days*), pedimos que façam
o favor de informarem para quando podem fazer a reserva (*in our
name, Sanders. We look forward to hearing from you.*)

## 23.6 Um apartamento mobilado *A furnished flat*

**23.6.1** Study the plan of a flat and its furniture (**os móveis**).

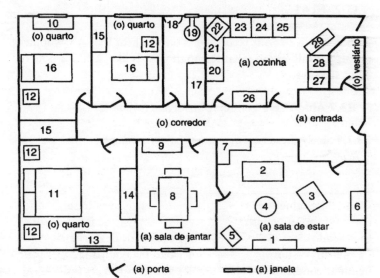

**(a) porta**     **(a) janela**

**1** a lareira *fireplace*
**2** o sofá *settee*
**3** a poltrona *armchair*
**4** a mesinha de centro *coffee table*

**5** o televisor *television set*
**6** o aparelho de som *hi-fi, stereo set*

**7** a estante de canto *corner shelf unit*
**8** a mesa e as cadeiras *table and chairs*

**9** o aparador *sideboard*
**10** a mesa para (o) computador e (a) impressora *work station for computer and printer*
**11** a cama de casal *double bed*
**12** a mesa de cabeceira *bedside table*
**13** o toucador (Eur.) / a penteadeira (Br.) *dressing table*
**14** o guarda-roupa *wardrobe*
**15** o armário *cupboard, storage unit*

**16** a cama de solteiro *single bed*
**17** a banheira *bathtub*
**18** o lavatório / a pia (Br.) *washbasin*
**19** a bacia / a retrete (Eur.) / o vaso sanitário (Br.) *toilet bowl*
**20** o fogão *stove, cooker*
**21** o balcão (Eur.) / a bancada (Br.) *work surface*
**22** o forno micro-ondas *microwave oven*
**23** o lava-louça / a máquina de lavar louça *dishwasher*
**24** a pia *sink*
**25** o frigorífico (Eur.) / o refrigerador *or* a geladeira (Br.) e o congelador *refrigerator and freezer unit*
**26** o armário *cupboard*
**27** a máquina de lavar roupa *washing machine*
**28** a máquina de secar roupa *clothes dryer*

**29** a tábua de passar roupa *ironing board*

Where context makes the meaning clear, some words are omitted, e.g., **a tábua de passar**.

**◆) CD2, TR 41**

**23.6.2** Listen to your recording. You will hear the lady who lives in this flat talk about what the apartment is like. Make a note of what she says.

### 23.7 Aluga-se e vende-se *To let and for sale*

**23.7.1** Study these two newspaper advertisements.

| i | ii |
|---|---|
| aluga-se<br>apartamento<br>mobilado<br>3 quartos de dormir<br>com ar condicionado<br>2° andar, elevador<br>serviço de limpeza (opcional)<br>Resposta ao número 27894 | vende-se<br>casa<br>6 quartos de dormir<br>cozinha equipada<br>aquecimento central<br>jardim e piscina<br>garagem<br>Resposta ao número 27036 |

**23.7.2** Sharon is interested in advert **i**. Help her write the text of her reply to the paper by entering the verbs in brackets in the correct form.

Em resposta ao anúncio n° 27894 desse jornal, tenho o prazer de comunicar que estou interessada em alugar um apartamento e esse talvez me (*convir*). Fico aguardando que (*fazer*) o favor de informar quando o (*poder*) ver.

(If you need help with these irregular verbs, look them up in the VG.)

**23.7.3** Reply to the following question, in Portuguese:

Quem poderá estar interessado no anúncio **ii**, uma pessoa que queira alugar ou uma pessoa que queira comprar?

Now write a reply to advert **ii**.

---

## Summary

1   Venho responder ao anúncio desse Jornal.
    Venho apresentar a minha candidatura ao cargo de tradutor / intérprete.
    Reúno todos os requisitos enumerados.
    Possuo um excelente domínio do Português, falado e escrito.
    Juntamente envio (Eur.) / estou enviando (Br.) o meu currículo e fotografia tipo passe.
    Espero que possam conceder-me uma entrevista.
    Fico aguardando resposta com grande interesse.
2 2.2 Formação educacional
    Geral
    Superior
    Pós-graduação
  2.3 Carreira profissional
    Emprego atual
    Empregos anteriores
3   Venho responder ao anúncio desse Jornal sobre um apartamento mobilado.
    Tenho o prazer de comunicar que estou interessada em alugar um apartamento.
    Esse talvez me convenha.
    Fico aguardando que façam o favor de informar quando o poderei ver.

# 24

..................................................................

# Irei, se puder
## I shall join in, if I can

In this revision unit you will learn about
- *Local culture and shows*
- *Family celebrations and parties*
- *Domestic work and a food recipe*

_____

## Exercises

**24.1 Indo ao teatro, ao cinema, à ópera ou a um concerto**
*A visit to the theatre, cinema, opera or a concert*

**QUICK VOCAB**

**(a) galeria** *gallery (balcony)*
**(o) 2° balcão** (Eur.)**/ balcão simples** (Br.) *upper circle*
**(o) 1° balcão** (Eur.)**/ balcão nobre** (Br.) *dress circle*
**(os) camarotes** *boxes*
**(a) plateia** *stalls*
**(a) orquestra** *orchestra*
**(o) palco** *stage*
**(o) bilhete** (Eur.) **(o) ingresso** (Br.) **= (a) entrada =** *ticket*

There are no tickets left for the gallery, upper circle and back stalls. Which of the following questions could be answered with **ainda** and which with **já não há mais**?

1 Ainda há entradas para a galeria?
2 Queria um camarote. Ainda tem?
3 Ainda tem lugares na plateia perto do palco?
4 Queria quatro ingressos para a plateia, nas filas atrás.
   Ainda há?
5 Ainda tem lugares no segundo balcão?
6 Queria dois lugares no primeiro balcão, no centro.
   Ainda tem?

**24.2**

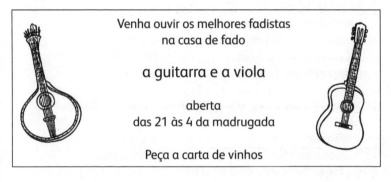

> Venha ouvir os melhores fadistas
> na casa de fado
>
> ## a guitarra e a viola
>
> aberta
> das 21 às 4 da madrugada
>
> Peça a carta de vinhos

**(a) guitarra portuguesa** *often shortened to*
**(a) guitarra** *Portuguese guitar*
**(a) guitarra** *or* **(a) viola**, in Brazil **(o) violão** *guitar*
**(o) instrumento dedilhado** *plucked stringed instrument*

Unscramble the words in brackets and find out about fado singing.

| | |
|---|---|
| **Margarida** | Já foi a uma casa de fados? |
| **Charles** | Não, nunca fui. O que é uma 'casa de fados'? |
| **Margarida** | (É / onde / restaurante, / o fado. / um lugar, um / se canta) |
| **Charles** | Mas o que significa 'fado'? |
| **Margarida** | (É / acerca da / experiência da vida. / uma canção / é / portuguesa / mas há / de temas. / O 'amor' / um tema frequente, / uma grande variedade) |
| **Charles** | E o que são a guitarra e a viola? |
| | *(Contd)* |

## Expressions

### a I believe, I agree

**Crer** and **acreditar em** translate *to believe*, but the latter is better left for trust in veracity rather than for conviction.

| **Creio** que ele tem razão. | *I believe that he is right.* |
|---|---|
| **Acredito** nas palavras dele. | *I believe his words.* |

**Concordar com** or **estar de acordo com** will translate *to agree with.*

| **Não concordo!** | *I disagree!* |
|---|---|
| **Concordo com** o senhor. / | *I agree with you.* |
| **Estou de acordo com** o senhor. | |

### b Leaving

Note the different renderings for *to leave* and *leave*.

**ir(-se) embora** *to leave, go away*

| **Fique. Não (se) vá embora.** | *Stay. Don't go.* |
|---|---|

**despedir-se** *to take one's leave*

| **Já é tarde. Tenho que (me) ir embora. Vou me despedir.** | *Time is getting on. I have to be going. I am going to say goodbye.* |
|---|---|

**partir / sair** *to leave, depart*

| **O comboio (Eur.) / trem (Br.) vai partir / sair às 8h35.** | *The train is going to leave at 8.35 hrs.* |
|---|---|

## c I miss...

*To miss* in the sense of *to fail to* e.g. *catch a plane* corresponds to **perder**.

> **Perdi** o avião. *I have missed the plane.*

*To miss* in the sense of *to lack* corresponds to **ter falta de**.

> **Tenho falta de** livros sobre esta matéria. *I lack books on this subject.*

*To miss* in the sense of *to feel the lack of* corresponds to **sentir (a) falta de**.

> **Sinto (a) falta de livros sobre esta matéria.** *I feel the need for books on this subject.*

*To miss* in the sense of *to notice with regret the absence or loss of* corresponds to **ter saudades de** or **estar com saudades de**.

> **Tenho saudades da Inglaterra. Estou com saudades da Inglaterra.**
> *I miss home (home being England).*

## d 'Sorry' and 'frightened'?

For emotions you can use the same format you learned in Unit 18 for expressions of feeling (pain. etc.) – **estar com** or **ter** + noun:

| Tenho | pena (*sorrow, pity*) de | I'm (feeling) | sorry for |
|-------|--------------------------|---------------|-----------|
| | inveja (*envy*) de | | envious of |
| Estou com | ciúme (*jealousy*) de | | jealous of |
| | medo (*fear*) de | | afraid of |

O bebé (Eur.) / bebê (Br.) **tem medo** das ondas do mar.
*The baby is afraid of the waves of the sea.*

## e Foi o máximo! *It was the best ever!*

If you want to be hyperbolical about someone or something, you can say **o máximo**.

> **Ela é o máximo!** *She is the greatest!*

*(Contd)*

You are quite impressed with the barbecue you have been invited to. You can express your appreciation in the following terms:

| | |
|---|---|
| **Eu nunca tinha ido a um churrasco tão bom.** | *I had never been to such a good barbecue.* |
| **Este é o melhor churrasco a que já fui.** | *This is the best barbecue I have ever been to.* |
| **Este é o melhor churrasco de sempre.** | *This is the best barbecue ever.* |
| **É o máximo!** | *It's the best ever!* |

---

## How it works

### a Bem – todo – mesmo – próprio: *Intensifiers*

You have come across certain words which sometimes appear to lose their literal meaning and are used as an intensifier instead. This is the case with **bem** (*well*), **todo** (*all*), **mesmo** (*same*) and **próprio** (*own*).

| | |
|---|---|
| Quer os ovos **bem** cozidos? | *Do you want the eggs hard boiled?* |
| Ele está **todo** molhado. | *He is soaking wet.* |
| Ela ficou **toda** contente quando o viu. | *She was extremely happy when she saw you.* |
| É isso **mesmo**. | *It's exactly that (what you said).* |

Also **eu mesmo**, etc. or **eu próprio**, etc. can translate *I myself*, etc. However, you are more likely to hear **Sou eu quem...** , etc.

**Sou eu quem** paga. *I am paying myself. (I am s/he who is paying)*

### b Tudo or todo? *Saying 'everything'*

**Tudo** translates *everything, all.* It usually functions as a pronoun and the neuter form of **todo**.

| Quanto é **tudo**? | *How much does it come to? (all the items)* |

Todo contains the notion of whole.

| Quanto é **ao todo**? | *How much does it come to? (in all, altogether)* |
| Ontem estudei o dia **todo** or **todo** o dia. | *Yesterday I studied all day.* |
| Estudo um pouco **todos** os dias. | *I study a bit every day.* |
| **Toda** a gente (Eur.) / **todo** (o) mundo (Br.) dança. | *Everyone / everybody dances.* |

### c Who does what?

▶ 'No-person' verbs:

You have come across some verbs that have no subject, expressed or implicit. It is so with the weather and other cases.

**Chove.** *(It) rains.*     **Dói.** *(It) hurts.*

▶ Different subject:

Note that different meanings can be obtained by changing the subject of the verb.

| Não me **lembro**; esqueci-me. | *I cannot remember; I have forgotten.* |
| **Lembre**-me. | *Remind me.* |

▶ Undefined subject:

When you wish to refer to an action without mentioning who actually does, or did, that action, use the third person of the verb and no expressed subject.

| **Disseram**-me que a 'Baixa' em Lisboa é em forma de rectângulo. | *I was told that Lisbon's 'Downtown' is in the shape of a rectangle. (lit. (they) told me...)* |

**d Que** or **quê – porque, por que** or **por quê – por causa de:**
*Saying 'why' and 'because'*

**Quê** is the strong form of **que**. The following dialogue will help you distinguish between the different forms.

**Por que** (*) comprou esse lenço?  *Why have you bought that scarf?*
**Por causa da** (**) cor.  *Because of its colour.*
**Por quê!?** or **Porquê!?** (Eur.) (***)  *Why!?*
**Por causa da cor. Porque** (****)  *Because of its colour. Because*
  **gosto da cor.**  *I like its colour.*

(*) Why, when you can also say **por que motivo** or **por que razão**, for what reason.
(**) *Because*, where followed by a noun, *because of*.
(***) *Why*, on its own.
(****) *Because*, other than (**)

---

## Exercises

### 24.3

◆) CD2, TR 42

**pôr a mesa** *to lay the table*
**tirar a mesa** *to clear the table*
**preparar** *to cook (food, meal)*
**fazer a cama** *to make the bed*
**limpar** *to clean, wipe clean*
**passar o aspirador em / aspirar** *to vacuum*
**passar a ferro** *to iron*

**24.3.1** Listen to your recording. The domestic help (**a empregada doméstica**) is being told her tasks for today. Make a note of what you hear.

**24.3.2** Reword the instructions you heard in **24.3.1** but present them in a different way, starting with **Hoje precisa...**

## 24.4 Uma receita para a festa *A recipe for the party*

**Ovos com recheio de anchova**          *Eggs with anchovy stuffing*

### 24.4.1 Os ingredientes *The ingredients*

Find the right translation in **a–f** for the ingredients in 1–6.

1 meia dúzia de ovos
2 uma lata pequena de anchova em filete
3 sumo (Eur.) / suco (Br.) de meio limão
4 um boião (Eur.) / vidro (Br.) pequeno de azeitonas recheadas
5 um boião (Eur.) / vidro (Br.) pequeno de maionese
6 uma alface
   **a** a lettuce                    **d** a small can of anchovy
   **b** a small jar of stuffed           fillets
      olives                        **e** juice of half a lemon
   **c** half a dozen eggs          **f** a small jar of
                                        mayonnaise

### 24.4.2 O procedimento *The method*

Now work out what to do.

Cozer bem os ovos. Descascá-los. Com uma faca, abri-los ao meio ao comprido. Com uma colher, tirar a gema para fora. Cortar a anchova em bocadinhos. Num prato grande, misturá-la com as gemas e o limão, usando um garfo. Encher as claras com a mistura. Por cima colocar um pouco de maionese e uma azeitona no meio. Cobrir o fundo de uma travessa com a alface cortada em tirinhas. Colocar os ovos recheados no leito de alface.

**24.4.3** Beginning with **Cozi bem os ovos,** explain to your friend how you have prepared the ingredients.

### 24.5 Palavras para a festa *Words for the party*

Fill in the gaps in the 'party talk' below with words from the box.

In some cases you have more than one choice. Use all the options.

**1** **i** *Someone is going to a party. Tell him/her to have a good time.*
Divirta-se! *or* _____

**ii** *Tell a group of people that you hope they'll have a good time at the party:*
Desejo que _____ na festa.

**2** **i** *You want to make a guest feel particularly welcome to your party. When your special guest arrives say 'It's good to see you':*
É bom _____ *or* _____ *or* _____ .

**ii** *You want to stress your appreciation for a present a guest brought you:*
Gosto muito do seu presente. _____ muito contente.

**3** **i** *You are going to a party and are buying something to give your host or hostess. In the shop ask to have the item gift-wrapped:*
Pode _____ embrulhar para presente?

**ii** *You arrive at the party with your gift and say:*
Isto é para _____ *or* _____ *or* _____ .

**4** *Join in the party toast:*
–Saúde! –Saúde! – _____ –Saúde!

................................................................
| | Diverte-te! | ver você | | Fiquei |
| ti | você | ver-te | si | Saúde! |
| se divirtam | | vê-lo / vê-la | | fazer o favor de |
................................................................

### 24.6 Quando é o seu aniversário? *When is your birthday?*

**o dia de anos** (Eur.) = **o aniversário**

– Quando é o seu aniversário?
– No dia 3 de dezembro. E o seu?
– O meu é hoje.
– Então parabéns! Quantos anos é que você faz?
– Faço vinte anos.
– Tenho de ir comprar um presente para você/para si (Eur.).
– Não, não se incomode.

Rewrite the above dialogue in the **tu** approach throughout, starting with **Quando é o dia dos teus anos?**

_____

## Summary

1 Ainda há entradas para a galeria? – Ainda tem lugares na plateia, perto do palco? – Queria quatro ingressos.
2 O que é uma 'casa de fados'? – Até que horas está aberta?
3 Divirta-se ! / Diverte-te! / Divirtam-se!
  Gosto muito do seu presente. Fiquei muito contente.
  Saúde!
4 Ponha / Tire a mesa. – Faça as camas. – Prepare o jantar. – Limpe a cozinha. – Passe o aspirador na sala de estar / jantar.

# 25

**Gostaria de praticar mais**
I should like to practise further

This concluding unit gives you tips on how to
- *Talk about the Portuguese you have learned*
- *Make the most of your Portuguese now and always*

This last revision unit gives you advice for your continued success in Portuguese in the future.

### 25.1 Português como Língua Estrangeira (PLE)
*Portuguese as a Foreign Language (PFL)*

◀) **CD2, TR 43**

Jenny is a very successful student of Portuguese as a foreign language. She has been interviewed for a radio broadcast. Below you will find Jenny's replies to Luísa's questions. The latter are on your recording. Listen to the recording and put questions and replies together in a dialogue.

– Aprendi principalmente ensinando a mim própria como autodidata. Mas sentia a falta de pessoas com quem pudesse falar. Então resolvi passar um tempo em Portugal, dois meses, a praticar e estudar a língua.

– Frequentei um curso de PLE na Universidade Nova de Lisboa. Tínhamos aulas de língua todos os dias e de cultura três vezes por semana. No fim do curso submeti-me a um exame. Passei com distinção. Fiquei muito contente.

– Obrigada. E aproveitei todas as oportunidades para falar, nas lojas, nos restaurantes, em todos os lados. Gostei muito de Portugal e da sua capital, das pessoas... de tudo. Tive muita pena de vir embora.

– Vou... vou voltar para um país de língua portuguesa, mas vai ser outro. Quero ir ao Brasil, quero passar dois ou três meses lá.

– Ainda não sei, mas gostaria de visitar Brasília.

– Não sei bem... Talvez porque é a capital federal. Talvez (*rindo*) também porque me disseram que Brasília foi construída em forma de avião. Não sei se acredite ou não. O melhor é ir ver.

– Ir ao Brasil é também uma boa oportunidade para ouvir outro sotaque e outras expressões.

– Hei de ir, mas quando ainda não sei.

### 25.2 Procure e descubra *Look for and find out*

For your continued success after completing this course, always try to 'think Portuguese' when you want to speak Portuguese. This is a golden rule.

Imagine that you are being shown several brands of **vinho tinto** at a wine shop. You make your choice and use the verb **ter** meaning to say *I'll have that one*. To your surprise, though, the assistant puts the bottle away. He thinks you are trying to say that you *already have* that one. As we saw earlier, **Quero esse** or **Levo esse** would have conveyed the right meaning.

The key lies in remaining aware of the boundary line in the area of meaning covered by a word. One English word may cover the main area of meaning of more than one Portuguese word, and vice versa.

**25.2.1** Find one single English word that will translate the different Portuguese words in each set.

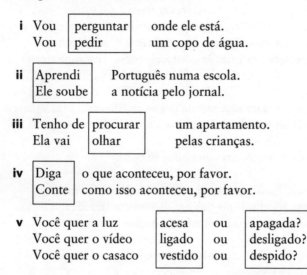

i   Vou [perguntar] onde ele está.
    Vou [pedir] um copo de água.

ii  [Aprendi] Português numa escola.
    [Ele soube] a notícia pelo jornal.

iii Tenho de [procurar] um apartamento.
    Ela vai [olhar] pelas crianças.

iv  [Diga] o que aconteceu, por favor.
    [Conte] como isso aconteceu, por favor.

v   Você quer a luz [acesa] ou [apagada?]
    Você quer o vídeo [ligado] ou [desligado?]
    Você quer o casaco [vestido] ou [despido?]

**25.2.2** Now find the words that go into the 'question mark' boxes in the sentences below (one for each set). They are hidden in the word search grid opposite.

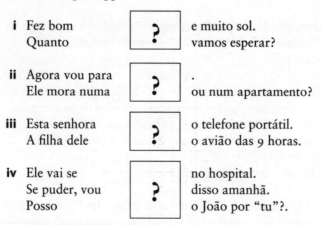

i   Fez bom [?] e muito sol.
    Quanto [?] vamos esperar?

ii  Agora vou para [?].
    Ele mora numa [?] ou num apartamento?

iii Esta senhora [?] o telefone portátil.
    A filha dele [?] o avião das 9 horas.

iv  Ele vai se [?] no hospital.
    Se puder, vou [?] disso amanhã.
    Posso [?] o João por "tu"?.

**v**  Você não me ☐?☐ esse dinheiro.
O Nuno ☐?☐ chegar em breve.
O senhor ☐?☐ reservar lugar.

**vi**  A que horas é que ☐?☐ o jantar?
Para que é que ☐?☐ isto?
Este casaco não me ☐?☐ . Está apertado.

**vii**  ☐?☐ 20 para as 8.
☐?☐ duas pessoas no grupo.
☐?☐ os guardanapos na mesa.

**viii**  Você já ☐?☐ a Teresa?
Ela não ☐?☐ ninguém aqui.
Peter não ☐?☐ Belém.

**ix**  Peter ☐?☐ onde fica Belém.
O senhor ☐?☐ falar Português?
Você ☐?☐ se ela chegou bem?

**x**  Onde ☐?☐ o seu apartamento?
Quem ? ☐?☐ em casa e quem vai sair?
Ela ☐?☐ contente quando o vê.

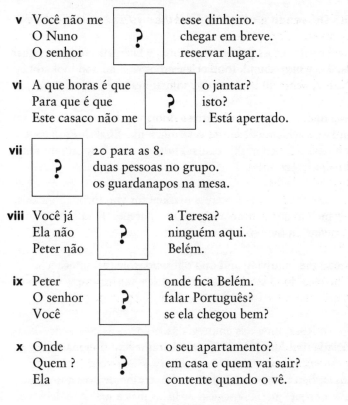

| C | O | N | H | E | C | E | R | A |
|---|---|---|---|---|---|---|---|---|
| O | C | A | S | D | E | V | A | S |
| F | A | T | T | E | M | P | O | S |
| A | O | R | E | V | I | E | R | E |
| L | P | A | M | E | D | R | O | R |
| T | I | T | O | V | Z | D | E | V |
| A | C | A | S | A | G | E | M | E |
| M | O | R | U | H | L | U | M | J |
| S | A | B | E | U | F | I | C | A |

## 25.3 Desvenda o mistério *Solve the mystery*

You will come across Portuguese words which will suggest English words. They may sound, look or even both sound and look alike, but the meaning will be different, sometimes 'dangerously' so.

Imagine that, on heading towards a door, you hear your friend say to you **Puxe**, which will sound very much like English *Push*. But (as you have learned in this course) *push* is exactly what you must not do – *pull* instead!

Other 'false friends' have been unmasked for you throughout this course, such as *cup* – **copo** and *parent* – **parente**. Find some more 'false friends' in the box.

Now read the following and find out who stole the quince 'cheese' from the local food store that morning, leaving an empty box on the shelf!

*10h00.* D. Rosa, uma das empregadas, colocou as caixas de marmelada nas duas primeiras prateleiras a contar de baixo.

*10h10.* D. Berta entrou com Joãozinho, o filho de dois anos, que chorava porque queria descalçar as luvas mas a mãe não deixava; é uma criança muito sensível. D. Maria, a empregada da caixa, diz que D. Berta não comprou nada e parecia preocupada ao sair.

*10h15.* D. Zulmira, senhora de sessenta anos, entrou com o seu cachorro Piloto. Conversou durante uns cinco minutos com D. Rosa junto às prateleiras da marmelada.

*10h20.* Sr. Olavo, homem de ar absorto, entrou na loja. Ele parecia pretender alguma coisa especial. Encontraram-se as suas impressões digitais na caixa vazia.

*10h30.* Sr. José, o gerente, notou que uma das caixas de marmelada não tinha nada dentro, estava vazia. A marmelada tinha desaparecido mas a caixa estava na prateleira.

| | 'false friend' | meaning* | |
|---|---|---|---|
| P | (a) marmelada | *quince cheese* | E |
| E | *marmalade* | (a) geleia de laranja | P |
| P | preocupado | *worried* | E |
| E | *preoccupied* | absorto | P |
| P | pretender | *to go for, to intend* | E |
| E | *to pretend* | fingir | P |
| P | sensível | *sensitive* | E |
| E | *sensible* | sensato | P |

*not necessarily the only one.

**25.4 Não ao pé da letra...** *Not literally...*

Similarly to what happens with some English words, throughout this course you have come across Portuguese words which sometimes lose their literal meaning in order to be used some other way. This includes verbs such as **andar, voltar, deixar, começar, acabar** and others.

Below you have two sets of sentences. Pair up the sentences in 1 to 5 with another way of saying the same in a to e.

**1** Eu **comecei a** estudar Português há seis meses.
**2** Mas em breve **deixei de** estudar Português por falta de tempo.
**3** Depois de um intervalo **voltei a** estudar Português.
**4** E **ando a estudar** (Eur.) / **ando estudando** muito.
**5** **Acabo de** fazer o penúltimo exercício deste curso.

**a** Depois de um intervalo estudei Português novamente.
**b** Fiz agora mesmo o penúltimo exercício deste curso.
**c** Eu estudei Português pela primeira vez há seis meses.
**d** E tenho estudado muito ultimamente.
**e** Mas em breve parei de estudar Português por falta de tempo.

### 25.5 A cultura do país *The country's culture*

**25.5.1** Study the information shown below. It appeared in a leaflet from the Arts Centre of a Brazilian University – Centro de Artes da Universidade Federal Fluminense.

literatura cinema

teatro

música

**INTRODUÇÃO À CULTURA BRASILEIRA**

**Participe!**

artes

plásticas

**Organização – Secretaria de Cultura de Niterói
de 03 de agosto a 10 de dezembro
TEATRO DA UFF das 15 às 18 horas**

**25.5.2** Reply to the following questions, in Portuguese:

  **i** Qual é o tema geral deste curso da UFF?
  **ii** Quem são os organizadores?
 **iii** Onde é que se vai realizar?
  **iv** Quando é que se vai realizar?

**25.5.3** Write to UFF:

*(You intend to spend six months in Brazil this coming year, July to December / Interested in an introductory course on Brazilian culture / Would like to take part in UFF's course / Applying and enclosing CV / Looking forward to a reply and hoping to be granted a place.)*

# Summary

**1** Aprendi Português principalmente como autodidata.
Resolvi passar um tempo em Portugal.
Lá frequentei um curso de PLE na Universidade Nova de Lisboa.
Passei o exame com distinção. Fiquei muito contente.
Gostei muito de lá estar e tive muita pena de (me) vir embora.
Vou voltar para um país de língua portuguesa, mas vai ser outro.
Vai ser o Brasil, para ouvir outro sotaque e outras expressões.

**2** Ao Centro de Artes da Universidade Federal Fluminense:
Tenciono passar seis meses no Brasil.
Estou interessada num curso de introdução à cultura brasileira.
Gostaria de participar no curso da UFF.
Venho apresentar a minha candidatura.
Juntamente estou enviando o meu currículo.
Espero que possam conceder-me lugar no curso.
Fico aguardando resposta.

# Testing yourself

Units 6, 11 and 16 are for consolidation and revision of what you have learned. There you will find plenty of additional opportunities to check your progress. The same applies to the last four units in the course, which contain material for overall revision of structures and for vocabulary expansion. Throughout you can monitor your progress by comparing your results with the **Key to the exercises** at the end of the book.

Unit 6 is the first main landmark in your progress. When you check your exercises against the **Key to the exercises** make a written note of how many you got right. If more than half were wrong, go back to Units 1–5 before you move forward to the next units. Do the same in Unit 11 and Unit 16. If your results are low in Units 22 to 25, go once more through the previous units.

Here are a few guidelines to help your performance:

| | |
|---|---|
| 80%–100% | Congratulations! **Parabéns!** You are doing extremely well. |
| 60%–79% | Very good. **Muito bem.** You have mastered most of the points covered in the last units. Try to clarify the areas that still need some work. |
| 51%–59% | Well done, but it might be advisable to clarify the areas where you are not so confident before you move on to the next units. |
| below 50% | Not bad, but I would strongly advise you to go back over the last units. When you have done so, test yourself again and see how much you have improved. |

Always remember that learning a new language does take time. If it seems a bit difficult, don't let yourself be discouraged. Come back to it another day and things will begin to make more sense again.

# Key to the exercises

**Unit 1**
1A.3: **a** Boa noite. **b** Bom dia. **c** Boa tarde. 1A.6: **a** Boa tarde,
Dona/dona Laura. **b** Olá! *or* Oi! (Br.) 1C.2: 2 d f; 3 c e; 4 a g.
1C.4: **a** Bom dia. **b** Boa tarde. (*on a more personal note, you can
also say the other parting words you have learnt, for example* até
breve / logo *to reassure the shopkeeper and the waiter that you will
be back*). **c** Adeus, até à próxima. **d** Tchau. *You can add* até mais /
logo / breve / a próxima , *depending on what you mean.*

**Unit 2**
2.1 certo 2 3, errado 1.
2.2 1 b. 2 a. 3 b.
2.3.1 ii A+C, iii B+C, iv B+C, v A+B.
2.3.2 **i** Faz favor, pode me dizer onde é a recolha de bagagem?
A recolha de bagagem é à direita, em frente do controle de
passaporte. Obrigada. **ii** Onde são as informações, por favor? As
informações são lá em cima, à direita. Obrigado. **iii** Desculpe, onde
são os sanitários para senhoras? Os sanitários para senhoras são
à esquerda, a seguir aos sanitários para homens. Muito obrigada.
**iv** Faz favor, pode me dizer onde é o aluguer de carros? O aluguer
de carros é a seguir às informações e ao ponto de encontro. Muito
obrigado. **v** Por favor, onde é a praça de táxis? A praça de táxis é
lá em baixo (Eur.) / lá embaixo (Br.), em frente. Muito agradecida.
2.4.1 Por favor / Faz favor / Desculpe, **a** pode me dizer onde é a
farmácia? or simply onde é a farmácia? **b** (pode me dizer) onde é
o banco? **c** (pode me dizer) onde são as informações? **d** (pode me
dizer) onde são os sanitários para homens?
2.4.2 Como? / Como? Mais devagar, por favor / faz favor (Eur.).
2.4.3 (Muito) obrigado / obrigada. *Your reply is also right if you
said* (Muito) agradecido / agradecida.
2.5 **i** À esquerda **ii** Em frente.
2.6 Por favor, pode me dizer onde é o câmbio?
2.7 Por favor, onde posso encontrar acesso a email?

**Unit 3**

3.1 certo 1 2, errado 3.

3.2 1 a. 2 a. 3 c.

3.3 1 closed, 2 closed, 3 engaged (occupied), 4 Non-smokers,
5 Wait in the queue (*as an instruction*), 6 No stopping or parking
(*as a prohibition*), 7 No camping (*as a prohibition*), 8 No
smoking, please (*as a polite request rather than an instruction or
prohibition*). 9 A reminder that litter should be disposed of in the
litter-bin, not on the floor, lit., 'litter on the floor, no, in here, yes'.

3.4.1 i 2, ii 1, iii 5, 6, iv 10, v 3, 4 vi 8, vii 7, viii 9.

3.4.2 i Faz favor (Eur.), queria um mapa. ii Queria dois cafés.
iii Por favor, quatro sandes (Eur.). / Por favor, quatro sanduíches.
iv Por favor, queria papel de carta e uma caneta. v Queria um
penso adesivo (Eur.) / Queria um esparadrapo (Br.). vi Faça o
favor de me dar alguma coisa para dor de cabeça. vii Pode me dar
alguma coisa para indigestão? viii Faça o favor de me dar alguma
coisa para queimadura de sol.

3.5.1 i três – ida, ii quatro – ida e volta, iii dez – ida e volta,
iv oito – simples, v seis – ida e volta, vi cinco – ida, vii nove – ida
e volta, viii sete – ida.

3.5.2 i Queria três bilhetes de ida para Faro. ii Quatro de ida e
volta para o Porto, faça favor. iii Dez de ida e volta para Cacilhas,
por favor. iv Faz favor, oito simples para o Estoril. v Queria seis
passagens de ida e volta para Manaus. vi Por favor, cinco de ida
para Belo Horizonte. vii Nove para o Rio, ida e volta, por favor.
viii Por favor, queria sete para Salvador, somente ida.

3.5.3 Queria ... i duas passagens de ida para Belo Horizonte.
ii dois bilhetes de ida e volta para Faro. iii quatro passagens de
ida para Manaus. iv oito bilhetes de ida e volta para Cacilhas.
*Your answer will also be correct if you have worded it in any of
the following ways:* i (Queria) duas (passagens) de ida para Belo
Horizonte. / Duas (passagens) para Belo Horizonte, (somente)
ida. ii (Queria) dois (bilhetes) de ida e volta para Faro. / Dois
(bilhetes) para Faro, ida e volta. iii (Queria) quatro (passagens) de
ida para Manaus. / Quatro (passagens) para Manaus, (somente)
ida. iv (Queria) oito (bilhetes) de ida e volta para Cacilhas. / Oito
(bilhetes) para Cacilhas, ida e volta. (*Adding* por favor / faz favor /
faça favor *at the beginning or end.*)

**3.6.1 i** Pode me dar a lista dos telefones? **ii** Pode me ligar para este número?
**3.6.2 i** cabine 5. **ii** caixa 7.

## Unit 4

**4.1** certo 2 3, errado 1.
**4.2 1** b. **2** c. **3** b.
**4.3.1 i** 2; **ii** 4; **iv** 3; **v** 5.
**4.3.2** Queria **i** um apartamento simples, com chuveiro, para cinco noites. **ii** dois quartos individuais, com banheira, para oito noites. **iii** um quarto duplo, com banheira, para nove noites. **iv** dois apartamentos duplos, com chuveiro e banheira, para dez noites. **v** um quarto de casal e dois quartos simples, com chuveiro, para sete noites.
**4.4** Queria **a** um quarto simples / individual, com chuveiro, para uma noite. **b** um quarto duplo / de casal, com banheira, para duas noites. **c** um quarto duplo / de casal e um quarto simples / individual, com chuveiro e banheira, para sete noites. **d** um quarto duplo / de casal, com chuveiro, para cinco noites. Queria duas camas.
**4.5.2** Stewart é o nome de batismo *or* Stewart é o nome próprio (Eur.) / prenome (Br.) e Martin é o nome de família *or* Martin é o apelido (Eur.) / sobrenome (Br.).
**4.6.1** supermercado, 1; restaurante, 2; museu, 3; igreja, 4; praia, 5; bombas de gasolina, 6; passagem subterrânea, 7; Hotel Sol-Mar, 8; parada de ônibus, 9; paragem de autocarros, 10; o turismo, 11; Estrada do Aeroporto, 12.
**4.6.2 i** Por favor, pode me dizer onde é o supermercado? **ii** Faz favor, pode me dizer onde é o restaurante? **iii** Faz favor, onde fica o museu? **iv** Desculpe, pode me dizer onde é a igreja? **v** Por favor, onde é a praia? **vi** Por favor, onde ficam as bombas de gasolina? **vii** Faz favor, onde é a passagem subterrânea? **viii** Faz favor, pode me dizer onde fica o Hotel Sol-Mar? **ix** Por favor, onde é a parada de ônibus? **x** Faz favor, onde é a paragem de autocarros? **xi** Desculpe, onde fica o turismo? **xii** Faz favor, onde é a Estrada do Aeroporto?
**4.6.3** Por favor, pode me dizer onde **i** é a Estrada do Aeroporto? **ii** fica a praia? **iii** é a passagem subterrânea? **iv** fica o museu? **v** fica o supermercado? **vi** é a paragem de autocarros (Eur.) / a parada de ônibus / o ponto de ônibus (Br.)? **vii** são as bombas de gasolina? **viii** fica o Hotel Sol-Mar?

## Unit 5

**5.1** certo 1, errado 2 3.

**5.2** 1 b. 2 b. 3 a.

**5.3.1** Desculpe, tem pão e leite?

**5.3.2** Queria i duas garrafas de leite, ii dois pães, iii duas bananas iv e duas maçãs.

**5.4.1** i de sexta-feira a domingo. ii sete dias por semana. iii dez minutos a pé. iv dez minutos de carro.

**5.4.2** Há um parque de campismo (Eur.) / um camping (Br.) perto daqui com. ii loja, chuveiro frio e quente e sala de televisão? iii tomada de corrente, frigorífico (Eur.) / geladeira (Br.) e sala de televisão? iv chuveiro frio e quente, lavandaria (Eur.) / lavanderia (Br.) e gás para campistas? *Your answer will also be correct if instead of* perto daqui *you used* aqui perto *or* por aqui.

**5.4.3** Tem vaga para i um trailer, isto é, carro de moradia rebocado, e uma barraca? ii uma caravana, isto é, carro de moradia rebocado, e duas tendas? iii um carro-cama, isto é, carro de moradia motorizado, um reboque pequeno e uma tenda? iv um carro de moradia motorizado, um reboque pequeno, uma rulote, isto é, um carro de moradia rebocado, e uma barraca?

**5.4.4** Tem vaga para ii um carro-cama, isto é, carro de moradia motorizado, e uma tenda? iii uma caravana / rulote / trailer, isto é, carro de moradia rebocado, e uma barraca? iv dois reboques pequenos e duas tendas?

**5.5** 1 Queria uma garrafa de vinho. 2 Tem um saca-rolhas? 3 Tem óculos de sol? 4 Queria uma escova de dentes e pasta de dentes. *Saying simply* Queria escova e pasta de dentes *would also be correct.*

**5.6.1** Queria fazer uma chamada a cobrar para o Canadá.

**5.6.2 A** i Tem cartões credifone? ii Tem telemóveis? **B** i Tem cartões de telefone? ii Tem celulares?

**5.7** Por favor, quanto custa meia hora na Internet?

## Unit 6

**6.1.3** Faça o favor de i repetir, mais devagar. ii escrever aqui quanto é. iii escrever aqui o nome, (o) endereço e (o) número do telefone. iv escrever aqui essa(s) palavra(s). v me mostrar essa palavra no dicionário *or* me mostrar no dicionário essa palavra. vi me mostrar no mapa onde fica. vii me mostrar no mapa onde estou. viii me mostrar as horas.

**6.2** Não, não tenho nada a declarar.

**6.3.1** i o meu ii a minha iii meu iv minha

**6.3.2** Aqui tem i o meu passaporte. ii a minha carta de condução. iii meu passaporte. iv minha carteira de motorista.

**6.4.2** i Pode me mostrar a lista dos modelos e preços? ii Quanto é por semana? iii Quanto é por dia? iv Quanto é por quilómetro rodado? v Quanto é por quilômetro rodado? vi Quanto é a caução? vii Quanto é o seguro contra todos os riscos? viii Queria este carro, pagando por semana. ix Queria este carro, pagando por dia. x Queria o carro sem motorista. xi Queria o carro com motorista. xii Queria o carro para cinco dias. xiii Pode me dar os documentos do carro? xiv Pode me dar um recibo?

**6.4.3** i Pode me mostrar a lista dos modelos e preços? ii Quanto é por dia? iii Quanto é o seguro? E a caução? iv Queria este carro, pagando por dia. v Queria o carro para dois dias, e sem motorista. vi Pode me dar um recibo? vii Pode me dar os documentos do carro?

**6.5** 1 b, 2 a, 3 d, 4 c.

**6.6.2** 2 A câmara municipal fica à esquerda. 3 Os bombeiros ficam à esquerda. 4 O centro de saúde fica à direita. *Your replies will still be correct if instead of* fica-ficam *you used* é-são.

**6.7.1** i três ii cais; um iii plataforma; cinco iv o trem; plataforma.

**6.7.2** i Do cais três. ii Do cais número um. iii Da plataforma cinco. iv Da segunda plataforma.

**6.7.3** i De que cais parte o comboio para o Porto? ii De que cais parte o comboio para Braga? iii De que plataforma parte o trem para o Rio? iv De que plataforma parte o trem para Campinas?

**6.8.1** i 4, ii 5, iii 2, iv 3, v 1.

**6.8.2** i Tem varanda? ii Tem vista para o mar? iii Queria um apartamento com ar condicionado. iv Tem aparelho de televisão? v Queria um apartamento sem barulho.

**6.8.3** Tem i ar condicionado? ii aparelho de televisão? iii varanda / sacada e vista para o mar?

**6.8.4** Queria um quarto / apartamento sem barulho.

**6.9.1** Por favor, pode me trazer mais ii um lençol. iii um edredão (Eur.) /edredom (Br.). iv um cobertor. v uma toalha. vi um sabonete. vii um rolo de papel higiénico (Eur.) / higiênico (Br.). viii um cabide.

**6.9.2** Por favor, pode me trazer mais i duas almofadas (Eur.) / dois travesseiros (Br.). ii dois lençóis. iii dois edredões (Eur.) / edredons

(Br.). **iv** dois cobertores. **v** duas toalhas. **vi** dois sabonetes. **vii** dois rolos de papel higiénico (Eur.) / higiênico (Br.). **viii** dois cabides.
**6.9.3** Por favor, pode me trazer mais quatro cabides e (mais) dois cobertores. Obrigado/a.
**6.10.1** a **i** Não, não há. **ii** Há. **iii** Há. **iv** Não, não há. **b** Não há um mecânico perto daqui. Não há um médico aqui perto, mas há um enfermeiro. Há um dentista muito perto, na primeira rua à direita.
**6.10.2** Pode chamar **i** um médico **ii** um enfermerio **iii** um mecânico **iv** um táxi para mim?
**6.11** **a** desculpar, **d** fazer, **e** ficar, **g** partir, **h** poder.
**6.12** Por favor, queria três pães, meia dúzia de maças, uma garrafa pequena de leite e uma garrafa grande de água.
**6.13.1** Por favor, pode me ajudar?
**6.13.2** Por favor, pode mudar a língua para inglês?
**6.13.3.1** Não consigo entrar.
**6.13.3.2** Não consigo acesso ao meu email.
**6.13.3.3** Não consigo accesso a este sítio.
**6.15** Across: **1** Não tem importância. **2** Com licença. **3** Desculpe. **4** Agradecido/a. **5** De nada. **6** Muito obrigado/a. Down: **1** Não tem de quê. **2** Obrigado/a. **3** De nada. **4** Por favor.

## Unit 7
**7.1** certo 2, errado 1 3.
**7.2** **1** b. **2** b. **3** c.
**7.3** Este é (o) Nuno, essa é (a) Rosa e aquela é (a) Mariana.
**7.4.1** **ii** Natal, Rio Grande do Norte; 34 anos, professora; noiva, não tem filhos. **iii** Porto Alegre, Rio Grande do Sul; 75 anos, homem de negócios aposentado; viúvo, tem um filho e uma neta. **iv** Funchal, Madeira; 41 anos, dona de casa; casada, tem um filho e uma filha.
**7.4.2** **i** O meu nome é José Fontes. Sou de Faro, no Algarve. Tenho vinte e dois anos e sou estudante. Não tenho filhos. Sou solteiro. **ii** Eu me chamo Glória Fonseca e sou de Natal, no Rio Grande do Norte. Tenho trinta e quatro anos de idade. Sou professora. Não tenho filhos. Não sou casada, mas estou noiva. **iii** Me chamo Osvaldo Medeiros e sou de Porto Alegre, no Rio Grande do Sul. Tenho muitos anos, setenta e cinco. Sou homem de negócios aposentado. Sou viúvo, mas tenho um filho e uma neta. **iv** Chamo-me Amélia Sarmento. Sou do Funchal, na Madeira. Tenho quarenta e um anos de idade. Sou dona de casa. Sou casada e tenho um filho e uma filha.

7.5 Não, não sou. Eu sou inglês. // (Eu) chamo-me Matthew
Smith (Eur.) / (Eu) me chamo Matthew Smith (Br.). (Eu) sou de
Manchester. *Your answer is equally right if you have said* O meu
nome é Matthew Smith (Eur.) / Meu nome é Matthew Smith (Br.)
// (Eu) estou sozinho e vou ficar oito dias, de férias. // Aqui está.
*or* Aqui tem. *You can also say* Aqui está or tem a minha carta de
condução (Eur.) / Aqui está *or* tem minha carteira de motorista (Br.).

## Unit 8

8.1 certo 1 2, errado 3 4.

8.2 1 b. 2 c.

8.3 domingo, segunda-feira, terça-feira, quarta-feira, quinta-feira,
sexta-feira, sábado.

8.4.1 i abre ii fecha iii começa iv parte v chega vi parte vii chega
viii passa.

8.4.2 ii À meia-noite. iii Ao meio-dia. iv Às duas e um quarto
(*or* quinze) da tarde. v Às dez e meia (*or* trinta) da noite. vi À uma
da tarde. vii Às dez e vinte da manhã. viii Às quatro da tarde menos
um quarto *or* A um quarto para as quatro da tarde. *Your answers
are also right if you have used the words* hora(s) *and* minutos
*throughout, e.g., for* viii Às quatro horas da tarde menos quinze
minutos *or* Aos quinze minutos para as quatro horas da tarde.

8.5.2 Tenho 1 cabelo louro, ondulado, comprido, tenho olhos
verdes e pele clara. 2 cabelo loiro, liso, curto, tenho olhos
castanhos e pele clara. 3 cabelo castanho, ondulado, comprido,
tenho olhos azuis e pele morena. 4 cabelo grisalho, frisado, curto,
tenho olhos castanhos e pele morena. 5 cabelo preto, crespo, curto,
tenho olhos pretos e pele morena. 6 cabelo ruivo, liso, comprido,
tenho olhos azuis e pele clara.

8.5.3 i Ela tem cabelo louro (*or* loiro), muito liso e comprido,
tem olhos azuis e pele clara. ii Ele tem cabelo grisalho, ondulado
e curto, tem olhos pretos e pele muito morena. iii Ele tem cabelo
castanho, frisado/crespo e muito curto, tem olhos castanhos e pele
morena. iv Ela tem cabelo ruivo, ondulado e muito comprido, tem
olhos verdes e pele clara.

## Unit 9

9.1 certo 3, errado 1, 2.

9.2 1 a. 2 c. 3 b.

**9.3.1** Naquela esquina ali com o semáforo, você vira à esquerda, depois segue em frente, na terceira transversal vira à direita e depois toma a primeira rua à esquerda. A piscina é aí, à esquerda.
**9.3.2** Naquela esquina ali com o semáforo, a senhora vira à esquerda, depois segue em frente... (*as above*).
**9.4.2** 1 Vou vestir terno marrom claro. 2 Vou estar vestida de saia e jaqueta cinza e blusa vermelha. 3 Vou vestir casaco laranja escuro, calças verdes e camiseta branca. 4 Vou estar vestido de blusão preto, calças de ganga azuis e camisa amarela.
**9.4.3** Para viajar normalmente visto 2 (uma) saia e jaqueta e (uma) blusa. 3 (um) casaco, (umas) calças e (uma) camiseta. 4 (um) blusão, (umas) calças de ganga e (uma) camisa.
**9.4.4** *Numbers 1 and 2* (terno marrom, saia e jaqueta cinza).
**9.4.5** i É aquela senhora de blusa (cor de) rosa e saia verde. ii É aquele senhor de camisa branca e calças castanhas (Eur.)/ calça marrom (Br.). *Your reply would also have been correct if you had said* com (uma/s) *throughout:* É aquela senhora com blusa, etc. *or* É aquela senhora com uma blusa, etc.
**9.5** 1 O senhor, por favor, como se chama? 2 Eu? Chamo-me Valdemar Nascimento. 3 Por favor! Esta é a pessoa que se chama Mauro de Sá. 4 Aquele senhor? Eu penso que ele se chama Fernando Camargo. 5 Desculpe a pergunta, a senhora chama-se Flávia Couto? 6 Não, não me chamo Flávia Couto. Chamo-me Rute Bento.

## Unit 10
**10.1** certo 1, errado 2 3.
**10.2** 1 c. 2 b. 3 c.
**10.3** Onde eles moram faz vento no outono, neva no inverno, chove na primavera e faz (muito) sol e calor / está (muito) quente no verão.
**10.4.1** ii junho, julho; mau tempo iii agosto; muito calor iv março, abril; chove muito v dezembro, janeiro, fevereiro; muito quente vi setembro, outubro, novembro; sol, um pouco frio.
**10.4.2** i Na minha terra maio é na primavera e faz bom tempo. ii Na terra do meu marido em junho e julho é inverno e faz mau tempo. iii Na terra da minha esposa agosto é um mês de verão e faz muito calor. iv Na terra dos meus avós é outono em março e abril e chove muito. v Aquele rapaz é de uma terra onde em dezembro, janeiro e fevereiro é verão e está muito quente. vi Estas crianças são

de uma terra onde em setembro, outubro e novembro é primavera
e faz sol mas está um pouco frio.
10.4.3 Fez mau tempo. Esteve / fez frio, fez vento, choveu, houve
nevoeiro e não fez sol (estava ventando... (Br.)).
10.5.1 Normalmente eu levanto-me / me levanto (Br.) às sete
(horas), saio de casa às oito, volto para casa às oito e meia da noite
e deito-me às onze (da noite).
10.5.2 Ontem eu levantei-me / me levantei (Br.) às oito (horas), saí de
casa às nove, voltei para casa às dez da noite e deitei-me à meia noite.
10.5.3 Normalmente ele levanta-se / se levanta (Br.) às sete
(horas), sai de casa às oito, volta para casa às oito e meia da noite e
deita-se às onze (da noite).
10.5.4 Ontem ele levantou-se / se levantou (Br.) às oito (horas),
saiu de casa às nove, voltou para casa às dez da noite e deitou-se à
meia noite.

## Unit 11
11.1.1 i norte. ii sul. iii este. iv leste. v oeste. vi nordeste.
vii sudeste. viii noroeste. ix sudoeste.
11.1.2 (Fica / É) no + *cardinal point as above.*
11.2.1 i d; ii c; iii f; iv e; v b; vi a.
11.2.2 i fez sol a sul do Rio Tejo; ii fez vento nordeste-sudoeste;
iii choveu a norte do Rio Tejo; iv esteve muito nublado a norte do
Rio Douro; v estiveram vinte e seis graus centígrados em Lisboa;
vi estiveram vinte e quatro graus centígrados no Porto.
11.2.3 i Fez mais calor em Lisboa. ii A temperatura esteve mais
baixa no Porto. iii Fez bom tempo no Sul. iv Esteve muito nublado
a norte do Rio Douro. v Fez (sim), fez vento / ventou (Br.) de
nordeste. vi Choveu a norte do Rio Tejo.
11.3.1 Queria fazer uma reserva para Curitiba para amanhã à
noite.// À noite tem o Executivo.// A que horas parte?// Às vinte
e duas e quarenta e cinco.// Está bem. Queria "não fumante",
somente ida.// O ônibus é todo "não fumante". É proibido fumar.//
Certo.// Aqui está a passagem da senhora. Poltrona quinze no
Executivo das dez e quarenta e cinco amanhã à noite. O ônibus sai
da primeira plataforma.
11.3.2 Queria fazer uma reserva para Lisboa para amanhã de
manhã.// De manhã tem o Intercidades.// A que horas parte?// Às dez
e vinte e cinco.// Está bem.// "Fumador" ou "não fumador"?// "Não

fumador", somente ida.// Quer lugar junto à janela?// Quero, sim.
Obrigada.// Aqui está o bilhete da senhora. Lugar vinte e dois
na carruagem vinte e um do Intercidades das dez e vinte e cinco
amanhã de manhã. O comboio sai da linha número dois.

11.4.2 a de água, l de longe, p de praia e h de homem.

11.5.1 i Onde é que o senhor mora? ii Onde é que tu moras?

11.5.2 ii Moro na Rua da Aldeia Norte, número 42 (quarenta
e dois).

11.6.1 i Pode me levar para este endereço? ii Can you take me
to this address? iii a Pode me levar para a Rua do Atlântico
número cem? b Faça o favor de me levar para a Rua do Atlântico
número cem.

11.7.1 i B; ii A; iii C.

11.7.2 i Esta rua é perpendicular à rua do jardim. Você segue em
frente até chegar lá. ii Você toma a primeira rua à direita, depois
(você) vira à esquerda e continua nessa rua. O jardim fica em
frente. iii Você vai em frente. Na primeira transversal (você) vira
à esquerda. O jardim fica nessa rua, mas antes de chegar lá (você)
tem que passar duas ruas à direita.

11.7.3 *With* o senhor / a senhora (*no other changes*).

11.8.1 i A minha filha é aquela senhora de biquíni (cor de) rosa.
ii Minha irmã é aquela senhora de maiô (cor de) laranja e cabelo
loiro comprido. iii O meu pai é aquele senhor de calções de banho
pretos e muito moreno.

11.8.2 i A minha neta é aquela senhora que está sentada. ii A
minha mãe é aquela senhora que está deitada. iii Meu avô é aquele
senhor que está em pé *or* de pé.

11.8.3 i A minha (Eur.) / Minha (Br.) amiga é aquela senhora de
biquíni vermelho e muito morena, que está em pé or de pé. ii O
meu (Eur.) / Meu (Br.) amigo é aquele senhor de calções de banho
verdes (Eur.) / calção de banho verde (Br.) e cabelo preto, que está
deitado. *Alternative:* de tanga (Eur.) / sunga (Br.) verde.

11.9.1 i Chamo-me Álvaro Maia. ii Sou de Maputo, em
Moçambique. iii Tenho dezoito anos. iv Moro aqui na África
do Sul. v Moro aqui há dois anos. vi Vou sair daqui no próximo
ano. vii Moro com os meus pais, a minha irmã e o meu irmão.
viii A terra dos meus pais é Portugal. ix No próximo ano vou

para o norte de Portugal. **x** Quero ser médico. **xi** Vou estudar na Universidade do Porto.

**11.9.2 ii** De onde é que tu és? **iii** Quantos anos é que tu tens? **iv** Onde é que tu moras? **v** Há quanto tempo é que moras aqui? **vi** Quando é que vais sair daqui? **vii** Com quem é que tu moras? **viii** Qual é que é a terra dos teus pais? **ix** Para onde é que tu vais no próximo ano? **x** O que é que tu queres ser profissionalmente? **xi** Em que universidade é que tu vais estudar?

**11.11** Parabéns no seu vigésimo quinto aniversário. Muitas felicidades. *or* Parabéns pelo seu vigésimo quinto aniversário. Muitas felicidades.

**11.12** e Feliz Ano Novo *or* e Próspero Ano Novo *or* e Boas entradas.

## Unit 12

**12.1 1** b. **2** a. **3** b. **4** a. **5** c.

**12.2.2 ii** A senhora tem que introduzir as moedas, pressionar a tecla onde diz "açúcar", esperar um pouco e depois retirar o troco e o café.

**12.2.3 ii** A senhora introduz as moedas, pressiona a tecla onde diz "açúcar", espera um pouco e depois retira o troco e o café.

**12.2.4 ii** Introduza as moedas, pressione a tecla onde diz "açúcar", espere um pouco e depois retire o troco e o café.

**12.2.5** The machine is out of order.

**12.3 1** Queria... **2** Quanto é? / custa? **3** Prefiro... **4** Um pouco mais / menos, por favor / faz favor (Eur.). **5** Está bem / certo. **6** Só isso, obrigado/a *or* É tudo, obrigado/a **7** Quanto é tudo? / custa tudo? *or* Quanto é / custa ao todo? **8** Pode me dar um saco / uma sacola (Br.)?

**12.4** Queria **i** isso que está à sua frente. **ii** esta lata de cerveja. **iii** quatro fatias daquele fiambre (Eur.) / presunto (Br.). **iv** mais ou menos meio quilo destas maçãs. **v** uma garrafa de vinho, uma dessas de litro. **vi** duzentos e cinquenta gramas daquele queijo, o terceiro a contar da esquerda.

**12.5.1** Stand on the right, walk on the left.

**12.5.2** Na escada rolante mantenham-se à direita, caminhem pela esquerda.

**12.5.3** Na escada rolante mantém-te à direita, caminha pela esquerda.

## Unit 13

**13.1** 1 c. 2 c. 3 b. 4 a. 5 a.

**13.2.1** i o ii 4, 6 iii o, 2 iv 3, 5, 7 v 4, 5, 9 vi 5, 3, 47.

**13.2.2** i Custa nove mil e oitocentos. ii Vai custar quarenta e quatro mil, quinhentos e sessenta. iii Vai custar setecentos mil, cento e vinte e dois. iv Custará talvez treze milhões, seiscentos e trinta e cinco mil, setecentos e setenta e um. v Não sei se custará quarenta e oito milhões, quinhentos e sete mil, novecentos e seis. vi Há de custar menos de noventa e cinco milhões, trezentos e trinta mil, oitocentos e quarenta e sete.

**13.2.3** ii Noventa e nove reais. iii Quinhentos reais. iv Dois mil e vinte e cinco reais. v Trinta e um euros e meio. vi Quarenta e sete euros. vii Duzentos euros. viii Dois mil e setenta euros.

**13.3.2** *The following items in this or other order:* Três sandes (Eur.) / sanduíches de fiambre, uma sandes (Eur.) /sanduíche de queijo, um iogurte de banana, duas cervejas, um café com leite e sem açúcar, um café sem leite e com açúcar e uma água mineral.

**13.3.4** Teremos que esperar muito tempo?

**13.3.5** A água mineral e o iogurte são para a senhora de camiseta / t-shirt vermelha e o café com leite e uma das sandes (Eur.) / sanduíches de fiambre são para o senhor de camisa verde.

**13.3.6** A conta, por favor.

**13.3.7** Pode ficar com o troco.

**13.4.1** i É favor não incomodar. ii Não incomode, por favor.

**13.4.2** i Já pode arrumar o quarto, por favor. ii Quando é que o quarto estará pronto?

**13.5.2** Será possível ter os roupões prontos antes de 5ª.-feira? Obrigada.

## Unit 14

**14.1** 1 c. 2 i c, ii b. 3 c. 4 b. 5 b.

**14.2.2** Comprei esta quando estava no Algarve e esta quando estava na Serra da Estrela.

**14.2.3** *In the preterite* (comprei) *and the imperfect* (estava), *for a point in time* (comprei) *within the period of time of her stay* (estava).

**14.2.4** Estive lá no ano passado. Fui em março e voltei dois meses depois, em maio.

14.2.5 i Quando é que você esteve lá? ii Quando é que (tu) estiveste lá?

14.3.1 i Este vestido está muito curto. Tem outro mais comprido do que este? ii Este vestido está muito apertado. Tem outro mais folgado do que este?

14.3.2 i Este vestido está muito comprido. Tem outro menos comprido do que este? ii Este vestido está muito folgado. Tem outro menos folgado do que este?

14.4.1 b, g, d, c, f, a, e.

14.4.2 – No meu país calço n° 5 mas aqui não sei que número é.// Cinco… isso será número 37 ou 38. Eu trago três ténis (Eur.) / tênis (Br.), um em 37, um em 38 e um em 39.// (experimentando o n° 37) Este ténis (Eur.) / tênis (Br.) está muito apertado.// Então quer experimentar o n° 38?// (experimentando o n° 38) Este está menos apertado do que o 37, mas está um pouco apertado. // Talvez o número acima, o 39.// (experimentando o n° 39) Este está bem, obrigada. Levo este par.

14.4.3 estava *throughout*.

14.5.1 Por favor, queria ii uns sapatos iii um vestido iv uma gravata v uma saia.

14.5.2 As 14.5.1 *plus* de ii pelica iii linho iv seda v fibra sintética.

14.5.3 As 14.5.2 *plus* ii lisos iii estampado iv listrada / às riscas (Eur.) v xadrez.

14.5.4 As 14.5.3 *plus* em ii azul escuro iii amarelo e verde iv preto e vermelho v duas ou três cores diferentes.

14.5.5 i Comprei estes sapatos na semana passada. ii Comprei esta camisa na 2ª.-feira passada e esta gravata na 4ª.-feira passada. iii Quando é que (tu) compraste esses sapatos / essa camisa e essa gravata?

## Unit 15

15.1 1 b. 2 c. 3 b. 4 c. 5 b. 6 b.

15.2.1 i Não, não vai. ii (Ela) vai a cavalo.

15.2.2 i Gosto de andar a cavalo. ii Ando a cavalo todos os sábados. iii Andei a cavalo no sábado passado.

15.2.3 Eu encontrei o Raul quando (eu) estava a andar a cavalo (Eur.) / estava andando a cavalo (Br.) no sábado passado. Ele também estava a andar (Eur.) / estava andando (Br.) a cavalo.

15.2.4 I met Raul when I was horse riding last Saturday. He was also horse riding *or* riding a horse. (*Sally met Raul when she was horse riding, and they were both horse riding at the same time.*)

15.3.1 a, f, c, b, e, d.

15.3.2 Tu falas Português muito bem. / Obrigado. Tu és muito amável. Eu ainda faço muitos erros. Corrige-me, está bem? / Está. Há quanto tempo aprendes Português? / Há dois meses. / Há só dois meses!? Como consegues aprender tão rapidamente? / Estudando um pouco todos os dias.

15.4.1 Do you accept this credit card? / Yes, we do.

15.4.2 i Aceitamos. ii Pode. iii Não, não tem.

15.5.2 i O clube abre às oito horas da noite. ii O jantar começa às oito horas e trinta (da noite). iii O museu está aberto até às dezasseis (Eur.) / as dezesseis (Br.) horas. iv A primeira matiné começa às quinze horas. v Há futebol no domingo. vi Não, não está. (Fecha às seis horas). vii A piscina está aberta a partir das oito horas da manhã. viii A biblioteca fecha às nove horas da noite. ix Pode. (A partir das nove horas.) x Não, não está. (Está aberta toda a noite.) xi O horário de atendimento do médico de clínica geral é das dezassete (Eur.) / dezessete (Br.) às vinte horas. xii Sim, ainda vai. (A terceira tiragem (Eur.) / coleta (Br.) é às vinte e uma horas.)

15.5.3 i Não, começa às nove e meia. ii Está aberta toda a noite. iii Não, só a partir das dezassete (Eur.) / dezessete (Br.) horas. iv Às onze horas.

15.5.4 i A soiré começa antes das nove horas? ii Até que horas é que a farmácia está aberta? iii No médico, há consultas de manhã? iv À que horas abre a galeria de arte?

15.5.5 i A que horas é que o restaurante abre? ii A que horas é que a soiré começa? iii Até que horas é que a farmácia está aberta hoje à noite / esta noite? iv A que horas é que o museu fecha?

## Unit 16

16.1 1 b, 2 a, 3 d, 4 c, 6 e, 7 f.

16.2 1 Amanhã, sábado, trabalho. 2 Amanhã vou trabalhar. 3 Provavelmente trabalharei amanhã *or* amanhã trabalharei. 4 Amanhã hei de trabalhar. 5 Agora não posso. Estou a trabalhar. (Eur.) / Agora não posso. Estou trabalhando. (Br.) 6 Trabalhei ontem, sábado. 7 Hugo telefonou ontem quando eu estava a trabalhar

(Eur.) / Hugo telefonou ontem quando eu estava trabalhando (Br.)
8 Eu trabalhava aos sábados, mas agora não trabalho. *or*
Eu costumava trabalhar aos sábados, mas agora não trabalho.
**16.3.1** i Está atrasado. ii Está adiantado.
**16.3.2** i Bernardo. ii Gonçalo.
**16.4.1** Importa-se de verificar esta conta. A conta está errada. Três
mil, trezentos e sessenta de bolos e bebidas mais trezentos e trinta e
seis de serviço não são três mil, setecentos e noventa e seis. São três
mil, seiscentos e noventa e seis.
**16.4.2** três mais três igual a seis, não igual a sete *or* três mais três
são seis, não são sete.
**16.5** 1 Façam o favor de falar mais baixo. 2 Por favor, queiram
falar mais baixo. 3 Querem falar mais baixo, por favor? 4 Falem
mais baixo!
**16.6.1** i carregue. ii Press to open. iii To obtain 'green' press here.
Thank you. iv Carregar para abrir. Para obter verde carregar aqui.
(Eur.)
**16.6.2** i Carregue para abrir. ii Tem que carregar para abrir.
iii Quer carregar para abrir? iv Queira carregar para abrir. v Faça o
favor de carregar para abrir. (Eur.)
**16.6.3** i Carregue para obter verde. ii Tem que carregar para obter
verde. iii Quer carregar para obter verde? iv Queira carregar para
obter verde. v Faça o favor de carregar para obter verde. (Eur.)
**16.6.4** a Aperte para abrir. b Para obter verde aperte aqui.
Obrigado. (Br.)
**16.6.5** Apertar para abrir. Para obter verde apertar aqui. (Br.)
**16.6.6** i Aperte para abrir. ii Tem que apertar para abrir. iii Quer
apertar para abrir? iv Queira apertar para abrir. v Faça o favor de
apertar para abrir. (Br.)
**16.6.7** i Aperte para obter verde. ii Tem que apertar para obter
verde. iii Quer apertar para obter verde? iv Queira apertar para
obter verde. v Faça o favor de apertar para obter verde. (Br.)
**16.7.1** a pé.
**16.7.2** Ontem fui a pé.
**16.7.3** Amanhã vou a pé.
**16.7.4** Como é que tu vais para as aulas de Português? *or* Como é
que vais para as aulas de Português? *or* Como vais para as aulas de
Português?

**16.8 a** Pode me dar o horário dos comboios? **b** Pode me dar a tabela de horário dos trens? *or* Pode me dar o horário dos trens?

**16.9.1** Tem um voo para Brasília amanhã de manhã sem escala?// Não, o voo faz escala no Rio.

**16.9.2** Tem um voo para Lisboa amanhã de manhã sem escala?// Não, o voo faz escala no Rio.

**16.10 1 i** O comboio das 15.25 para Tomar é direto ou tem transbordo?// É direto. **ii** O comboio das 15.25 para a Guarda é direto ou tem transbordo?// É direto. **2** trem.

**16.11 1** b, 1 d, 1 e, 2 a, 3 c.

**16.12.2 a 1** trabalho; metro; 20 minutos. **2** colégio; trem; 1/2 hora. **3** biblioteca; autocarro; 1/4 hora. **4** estádio; comboio; 3/4 hora. **5** cinema; ônibus; 10 minutos. **b 1** Normalmente vou para o trabalho de metro. Levo vinte minutos. **2** Eu vou para o colégio de trem (Br.). Levo meia hora. **3** Vou para a biblioteca de autocarro (Eur.). Levo um quarto de hora. **4** Eu vou para o estádio de comboio (Eur.). Levo três quartos de hora. **5** Eu vou para o cinema de ônibus (Br.). Levo dez minutos. **6** Eu vou para a praia de bicicleta. Levo cinco minutos mais ou menos.

**16.12.3 ii** Agora normalmente vou de autocarro mas costumava ir de metro. (Eur.) / Agora normalmente vou de ônibus mas costumava ir de metrô. (Br.) **iii** Agora normalmente vou de comboio mas costumava ir de carro. (Eur.) / Agora normalmente vou de trem mas costumava ir de carro. (Br.) **iv** Agora normalmente vou de autocarro mas costumava ir de bicicleta. (Eur.) / Agora normalmente vou de ônibus mas costumava ir de bicicleta. (Br.)

**16.13 1** Aquela menina de cabelo louro (*or* loiro) comprido e vestido vermelho e branco. **2** Aquele rapaz que está em pé (*or* de pé) junto da (*or* à) venda automática de café. *Your reply is equally correct if you have said* máquina de venda automática de café. **3** Aquela senhora de biquíni preto que está a falar (Eur.) / falando (Br.) junto do (or ao) carro amarelo. **4** Aquele senhor de cabelo preto curto e camisa listrada / às/com riscas (Eur.) que está sentado a ler (Eur.) / lendo (Br.) o jornal.

**16.14.2 1** Para a cave. **2** Para o segundo. **3** Para o rés-do-chão (Eur.).

**16.14.3 i** Por favor, pode me dar a chave do quarto (*or* do apartamento, *depending on type of hotel*) número quatro – três – nove. **ii** Por favor, pode me dar a chave do quarto (*or* do apartamento) número quatrocentos e trinta e nove.

**16.15.1** *Boxes ticked for:* 08.00–08.30; torradas; geleia; manteiga; laranja; café; leite; ovos cozidos; presunto. *Special requirements:* ovo bem cozido, leite magro (Eur.) e pão integral.

**16.15.2** Before going to bed, please hang your breakfast order form on the outside handle of your door. (*lit. Before going to bed, could you please hang (this form) on the outside door handle.*)

**16.15.3** Bom dia. Esqueci-me de pendurar na maçaneta da porta o cartão para pedir o pequeno-almoço (Eur.) (café da manhã (Br.) *if you were in Brazil*). Ainda posso pedir? // Pode, sim. O que deseja? // Queria ovo cozido, torradas, presunto, manteiga, geleia, sumo (Eur.) de laranja, café e leite.// Prefere o ovo bem ou mal cozido? // Bem cozido. E só mais duas coisas, desculpe. Prefiro leite magro (Eur.) e pão integral. Terei que esperar muito tempo? // Não, meia hora mais ou menos.

**16.16** 1 c, 2 a, 3 d, 4 n, 5 g, 6 b, 7 j, 8 m, 9 e, 10 f, 11 h, 12 k, 13 i, 14 l.

**16.17.1** i The word 'alimentação', food store. ii The shop window. iii In the centre. iv Shelves. v A door to the back.

**16.17.2** ii a A caixa que A quer está em cima do balcão. b A caixa que B quer está perto da montra (Eur.) / vitrine (Br.). c A caixa que D quer está dentro do balcão. d A pessoa que prefere uma das caixas pequenas em volta da caixa grande é D *or* D é a pessoa que prefere... e Quem quer uma caixa que está na segunda prateleira a contar de baixo, atrás do balcão, é C *or* C é quem quer uma caixa...

**16.18.1** Estou só a ver (Eur.) / Estou só olhando (Br.).

**16.18.2** Onde posso encontrar uma loja que vende guarda-sóis? *or* Onde é que posso encontrar uma loja que venda guarda-sóis?

**16.18.3** Pay at the cash desk and take the voucher / receipt stub back to the assistant who has been serving you.

**16.19.1** i Às oito (horas) e quarenta e três (minutos). ii Às vinte e cinquenta e cinco. iii Às duas e cinquenta. iv Às quinze e quinze.

**16.19.2** i Estará, sim. *or* Está, sim. (*no doubt*). ii Estará, sim *or* Está, sim.

**16.20.1** Pode me dizer onde é o aluguer (Eur.) / aluguel (Br.) de cadeiras de praia e guarda-sóis? *Alternatives:* Pode me dizer onde se alugam cadeiras de praia e guarda-sóis? *or* Pode me dizer onde posso alugar cadeira / cadeiras de praia e um guarda-sol?

**16.20.2** i Queria alugar duas cadeiras de praia por um dia. ii Queria alugar um guarda-sol por meio dia.

**16.20.3** i Quanto são as cadeiras de praia por um dia? *or* Quanto custam as cadeiras de praia por um dia? ii Quanto é o guarda-sol por meio dia? *or* Quanto custa o guarda-sol por meio dia?

## Unit 17

**17.1** 1 c. 2 b. 3 b. 4 b. 5 b.

**17.2.1** i Quer deitar-se? ii Quer levantar-se e sentar-se? iii Quer levantar-se? *Your reply is also correct if you have said* i Quer se deitar? ii Quer se levantar e sentar? iii Quer se levantar?

**17.2.2** Faça favor de i sentar-se ii deitar-se iii levantar-se. *Your reply is also correct if you have said* Faça o favor de i se sentar ii se deitar iii se levantar.

**17.2.3** Queira i sentar-se ii deitar-se iii levantar-se. *Your reply is also correct if you have said* Queira i se sentar ii se deitar iii se levantar.

**17.2.4** Sente-se ii Deite-se iii Levante-se.

**17.2.5** ii Deitem-se iii Levantem-se.

**17.2.6** ii Deita-te iii Levanta-te.

**17.2.7** i Sentem-se ii Deitem-se iii Levantem-se.

**17.3** Queira i despir *or* tirar o (seu) casaco. ii descalçar *or* tirar as (suas) botas. iii tirar o (seu) chapéu.

**17.4.1** Dói-me i muito a garganta desde domingo passado. ii um dente há dois dias. iii muito o ouvido direito desde ontem à noite. iv um pouco aqui desde quarta-feira passada.

**17.4.2** i Já me despi. ii Já tirei a roupa.

**17.4.3** i every six hours. ii twice a day. iii every other day.

**17.5** 1 Sim, sou. 2 Sofro do coração. 3 (Sou,) sim, sou alérgica a penicilina. 4 Não, não tomei. 5 Deve avisar meu marido, Óscar Campos. O número do telefone é quatro três oito, um zero, dois dois.

**17.6** 1 Cuidado! 2 Tem perigo! 3 Depressa! 4 É perigoso! 5 Aqui há perigo! 6 Fogo! 7 Socorro!

**17.7.1** i Walk on the right-hand side of the pavement or hard shoulder. ii Caminhe pelo lado direito do passeio ou da berma.

**17.7.2** i To cross the road (*cross over*) / – Stop on the pavement / – Look first left and then right to see whether there is a car coming / – If no car is coming, cross over, but keep looking, left the first half of the road and then right. ii Para atravessar / Pare no passeio /

Olhe primeiro para a esquerda e depois para a direita para ver se vem algum carro / Se não vier nenhum, atravesse, olhando novamente para a esquerda até ao meio da rua e depois para a direita.
17.7.3 i Caminhe pelo lado direito da calçada ou do acostamento. ii Para atravessar / Pare na calçada / Olhe primeiro para a esquerda e depois para a direita para ver se vem algum carro / Se não vier nenhum, atravesse, olhando novamente para a esquerda até o meio da rua e depois para a direita.

## Unit 18

18.1 1 c. 2 a. 3 b. 4 a. 5 b.

18.2.1 Afonso, car B; Olavo, car A.

18.2.2 Onde é que o senhor está? // Na estrada de Sagres para Lagos, a mais ou menos 10 km de Sagres. // Precisa de ambulância ou de rebocador? // Não preciso de ambulância. Não há feridos, nem mortos. Mas preciso de um rebocador. O meu carro não funciona / está funcionando (Br.).

18.2.3 1 b, 2 c, 3 a.

18.2.4 Eu seguia / estava seguindo (Br.) pela estrada a 60 km por hora. Na minha frente seguia / estava seguindo (Br.) o carro C, muito lentamente. Eu vi o carro A, que parecia que tinha parado no cruzamento. Eu ultrapassei o carro C, mas o carro A avançou e bateu no meu.

18.3.1 Nunca bebo quando conduzo.

18.3.2 Nunca bebo quando dirijo / estou dirigindo.

18.4.2 i c, ii e, iii a, iv d, v b.

18.5.1 i um pendente / pingente (Br.) (feito) de ouro e em forma de estrela. ii tem cabelo preto e está vestido de camiseta / t-shirt branca e calças de ganga azuis (Eur) / calça de zuarte or brim azul (Br.). *Your answer would also be correct in the past tense (he might have changed his clothes or dyed his hair a different colour in the meantime)* tinha cabelo preto e estava vestido de camiseta / t-shirt branca e calças de ganga azuis (Eur) / calça de brim azul (Br.).

18.5.2 i é/era um carro verde escuro. *or* o carro é/era verde escuro. ii tem (*or* deve ter) uns quarenta anos (*or* mais ou menos quarenta anos), tem/tinha cabelo louro curto e está/estava vestido de camisa amarela.

**18.6** 1 b, 2 a.

**18.7.1** i É grave. ii A partir de 53 km/hr. iii Suspensão da carteira da habilitação (Br.) / carteira de motorista (Br.) / carta de condução (Eur.) por 2 a 7 meses.

**18.7.2** i Watch out if you speed / Beware of speeding. ii Rushing and safety never go well together (*lit.* never go the same way), *play on the different meanings of the word* mão: hand *and* flow of traffic.

## Unit 19

**19.1** 1 b. 2 c. 3 a. 4 a. 5 c.

**19.2.1** i B, ii A, iii B, iv B, v A.

**19.2.2** Todos os dias, faço jogging / cooper (Br.) de manhã cedo. Aos fins de semana, pratico esqui aquático, quando faz bom tempo; e praticaria mais vezes, se tivesse mais tempo.

**19.3.2** A Madeira tem plantas raras? E animais?// Sim, tem. A Madeira é praticamente uma reserva natural, sendo dois terços do território Área Protegida onde abunda fauna e flora raras. // Que passeios a pé tem para pessoas que não estão em boa forma? // Tem passeios suaves. Para os que não se querem meter em grandes aventuras, tem os belos passeios ao longo das "levadas". // Desculpe. Não compreendo. O que significa "levadas"? // "Levadas" significa pequenos canais de irrigação artificiais. // E que passeios tem para os mais aventureiros? // Para os mais aventureiros tem muitos trilhos, que estão bem assinalados com placas e que levam às montanhas. // O que tem para quem joga golfe? // Para quem joga golfe tem muita coisa, incluindo dois campos para campeonatos. // Pode fazer-se mergulho e vela? // Pode, sim. A Madeira, sendo uma ilha, é rica em desportos aquáticos. // Só mais uma pergunta. Seria possível fazer pesca de alto mar? // É, sim. E é possível pescar espadim azul com mais de 500 kg.

**19.4.1** à sombra. ao sol.

**19.4.2** i Não comprou. ii Porque já não havia mais lugares nas bancadas à sombra. iii Teria. *or* Teria, sim.

**19.5** 2 O Carnaval. 3 Com muita antecedência. 4 Escolas de samba. 5 Por toda a parte. Na rua. 6 **a** os passistas, **b** a bateria, **c** as fantasias.

**19.6.1** trezentos e três (*or* zero zero três, zero três), setor nove, fila C, lugar um (*or* primeiro *or* número um *or* zero zero um).

**19.6.2** i You have an odd number but are on the even-number side. ii Go to the southern side, the other side of the boulevard.

19.7 1 Desculpe. Parece que perdi o bilhete de transporte. 2 Achei o bilhete de transporte. Aqui tem. *or* Aqui está.

## Unit 20

20.1 1 a. 2 b. 3 c. 4 c. 5 b.

20.2 1 Faz favor, traga-me a ementa. 2 O cardápio, por favor. 3 Queríamos uma mesa para quatro, longe da porta, se possível. 4 Pode trazer mais pão? 5 Queria experimentar um prato típico desta região.

20.3 Traga-me 1 um copo de água, por favor. 2 uma chávena (Eur.) / xícara (Br.) de chá, por favor. 3 uma chávena (Eur.) / xícara (Br.) de café, por favor. 4 uma caneca de cerveja, por favor. 5 um cálice de porto, por favor. 6 uma taça de champanhe, por favor.

20.4.2 Paraty ↔ para ti: Paraty in August is for you (para ti), always.

20.4.3 Vou ao festival da pinga em Paraty. Lá a terra é propícia ao cultivo da cana de açúcar e há séculos que fazem aguardente. Vou beber o que dizem ser uma das melhores pingas do Brasil.

20.4.4 Infelizmente eu não pude ir ao festival. Se tivesse ido, teria bebido o que dizem ser uma das melhores pingas do Brasil.

20.5 A minha / minha (Br.) cidade natal fica (*or* é) 1 na margem de um rio. 2 numa região montanhosa. 3 na costa norte do país. A minha / minha (Br.) cidade natal tem 4 um milhão de habitantes. 5 um clima frio no inverno. 6 indústria de computadores.

20.6 1 Sou escocês. Nasci em Dundee, uma cidade na costa leste da Escócia. Dundee tem um porto grande e um tipo famoso de bolo. 2 Sou galês. Nasci em Caerphilly, uma cidade no sul do País de Gales. Caerphilly tem um castelo antigo e um tipo famoso de queijo.

20.7.2 i Em que consiste o bacalhau Gomes de Sá? ii Em que consiste o bacalhau tropical? iii Em que consiste o bacalhau à moda da casa?

20.7.3 i Preferia um prato que não tivesse cebola. ii Preferia um prato que não tivesse ovo. iii Preferia um prato que não tivesse couve. iv Preferia um prato que não tivesse leite de coco.

## Unit 21

21.1 1 b. 2 b. 3 c. 4 b.

21.2 1 À ordem de Fernando Costa Machado. 2 Sessenta mil euros. 3 Falta o ano na data.

21.3 1 Queria descontar este cheque. 2 Onde é que estão as guias de depósito? 3 Isto é o recibo de depósito? 4 Queria ver o meu saldo. 5 A quanto está a libra hoje? E quanto é a comissão?

21.4.1 *At service hatch* 1: b, e, f. *At service hatch* 2: no one. *At service hatch* 3: a, c, d.

21.4.2 a Que preciso fazer para ter uma posta restante? b Faz favor, queria enviar esta carta registada. c Tem algumas cartas para Donald Cooper? d Tem alguma coisa em nome de Alison Davies? e Quanto custa enviar isto para os Estados Unidos, registado? f Quanto custa enviar este pacote para Inglaterra, por via aérea, registrado (Br.)?

21.5.2 i a, c. ii e, d, b, f.

21.6.2 1 A Torre de Belém. 2 A UNESCO 3 O estilo manuelino é um estilo ornamental arquitetónico (Eur.) / arquitetônico (Br.) português. (Data do fim do século quinze e principalmente do século dezasseis (Eur.) / dezesseis (Br.), época de grandeza para Portugal que coincide com o reinado de Dom Manuel; daí o nome "manuelino".) 4 Cabo da Boa Esperança. 5 Vasco da Gama chegou à Índia em 1498 e Álvares Cabral chegou ao Brasil em 1500. 6 *Three out of* pilares em espiral, cordame, esferas armilares e a cruz da Ordem de Cristo.

21.7.2 Olá, Georgina! / Tudo bem? Aqui faz bom tempo, a comida é boa e eu estou bem. Ontem fui visitar a Torre de Belém. Data do século XVI e tem (*or* apresenta) todas as características individualizantes do estilo manuelino. O estilo manuelino é um estilo ornamental arquitetónico (Eur.) / arquitetônico (Br.) português. Inclui pilares em espiral, cordame, esferas armilares e a cruz da Ordem de Cristo. / Um beijo do Phil.

### Unit 22

22.1.2 i Como é que a senhora quer o cabelo? // Eu quero uma franja bem curta, e dos lados e atrás quero cortar só um pouco. ii Como é que o senhor quer o cabelo? // Quero bem curto atrás e penteado para trás. iii Como é que a senhora quer as unhas? // Quero cortar só um pouco e quero esmalte incolor. iv De que cor é que a senhora quer o verniz?// Vermelho escuro.

22.1.3 Quero i bem curto. ii cortar só um pouco dos lados e atrás. iii penteado para trás. iv penteado para o lado direito.

**22.2.2** Você retira o auscultador (Eur.) / fone (Br.) do gancho e aguarda o sinal de discar; disca primeiro estes números e depois o número do telefone desejado; e aguarda o sinal de tocar.

**22.2.3** Retire o auscultador (Eur.) / fone (Br.) do gancho e aguarde o sinal de discar; disque primeiro estes números e depois o número do telefone desejado; e aguarde o sinal de tocar.

**22.3.1** (A) Qual é o indicativo (Eur.) da região? (B) Qual é o código (Br.) da região?

**22.3.2** Este sinal quer dizer ocupado?

**22.3.3** Penso que a ligação foi cortada.

**22.4.1** i "Trenzinho" significa "pequeno trem" ou "trem pequeno" *or* "Trenzinho" quer dizer "pequeno trem" ou "trem pequeno". ii O Cristo Redentor é o principal ponto turístico do Rio. iii Passear no trem é fazer uma viagem pela história do Brasil.

**22.4.2** Querido Simão // (Aqui) faz bom tempo, a comida é boa e eu estou bem. Ontem fui ao Corcovado de trenzinho. Este ponto turístico é visitado por mais de 250 mil pessoas por ano. Na viagem aprecia-se (o passageiro aprecia) uma linda vista. / Um beijo do + *your name* (*if you are male*) // Um beijo da + *your name* (*if you are female*) *Alternatives*: Saudades e beijinhos / Saudades. Um abraço.

**22.5** Como é que se diz "dot" em Português?

**22.6.1** i (Eu) tenciono passar uma semana nesse país. Estou especialmente interessado (*if you are male*) / interessada (*female*) num hotel perto de uma praia. Peço que façam o favor (*or* tenham a gentileza) de me enviarem a lista dos hotéis perto de uma praia. Fico aguardando resposta e desde já agradeço. ii (Eu) tenciono passar dois meses nesse país. Estou especialmente interessado (*if you are male*) / interessada (*female*) num parque de campismo (Eur.) / camping (Br.) com facilidades / instalações para crianças. Peço que façam o favor (*or* tenham a gentileza) de me enviarem a lista dos parques de campismo (Eur.) / campings (Br.) com facilidades para crianças. Fico aguardando resposta e desde já agradeço. iii (Eu) tenciono passar um mês nesse país. Estou especialmente interessado (*if you are male*) / interessada (*female*) num albergue (da juventude) com facilidades / instalações para deficientes físicos. Peço que façam o favor (*or* tenham a gentileza) de me enviarem a lista dos albergues (da juventude) com facilidades / instalações para deficientes físicos. Fico aguardando resposta e desde já agradeço.

**22.6.2** i Caros Senhores *or* Prezados Senhores. ii Cordialmente.

**Unit 23**

23.1.2 reuno; possuo; possam.

23.1.3 Tenho / Possuo i um diploma profissional. ii bons conhecimentos de informática. iii um elevado grau de autonomia e professionalismo.

23.2 Incomplete address, not providing enough information.

23.3.2 i Em Guimarães. ii Ana Isabel Vieira Gama. iii Não, sou médica. iv Na Universidade de Coimbra. v Não, não fiz. vi Não, trabalho numa clínica.

23.4 1 and 4.

23.5 Tencionamos visitar esse país em junho do ano que vem. Precisamos de um apartamento para casal. Preferíamos a primeira semana do mês. / Se o hotel não tiver vagas nesses dias, pedimos que façam o favor de informarem para quando podem fazer a reserva em nosso nome, Sanders. Ficamos aguardando resposta (com grande interesse).

23.6.2 O apartamento tem três quartos de dormir, um sendo de casal. A sala de estar fica à esquerda de quem entra e, a seguir, fica a sala de jantar. A cozinha fica mais ou menos em frente da sala de estar e tem uma porta perto da sala de jantar. A cozinha tem fogão, micro-ondas, lava-louça..., tudo o que precisamos. A sala de estar tem uma lareira, para os dias frios. Claro que tem sofá, poltrona, mesinha de centro e televisor. Tem também uma estante e aparelho de som. O apartamento não é muito grande mas é bom.

23.7.2 convenha; façam; poderei *or* vou poder *or* posso.

23.7.3 Uma pessoa que queira comprar.

23.7.4 Em resposta ao anúncio n° 27036 desse jornal, tenho o prazer de comunicar que estou interessada em comprar uma casa e essa talvez me convenha. Fico aguardando que façam o favor de informar quando a poderei ver. (*or* vou poder *or* posso)

**Unit 24**

24.1 já não há mais 1, 4, 5; ainda 2, 3, 6.

24.2 É um lugar, um restaurante, onde se canta o fado. // É uma canção portuguesa acerca da experiência da vida. O "amor" é um tema frequente, mas há uma grande variedade de temas. // São os dois instrumentos dedilhados que normalmente acompanham a pessoa que canta o fado, o fadista ou a fadista.

24.3.1 i Faça as camas todas. ii Limpe a casa de banho (Eur.) / o banheiro (Br.). iii Arrume a sala de estar. iv Passe o aspirador na sala de estar e na sala de jantar. v Passe a ferro a roupa que foi lavada ontem. vi Prepare o jantar. vii Ponha a mesa para o jantar. viii Depois do jantar, tire a mesa e lave a louça. ix Leve o lixo lá para baixo. x Dê de comer ao gato.

24.3.2 Hoje precisa (de) i fazer as camas todas. ii limpar a casa de banho (Eur.) / o banheiro (Br.). iii arrumar a sala de estar. iv passar o aspirador na sala de estar e na sala de jantar. v passar a ferro a roupa que foi lavada ontem. vi preparar o jantar. vii pôr a mesa para o jantar. viii depois do jantar, tirar a mesa e lavar a louça. ix levar o lixo lá para baixo. x dar de comer ao gato.

24.4.1 1 c; 2 d; 3 e; 4 b; 5 f; 6 a.

24.4.2 Hard-boil the eggs. Shell them. With a knife, cut them in half lengthways. With a spoon, take out the yolk. Cut the anchovy fillets into small pieces. On a large plate, mix the cut-up anchovy fillets with the egg-yolks and the lemon juice, using a fork. Fill the egg-whites with the mixture. Over the eggs put a bit of mayonnaise and a stuffed olive in the middle. Shred the lettuce and use it to cover the bottom of a serving dish. Place the stuffed eggs on the bed of shredded lettuce.

24.4.3 Descasquei-os. Com uma faca, abri-os ao meio ao comprido. Com uma colher, tirei a gema para fora. Cortei a anchova em bocadinhos. Num prato grande, misturei-a com as gemas e o limão, usando um garfo. Enchi as claras com a mistura. Por cima coloquei um pouco de maionese e uma azeitona no meio. Cobri o fundo de uma travessa com a alface cortada em tirinhas. Coloquei os ovos recheados no leito de alface.

24.5 1 i Diverte-te! ii se divirtam 2 i vê-lo/la / ver você / ver-te ii Fiquei 3 i fazer o favor de ii si / você / ti 4 Saúde!

24.6 No dia 3 de dezembro. E o teu? / O meu é hoje. / Então parabéns! Quantos anos é que tu fazes? / Faço vinte anos. / Tenho de ir comprar um presente para ti. / Não, não te incomodes.

## Unit 25

25.1
– Você sabe falar Português muito bem. Onde aprendeu?
– Aprendi principalmente ensinando a mim própria como autodidata. Mas sentia a falta de pessoas com quem pudesse falar.

Então resolvi passar um tempo em Portugal, dois meses, a praticar e estudar a língua.

– E em Portugal, como estudou?

– Frequentei um curso de PLE na Universidade Nova de Lisboa. Tínhamos aulas de língua todos os dias e de cultura três vezes por semana. No fim do curso submeti-me a um exame. Passei com distinção. Fiquei muito contente.

– Muitos parabéns!

– Obrigada. E aproveitei todas as oportunidades para falar, nas lojas, nos restaurantes, em todos os lados. Gostei muito de Portugal e da sua capital, das pessoas... de tudo. Tive muita pena de vir embora.

– Então vai voltar?

– Vou... vou voltar para um país de língua portuguesa, mas vai ser outro. Quero ir ao Brasil, quero passar dois ou três meses lá.

– E no Brasil, onde vai ficar?

– Ainda não sei, mas gostaria de visitar Brasília.

– Brasília? Por quê?/Porquê? (Eur.)

– Não sei bem... Talvez porque é a capital federal. Talvez (*rindo*) também porque me disseram que Brasília foi construída em forma de avião. Não sei se acredite ou não. O melhor é ir ver.

– (*rindo*) Tem razão. O melhor é ver.

– Ir ao Brasil é também uma boa oportunidade para ouvir outro sotaque e outras expressões.

– Concordo. Acho que faz muito bem. E irá também a alguns países de África onde se fala Português?

– Hei de ir, mas quando ainda não sei.

– Muito obrigada pela entrevista. E muitos parabéns por saber falar Português tão bem, fluentissimamente... e sem erros. Boa sorte para o futuro!

25.2.1 i ask (for). ii (I/he) learned. iii look (for/after). iv tell. v on; off.

25.2.2 i tempo. ii casa. iii perdeu. iv tratar. v deve. vi serve. vii faltam. viii conhece. ix sabe. x fica.

25.3 The quince 'cheese' was stolen by the dog. Johnny took the lid off the box. Piloto knocked the box off the shelf and ate its contents. Absent-minded Sr. Olavo placed the box back on the shelf.

25.4 1 c; 2 e; 3 a; 4 d; 5 b.
25.5.2 i A cultura brasileira. ii A Secretaria de Cultura de Niterói.
iii No Teatro da UFF. iv De 3 de agosto a 10 de dezembro.
25.5.3 Ilmos Senhores, // Tenciono passar seis meses no Brasil no
ano que vem, de julho a dezembro. Estou interessado/a num curso
de introdução à cultura brasileira; e gostaria de participar no curso
da UFF. Venho apresentar a minha candidatura e juntamente envio
(Eur.) / estou enviando (Br.) o meu currículo. Fico aguardando
resposta (com grande interesse) e espero que possam conceder-me
lugar no curso. // Atenciosamente, (*signature*).

---

## Congratulations on reaching the end of
*Complete Portuguese*

I hope you have enjoyed working your way through the course.
I am always keen to receive feedback from people who have used my
course, so why not contact me and let me know your reactions?

You can contact me through the publishers at:

Teach Yourself Books, Hodder Headline Ltd, 338 Euston Road,
London NW1 3BH, UK, or directly via e-mail at the following address:
mcook_typort@hotmail.com

I hope you will want to build up your knowledge of Portuguese and
have made a few suggestions to help you do this in the section
entitled **Taking it further**.

All the best!

*Boa sorte para o futuro!*

Manuela Cook

---

# Glossary of grammatical terms

**adjective** describes or qualifies a noun. The hotel is *good*.
**O hotel é bom.**

**adverb** gives information about a verb. He speaks Portuguese *fluently*. **Ele fala Português *fluentemente*** (Portuguese **-mente** corresponding to English *-ly*). She went *there*. **Ela foi lá.** I can't *now*. **Não posso *agora*.** Some adverbs can also give information about an adjective. *Very* good. ***Muito bom.***

**article** see **definite article** and **indefinite article**.

**clause** is a group of words with a verb that makes sense on its own, as a sentence or as part of a sentence. In a two-clause sentence, one of the clauses is often more important. This is the **main clause**. The other is the **subordinate clause**. I shall phone, when he arrives. **Eu telefonarei, quando ele chegar.** (*when he arrives* / ***quando ele chegar*** is the subordinate clause).

**conjugation** the different endings and forms given to a verb. I *phone*. **Eu *telefono*.** He *phones*. **Ele *telefona*.** He *phoned*. **Ele *telefonou*.**

**conjunction** joins two **clauses** together. I shall phone *when* he arrives. **Eu telefonarei *quando* ele chegar.**

**consonant** a speech-sound such as that represented by the letters **t**, **b** or **m** in which the breath is at least in part obstructed at some point in your mouth or lips. Consonants combine with vowels to form syllables.

**definite article** in English *the*, precedes a noun which is presented as a specific item. *The* hotel is good. ***O* hotel é bom.**

**demonstrative** determines which noun you mean (more precisely than *the*) and it may stand for a noun as a pronoun. *This* hotel is good. ***Este* hotel é bom.** *This* is new. ***Isto* é novo.**

**direct speech** is when you report what someone has said using the person's exact words. He said, '*I have a puncture*'. **Ele disse: "*Estou com um pneu furado*".**

**gender** nouns (adjectives, adjective-like words and some pronouns) may be **masculine** or **feminine** even if they do not refer to a gendered being – *car*, ***carro*** is masculine in Portuguese. Some nouns are **common**, i.e., the same for male and female  dentist, ***dentista***. There are also neuter words – this (thing), *isto* (the Portuguese word has a masculine ending, *-o*, but acts as a neuter).

**indefinite** refers to the noun you mean (more selectively than *a/an*) and it may stand for a noun as a pronoun. I am going to visit *some of* these museums. **Eu vou visitar *alguns* destes museus.**

**indefinite article** in English *a/an*, precedes a noun which is presented in an unspecified manner. I am going to visit *a* museum. **Eu vou visitar *um* museu.**

**indicative** is a set of verb forms mainly for statements of fact. I *live* here. **Eu *moro* aqui.** It *was* cold. ***Estava* frio.**

**indirect speech** is when you report what someone has said without using the person's exact words, hence also known as reported speech. He said *that he had a puncture*. **Ele disse *que estava com um pneu furado*.** Also see **direct speech**.

**infinitive** the basic form of the verb. It is in this form that you should look up a verb in a dictionary. Portuguese infinitives end in **-ar**, **-er**, **-ir** and **-or**.

**interrogative word** it often starts a question and may belong to different categories of words, such as a pronoun (*Who* is it? *Quem* é?) or an adverb (*Where* is it? *Onde* é?).

**noun** is a naming word – *car*, *carro*; *beach*, *praia*; *John*, *João*.

**object** is what receives the action expressed by the verb. He ate *the apple*. **Ele comeu *a maçã*.**

**person** is the subject of an action or state of being. For example, **1st person** is the person speaking; **2nd person** the person spoken to; and **3rd person** the person spoken of. She is *nice*. ***Ela é simpática.*** (*she* / *ela* = 3rd person).

**personal pronoun** the words for I, **eu**, me, **me** or **mim**, etc.

**phrase** is a group of words which is part of a clause or sentence but does not make sense on its own – *by him*, ***por ele***.

**possessive** shows ownership or belonging. This car is *hers*. **Este carro é *dela*.**

**preposition** shows the relationship of one thing to another. I have come *from* the beach. **Eu vim *da* praia.** The book is *on top* of the table. **O livro está *em cima da* mesa.**

**pronoun** stands in place of a noun. *I*, ***eu*** (says John talking about himself; where pronoun I = noun *John*).

**reflexive** where subject and object are the same. ***Eu lavo-me.*** *I wash myself.*

**relative pronoun** it both stands for a noun and joins two clauses together like a conjunction. This is the dish *which* I am going to order. **Este é o prato *que* eu vou pedir** (*which / que* relates to *dish / **prato*** and links the two clauses).

**reported speech** see **indirect speech**.

**sentence** is a group of words complete in itself. It may consist of one or more clauses. *I shall phone.* **Eu telefonarei.**

**subject** is what does the action or bears the state of being expressed by the verb. It is often referred to as **person**.

**subjunctive** is a set of verb forms mainly for what is imagined or wished for. If I *were* a millionaire. **Se eu *fosse* milionário.**

**subordinate** see **clause**.

**syllable** is a short uninterrupted unit of pronunciation. The word **ca-fé** has two syllables and the word **con-cer-to** three.

**tense** means the verb changes to express meanings such as 'present', 'past' and 'future'. *I write / wrote / shall write.* **Eu escrevo / escrevi / escreverei.**

**verb** is a doing or being word.

**vowel** is a speech-sound such as that represented by the letter *a* or *o* where the vibration of the vocal cords is the main characteristic. It is more open than a consonant and in some cases may stand on its own as a syllable.

**voice** is the relationship between the verb and the subject. It is active when the subject does the action. It is **passive** when the subject has the action done to it: *The apple* was eaten by him. **A maçã foi comida por ele.**

# Pronunciation and spelling

### Stress and accentuation

Portuguese words in general are stressed on the penultimate syllable:

**passa'porte** (*passport*)

The chief constituent, or centre, of the syllable is a vowel element:

**passa'porte**

In words which do not end in a single **a**, **e**, or **o**, the stress usually falls on the last syllable:

**ho'tel** (*hotel*) **esta'ção** (*station*)

Words which are an exception to the above stress rules usually bear a written accent:

**al'fândega** (*customs*)

In Portugal, contrast between stressed and unstressed syllables is sharp. There is a tendency to linger on the stressed syllable and glide over the intermediate sounds. As a result, unstressed vowels become 'neutralized' and final **e** tends to disappear. Brazilian stress is more evenly spaced out, and a secondary stress often emerges in a single word:

**humani'dade** (Eur.) (*humankind*)

**hu'mani'dade** (Br.)

## Portuguese sounds

The chart in this section will give you a detailed description of the Portuguese sounds. Differences between European and Brazilian practice are highlighted with the abbreviations (Eur.) and (Br.).

In the first column you will see a letter or group of letters as used in normal spelling. The sound that letter (or group of letters) stands for is represented in the second column by a phonetic symbol from the International Phonetic Alphabet. You needn't worry if you are not familiar with phonetic symbols. Just move on to the third column. It compares the Portuguese sound with an English sound. In some cases a French sound-alike is given too. The fourth column tells you the position of the sound in the word. In the last column you will be able to see an example of a Portuguese word including the respective sound.

### Liaison and elision

In the flow of speech, consecutive words are often linked together and the faster a person speaks the more this happens. E.g., **dois endereços** (*two addresses*) [doizẽde'resoʃ] (Eur.) / [doizẽde'resos] (Br.). The final s in **dois** is now between vowels (see chart of sounds page 294).

A word ending in a vowel tends to be run together with a word beginning with a vowel. E.g., **De onde é?** (*Where do you come from?*) ['dõ'dɛ] (Eur.) / ['dõ'dji'ɛ] (Br.). (A careful speaker, though, will pronounce the unstressed vowel element as a semi-vowel.)

Elision of vowels often occurs in relaxed speech, as shown in some unconventional spellings. E.g., **p'ra** or **pra** instead of **para** (*to*) ['prɐ]. Also, this tendency is sometimes taken to extremes.

**n'é** or **né** instead of **não é** ? (*in't it?*)

**t'obrigado** or **tobrigado** instead of **muito obrigado** (*thank you very much*)

## Hyphen

▸ Hyphens (-) serve to link separate words and particles. They are used mainly:

▸ in cases such as **segunda-feira** (*Monday*) and **guarda-chuva** (*umbrella*), where the components have to some extent lost their independent meaning.

▸ with some particles (prefixes) that precede the main word, as in **pré-escola** (*preschool*) and **pós-graduado** (*postgraduate*).

▸ with object and reflexive pronouns – *me*, *myself*, etc. – but word order plays a role. As a general principle, a hyphen is used where the pronoun follows the verb: **Pode dizer-me onde é a saída?** (*Can you tell me where the exit is?*). However, the following construction is more widely used: **Pode me dizer onde é a saída?** In this construction, the pronoun (**me**) comes before, not after, the verb to which it relates (**dizer**). Notwithstanding, there are those who prefer to hyphenate the pronoun to the verb that now precedes it (**Pode**): **Pode-me dizer onde é a saída?**

| spelling | IPA symbol | sound-alikes | position | examples |
|---|---|---|---|---|
| a | [a] | more open than English *a*, approaching *ah* | stressed | falo (*I speak*); fala (*you speak*); pare! (*stop*); mapa (*map*); mala (*suitcase*) |
| a | [ɐ] | resembling *a* as in *among* but longer | stressed, before **m** or **n** starting a new syllable | cama (*bed*); ano (*year*); falamos (*we speak*) |
| a | [ɑ] | between *a* and *ah*, as above, but pronounced further back in the mouth | before **l** or **u** in the same syllable | hospital (*hospital*); mau (*bad*); carnaval (*carnival*) |
| á, à | [a] | between *a* and *ah*, as above | stressed | há (*there is*); lá (*there*) |
| â | [ɐ] | resembling *a* as in *among*, as above | stressed | câmara (*council*) |
| a | [ɐ] | resembling *a* as in *among* | unstressed, at the end of word, and elsewhere | mala (*suitcase*); cama (*bed*); falamos (*we speak*); para (*to, for*) |

*(Contd)*

| | | | | |
|---|---|---|---|---|
| e | [ɛ] | resembling e in tell | stressed | zero (zero); ela (she) |
| e | [e] | like e in they but without the final glide (like the French word et) | stressed and unstressed depending on the origin of the word and / or its surrounding sounds | mesa (table); caneta (pen); esteve (it was); ele (he); comer (to eat) |
| ê | [ɛ] | resembling e in tell | stressed | café (coffee); pé (foot) |
| ê | [e] | like e in they, as above | stressed | você (you); mês (month) |
| e | [I] | resembling i in cigarette | unstressed, particularly before a vowel or at the beginning of syllable | compreendo (I understand); está (it is); exame (exam) |
| e | [ə] | like e in butter, or disappears (Eur.) | at the end of word | noite (night); vinte (twenty); nome (name); me (me); envelope (envelope) |
| | [I] | resembling i in cigarette (Br.) | | |
| i | [i] | like ee in meet but usually shorter | stressed and semi-stressed | dizer (to to say); aqui (here); fazia (she used to do) |
| i | [I] | resembling i in cigarette | unstressed | cigarro (cigarette) |

| | | | |
|---|---|---|---|
| i | [I] | like *i* in *pill* | before l or u in the same syllable | mil (*thousand*); partiu (*s/he left*) |
| í | [i] | like *ee* in *meet* but usually shorter | stressed | saí (*I got out*) |
| i | [j] | like *y* in *yet* | before a stressed vowel | diária (*daily rate*) |
| o | [ɔ] | resembling *o* in *jolly* | stressed | ovos (*eggs*); come (*you eat*) |
| o | [o] | a bit like *o* in *note* (like French *au* in *chaud*) | stressed and unstressed depending on the origin of the word and/or its surrounding sounds | ovo (*egg*); bolo (*cake*); fogo (*fire*); porto (*port*); como (*I eat*); como (*how; as*); todo (*all*) |
| ó | [ɔ] | resembling *o* in *jolly* | stressed | avó (*grandmother*); próximo (*next*) |
| ô | [o] | a bit like *o* in *note*, as above | stressed | avô (*grandfather*); pôr (*to put*) |
| o | [u] | resembling *u* in *put* | unstressed, at end of word | ovo, ovos (*egg/s*) |

(*Contd*)

| | | | | |
|---|---|---|---|---|
| u | [u] | resembling oo in soon (like French ou in où) | stressed | tudo (*everything*); uva (*grape*); aluno (*pupil, student*) |
| ú | [u] | a bit like oo in *soon*, as above | stressed | número (*number*) |
| u | [°u] | like ou in *could* | before l in the same syllable | azul (*blue*); sul (*south*) |
| u | [w] | like w in *water* | after **g** or **q** and before **a** or **o** | quando (*when*); quanto (*how much*); água (*water*) |
| u | [ ] | silent | after **g** or **q** and before **e** or **i**, in general | aqui (*here*); quero (*I want*); seguir (*to follow*) |
| u | [w] | like w in *water* | after g or q and before e or i, in some cases | cinquenta (*fifty*); aguentar (*to stand, bear*) |
| ai | [aj] | like y in *my* | any position | pai (*father*); mais (*more*) |
| au | [au] | resembling ow in *bow* | any position | mau (*bad*) |

| | | | |
|---|---|---|---|
| ei | [ɐj] | resembling *ay* in *pay* (Eur.) | any position | direita (*right*); leite (*milk*); sei (*I know*) |
| | [ej] | resembling *e* in *they* (Br.) | | |
| eu | [eu] | a bit like *e* in *they* plus *oo* in *soon* (like the French word *et* plus the French spelling *ou*) | any position | eu (*I*); meu (*my*); seu (*your*); Europa (*Europe*) |
| oi | [oj] | a bit like *o* in *note* (like French *au* in *chaud*) plus *y* in *yet* | any position | coisa (*thing*); dois (*two*) |
| ou | [o] | a bit like *o* in *note* (French *au* in *chaud*) (Eur.) | any position | sou (*I am*); vou (*I go*); outro (*other*) |
| | [ou] | resembling *o* in *note* (Br.) | | |
| ui | [uj] | a bit like *oo* in *soon* plus *y* in *yet* | in general, but in the word muito (*much; very*) it is often pronounced like *ui* in *ruin* | fui (*I went*) |

*(Contd)*

## Nasal sounds

🔊 CD2, TR 45

| | | | |
|---|---|---|---|
| ã, am, an | [ɐ̃] | a bit like *an* in *anchor* | any position as one syllable (spelling **am** before **p** or **b**) | amanhã (*tomorrow*); ambos (*both*); banco (*bank*) |
| am, ão | [ɐ̃ũ] | like *ow* in *how* but nasalized, i.e., pronounced through your nose | any position (spelling **am** in unstressed 3rd-person verbal endings) | falam (*they speak*); não (*no*); pão (*bread*); irmão (*brother*) |
| em, ãe | [ɐ̃j] | like *ay* in *pay* but nasalized (Eur.) | end of word | em (*in, on*); bem (*well*); homem (*man*); mãe (*mother*); pães (*loaves*) |
| | [ẽj] | like *ey* in *they* but nasalized (Br.) | | |
| êm | [ɐ̃j] | (Eur.) the same as for the spelling em above but the sound should be repeated (Br.) | end of word (3rd-p. plural verb ending) | têm (*they have*) |
| | [ẽj] | | | |

394

| em, en | [ẽ] | like *e* in *they* but without the final glide and nasalized | any position (but not end of word) | emprego (*job, employment*); entre (*enter, come/go in*) |
|---|---|---|---|---|
| im, in | [ĩ] | like *ee* in *meet* but nasalized | any position | sim (*yes*); cinco (*five*) |
| om, on | [õ] | like *o* in *note* but nasalized | any position | bom (*good*); conta (*bill*) |
| õe | [õj] | like *o* in *note* plus *y* in *yet* but nasalized | any position | lições (*lessons*); põe (*s/he puts*) |
| um, un | [ũ] | like *oo* in *soon* but nasalized | any position | um (*one*); juntos (*together*) |

## Consonants

🎧 CD2, TR 46

| b | [b] | as in English, but softer | any position | belo (*beautiful*) |
|---|---|---|---|---|
| c | [s] | as English *s* | before e or i | cem (*a hundred*); cinco (*five*) |
| c | [ ] or [k] | silent or like *c* in *cat* | in words with original -ct- | facto (*fact*); acto (*act*) |
| c | [k] | like *c* in *cat* | elsewhere | carro (*car*); com (*with*) |

(*Contd*)

| ç | [s] | as English s | any position | informação (*information*) |
| ch | [ʃ] | like *sh* in *show* | any position | chave (*key*); achar (*to find*) |
| d | [d] | as in English, but with tip of tongue against teeth, not gum ridge | any position (Eur.) in general (Br.) | **dar** (*to give*); **tarde** (*late*); universidade (*university*) |
| d | [dj] | the same as explained for *d* above, plus *y* in *yet* | before sound [i], in most of Brazil | tarde (*late*); universidade (*university*) |
| f | [f] | as in English | any position | fácil (*easy*) |
| g | [ʒ] | like *s* in *pleasure* | before e or i | gente (*people*) |
| g | [g] | like *g* in good | elsewhere | grande (*large*); garrafa (*bottle*) |
| h | [ ] | silent | in general | hotel (*hotel*); homem (*man*) |
| j | [ʒ] | like *s* in *pleasure* | any position | loja (*shop*); hoje (*today*) |
| l | [ł] | as in English, but drawing your tongue back | at the end of syllable | sol (*sun*); mil (*thousand*); almoço (*lunch*) |
| l | [l] | as in English | elsewhere | lanche (*snack*); falar (*to speak*) |

| lh | [ʎ] | resembling *lli* in *million* | any position | filho (*son*); trabalho (*work*) |
| m | [m] | as in English | at beginning of syllable | mãe (*mother*); mesa (*table*) |
| n | [n] | as in English | at beginning of syllable | nome (*name*); nada (*nothing*) |
| nh | [ɲ] | resembling *ni* in *onion* | any position | vinho (*wine*); senhora (*lady*) |
| p | [p] | as in English, but softer | any position | pai (*father*); perto (*near*) |
| p | [ ] | silent or *p* (soft) | in words with original -pt- , -pc-. -pç- | rapto (*kidnapping*); apto (*capable*) |
| q | [k] | like *c* in *cat* | any position | quatro (*four*); quente (*hot*) |
| r | [rr] or [ʀ] | like the rolled Scottish *r*, with multiple trill, or like *ch* in *loch* or a very heavy English *h* | at the beginning of word and generally at the beginning of syllable | rua (*road*); rio (*river*); refeição (*meal*); repetir (*to repeat*) |
| r | [r] or [ɹ] | like the *r* in baker, or 'swallowed' | at end of word and generally at the end of syllable | jantar (*dinner*); fazer (*to do*); porta (*door*); norte (*north*) |
| r | [r] | like the *r* in *bakery* | elsewhere | caro (*dear*); barato (*cheap*) |

*(Contd)*

| | | | | |
|---|---|---|---|---|
| rr | [rr] or [ɹɹ] | as explained above for spelling *r* at the beginning of word and generally at the beginning of syllable | | carro (*car*) |
| s | [s] | like s in *so* | between vowels | sol (*sun*); semana (*week*); observar (*to watch*) |
| s | [ʃ] | like *sh* in *push* (Eur.) and (Br.) Rio de Janeiro<br><br>like s in *us* (Br.) but not in Rio de Janeiro | at the beginning of word or after a consonant<br><br>at the end of word or syllable | dois (*two*); homens (*men*); esquerda (*left*); nascer (*to be born*) |
| s | [ʒ] | like s in *pleasure* (Eur.) and (Br.) Rio de Janeiro<br><br>like English z (Br.) but not in Rio de Janeiro | before a voiced consonant | mesmo (*same*); desde (*since*); desfazer (*to undo*) |

| | | | |
|---|---|---|---|
| s | [z] | like English z | between vowels | casa (*house, home*) |
| ss | [s] | like s in so | between vowels | passaporte (*passport*) |
| t | [t] | as in English, but with tip of tongue against teeth, not gum ridge | in general | tudo (*everything*); tive (*I had*); noite (*night*) |
| t | [tʃ] | the same as explained for t above, plus y in *yet* | before sound [i], in most of Brazil | tive (*I had*); noite (*night*) |
| v | [v] | as in English | any position | vago (*vacant*) |
| x | [ʃ] | like *sh* in *show* | at the beginning of word or syllable and in some cases between vowels | xarope (*syrup*); xícara (*cup*); xadrez (*checked*); caixa (*check-out*); puxar (*to pull*) |
| x | [z] | like English z | where ex comes before a vowel | exame (*exam*) |
| x | [ks] | like x in *taxi* | in some words | táxi (*taxi*); fixo (*fixed*) |
| x | [s] | like s in so | between vowels, other than above | próximo (*next*); trouxe (*I brought*) |

*(Contd)*

| Letter | IPA | Description | Position | Example |
|---|---|---|---|---|
| x | [ʃ] | like *sh* in *push* (Eur.) and (Br.) Rio de Janeiro | before a consonant | extra (*extra*); sexta-feira (*Friday*) |
| | [s] | like *s* in so (Br.) but not in Rio de Janeiro | | |
| z | [z] | like English *z* | at the beginning of a word and between vowels | zero (*zero*); fazer (*to do*) |
| z | [ʃ] | like *sh* in *push* (Eur.) and (Br.) Rio de Janeiro | at end of word | luz (*light*); feliz (*happy*) |
| | [ʒ] | like *s* in *pleasure* (Br.) but not in Rio de Janeiro | | |
| z | [ʒ] | like *s* in pleasure | before a voiced consonant | Feliz Natal (*Happy Christmas*) |
| | [z] | like English *z* (Br.) but not in Rio de Janeiro | | |

**Spelling agreement** (*acordo ortográfico*)
(See also the Introduction)

Below you have a list of spelling updates and alternatives in accordance with the spelling agreement (*acordo ortográfico*) towards a single common orthography among the different Portuguese-speaking countries

## Spelling updates – main changes

**1** c is removed in **cc**, **cç** and **ct** where it is not pronounced.
**2** p is removed in **pc**, **pç** and **pt** where it is not pronounced.
**3** diaeresis is no longer used.
**4** acute accent is no longer used on stressed **oi** and **ei**, second syllable from the end.
**5** circumflex accent is no longer used on stressed double vowels, second syllable from the end, including first person plural of verbs **ler** and **ver**, present indicative, and verb **dar**, present subjunctive (see verb tables in VG).
**6** a graphic accent (circumflex or other) is no longer used on words with the same spelling as contracted words, etc. where meaning is clear from context.

|   | old spelling | | new spelling | |
|---|---|---|---|---|
| 1 | sele**cc**ionar | → | sele**c**ionar | *(to select)* |
|   | dire**cç**ão | → | dire**ç**ão | *(direction)* |
|   | a**ct**ual | → | a**t**ual | *(current)* |
| 2 | exce**pc**ional | → | exce**c**ional | *(exceptional)* |
|   | dece**pç**ão | → | dece**ç**ão | *(disappointment)* |
|   | ó**pt**imo | → | ó**t**imo | *(excellent)* |
| 3 | cinq**ü**enta | → | cinq**u**enta | *(fifty)* |
| 4 | id**éi**a | → | id**ei**a | *(idea)* |
|   | j**ói**a | → | j**oi**a | *(jewel)* |

| old spelling | | new spelling | |
|---|---|---|---|
| **5** | vôo | → | voo | *(flight)* |
| | vêem | → | veem | *(they see)* |
| **6** | pêlo, to distinguish from pelo = por + o (*by the, etc.*) | → | pelo | *(hair; fur)* |

Note: regarding the 'old' spellings listed in 1 and 2 above, there is tolerance of choice in a number of cases where these etymological spellings have been retained in some areas of the Portuguese-speaking world. Examples: facto *or* fato (*fact*), recepção *or* receção (*reception*).

### Spelling alternatives where there are variations

1 acute or circumflex accent on stressed **o**, third syllable from the end;
2 acute or circumflex accent on stressed **e**, end syllable;
3 acute or circumflex accent on **e** or **o** before syllable starting with **m** or **n**;
4 no graphic accent on **o** where the stress is on the second syllable from the end or a circumflex accent where the stress is on the end syllable;
5 acute accent or no graphic accent on second syllable from the end for first conjugation verbs, preterite, first person plural (see Unit 10:HIWe and verb tables in VG);
6 circumflex accent or no graphic accent on second syllable from the end for first person plural of verb **dar**, present subjunctive (see verb tables in VG).

| | mainly Eur. | | mainly Br. | |
|---|---|---|---|---|
| 1 | fenómeno | or | fenômeno | *(phenomenon)* |
| 2 | bebé | or | bebê | *(baby)* |
| 3 | ténis | or | tênis | *(tennis)* |
| | abdómen | or | abdômen | *(abdomen)* |
| 4 | metro | or | metrô | *(underground train / subway* (US)) |
| 5 | comprámos | or | compramos | *(we bought / we have bought)* |
| 6 | dêmos | or | demos | *(we may perhaps give)* |

# Verb guide

Verbs follow general conjugation patterns for present, past and future, as well as for other meanings they may express. However, there is a certain range of variation in the degree to which each verb conforms to the general pattern. This section explains the relevant differences in Portuguese verbs. It also contains a quick-reference table of the regular conjugation endings (for more detail see 'conjugations' in the cross-reference Grammar index) and tables of verbs with anomalous features.

### Regular verbs

Regular verbs simply follow the standard pattern for their conjugation, like the three model verbs used in this course, namely **comprar**, **vender** and **partir**.

### Special verbs

i *Orthography-changing verbs:* those which change their spelling in order to preserve the same pronunciation.
   – Conhece o Rio?       *Do you know Rio?*
   – Sim, conheço.       *Yes, I do*     (verb **conhecer**)

ii *Radical-changing verbs:* those which change their root vowel under certain conditions, as, for example, when the stress falls on the root or through the influence of a nearby vowel.
   – Prefere chá ou café?       *Do you prefer tea or coffee?*
   – Prefiro chá.       *I prefer tea.*    (verb **preferir**)

iii *Irregular verbs:* those which do not conform to the model endings for the three conjugations -**ar**, -**er**, -**ir**.
   Onde é o hotel?       *Where is the hotel?* (verb **ser**)
   **Vou** amanhã.       *I am going tomorrow.* (verb **ir**)

One single verb may display features from more than one group above (i / ii / iii).

| Quando eu **segui**a pela estrada. | *When I was going along the road.* |
| **Siga** em frente. | *Go straight on.* |

(verb **seguir** i + ii)

**Orthography-changing verbs**

The following chart shows the required changes.

| -c**a**r | -**ç**a**r | -**g**a**r | -**c**er | -**g**er<br>-**g**ir | -**gu**er<br>-**gu**ir |
|---|---|---|---|---|---|
| ↓ | ↓ | ↓ | ↓ | ↓ | ↓ |
| **-qu** | **-c** | **-gu** | **-ç** | **-j** | **-g** |
| before *e* | | | before *a* or *o* | | |

| ficar (*to stay*) | → fiquei; fique |
| começar (*to begin*) | → comecei; comece |
| pagar (*to pay*) | → paguei; pague |
| conhecer (*to know*) | → conheço; conheça |
| proteger (*to protect*) | → protejo; proteja |
| dirigir (*to drive*) | → dirijo; dirijam |
| erguer (*to lift*) | → ergo; erga |
| seguir (*to follow, go*) | → sigo; sigam |

Verbs whose infinitive ends in **o + er** have a spelling change in the 3rd person of the present indicative (the *it*, *s/he* form), where the end vowel is written **-i**. Also note the written accent in the example below.

   doer – dói aqui (*it hurts here*)

## Radical-changing verbs

Please refer to the following chart for the required changes.

| e | o | u |
|---|---|---|
| ↓ | ↓ | ↓ |

| i | u | o |
|---|---|---|
| *Present indicative, 1st person (**eu** form)<br>*Present subjunctive<br>*Command forms from present subjunctive | | *Present indicative, 2nd and 3rd persons and respective plurals (**tu**, **você(s)**, **ele(s)** forms)<br>*Command form for **tu** |

repetir (*to repeat, to say/do again*)
Pres. ind.: repito, repetes, etc.
Pres. subj.: repita, repitas, repita, repitamos, (repitais), repitam
Command: repita, repitam

dormir (*to sleep*)
Pres. ind.: durmo, dormes, etc.
Pres. subj.: durma, durmas, durma, durmamos, (durmais), durmam
Command: durma, durmam

subir (*to climb, to go/come up*)
Pres. ind.: subo, sobes, sobe, subimos, (subis), sobem
Command: sobe (tu)

Variations in the quality of the root vowel are not always registered in spelling. (See the chart for vowel sounds in the Pronunciation and spelling section.)

| | |
|---|---|
| – Falam Português? | *Do you speak Portuguese?* |
| – Sim, falamos. | *Yes, we do.*        (verb **falar**) |
| – Come carne? | *Do you eat meat?* |
| – Não, não como; sou vegetariano. | *No, I don't; I am a vegetarian*        (verb **comer**) |

There are cases in which an accent can be written over the vowel to prevent confusion with another form of the verb or indeed another word with a completely different meaning. This is the case with **pode**, for *you, s/he can*, and **pôde**, for *you, s/he could*, and with **pôr** (*to put*) and **por**, a preposition translating *for* or by.

### Other changes

Verbs with infinitive in **a** + **ir** retain the **i** throughout their conjugation except in the 3rd person plural of the indicative present (*they* form). Also this **i** is given a written accent where it forms a stressed syllable.

sair (*to go/come out*)
Pres. ind: saio, sais, sai, saímos, (saís), saem

Verbs with infinitive in **e** + **ar** add an **i** after stressed **e**. Only the present indicative, present subjunctive and command forms are affected.

passear (*to go for a walk / ride*)
Pres. ind: passeio, passeias, passeia, passeamos, (passeais), passeiam

The verb **odiar** (*to hate*) is conjugated similarly.

### Irregular past participles

| | | | |
|---|---|---|---|
| abrir (*to open*) | – aberto | escrever (*to write*) | – escrito |
| aceitar (*to accept*) | – aceito *or* aceite | ganhar (*to earn, win*) | – ganho |
| acender (*to light*) | – aceso | gastar (*to spend*) | – gasto |
| entregar (*to deliver*) | – entregue | pagar (*to pay*) | – pago |

Where both a regular and an irregular form are available, usually the former is used in compound perfect tenses and the latter is used as an adjective.

Eu tinha **acendido** a luz. A luz estava **acesa**. *I had switched the light on. The light was on.*

Also, sometimes a past participle is used as a noun.

Não tenho **trocado**. *I haven't got any change.*
**Perdidos** e **achados** *'Lost and found'*
**Chegadas** *Arrivals*

## Compound verbs

Please remember that compounds of special verbs normally exhibit the same features as the single verbs.

|  | from |
|---|---|
| **i Orthography-changing** | |
| conseguir (*to achieve*) | seguir |
| reconhecer (*to recognize*) | conhecer |
| | |
| **ii Radical-changing** | |
| conseguir (*to achieve*) | seguir |
| consentir (*to consent*) | sentir |
| descobrir (*to discover, to uncover*) | cobrir |
| preferir (*to prefer*) | ferir |
| referir (*to mention*) | ferir |
| | |
| **iii Irregular** | |
| compor (*to compose, to arrange together*) | pôr |
| condizer (*to match*) | dizer |
| conter (*to contain*) | ter |
| contradizer (*to contradict*) | dizer |
| convir (*to suit, to be convenient*) | vir |
| desfazer (*to undo*) | fazer |
| manter (*to maintain*) | ter |
| satisfazer (*to satisfy*) | fazer |
| supor (*to assume*) | pôr |

# Regular verbs (endings only)

| Infinitive | Present indicative | Preterite indicative | Imperfect indicative | Pluperfect indicative | Future indicative | 'Commands' (imperative) |
|---|---|---|---|---|---|---|
| -ar | -o | -ei | -ava | -ara | -arei | — |
| | -as | -aste | -avas | -aras | -arás | -a |
| | -a | -ou | -ava | -ara | -ará | -e |
| | -a | -ou | -ava | -ara | -ará | — |
| | -amos | -amos | -ávamos | -áramos | -aremos | -emos |
| | (-ais) | (-astes) | (-áveis) | (-áreis) | (-areis) | (-ai) |
| | -am | -aram | -avam | -aram | -arão | -em |
| | -am | -aram | -avam | -aram | -arão | — |
| -er | -o | -i | -ia | -era | -erei | — |
| | -es | -este | -ias | -eras | -erás | -e |
| | -e | -eu | -ia | -era | -erá | -a |
| | -e | -eu | -ia | -era | -erá | — |
| | -emos | -emos | -íamos | -êramos | -eremos | -amos |
| | (-eis) | (-estes) | (-íeis) | (-êreis) | (-ereis) | (-ei) |
| | -em | -eram | -iam | -eram | -erão | -am |
| | -em | -eram | -iam | -eram | -erão | — |
| -ir | -o | -i | -ia | -ira | -irei | — |
| | -es | -iste | -ias | -iras | -irás | -e |
| | -e | -iu | -ia | -ira | -irá | -a |
| | -e | -iu | -ia | -ira | -irá | — |
| | -imos | -imos | -íamos | -íramos | -iremos | -amos |
| | (-is) | (-istes) | (-íeis) | (-íreis) | (-ireis) | (-i) |
| | -em | -iram | -iam | -iram | -irão | -am |
| | -em | -iram | -iam | -iram | -irão | — |

| Present subjunctive | Imperfect subjunctive | Future subjunctive | Conditional | Personal infinitive | Present participle | Past participle |
|---|---|---|---|---|---|---|
| -e | -asse | -ar | -aria | -ar | -ando | -ado |
| -es | -asses | -ares | -arias | -ares | | |
| -e | -asse | -ar | -aria | -ar | | |
| -e | -asse | -ar | -aria | -ar | | |
| -emos | -ássemos | -armos | -aríamos | -armos | | |
| (-eis) | (-ásseis) | (-ardes) | (-aríeis) | (-ardes) | | |
| -em | -assem | -arem | -ariam | -arem | | |
| -em | -assem | -arem | -ariam | -arem | | |
| -a | -esse | -er | -eria | -er | -endo | -ido |
| -as | -esses | -eres | -erias | -eres | | |
| -a | -esse | -er | -eria | -er | | |
| -a | -esse | -er | -eria | -er | | |
| -amos | -êssemos | -ermos | -eríamos | -ermos | | |
| (-ais) | (-êsseis) | (-erdes) | (-eríeis) | (-erdes) | | |
| -am | -essem | -erem | -eriam | -erem | | |
| -am | -essem | -erem | -eriam | -erem | | |
| -a | -isse | -ir | -iria | -ir | -indo | -ido |
| -as | -isses | -ires | -irias | -ires | | |
| -a | -isse | -ir | -iria | -ir | | |
| -a | -isse | -ir | -iria | -ir | | |
| -amos | -íssemos | -irmos | -iríamos | -irmos | | |
| (-ais) | (-ísseis) | (-irdes) | (-iríeis) | (-irdes) | | |
| -am | -issem | -irem | -iriam | -irem | | |
| -am | -issem | -irem | -iriam | -irem | | |

Note: The verbal forms corresponding to 'vós' have been entered in brackets in view of their limited use.

## Irregular verbs

| Infinitive | Present indicative | Preterite indicative | Imperfect indicative | Pluperfect indicative | Future indicative |
|---|---|---|---|---|---|
| crer<br>to believe | creio<br>crês<br>crê<br>cremos<br>(credes)<br>creem | *Regular* | *Regular* | *Regular* | *Regular* |
| dar<br>to give | dou<br>dás<br>dá<br>damos<br>(dais)<br>dão | dei<br>deste<br>deu<br>demos<br>(destes)<br>deram | *Regular* | dera<br>deras<br>dera<br>déramos<br>(déreis)<br>deram | *Regular* |
| dizer<br>to say | digo<br>dizes<br>diz<br>dizemos<br>(dizeis)<br>dizem | disse<br>disseste<br>disse<br>dissemos<br>(dissestes)<br>disseram | *Regular* | dissera<br>disseras<br>dissera<br>disséramos<br>(disséreis)<br>disseram | direi<br>dirás<br>dirá<br>diremos<br>(direis)<br>dirão |
| estar<br>to be | estou<br>estás<br>está<br>estamos<br>(estais)<br>estão | estive<br>estiveste<br>esteve<br>estivemos<br>(estivestes)<br>estiveram | *Regular* | estivera<br>estiveras<br>estivera<br>estivéramos<br>(estivéreis)<br>estiveram | *Regular* |
| fazer<br>to do,<br>make | faço<br>fazes<br>faz<br>fazemos<br>(fazeis)<br>fazem | fiz<br>fizeste<br>fez<br>fizemos<br>(fizestes)<br>fizeram | *Regular* | fizera<br>fizeras<br>fizera<br>fizéramos<br>(fizéreis)<br>fizeram | farei<br>farás<br>fará<br>faremos<br>(fareis)<br>farão |
| haver<br>to exist,<br>there to<br>be, have | hei<br>hás<br>há<br>havemos<br>(haveis)<br>hão | houve<br>houveste<br>houve<br>houvemos<br>(houvestes)<br>houveram | *Regular* | houvera<br>houveras<br>houvera<br>houvéramos<br>(houvéreis)<br>houveram | *Regular* |

Note: the verbal forms corresponding to 'vós' are entered in brackets in view of their limited use.

| Command forms | Present subjunctive | Imperfect subjunctive | Future subjunctive | Conditional | Participles |
|---|---|---|---|---|---|
| — | creia | | | | *Pres.* crendo |
| crê | creias | | | | |
| creia | creia | *Regular* | *Regular* | *Regular* | *Past* crido |
| creiamos | creiamos | | | | |
| (crede) | (creiais) | | | | |
| creiam | creiam | | | | |
| — | dê | desse | der | | *Pres.* dando |
| dá | dês | desses | deres | | |
| dê | dê | desse | der | *Regular* | *Past* dado |
| demos/dêmos | dêmos | déssemos | dermos | | |
| (dai) | (deis) | (désseis) | (derdes) | | |
| deem | deem | dessem | derem | | |
| — | diga | dissesse | disser | diria | *Pres.* dizendo |
| diz(e) | digas | dissesses | disseres | dirias | |
| diga | diga | dissesse | disser | diria | *Past* dito |
| digamos | digamos | disséssemos | dissermos | diríamos | |
| (dizei) | (digais) | (dissésseis) | (disserdes) | (diríeis) | |
| digam | digam | dissessem | disserem | diriam | |
| — | esteja | estivesse | estiver | | *Pres.* estando |
| está | estejas | estivesses | estiveres | | |
| esteja | esteja | estivesse | estiver | *Regular* | *Past* estado |
| estejamos | estejamos | estivéssemos | estivermos | | |
| (estai) | (estejais) | (estivésseis) | (estiverdes) | | |
| estejam | estejam | estivessem | estiverem | | |
| — | faça | fizesse | fizer | faria | *Pres.* fazendo |
| faz(e) | faças | fizesses | fizeres | farias | |
| faça | faça | fizesse | fizer | faria | *Past* feito |
| façamos | façamos | fizéssemos | fizermos | faríamos | |
| (fazei) | (façais) | (fizésseis) | (fizerdes) | (faríeis) | |
| façam | façam | fizessem | fizerem | fariam | |
| — | haja | houvesse | houver | | *Pres.* havendo |
| há | hajas | houvesses | houveres | | |
| haja | haja | houvesse | houver | *Regular* | *Past* havido |
| hajamos | hajamos | houvéssemos | houvermos | | |
| (havei) | (hajais) | (houvésseis) | (houverdes) | | |
| hajam | hajam | houvessem | houverem | | |

*(Contd)*

| Infinitive | Present indicative | Preterite indicative | Imperfect indicative | Pluperfect indicative | Future indicative |
|---|---|---|---|---|---|
| ir<br>to go | vou<br>vais<br>vai<br>vamos<br>(ides)<br>vão | fui<br>foste<br>foi<br>fomos<br>(fostes)<br>foram | Regular<br>(ia, etc.) | fora<br>foras<br>fora<br>fôramos<br>(fôreis)<br>foram | Regular |
| ler<br>to read | leio<br>lês<br>lê<br>lemos<br>(ledes)<br>leem | Regular | Regular | Regular | Regular |
| ouvir<br>to hear | ouço<br>ouves<br>ouve<br>ouvimos<br>(ouvis)<br>ouvem | Regular | Regular | Regular | Regular |
| pedir<br>to ask for | peço<br>pedes<br>pede<br>pedimos<br>(pedis)<br>pedem | Regular | Regular | Regular | Regular |
| perder<br>to lose | perco<br>perdes<br>perde<br>perdemos<br>(perdeis)<br>perdem | Regular | Regular | Regular | Regular |
| poder<br>can, may | posso<br>podes<br>pode<br>podemos<br>(podeis)<br>podem | pude<br>pudeste<br>pôde<br>pudemos<br>(pudestes)<br>puderam | Regular | pudera<br>puderas<br>pudera<br>pudéramos<br>(pudéreis)<br>puderam | Regular |
| pôr<br>to put | ponho<br>pões<br>põe<br>pomos<br>(pondes)<br>põem | pus<br>puseste<br>pôs<br>pusemos<br>(pusestes)<br>puseram | punha<br>punhas<br>punha<br>púnhamos<br>(púnheis)<br>punham | pusera<br>puseras<br>pusera<br>puséramos<br>(puséreis)<br>puseram | Regular<br>(no accent ^) |

| Command forms | Present subjunctive | Imperfect subjunctive | Future subjunctive | Conditional | Participles |
|---|---|---|---|---|---|
| — | vá | fosse | for | | *Pres.* |
| vai | vás | fosses | fores | | indo |
| vá | vá | fosse | for | *Regular* | *Past* |
| vamos | vamos | fôssemos | formos | | ido |
| (ide) | (vades) | (fôsseis) | (fordes) | | |
| vão | vão | fossem | forem | | |
| — | leia | | | | *Pres.* |
| lê | leias | | | | lendo |
| leia | leia | *Regular* | *Regular* | *Regular* | *Past* |
| leiamos | leiamos | | | | lido |
| (lede) | (leiais) | | | | |
| leiam | leiam | | | | |
| — | ouça | | | | *Pres.* |
| ouve | ouças | | | | ouvindo |
| ouça | ouça | *Regular* | *Regular* | *Regular* | *Past* |
| ouçamos | ouçamos | | | | ouvido |
| (ouvi) | (ouçais) | | | | |
| ouçam | ouçam | | | | |
| — | peça | | | | *Pres.* |
| pede | peças | | | | pedindo |
| peça | peça | *Regular* | *Regular* | *Regular* | *Past* |
| peçamos | peçamos | | | | pedido |
| (pedi) | (peçais) | | | | |
| peçam | peçam | | | | |
| — | perca | | | | *Pres.* |
| perde | percas | | | | perdendo |
| perca | perca | *Regular* | *Regular* | *Regular* | *Past* |
| percamos | percamos | | | | perdido |
| (perdei) | (percais) | | | | |
| percam | percam | | | | |
| — | possa | pudesse | puder | | *Pres.* |
| pode | possas | pudesses | puderes | | podendo |
| possa | possa | pudesse | puder | *Regular* | *Past* |
| possamos | possamos | pudéssemos | pudermos | | podido |
| (podei) | (possais) | (pudésseis) | (puderdes) | | |
| possam | possam | pudessem | puderem | | |
| — | ponha | pusesse | puser | | *Pres.* |
| põe | ponhas | pusesses | puseres | | pondo |
| ponha | ponha | pusesse | puser | *Regular* | *Past* |
| ponhamos | ponhamos | puséssemos | pusermos | (no | posto |
| (ponde) | (ponhais) | (pusésseis) | (puserdes) | accent ^) | |
| ponham | ponham | pusessem | puserem | | |

*(Contd)*

| Infinitive | Present indicative | Preterite indicative | Imperfect indicative | Pluperfect indicative | Future indicative |
|---|---|---|---|---|---|
| querer *to want* | quero queres quer queremos (quereis) querem | quis quiseste quis quisemos (quisestes) quiseram | Regular | quisera quiseras quisera quiséramos (quiséreis) quiseram | Regular |
| saber *to know* | sei sabes sabe sabemos (sabeis) sabem | soube soubeste soube soubemos (soubestes) souberam | Regular | soubera souberas soubera soubéramos (soubéreis) souberam | Regular |
| ser *to be* | sou és é somos (sois) são | fui foste foi fomos (fostes) foram | era eras era éramos (éreis) eram | fora foras fora fôramos (fôreis) foram | Regular |
| ter *to have* | tenho tens tem temos (tendes) têm | tive tiveste teve tivemos (tivestes) tiveram | tinha tinhas tinha tínhamos (tínheis) tinham | tivera tiveras tivera tivéramos (tivéreis) tiveram | Regular |
| trazer *to bring* | trago trazes traz trazemos (trazeis) trazem | trouxe trouxeste trouxe trouxemos (trouxestes) trouxeram | Regular | trouxera trouxeras trouxera trouxéramos (trouxéreis) trouxeram | trarei trarás trará traremos (trareis) trarão |
| ver *to see* | vejo vês vê vemos (vedes) veem | vi viste viu vimos (vistes) viram | Regular | vira viras vira víramos (víreis) viram | Regular |
| vir *to come* | venho vens vem vimos (vindes) vêm | vim vieste veio viemos (viestes) vieram | vinha vinhas vinha vínhamos (vínheis) vinham | viera vieras viera viéramos (viéreis) vieram | Regular |

| Command forms | Present subjunctive | Imperfect subjunctive | Future subjunctive | Conditional | Participles |
|---|---|---|---|---|---|
| — | queira | quisesse | quiser | | *Pres.* |
| quer(e) | queiras | quisesses | quiseres | | querendo |
| queira | queira | quisesse | quiser | *Regular* | *Past* |
| queiramos | queiramos | quiséssemos | quisermos | | querido |
| (querei) | (queirais) | (quisésseis) | (quiserdes) | | |
| queiram | queiram | quisessem | quiserem | | |
| — | saiba | soubesse | souber | | *Pres.* |
| sabe | saibas | soubesses | souberes | | sabendo |
| saiba | saiba | soubesse | souber | *Regular* | *Past* |
| saibamos | saibamos | soubéssemos | soubermos | | sabido |
| (sabei) | (saibais) | (soubésseis) | (souberdes) | | |
| saibam | saibam | soubessem | souberem | | |
| — | seja | fosse | for | | *Pres.* |
| sê | sejas | fosses | fores | | sendo |
| seja | seja | fosse | for | *Regular* | *Past* |
| sejamos | sejamos | fôssemos | formos | | sido |
| (sede) | (sejais) | fôsseis | (fordes) | | |
| sejam | sejam | fossem | forem | | |
| — | tenha | tivesse | tiver | | *Pres.* |
| tem | tenhas | tivesses | tiveres | | tendo |
| tenha | tenha | tivesse | tiver | *Regular* | *Past* |
| tenhamos | tenhamos | tivéssemos | tivermos | | tido |
| (tende) | (tenhais) | (tivésseis) | (tiverdes) | | |
| tenham | tenham | tivessem | tiverem | | |
| — | traga | trouxesse | trouxer | traria | *Pres.* |
| traz(e) | tragas | trouxesses | trouxeres | trarias | trazendo |
| traga | traga | trouxesse | trouxer | traria | *Past* |
| tragamos | tragamos | trouxéssemos | trouxermos | traríamos | trazido |
| (trazei) | (tragais) | (trouxésseis) | (trouxerdes) | (traríeis) | |
| tragam | tragam | trouxessem | trouxerem | trariam | |
| — | veja | visse | vir | | *Pres.* |
| vê | vejas | visses | vires | | vendo |
| veja | veja | visse | vir | *Regular* | *Past* |
| vejamos | vejamos | víssemos | virmos | | visto |
| (vede) | (vejais) | (vísseis) | (virdes) | | |
| vejam | vejam | vissem | virem | | |
| — | venha | viesse | vier | | *Pres.* |
| vem | venhas | viesses | vieres | | vindo |
| venha | venha | viesse | vier | *Regular* | *Past* |
| venhamos | venhamos | viéssemos | viermos | | vindo |
| (vinde) | (venhais) | (viésseis) | (vierdes) | | |
| venham | venham | viessem | vierem | | |

# Portuguese–English vocabulary

The words listed below can be used on both sides of the Atlantic. Where there is a difference, the word is followed by the sign (Eur.) or (Br.), which stand, respectively, for European and Brazilian.

The abbreviations (m) and (f) mean masculine and feminine; (pl) means plural.

**a** *the (f); you (f); her, it; at, to*
**à (= a + a)**
**abaixo** *below*
**abdómen** *(Eur.)* / **abdômen** *(Br.)* *(m) abdomen*
**aberto** *open*
**abertura** *(f) opening*
**abril** *(m) April*
**abrir** *to open*
**abundar** *to abound*
**acabar** *to finish, be over*
**acabar de ...** *to have just ...*
**acampar** *to camp*
**aceitar** *to accept*
**acender** *to light (fire); to switch / turn on*
**acerca de** *about*
**aceso** *on (light)*
**acesso** *(m) access*
**achar** *to find; to think;* **que tal acha ...?** *what do you think of ...?*
**acidente** *(m) accident*
**acima** *above*
**acompanhar** *to accompany*
**aconselhável** *advisable*
**acontecer** *to happen*
**acordo** *(m) agreement;* **de acordo com** *according to*

**açoriano** *from the Azores, Azorean*
**acreditar** *to believe*
**açúcar** *(m) sugar*
**adequado** *appropriate*
**adeus** *goodbye*
**adiantado** *early; fast (time)*
**adoecer** *to fall ill*
**adorar** *to adore, love*
**adquirir** *to acquire; to obtain*
**adult** *(m) adult*
**aeromoço** *(m) (Br.) air steward / host*
**aeroporto** *(m) airport*
**afastar** *to move away*
**agência** *(f) agency, office*
**agência de viagens** *(f) travel agency*
**agora** *now*
**agosto** *(m) August*
**agradável** *pleasing, pleasant*
**agradecer** *to thank;* **desde já agradeço** *thanking you in anticipation (letter)*
**água** *(f) water*
**água mineral** *(f) mineral water*
**água potável** *(f) drinking water*
**água tónica** *(Eur.)* / **tônica** *(Br.) (f) tonic water*

**aguardar** *to await*
**aí** *there*
**ainda** *still;* **ainda não** *not yet*
**ajudar** *to help*
**albergue** *(m) hostel*
**álcool** *(m) alcohol*
**aldeia** *(f) village*
**além de** *beyond; besides*
**alface** *(f) lettuce*
**alfândega** *(f) Customs*
**algo** *something*
**algodão** *(m) cotton*
**alguém** *someone, somebody*
**algum** *some, any*
**alguma coisa** *something*
**ali** *there (see also* **lá***)*
**aliança (de casamento)** *(f)*
 *wedding ring*
**alimentação** *(f) food*
**alimento** *(m) foodstuff*
**almoçar** *to have lunch*
**almoço** *(m) lunch*
**almofada** *(f) cushion; pillow (Eur.)*
**alojamento** *(m) accommodation*
**altitude** *(f) altitude*
**alto** *tall; high;* **alto mar** *deep sea*
**alugar** *to hire, rent, let*
**aluguel** *(Br.),* **aluguer** *(Eur.) (m)*
 *rental*
**alvorada** *(f) dawn*
**amanhã** *tomorrow*
**amar** *to love*
**amarelo** *yellow*
**amável** *kind, polite*
**ambiente** *(m) environment;*
 *atmosphere*
**ambos** *both*
**ambulância** *(f) ambulance*
**americano** *from America,*
 *American*
**amigo** *(m) friend*
**amor** *(m) love*

**andar** *to walk, move along*
**andar** *(m) floor (level);* **andar**
 **térreo** *ground floor*
**anel** *(m) ring*
**angolano** *from Angola, Angolan*
**animal** *(m) animal*
**aniversário** *(m) birthday*
**aniversário de casamento** *(m)*
 *wedding anniversary*
**ano** *(m) year;* **ter ... anos** *to*
 *be ... years old;* **fazer ... anos** *to*
 *become ... years old;* **todos os**
 **anos** *every year*
**Ano Novo** *(m) New Year*
**antecedência** *(f):* **com**
 **antecedência** *in advance*
**anteontem** *the day before*
 *yesterday*
**anterior** *former*
**antes** *before*
**antigo** *ancient, former, old*
**anúncio** *(m) advertisement*
**ao (= a + o)**
**apagar** *to put out (fire); to switch*
 *off (light); to erase*
**aparecer** *to appear; to turn up*
**aparelho** *(m) apparatus*
**aparelho de rádio** *(m) radio set*
**aparelho digestivo** *(m) digestive*
 *system*
**apartamento** *(m) apartment,*
 *flat; bed sitter; hotel room with*
 *ensuite facilities*
**apelido** *(m) (Eur.) surname*
**apenas** *only*
**aperitivo** *(m) aperitif; appetizer*
**apertado** *tight*
**apertar** *to hold tight; to fasten*
**apertar a mão** *to shake hands*
**apontar** *to point*
**após** *after, upon*
**aposentado** *retired*

**apreciar** to appreciate; to enjoy
**aprender** to learn
**apresentar** to present; to introduce
**aproveitar** to take (opportunity, advantage)
**aproximadamente** approximately
**aproximar** to draw near
**aquário** (m) aquarium
**aquático** aquatic, water (sport)
**aquecimento central** (m) central heating
**aquele** that, that one (m); (see also **esse**)
**aqui** here
**aquilo** that; (see also **isso**)
**ar** (m) air; look (appearance)
**ar condicionado** (m) air conditioning
**área** (f) area
**armário** (m) cupboard; wardrobe
**armazém** (m) warehouse; grocery store
**arquitetura** (f) architecture
**arrumar** to tidy up, put in order
**arte** (f) art
**artes plásticas** (fpl) visual arts
**artesanal** craft (product)
**artificial** artificial; man-made
**artigo** (m) article; item
**artigos regionais** (mpl) regional craft
**ascensor** (m) lift / elevator (US)
**assim** like this
**assinalar** to mark
**assinar** to sign
**assinatura** (f) signature
**assistir** to watch (film, performance, etc.)
**até** until, up to, as far as

**atender a** to see to, attend to; to serve
**atividade** (f) activity
**atração** (f) attraction
**atrás (de)** behind; at the back
**atrasado** late; slow (time)
**atravessar** to cross (over)
**atropelado** run over
**atual** present, current
**atum** (m) tuna fish
**aula** (f) class lesson
**auscultador** (m) (Eur.) receiver (telephone)
**australiano** from Australia, Australian
**autocarro** (m) (Eur.) bus, coach
**autodidata** (mf) self-taught person
**autoestrada** (f) motorway / expressway (US)
**autolocadora** (f) car rental agency
**automóvel** (m) automobile, car
**autonomia** (f) autonomy, independence
**autosserviço** (m) self-service
**avariado** out of order, damaged
**ave** (f) bird; ave(s) poultry
**avenida** (f) boulevard
**aventura** (f) adventure
**avião** (m) aeroplane / airplane (US); aircraft
**avisar** to tell, let know, inform
**avó** (f) grandmother
**avô** (m) grandfather
**azeitona** (f) olive
**azul** blue

**bacalhau** (m) cod, dried cod
**bacon** (m) (Br.) bacon
**bagagem** (f) baggage
**baile** (m) dance; ball

**baixo** *low; short, small (people)*
**baixo: em baixo** *below;* **em baixo de** *(Eur.),* **embaixo de** *(Br.) underneath*
**baixo: lá / aqui em baixo** *downstairs, at the bottom*
**balcão** *(m) counter; circle (theatre)*
**banca de jornais** *(f) newspaper stand*
**bancada** *(f) bench*
**banco** *(m) bank; stool*
**banheira** *(f) bathtub*
**banheiro** *(m) (Br.) bathroom; toilet / washroom (US)*
**banho** *(m) bath*
**banho: tomar banho** *to have a bath (wash), bathe, go into the water (beach)*
**bar** *(m) bar*
**barato** *cheap, inexpensive*
**barba** *(f) beard;* **fazer a barba** *to have a shave*
**barbeiro** *(m) barber*
**barco** *(m) boat*
**barraca** *(f) hut, tent*
**barro** *(m) earthenware*
**barulhento** *noisy*
**barulho** *(m) noise*
**bastante** *enough*
**batata** *(f) potato;* **batata frita** *chip;* **batatinha de pacote** *crisp*
**baunilha** *(f) vanilla*
**bebé** *(Eur.),* **bebê** *(Br.) (mf) baby*
**beber** *to drink*
**bebida** *(f) drink, beverage*
**beijo** *(m) kiss*
**belo** *beautiful*
**bem** *well; thoroughly; properly, quite*
**bem: está bem** *that's all right, OK*
**bem: tudo bem** *all is well*

**bem-vindo** *welcome*
**biblioteca** *(f) library*
**bicha** *(f) (Eur.) line, queue; row*
**bife** *(m) (beef) steak*
**bilhete** *(m) ticket*
**bilhete de identidade** *(m) (Eur.) identity card*
**bilhete postal** *(m) (Eur.) postcard*
**bilheteira** *(Eur.),* **bilheteria** *(Br.) (f) ticket office*
**biquíni** *(m) bikini*
**bisnaga** *(f) tube*
**blusa** *(f) blouse*
**boa** *good (f)*
**boate** *(Br.),* **buate** *(Eur.) (f) night club*
**bocadinho** *(m) small bit*
**boião** *(m) (Eur.) jar*
**boletim meteorológico** *(m) weather report, forecast*
**bolo** *(m) cake*
**bolsa** *(f) handbag; purse*
**bom** *good (m)*
**bombeiro** *(m) fireman*
**bonde** *(m) (Br.) tram / streetcar (US)*
**bonito** *pretty, handsome*
**botão** *(m) button*
**branco** *white*
**brasileiro** *from Brazil, Brazilian*
**breve: em breve** *soon*
**brinquedo** *(m) toy*
**britânico** *from Britain, British*
**buscar** *to seek; ir / vir buscar to fetch, collect*

**cá** *here*
**cabeleireiro** *(m) hairdresser*
**cabelo** *(m) hair (on human head)*
**cabo-verdiano** *from Cape Verde, Cape Verdean*
**caça** *(f) game; shooting*

**cachecol** *(m) long scarf*
**cachorro** *(m) puppy; dog (Br.)*
**cada** *each*
**cada um** *(m) each one*
**cada uma** *(f) each one*
**cadeira** *(f) chair*
**café** *(m) coffee*
**café da manhã** *(m) (Br.) breakfast*
**cair** *to fall, fall over*
**cais** *(m) quay; platform (Eur.)*
**caixa** *(f) box; cashdesk; till;
  check-out*
**caixa de correio** *(f) letter box*
**calça** *(f)*, **calças** *(fpl) trousers /
  pants (US)*
**calçado** *(m) footwear*
**calção** *(m)*, **calções** *(fpl)
  swimming trunks*
**calçar** *to put on (shoes, gloves)*
**calçar-se** *to put one's shoes on*
**calmo** *calm*
**calor** *(m) heat*
**calor** *(m):* **faz calor** *it is hot
  (weather)*
**cama** *(f) bed*
**cama de casal** *(f) double bed*
**cama de solteiro** *(f) single bed*
**câmara** *(f) camera*
**câmara municipal** *(f) town
  council; town hall (Eur.)*
**câmbio** *(m) foreign exchange*
**caminhar** *to walk; to progress*
**caminho** *(m) way, route*
**caminho de ferro** *(m) (Eur.)
  railway / railroad (US)*
**camioneta** *(f) van*
**camioneta (para passageiros)** *(f)
  (Eur.) coach*
**campeonato** *(m) championship*
**campismo** *(m) camping*
**campista** *(mf) camper*

**campo** *(m) field; countryside;
  ground, court (sport)*
**canadense / canadiano** *(Eur.)
  from Canada, Canadian*
**canal** *(m) channel; canal*
**canção** *(f) song*
**candidato** *(m) candidate (exam,
  job)*
**candidatura** *(f) application*
**caneta** *(f) pen*
**cansado** *tired*
**cantar** *to sing*
**canto** *(m) corner (inside of angle)*
**cão** *(m) dog*
**capital** *(f) capital city*
**cara** *(f) face*
**característica / caraterística** *(f)
  characteristic, feature*
**caravana** *(f) caravan*
**cardápio** *(m) (Br.) menu card*
**cargo** *(m) post (job)*
**carnaval** *(m) carnival*
**carne** *(f) meat*
**caro** *dear, expensive*
**carro** *(m) car / auto(mobile) (US);*
  **de carro** *by car*
**carta** *(f) letter*
**carta de condução** *(f) (Eur.) driving
  licence / driver's licence (US)*
**cartão** *(m) card*
**cartão de crédito** *(m) credit card*
**cartão de visita** *(m) calling card*
**cartão postal** *(m) (Br.) postcard*
**carteira** *(f) wallet / billfold (US);
  small handbag*
**carteira de identidade** *(f) (Br.)
  identity card*
**carteira de motorista** *(f) (Br.) driving
  licence / driver's licence (US)*
**casa** *(f) house; home;* **em casa** *at
  home;* **para casa** *home (going to)*

casa de banho (f) (Eur.) bathroom; toilet / washroom (US)

casa de fado(s) (f) 'fado' house (see also fado)

casaco (m) coat

casado married

casal (m) couple

casamento (m) marriage, wedding

casar-se to get married

caso (m) case; (em) caso (de) in case of

castanho (Eur.) brown

castelo (m) castle

católico catholic

catorze fourteen

causa (f) cause; por causa de because

cavalheiro (m) gentleman

cebola (f) onion

cedo early

celular (m) mobile phone / cellphone (US)

cem a hundred

centavo, cêntimo (m) cent

cento (m) a hundred; por cento percent

central central

centro (m) centre

centro comercial (m) (Eur.) shopping centre

cereal (m) cereal

certeza (f) certainty; ter (a) certeza to be sure

certo right; certo! OK!

cerveja (f) beer

chá (m) tea

chamar to call; to send for

chamar-se to be called

chão (m) floor, ground

chave (f) key

chávena (f) (Eur.) cup

chegada (f) arrival

chegar to arrive

cheio full, complete

cheque (m) cheque / check (US)

cheque de viagem (m) traveller's cheque / check (US)

chorar to cry, weep

chumbo (m) lead

chuva (f) rain

chuveiro (m) shower (bath)

cidade (f) town, city

cidade natal (f) native town, home town

cima: em cima above; em cima de on top of; por cima de over

cima: lá / aqui em cima upstairs, at the top

cimo (m) top

cinco five

cinema (m) cinema

cinquenta fifty

cinto (m) belt

cinza (f) ash; grey (Br.)

cinzento grey (Eur.)

circundar to surround

clara (f) egg-white

claro light (luminosity)

classe (f) class

clima (m) climate

clube (m) club

cobertor (m) blanket

cobrar to cash

cobrir to cover

coco (m) coconut

coisa (f) thing

colcha (f) bedspread

colega (mf) colleague; classmate

colégio (m) school, college

colher (f) spoon

colocar to place, put

**com** *with*
**combinação** *(f) combination; slip (underwear)*
**combinar** *to arrange, agree*
**comboio** *(m) (Eur.) train*
**combustível** *(m) fuel*
**começar** *to start, begin*
**começo** *(m) start, beginning*
**comer** *to eat;* **dar de comer a** *to feed*
**comerciante** *(mf) business person*
**comida** *(f) food*
**comigo** *with me*
**como** *how; like; as*
**comparecer** *to attend (function)*
**completamente** *completely, totally*
**completo** *complete*
**compra** *(f) purchase;* **fazer compras** *to go shopping*
**comprar** *to buy*
**compreender** *to understand*
**comprido** *long;* **ao comprido** *lengthways*
**comprimento** *(m) length*
**computador** *(m) computer*
**comunicar** *to communicate, inform*
**conceder** *to grant; to give*
**concerto** *(m) concert*
**concordar** *to agree*
**conduzir** *(Eur.) to drive (vehicle)*
**conhecer** *to know; to get to know; to meet for the first time*
**conhecido** *(m) acquaintance*
**conhecimento** *(m) knowledge*
**conjunto** *(m) collection; group; outfit (clothes)*
**connosco** *(Eur.),* **conosco** *(Br.) with us*
**conseguir** *to get, obtain*

**conseguir fazer** *to manage to do, succeed in doing*
**consertar** *to repair, mend*
**considerar** *to consider; to regard*
**consigo** *with him, her; with you*
**consigo (conseguir): não consigo** *I can't*
**consistir em** *to consist of*
**constipação** *(f) (Eur.) cold (health condition)*
**constipado: estar constipado** *(Eur.) to have a cold*
**construir** *to build*
**consulado** *(m) consulate*
**consulta** *(f) consultation; appointment*
**consultório** *(m) surgery*
**conta** *(f) arithmetic work, sum; bill; account*
**contar** *to count;* **a contar de** *counting from*
**contar** *to narrate, tell*
**contente** *happy, pleased*
**contínuo** *continuous*
**conto** *(m) story, tale*
**contra** *against*
**controle, controlo** *(m) controle*
**conversa, conversação** *(f) conversation*
**conversar** *to talk*
**convidar** *to invite*
**convir** *to suit; to be convenient*
**convite** *(m) invitation*
**copo** *(m) glass, cup (no handle)*
**cor** *(f) colour*
**corredor** *(m) corridor; passageway*
**correio** *(m) post office; mail;* **pelo correio** *by post*
**correr** *to run*
**correspondência** *(f) mail, correspondence*

corrigir *to correct*
cortar *to cut*
costa *(f) coast, coastline*
costumar *to use to*
couro *(m) leather*
couve *(m) cabbage*
cozer *to boil, cook*
cozinha *(f) kitchen*
creme de barbear *(m) shaving
cream*
creme dental *(m) toothpaste*
crer *to believe*
criança *(f) child*
cruzamento *(m) crossroads,
junction*
cuidado *(m) care; cuidado! watch
out!*
cujo *whose, of which*
cultivo *(m) cultivation*
cultura *(f) culture*
cumprimentos *(mpl) regards*
currículo *(m) C.V.*
curso *(m) course, course of studies*
curto *short (length or duration)*
custar *to cost*

da (= de + a)
dali (= de + ali)
daquele (= de + aquele)
daqui (= de + aqui)
daquilo (= de + aquilo)
dar *to give*
dar para *to look on to*
data *(f) date*
de *of; from; by*
deceção *(f) disappointment*
décimo *tenth*
declarar *to declare, say*
defeito *(m) defect; com defeito
out of order (Br.)*
deficiente *(mf) disabled person*

deitar-se *to lie down; to go to bed*
deixar *to leave (abandon);
to allow; deixar de …
to stop …*
dela (= de + ela)
dele (= de + ele)
demais *too, too much*
demorar *to take time; to delay*
dentista *(mf) dentist*
dentro *in, inside; dentro de within
(time)*
depois *after, afterwards, then*
depois: depois de amanhã *the
day after tomorrow*
depositar *to put in, deposit*
depressa *quickly; depressa! hurry!*
desafiador *challenging*
desaparecer *to disappear*
desarranjado *out of order (Br.)*
descalçar *to take off (shoes, gloves)*
descalçar-se *to take one's
shoes off*
descansar *to rest*
descascar *to remove shell or peel*
descer *to go / come down*
descobrir *to discover*
desconhecido *unknown*
descontar *to cash (cheque / check
(US))*
desculpar *to excuse; to forgive*
desculpe *sorry; excuse me*
desde *since; desde já from now*
desejar *to desire, wish; o que
deseja? what would you like?*
desfiar *to reduce to threads*
desfile *(m) parade*
desligar *to disconnect*
desodorante *(m) (Br.) deodorant*
desodorizante *(m) (Eur.)
deodorant*
despir *to take off (clothes)*

**despir-se** to get undressed
**desporto** (m) (Eur.) sport
**desse** (= de + esse); (see also **dar**)
**deste** (= de + este); (see also **dar**)
**destinatário** (m) addressee
**destino** (m) destination
**detestar** to dislike strongly, detest
**devagar** slowly
**dever** to owe; should, must, ought to; to be likely to
**dez** ten
**dezanove** (Eur.), **dezenove** (Br.) nineteen
**dezasseis** (Eur.), **dezesseis** (Br.) sixteen
**dezassete** (Eur.), **dezessete** (Br.) seventeen
**dezembro** (m) December
**dezoito** eighteen
**dia** (m) day; **bom dia** good morning; **dia útil** working day
**dia de anos** (m) (Eur.) birthday
**dia-a-dia** (m) daily life
**diálogo** (m) dialogue
**diária** (f) daily charge, rate
**diário** daily
**diarreia** (f) diarrhoea
**dicionário** (m) dictionary
**dieta** (f) diet
**diferente** different
**diga** (see **dizer**)
**dinheiro** (m) money; (**dinheiro**) **trocado** small change
**diploma** (m) certificate, diploma
**direção** (f) direction
**direita** (f) right; **à direita** on / to the right
**direito** right; straight
**direito de importação** (m) import duty
**direto** direct

**dirigir** to direct; to drive (vehicle) (Br.)
**discoteca** (f) discotheque, disco
**disse** (see **dizer**)
**disso** (= de + isso)
**distinção** (f) distinction
**disto** (= de + isto)
**divertir-se** to enjoy oneself, to have a good time
**divorciado** divorced
**diz** see **dizer**
**dizer** to say, inform, tell
**dizer: querer dizer** to mean
**do** (= de + o)
**doce** sweet
**doce** (m) sweet, pudding
**documento** (m) document
**doente** ill
**doer** to hurt; **dói** it hurts
**dois** (m) two; **os dois** both
**dólar** (m) dollar
**domicílio** (m) home, residence
**domingo** (m) Sunday
**domínio** (m) command (language)
**dona de casa** (f) housewife
**dor** (f) pain, ache
**dormida** (f) sleep; sleeping accommodation
**dormir** to sleep
**doze** twelve
**duas** (f) two; **as duas** both
**ducha** (f) (Br.), **duche** (m) (Eur.) shower (bath)
**duplo** double
**durante** for, during
**duzentos** two hundred
**dúzia** (f) dozen; **meia dúzia** half a dozen

**e** and
**é** (see **ser**)

**edifício** (m) building
**efeito** (m) effect
**ela** she, it
**ele** he, it
**elétrico** (m) (Eur.) tram / streetcar (US)
**elevado** high
**elevador** (m) lift / elevator (US)
**em** in, on, at
**embarcar** to board
**embora** although; (see also **ir(-se) embora**)
**embrulhar** to wrap up
**ementa** (f) (Eur.) menu card
**emergência** (f) emergency
**emitir** to issue
**empregado** (m) employee, assistant
**emprego** (m) employment, job
**empresa** (f) firm
**empurrar** to push
**encerrar** to close, shut
**encerrar** (computer) to log out
**encher** to fill
**encomenda** (f) parcel
**encontrar** to find, meet
**encontro** (m) meeting
**endereço** (m) address
**enganar-se** to be mistaken
**engenheiro** (m) engineer
**enorme** huge
**enquanto** while, whilst
**ensinar** to teach
**então** then
**entender** to understand
**entrada** (f) way in; entry; entrance; hallway; admission ticket
**entrar** to enter; to go / come in
**entrar** (computer) to log on
**entre** between, among; (see also **entrar**)

**entregar** to deliver; to hand in / over
**entregue** delivered
**entrevista** (f) interview
**enumerar** to list
**envelope** (m) envelope
**enviar** to send
**equipado** equipped
**errado** wrong, incorrect
**erro** (m) error, mistake
**escada** (f) stairs
**escada rolante** (f) escalator
**escocês** from Scotland, Scottish
**escola** (f) school
**escolher** to choose
**escova de dentes** (f) toothbrush
**escrever** to write; **como se escreve?** how do you spell it?
**escrito** written
**escritório** (m) office
**escudo** (m) former unit of Portuguese currency
**escuro** dark
**escutar** to listen
**esforço** (m) effort
**esgotado** sold out
**espadim** (m) large fish akin to tuna
**especial** special
**especialmente** particularly
**espécie** (f) species; kind
**esperança** (f) hope
**esperar** to wait, expect, hope
**esporte** (m) (Br.) sport
**esposa** (f) wife
**esposo** (m) husband
**esquecer(-se)** to forget
**esquerda** (f) left; **à esquerda** on / to the left
**esquina** (f) corner (outside of angle)

**esse** *that, that one (m); (see also* **aquele***)*
**está** *(see* **estar***)*
**esta** *this, this one (f)*
**estação** *(f) station; season*
**estacionamento** *(m) parking*
**estacionar** *to park, wait*
**estada, estadia** *(f) stay*
**estádio** *(m) stadium*
**estado** *(m) state*
**estado civil** *(m) marital status*
**estar** *to be;* **está bem** *it's all right*
**este** *this, this one (m)*
**este** *(m) east; (see also* **leste***)*
**estimar** *to appreciate*
**estimar** *to wish;* **estimo as suas (rápidas) melhoras** *I wish you a speedy recovery*
**estiver** *(see* **estar***)*
**estômago** *(m) stomach*
**estrada** *(f) open road*
**estrada de ferro** *(f) (Br.) railway / railroad (US)*
**estrangeiro** *foreign*
**estrangeiro** *(m) abroad*
**estreito** *narrow*
**estrela** *(f) star*
**estudante** *(mf) student*
**estudar** *to study*
**eu** *I*
**euro** *(m) euro*
**europeu** *from Europe, European*
**exame** *(m) examination*
**exatamente** *exactly*
**excecional** *exceptional*
**excelente** *excellent*
**excesso de velocidade** *(m) speeding*
**exceto** *except*
**excursão** *(f) excursion*
**exemplo** *(m) example;* **por exemplo** *for instance*

**exercício** *(m) exercise*
**êxito** *(m) success*
**experiência** *(f) experience*
**experimentar** *to experiment, try*
**expressão** *(f) expression*
**exterior** *(m) outside, exterior*

**faca** *(f) knife*
**faça** *(see* **fazer***)*
**fácil** *easy*
**facilidade** *(f) facility*
**facto** *(Eur.),* **fato** *(Br.) (m) fact*
**fadista** *(mf) 'fado'-singer*
**fado** *(m) traditional Portuguese song*
**falar** *to speak*
**falta** *(f) lack*
**faltar** *to miss, be missing*
**família** *(f) family*
**farmácia** *(f) chemist's (shop)*
**fatia** *(f) slice*
**fato** *(m) (Eur.) suit; (see also* **facto***)*
**fato de banho** *(m) (Eur.) bathing costume / bathing suit (US)*
**fator** *(m) factor*
**fauna** *(f) fauna*
**favor** *(m) favour;* **faça / faz / por favor** *please, excuse me; please do*
**favorito** *favourite*
**faz** *(see* **fazer***)*
**faz: tanto faz** *I don't mind (it's all the same)*
**fazer** *to do; to make*
**fechar** *to close, shut*
**federal** *federal*
**feito** *(see* **fazer***)*
**felicidades** *(fpl) all the best (wish)*
**feliz** *happy*
**felizmente** *fortunately*
**feminino** *female, feminine*

**fenómeno** (Eur.) / **fenômeno** (Br.)
  (m) phenomenon
**feriado** (m) holiday
**férias** (fpl) holidays / vacation (US)
**ferir** to hurt, wound, bruise
**ferro** (m) iron
**festa** (f) party, celebration
**fevereiro** (m) February
**fiambre** (m) (Eur.) ham
**fica** (see **ficar**)
**ficar** to be; to be situated; to stay;
  to become
**ficar com** to take, keep
**ficha** (f) form card; token
**fila** (f) line, queue; row
**filha** (f) daughter
**filho** (m) son
**fim** (m) end
**fim de semana** (m) weekend
**finalidade** (f) purpose
**finalmente** finally, at last
**fingir** to pretend
**fique** (see **ficar**)
**flexibilidade horária** (f) flexible
  time (work)
**flor** (f) flower
**flora** (f) flora
**fluentemente** fluently
**fogo** (m) fire
**foi** (see **ser** and **ir**)
**folheto** (m) leaflet
**fome** (f): **estar com / ter fome** to
  be hungry
**fone** (m) (Br.) receiver (telephone)
**fora** out, outside
**força** (f) strength; **força!** take
  heart!
**forma** (f) shape; **em boa
  forma** fit
**formação** (f) studies, training
**formar-se** to graduate
**formulário** (m) form

**fotografia** (f) photograph;
  photography
**fotografia tipo passe** (f) ID
  photograph
**freguês** (m) customer
**frente** (f) front; **em frente de / a**
  straight on, opposite; **à frente de**
  facing
**frequentar** to attend (course)
**frequente** frequent
**frequentemente** often
**frigorífico** (m) (Eur.) refrigerator
**frio** cold
**frio** (m): **faz frio** it is cold
  (weather)
**frito** fried
**fronteira** (f) frontier, border
**fruta** (f) fruit
**fui** (see **ser** and **ir**)
**fumador** (m) (Eur.) smoker
**fumante** (m) (Br.) smoker
**fumar** to smoke
**função** (f) function; role (job)
**funcionar** to work, function,
  operate
**fundo** (m) bottom; back (room)
**futebol** (m) soccer
**futuro** (m) future

**galeria** (f) gallery (theatre)
**galeria de arte** (f) art gallery
**galês** from Wales, Welsh
**ganhar** to earn, win
**garagem** (f) garage
**garantir** to guarantee
**garfo** (m) fork
**garrafa** (f) bottle (beverage)
**gás** (m) gas; **com gás** fizzy; **sem
  gás** still
**gasóleo** (m) diesel oil
**gasolina** (f) petrol / gas(oline)
  (US)

**gato** *(m)* cat
**geladeira** *(f) (Br.)* refrigerator
**gelado** *frozen; ice-cold*
**gelado** *(m) (Eur.)* ice cream; ice
lolly
**geleia** *(f)* fruit jelly / jam
**gema** *(f)* egg-yolk
**genro** *(m)* son-in-law
**gente** *(f)* people; **toda a gente**
everyone *(Eur.)*
**gentil** *courteous, charming, kind*
**geral** *general*
**gerente** *(mf)* manager,
manageress
**golfe** *(m)* golf
**gordo** *fat*
**gostar de** *to like;* **gostar muito de**
... *to like ... very much*
**governo** *(m)* government
**grama** *(m)* gram
**grande** *large, big*
**grátis, gratuito** *free, without*
charge
**grau** *(m)* degree
**grave** *serious*
**grisalho** *grey (hair)*
**grupo** *(m)* group, party
**guarda** *(f)* guard, police
**guarda-chuva** *(m)* umbrella
**guardanapo** *(m)* napkin
**guarda-sol** *(m)* parasol; beach
parasol, sunshade
**guichê** *(m)* service window (bank,
etc.)
**guineense, guinéu** *from Guinea,
Guinean*
**guitarra** *(f)* Portuguese guitar;
guitar, traditionally known as
**viola**

**há** *for; ago; how long; (see also*
**haver)**

**habitante** *(mf)* inhabitant
**habitualmente** *usually*
**haver** *there to be; to exist; have
(auxiliary)*
**hei de** *I will; (see also* **haver)**
**hipermercado** *(m)* hypermarket
**história** *(f)* history
**hoje** *today*
**homem** *(m)* man
**hora** *(f),* **horas** *(fpl)* hour(s);
o'clock; **meia (hora)** *half an hour,
half past*
**hora: a que horas ... ?** *at what
time ... ?*
**hora: que horas são?** *what time
is it?*
**horário** *(m)* timetable
**horas de abertura** *(fpl)* opening
hours
**hospedeiro (de bordo)** *(m) (Eur.)
air steward / host*
**hospital** *(m)* hospital
**hotel** *(m)* hotel

**ida** *(f)* going, departure; one-way
(ticket)
**ida e volta** *(f)* return, round-trip
(ticket)
**idade** *(f)* age
**ideia** *(f)* idea
**identidade** *(f)* identity
**idioma** *(m)* language
**igreja** *(f)* church
**igual a** *equal to; the same as*
**igualmente** *equally; likewise*
**ilha** *(f)* island
**ímpar** *odd (number)*
**importância** *(f) importance;* **não
tem importância** *not to worry,
it's all right*
**importante** *important; main*
**importar** *to import*

**importar-se** *to mind;* **importa-se...?** *can you please...?*
**imposto** *(m) tax*
**impressão digital** *(f) fingerprint*
**impresso** *(m) printed paper; form*
**incluir** *to include; to enclose*
**incomodar** *to inconvenience, disturb*
**incómodo** *(Eur.),* **incômodo** *(Br.) (m) inconvenience*
**indigestão** *(f) indigestion*
**individual** *individual*
**individualizar** *to individualize*
**indivíduo** *(m) individual*
**indústria** *(f) industry*
**inesquecível** *unforgettable*
**informação** *(f) information*
**informar** *to inform; to report*
**informática** *(f) computing; computer science*
**infração** *(f) infringement*
**inglês** *from England, English*
**Inglês / inglês** *(m) English (language) (discipline of study)*
**ingresso** *(m) (Br.) admission ticket*
**inicial** *initial*
**iniciar** *to start*
**iniciar** *(computer) to log in*
**instalação** *(f) facility*
**instalar** *to install*
**instrução** *(f) instruction; education*
**insuficiente** *insufficient*
**integrado (em)** *as part of*
**interessado** *interested*
**interessante** *interesting*
**interesse** *(m) interest*
**interior** *inner; inside*
**internacional** *international*
**intérprete** *(mf) interpreter*
**interurbano** *long distance*
**intervalo** *(m) interval, break*
**introdução** *(f) introduction*

**introduzir** *to introduce, insert*
**inverno** *(m) winter*
**iogurte** *(m) yogurt*
**ir** *to go;* **ir para casa** *to go home*
**ir(-se) embora** *to go away*
**irlandês** *from Ireland, Irish*
**irmã** *(f) sister*
**irmão** *(m) brother*
**irrigação** *(f) irrigation*
**isso** *that; (see also* **aquilo***)*
**isto** *this;* **isto é** *that's to say, I mean*

**já** *now, immediately; presently; already; ever;* **já não (mais)** *no longer;* **já está!** *done!*
**janeiro** *(m) January*
**janela** *(f) window*
**jantar** *to have dinner, the evening meal;* **jantar fora** *to eat out*
**jantar** *(m) dinner, evening meal*
**jardim** *(m) garden*
**jardim zoológico, zoo** *(m) zoo*
**jogar** *play (game)*
**joia** *(f) jewel*
**jornal** *(m) newspaper*
**jovem** *young*
**julho** *(m) July*
**junho** *(m) June*
**juntamente** *together; attached*
**junto** *next to, (close) by*

**la** *you, her, it*
**lá** *there (see also* **ali***)*
**lã** *(f) wool*
**lado** *(m) side;* **ao lado de** *beside;* **todo(s) o(s) lado(s)** *everywhere*
**lanche** *(m) snack*
**laranja** *(f) orange*
**largo** *wide; loose (clothes)*
**largo** *(m) square, precinct*
**largo: ao largo** *off (coast)*

**largura** *(f) width*
**lata** *(f) tin, can*
**lavabo** *(m) toilet / washroom (US)*
**lavagem de roupa** *(f) laundry service*
**lavandaria** *(Eur.),* **lavanderia** *(Br.) (f) launderette*
**lavar** *to wash*
**lavar-se** *to have a wash*
**lazer** *(m) leisure*
**leitaria** *(Eur.),* **leiteria** *(Br.) (f) dairy (shop)*
**leite** *(m) milk*
**leito** *(m) bed*
**lembrança** *(f) souvenir*
**lembrar** *to remind*
**lembrar(-se)** *to remember*
**lençol** *(m) sheet (bed)*
**lente de contacto** *(Eur.)* **/ contato** *(Br.) (f) contact lens*
**ler** *to read*
**leste** *(m) east; (see also* **este** *and* **ler***)*
**levantar** *to stand, pick up*
**levantar-se** *to stand up, get up; to get up from bed*
**levar** *to take, to carry; to lead to*
**levar tempo** *to require or take time*
**leve** *light (weight); (see also* **levar***)*
**lhe** *(to) you, him, her, it*
**libra** *(f) pound*
**lição** *(f) lesson*
**licença** *(f) permission*
**ligar** *to connect*
**limão** *(m) lemon*
**limpar** *to clean, wipe clean*
**limpeza** *(f) cleaning*
**limpo** *clean*
**lindo** *beautiful*
**língua** *(f) tongue; language*

**linha** *(f) thread*
**linha férrea** *(f) railway*
**linho** *(m) linen (material)*
**liso** *straight; plain (pattern)*
**lista** *(f) list*
**lista dos telefones / telefónica** *(Eur.)* **/ telefônica** *(Br.) (f) telephone directory*
**literatura** *(f) literature*
**litoral** *(m) coast, seaboard*
**litro** *(m) litre*
**livraria** *(f) bookshop*
**livre** *free, vacant; for hire*
**livro** *(m) book*
**lixo** *(m) litter; rubbish / garbage (US)*
**lo** *you, him, it*
**local** *(m) site, place*
**local** *local*
**localização** *(f) location*
**logo** *later; straightaway*
**loja** *(f) shop*
**longe** *far*
**longo** *long;* **ao longo de** *along*
**louro** *light brown; blond*
**lua-de-mel** *(f) honeymoon*
**lugar** *(m) place, space; seat*
**lusófono** *Portuguese-speaking*
**luva** *(f) glove*
**luz** *(f) light*

**má** *bad, evil (f)*
**maçã** *(f) apple*
**macaense** *from Macau, Macanese*
**maçaneta** *(f) knob, handle*
**machucar** *(Br.) to hurt, wound, bruise*
**madeira** *(f) wood (material)*
**madeirense** *from Madeira, Madeiran*

**madrugada** (f) early hours of the day, past midnight
**mãe** (f) mother
**magro** thin, slim
**maiô** (m) (Br.) bathing costume / bathing suit (US)
**maio** (m) May
**maior** larger; **o maior** the largest
**mais** more; **o mais** the most; **mais (do) que** more than
**mal** badly
**mal** (m) harm; **não faz mal** never mind; it's all right (in response to an apology)
**mala (de viagem)** (f) suitcase
**mandar** to be in charge; to order; to send
**mandar consertar** ... to have ... repaired
**manhã** (f) morning
**manteiga** (f) butter
**manter-se** to remain; to stand / stay still
**manuscrito** handwritten
**mão** (f) hand; flow of traffic
**mapa** (m) map
**máquina** (f) machine
**máquina de filmar** (f) movie / video camera
**máquina fotográfica** (f) (photo) camera
**mar** (m) sea
**maravilhoso** wonderful
**marcar** to mark; to book
**março** (m) March
**marido** (m) husband
**marisco** (m) shellfish
**marmelada** (f) quince paste
**marrom** (Br.) brown
**mas** but
**masculino** male, masculine

**mau** bad, evil (m)
**máximo** maximum
**me** me, to me, for me
**medicamento** (m) medicine
**médico** (m) doctor
**meia** (f) sock, stocking
**meia-noite** (f) midnight
**meio** (m) half; **ao meio** in half; **no meio** in the middle
**meio-dia** (m) midday
**melhor** better; **o melhor** the best
**melhora** (f) improvement; **melhoras!** get well soon!
**melhorar** to improve, make / get better
**menina** (f) young girl
**menino** (m) young boy
**menor** smaller; **o menor** the smallest
**menos** less, fewer; **o menos** the least, fewest
**mensalmente** monthly
**mercearia** (f) grocer's (shop)
**mês** (m) month
**mesa** (f) table
**mesmo** same; really; right
**mesmo** que even if
**meter** to put (in)
**meter-se em** to get involved in
**metro** (Eur.), **metrô** (Br.) (m) underground train / subway (US)
**meu** my, mine (m)
**mil** thousand
**milhão** (m) million
**mim** (to / for) me
**minha** my, mine (f)
**minuto** (m) minute
**misturar** to mix
**mobilado** furnished
**moçambicano** from Mozambique, Mozambican

**moço** *(m) boy, young man*
**moderno** *modern*
**moeda** *(f) coin*
**momento** *(m) moment*
**montanha** *(f) mountain*
**montra** *(f) (Eur.) shop window*
**morango** *(m) strawberry*
**morar** *to live, be resident*
**moreno** *dark (skin)*
**morrer** *to die*
**mostrar** *to show*
**motorista** *(mf) driver*
**mudar** *to change*
**mudar-se** *to move house, residence*
**muito** *much; a lot of; very*
**muitos** *(mpl)*, **muitas** *(fpl) many*
**mulher** *(f) woman; wife*
**multa** *(f) fine*
**mundo** *(m) world; todo (o) mundo (Br.) everyone*
**museu** *(m) museum*
**música** *(f) music*

**na (= em + a)**
**nacional** *national*
**nacionalidade** *(f) nationality*
**nada** *nothing;* **de nada** *not at all;* **não foi nada** *not to worry, it's all right*
**nadar** *to swim*
**não** *no; not;* **não mais** *no longer*
**nascer** *to be born*
**nascimento** *(m) birth*
**natal** *native*
**Natal** *(m) Christmas*
**natural** *natural; native*
**naturalmente** *naturally*
**natureza** *(f) nature*
**navegador** *(m) navigator*

**necessário** *necessary*
**negócio** *(m) business*
**negro** *black*
**nem** *nor;* **nem … nem …** *neither … nor …*
**nenhum** *no, none*
**neozelandês** *from New Zealand, New Zealander*
**neste (= em + este)**
**neta** *(f) granddaughter*
**neto** *(m) grandson*
**ninguém** *no-one*
**nível** *(m) level*
**no (= em + o)**
**noite** *(f) night;* **boa noite** *good night / evening*
**noivado** *(m) engagement*
**noivo** *engaged;* **noivo** *(m) fiancé*
**nome** *(m) name*
**nome completo** *(m) full name*
**nomeadamente** *namely*
**nono** *ninth*
**nora** *(f) daughter-in-law*
**normalmente** *normally; usually*
**norte** *(m) north*
**Norte: o Norte** *the North, Northern part of the country*
**nós** *we*
**nos (= em + os);** *(to / for) us, (to) ourselves*
**nosso** *our, ours*
**nota** *(f) note*
**notar** *to notice*
**notícia** *(f) news*
**noticiário** *(m) news bulletin*
**noutro (= em + outro)**
**novamente** *anew, again*
**nove** *nine*
**novecentos** *nine hundred*
**novembro** *(m) November*
**noventa** *ninety*

**novo** *new; young*
**nublado** *cloudy*
**número** *(m) number*
**nunca** *never*

**o** *the (m); you (m); him, it*
**obrigada** *thank you (said by a female),* **obrigado** *thank you (said by a male)*
**obrigatório** *obligatory*
**observação** *(f) observation*
**obter** *to obtain, get*
**ocasionalmente** *occasionally*
**oceano** *(m) ocean*
**oculista** *(mf) optician*
**óculos** *(mpl) glasses, spectacles*
**óculos de sol** *(mpl) sun glasses*
**ocupação** *(f) occupation*
**ocupar** *to occupy*
**oeste** *(m) west*
**oferecer** *to offer; to make a gift of*
**oficial** *official*
**oi!** *(Br.) hi! (greeting)*
**oitavo** *eighth*
**oitenta** *eighty*
**oito** *eight*
**oitocentos** *eight hundred*
**olá!** *hello!; hi! (greeting)*
**óleo** *(m) oil*
**olhar** *to look*
**olhar por** *to look after*
**onde** *where*
**ônibus** *(m) (Br.) bus, coach*
**ontem** *yesterday*
**onze** *eleven*
**opcional** *optional*
**opinião** *(f) opinion*
**oportunidade** *(f) opportunity*
**ora** *now; well*
**ordem** *(f) order*

**ordem: à ordem de** *made out to (cheque / check (US))*
**organização** *(f) organization; organizing committee*
**organizador** *(m) organizer*
**ótimo** *excellent*
**ou** *or;* **ou … ou …** *either … or …*
**ouro** *(m) gold*
**outono** *(m) autumn / fall (US)*
**outro** *other, another*
**outubro** *(m) October*
**ouvir** *to hear;* **ouvir com atenção** *to listen to*
**ovo** *(m) egg*

**pacote** *(m) packet; carton*
**padaria** *(f) bakery, baker's (shop)*
**pagamento** *(m) payment*
**pagar** *to pay*
**pai** *(m) father*
**país** *(m) country*
**pais** *(mpl) parents*
**paisagem** *(f) scenery*
**palácio** *(m) palace*
**palavra** *(f) word*
**pane** *(f) breakdown*
**pão** *(m) bread, loaf*
**pãozinho** *(m) roll (bread)*
**papel** *(m) paper*
**papel higiénico** *(Eur.) /* **higiênico** *(Br.) (m) toilet paper*
**par** *even (number)*
**para** *to, for; (see also* **parar***)*
**parabéns** *(mpl) congratulations; happy birthday*
**parada** *(f) (Br.) stop;* **parada de ônibus** *bus / coach stop*
**paragem** *(f) (Eur.) stop;* **paragem de autocarros** *bus / coach stop*
**paraíso** *(m) paradise*
**parar** *to stop*

**parcómetro** (m) (Eur.) parking meter

**parecer** to appear, seem

**parede** (f) wall

**parente** (m) relative, relation

**parque** (m) park

**parque de campismo** (m) (Eur.) camping / caravanning site

**parque infantil** (m) children's playground

**parquímetro** (m) (Br.) parking meter

**parte** (f) part; **outra parte** somewhere else; **toda a parte** everywhere

**parte da frente** (f) front

**parte de trás** (f) back

**participar** to take part

**partida** (f) departure

**partir** to leave, depart, set off; to break; **a partir de** starting from

**Páscoa** (f) Easter

**passado** last, past

**passado: bem / mal passado** well done / rare (food)

**passageiro** (m) passenger

**passagem** (f) fare

**passaporte** (m) passport

**passar** to go past, by; to go through

**passar** to iron (clothes)

**passar** to pass (exam)

**passar** to spend (time)

**passatempo predileto** (m) hobby

**passe** (m) pass; (see also **passar**)

**passear** to go for a leisurely walk or ride; to take for a walk

**passeio** (m) leisure walk or ride

**pasta de dentes** (f) toothpaste

**pastelaria** (f) cake shop

**património** (Eur.), **patrimônio** (Br.) (m) heritage

**pé** (m) foot

**pé: a pé** on foot; **em / de pé** standing

**peão** (m) (Eur.) pedestrian

**pedaço** (m) piece

**pedestre** (m) (Br.) pedestrian

**pedir** to ask for

**pegar** to grab, pick up; to take hold of

**peixe** (m) fish

**pele** (f) skin

**pelo** (m) hair; fur

**pelo** (= por + o)

**pena** (f) pity; **ter pena** to feel sorry

**penalidade** (f) penalty

**pendurar** to hang

**pensão** (f) boarding house

**pensar** to think; **pensar em** to think of / about

**penúltimo** penultimate

**pequeno** small

**pequeno-almoço** (m) (Eur.) breakfast

**perceber** to understand; to realize

**perder** to lose; to miss

**perfil** (m) profile

**pergunta** (f) question; **fazer uma pergunta** to ask a question

**perguntar** to ask, enquire

**perigo** (m) danger

**permanente** permanent

**permitir** to allow

**pertencer a** to belong to

**perto** near; **perto daqui / aqui perto** nearby

**pesado** heavy

**pesca** (f) fishing

**pessoa** (f) person

**pessoal** *(m) personnel, staff*
**pessoas** *(fpl) people*
**picolé** *(m) (Br.) (ice) lolly*
**pimenta** *(f) pepper*
**pior** *worse;* **o pior** *the worst*
**piorar** *to get worse*
**piscina** *(f) swimming pool, pool*
**piso** *(m) floor, level*
**placa** *(f) plate; signpost*
**placa de matrícula** *(Eur.)* **/**
  **licença** *(Br.) (f) car registration*
  *plate*
**plano** *(m) plan*
**plástico** *plastic*
**plataforma** *(f) platform*
**pneu** *(m) tyre*
**pode** *(see* **poder**)
**poder** *can; may*
**pois** *so; since, because; but;* **pois**
  **bem** *well then*
**pois não** *(Br.) please do; how can I*
  *help you?*
**pois não!** *of course!, certainly!, yes*
  *with pleasure!*
**pois sim!** *(ironically) oh sure!*
**polícia** *(f) police*
**ponte** *(f) bridge*
**ponto** *(m) point; dot*
**ponto de encontro** *(m) meeting*
  *point*
**ponto de táxi** *(m) taxi-rank*
**popular** *popular; pop*
**por** *for; per; a / an; by*
**pôr** *to put; to put on (clothes,*
  *shoes)*
**por aqui** *hereabouts; this way*
**por causa de** *because*
**por que ... ?** *why ... ?*
**por quê?** *why?*
**por quem?** *by whom?*
**porção** *(f) portion*

**porque** *because*
**porta** *(f) door*
**porto** *(m) port (drink)*
**porto** *(m) port; harbour*
**português** *from Portugal,*
  *Portuguese*
**Português / português** *(m)*
  *Portuguese (language) (discipline*
  *of study)*
**possível** *possible*
**posso** *(see* **poder**)
**possuir** *to possess, have*
**posta** *(f) fish steak*
**postal** *(m) postcard*
**posto de abastecimento /**
  **combustível / gasolina** *(m)*
  *filling station*
**pouco** *little, few;* **um pouco**
  *a little*
**praça** *(f) square; market place*
**praça de táxis** *(f) taxi-rank*
**praia** *(f) beach; seaside*
**prata** *(f) silver*
**prateleira** *(f) shelf*
**praticamente** *practically*
**praticar** *to practise*
**prato** *(m) plate; dish*
**prazer** *(m) pleasure;* **muito prazer**
  *delighted to meet you*
**prazo** *(m) period; time limit*
**precisar** *(de) to need*
**preço** *(m) price, cost*
**preencher** *to complete*
**prefeitura** *(municipal) (f) (Br.)*
  *town hall*
**preferir** *to prefer*
**premer** *to press*
**preocupado** *worried*
**preocupar-se** *to worry*
**preparar** *to prepare*
**presente** *present*

**presente** (m) present, gift
**pressa** (f) hurry; haste
**pressionar** to put on pressure; to press (button)
**presunto (cozido)** (m) (Br.) ham
**presunto** (m) (Eur.) bacon
**pretender** to intend; to ask for (requirement)
**preto** black
**primavera** (f) spring
**primeiro** first
**primeiro** plano (m) forefront
**principal** principal, main
**principalmente** mainly
**prioridade** (f) priority, right of way
**prisão de ventre** (f) constipation
**privado** private
**procurar** to look for
**produzir** to produce
**professor** (m) teacher
**profissão** (f) profession, job
**profissional** professional
**profissionalismo** (m) professionalism
**progresso** (m): **fazer progressos** to make progress
**proibição** (f) prohibition
**proibir** to forbid
**pronto** ready
**pronunciar** to pronounce
**propício** propitious, favourable
**próprio** own; **a mim próprio** (to) myself
**proteger** to protect
**protetor solar** (m) sunscreen
**prova** (f) proof; test (exam)
**prova de pagamento** (f) proof of payment
**provar** to try, taste; to prove
**próximo** next; near

**publicação** (f) publication
**publicar** to publish
**puder** (see **poder**)
**puxar** to pull

**qual** which, what
**qualidade** (f) quality
**qualquer** any
**quando** when
**quantas** (fpl), **quantos** (mpl) how many
**quantia** (f) amount, sum
**quantidade** (f) quantity
**quanto** how much
**quarenta** forty
**quarta-feira** (f) Wednesday
**quarto** fourth
**quarto (de dormir)** (m) bedroom; hotel room
**quarto** (m) quarter
**quarto** (m) room
**quase** almost
**quatocentos** four hundred
**quatorze** see **catorze**
**quatro** four
**que** what, which, that, who; that (conjunction)
**quê** what; **para quê?** what for?
**quê: não tem de quê** not at all
**quebrar** to break
**queijo** (m) cheese
**queimadura de sol / solar** (f) sunburn
**queira** (see **querer**)
**quem** who
**quente** hot, warm
**querer** to want, will, wish
**queria** (see **querer**)
**quilo, quilograma** (m) kilogram
**quilómetro** (Eur.), **quilômetro** (Br.) (m) kilometre

**quinhentos** *five hundred*
**quinta-feira** *(f) Thursday*
**quinto** *fifth*
**quinze** *fifteen*
**quinze dias** *(mpl) a fortnight, two weeks*

**rádio** *(m) radio; (f) radio station*
**rapaz** *(m) boy, young man, lad*
**rápido** *rapid, quick*
**raramente** *seldom*
**raro** *rare*
**razão** *(f) reason;* **ter razão** *to be right*
**real** *(m) unit of Brazilian currency*
**realizar-se** *to take place; to come true (dream)*
**receber** *to receive*
**receção / recepção** *(f) reception*
**receita** *(f) recipe; prescription*
**recheado** *stuffed*
**recibo** *(m) receipt*
**recomendar** *to recommend*
**reconhecer** *to recognize; to acknowledge; to identify*
**refeição** *(f) meal*
**refogar** *to sauté*
**reformado** *(Eur.) retired*
**região** *(f) region*
**regra** *(f) rule*
**regressar** *to return*
**regresso** *(m) return*
**regularmente** *regularly*
**reinado** *(m) reign*
**relógio** *(m) watch, clock*
**remédio** *(m) medicine; remedy*
**remoto** *remote, distant, far off*
**remuneração** *(f) remuneration*
**repetir** *to repeat*
**repor** *to put back*
**repouso** *(m) rest*

**reputação** *(f) reputation*
**requisito** *(m) requirement*
**rés-do-chão** *(m) (Eur.) ground floor*
**reserva** *(f) reservation, booking*
**reserva natural** *(f) nature reserve*
**reservar** *to reserve, book*
**resfriado** *(m) (Br.) cold (health condition)*
**resfriado: estar resfriado** *(Br.) to have a cold*
**residência** *(f) residence*
**residencial** *residence / home (address)*
**resolver** *to solve (problem); to decide*
**respeitar** *to respect, observe*
**responder** *to answer; to reply*
**resposta** *(f) answer; reply*
**ressalva** *(f) correction (in document)*
**restaurante** *(m) restaurant*
**resultado** *(m) result*
**retrete** *(f) (Eur.) toilet / washroom (US)*
**reunião** *(f) meeting*
**reunir** *to bring together; to combine*
**revista** *(f) magazine*
**rico** *rich*
**rio** *(m) river*
**rolha** *(f) cork, stopper*
**rolo** *(m) roll*
**roubar** *to steal*
**roupa** *(f),* **roupas** *(fpl) clothes / apparel (US)*
**roupão** *(m) dressing gown*
**rua** *(f) street, urban road*
**ruim** *bad*

**sábado** *(m) Saturday*
**saber** *to know; to learn; can*

**sabonete** (m) toilet soap
**sabor** (m) flavour
**saca-rolhas** (m) corkscrew
**saco** (m) bag, carrier bag
**saia** (f) skirt
**saia** (see **sair**)
**saída** (f) exit, way out
**sair** to exit; to go / come out; to leave
**sair** (computer) to log off
**sal** (m) salt
**sala** (f) room (house)
**salada** (f) salad
**saldo** (m) balance (account)
**salsicha** (f) sausage
**sandes** (f) (Eur.) sandwich
**sanduíche** (f) (Eur.), **sanduíche** (m) (Br.) sandwich
**sanitário** (m) toilet / washroom (US)
**são** (see **ser**)
**são-tomense, tomeense** from São Tomé and Príncipe, São Toméan
**sapato** (m) shoe
**satisfeito** pleased, satisfied
**saudade** (f) longing
**saúde** (f) health
**saúde!** cheers! (toasting)
**se** one, oneself; if, whether
**secador de cabelo** (m) hairdryer
**século** (m) century
**sede** (f): **estar com / ter sede** to be thirsty
**seguinte** following
**seguir** to go, follow
**segunda-feira** (f) Monday
**segundo** second (sequence)
**segundo** (m) second (clock)
**segurança** (f) security; safety
**seguro** (m) insurance

**seguro** safe
**sei** (see **saber**)
**seis** six
**seiscentos** six hundred
**selecionar** to select
**selo** (m) stamp
**sem** without
**semáforo** (m) traffic lights
**semana** (f) week
**sempre** always
**senhor** (m) gentleman, sir; you
**senhora** (f) lady, madam; you
**sensível** sensitive
**sentar** to sit
**sentar-se** to sit down
**sentir** to feel; **sentir a falta** to miss
**ser** to be
**sério** serious; **a sério** seriously, in earnest
**serviço** (m) service; **de serviço** on duty
**servir** to serve; to be fitting; to fit
**sessenta** sixty
**sete** seven
**setecentos** seven hundred
**setembro** (m) September
**setenta** seventy
**sétimo** seventh
**seu** (m) (Br.) casual alternative to **senhor**
**seu** your, yours, his, her, hers, its, their, theirs (m)
**sexo** (m) sex
**sexta-feira** (f) Friday
**sexto** sixth
**siga** (see **seguir**)
**significar** to mean
**sim** yes
**simpático** nice, friendly
**simples** single (hotel room, etc.)
**sinal** (m) sign; signal

**sinto** (see **sentir**)

**sítio** (m) (computer) site

**só, somente** only; **não só ...**
  **mas também ...** not only ...
  but also ...

**só, sozinho** alone, by oneself

**sob** under

**sobre** on; upon (subject)

**sobremesa** (f) dessert

**sobrenome** (m) (Br.) surname

**socorro!** (distress) help!

**sofrer** to suffer

**sofrido** long-suffering

**sogra** (f) mother-in-law

**sogro** (m) father-in-law

**sol** (m) sun; sunshine

**solteiro** single, unmarried

**sonho** (m) dream

**sopa** (f) soup

**sorriso** (m) smile

**sorte** (f) luck; **boa sorte!** good
  luck!, all the best!

**sorvete** (m) ice cream, sorbet

**sotaque** (m) accent (speech)

**sou** (see **ser**)

**sua** your, yours, his, her, hers, its,
  their, theirs (f)

**suave** gentle

**subir** to go / come up

**submeter-se a** to take (exam)

**suco** (m) (Br.) juice; **suco de**
  **laranja** orange juice

**sugerir** to suggest

**sujo** dirty

**sul** (m) south

**Sul: o Sul** the South, Southern part
  of the country

**sul-africano** from South Africa,
  South African

**sumo** (m) (Eur.) juice; **sumo de**
  **laranja** orange juice

**superfície** (f) area (dimension)

**supermercado** (m) supermarket

**suspensão** (f) suspension


**tal** such

**talvez** perhaps

**tamanho** (m) size

**também** also, too, as well

**tanto** so much

**tanto ... como ...** both ...
  and ...

**tanto ... quanto / como ...**
  as / so much ... as ...

**tantos ... quanto / como ...** as /
  so many ... as ...

**tão** so; **tão ... quanto / como ...**
  as / so ... as ...

**tapete rolante de bagagens** (m)
  baggage conveyor belt

**tarde** late

**tarde** (f) afternoon / evening; **boa**
  **tarde** good afternoon / evening

**tarifa** (f) rate

**táxi** (m) taxi

**teatro** (m) theatre; drama

**tecla** (f) key (pressing)

**telefonar** to telephone

**telefone** (m) telephone

**telefone portátil** (m) portable
  phone, mobile phone

**telefonista** (mf) telephone
  operator

**telemóvel** (m) mobile phone /
  cellphone (US)

**televisão** (f) television

**televisor** (m) television set

**tem** (see **ter**)

**tema** (m) topic

**temperatura** (f) temperature

**tempo** (m) time; weather

**tencionar** to intend, plan

**tenda** (f) tent
**tenho** (see **ter**)
**ténis** (Eur.) **/ tênis** (Br.) tennis
**ter** to have; **ter de / que** to have to
**terça-feira** (f) Tuesday
**terceiro** third
**terço** (m) third (part)
**terno** (m) (Br.) suit
**terra** (f) earth; soil; land; (home) land
**terra natal** (f) native / home land
**território** (m) territory; land
**teto** (m) ceiling
**teu** your, yours (familiar)
**tia** (f) aunt
**timorense** from Timor, Timorese
**tio** (m) uncle
**tipicamente** typically
**típico** typical
**tira** (f) strip; **em tirinhas** shredded
**tirar** to take away / out / off
**toalete** (Br.). **toilete** (Eur.) (m) toilet / washroom (US)
**toalha** (f) towel; table cloth
**tocar** to touch; to ring (bell); to play (instrument)
**todo** the whole; all; every (one)
**toldo** (m) awning, sunshade
**tomada de corrente** (f) power point
**tomar** to take; to have (drink, food, medicine)
**tomate** (m) tomato
**torcer** to twist; to sprain (foot)
**torre** (f) tower
**trabalhar** to work
**trabalho** (m) work; job
**tradição** (f) tradition
**tradutor** (m) translator
**traga** (see **trazer**)
**transbordo** (m) change, transfer (passengers)

**transeunte** (mf) passer-by
**transportar** to carry; to transport
**transporte público** (m) public transport
**transversal** cross (street, road)
**tratar (de)** to treat; to deal with
**tratar por** to address as
**travessa** (f) serving dish; alley
**travesseiro** (m) bolster (Eur.); pillow (Br.)
**trazer** to bring, carry
**treino** (m) training
**trem** (m) (Br.) train
**três** three
**treze** thirteen
**trezentos** three hundred
**trilho** (m) path; track
**trinta** thirty
**trocar** to change
**troco** (m) change
**trouxe** (see **trazer**)
**tu** you
**tubo** (m) tube (container)
**tudo** all, everything
**turismo** (m) tourism; tourist office
**turista** (mf) tourist

**uísque** (m) whisky
**ultimamente** lately
**último** last; latest; **nos últimos dias** in the last few days
**ultrapassar** to overtake
**um** (m) a, an; one
**uma** (f) a, an; one
**universidade** (f) university
**urgência** (f) emergency
**urgente** urgent
**usar** to use; to wear
**útil** useful

**vacina** (f) vaccine
**vaga** (f) vacancy, space (camping)

**vago** vacant
**vai** (see **ir**)
**válido** valid
**valor** (m) value
**varanda** (f) balcony; verandah
**variedade** (f) variety
**vários** several
**vazio** empty
**vê** (see **ver**)
**vejo** (see **ver**)
**vela** (f) sail; sailing (sport)
**velho** old; (see also **ano**)
**velocidade** (f) speed
**vem** (see **vir**); **que vem** coming, next
**venda** (f) sale
**vendedor** (m) shop assistant; seller
**vender** to sell
**venho** (see **vir**)
**vento** (m) wind
**ver** to see
**verão** (m) summer
**verdade: é verdade que…?** is it true that…?
**verde** green; type of wine
**verificar** to check
**vermelho** red
**vestido** (m) dress, frock
**vestir** to put on (clothes)
**vestir-se** to get dressed
**vez** (f) time, occasion; **sua vez** your turn; **outra vez** again; **alguma vez** sometime, ever
**vezes** (fpl) occasions; **às vezes** sometimes; **muitas vezes** often; **poucas vezes** seldom
**viagem** (f) journey, trip; voyage; **boa viagem!** have a nice journey!

**vida** (f) life
**vídeo** (m) video
**vidro** (m) glass; glass jar, bottle (Br.)
**vigilância** (f) vigilance
**vinho** (m) wine; lista / carta dos vinhos (f) wine list
**vinte** twenty
**viola** (f) guitar
**violão** (m) guitar
**vir** to come
**virar** to turn; to turn over
**visita** (f) visit; **fazer uma visita a …** to visit … , pay a call to …
**visita de negócio(s)** (f) business visit
**visitar** to visit
**vista** (f) view
**visto** (m) visa
**vitrine** (f) (Br.) shop window
**viúva** (f) widow
**viúvo** (m) widower
**viver** to live
**você** you
**volta** (f) turn; **estar de volta** to be back
**voltar** to return, go / come back
**voltar a …** to (do) again
**vontade** (f) will, wish; **à vontade** at ease
**voo** (m) flight
**vou** (see **ir**)

**xerez** (m) sherry
**xícara** (f) (Br.) cup

**zero** zero, nought
**zona** (f) zone

# English–Portuguese vocabulary

The Portuguese words given below can be used on both sides of the Atlantic. Where there is a difference, the word is followed by the sign (Eur.) or (Br.), which stand, respectively, for European and Brazilian.

The abbreviations (m) and (f) mean masculine and feminine; (pl) means plural.

*a / an* **um** *(m)*, **uma** *(f)*
*able (to be able to)* **ser capaz de, poder**
*about* **acerca de**
*access (to get Internet access)* **ter acesso à Internet** *or* **à Rede**
*accident* **acidente** *(m)*
*accommodation* **alojamento** *(m)*, **acomodação** *(f)*
*account* **conta** *(f)*
*ache* **dor** *(f)*
*act (to), behave* **agir**
*adaptor* **adaptador** *(m)*
*address* **endereço** *(m)*
*admission ticket (show)* **entrada** *(f)* **/ ingresso** *(m) (Br.)*
*adult* **adulto** *(m)*
*aerial* **antena** *(f)*
*aeroplane* **avião** *(m)*
*afraid* **receoso**
*Africa* **África** *(f)*
*after, afterwards* **depois**
*afternoon* **tarde** *(f); good afternoon* **boa tarde**
*afternoon: good afternoon (when dark)* **boa noite**
*after-shave (lotion)* **loção após-barba** *(f)*

*again* **outra vez, novamente**
*age* **idade** *(f)*
*ago* **há**
*agree (to)* **concordar, estar de acordo**
*ahead (straight on)* **em frente**
*air* **ar** *(m)*
*air conditioning* **ar condicionado** *(m)*
*air host* **hospedeiro (de bordo)** *(Eur.)* **/ aeromoço** *(m) (Br.) (m)*
*air hostess* **hospedeira (de bordo)** *(Eur.)* **/ aeromoça** *(f) (Br.) (f)*
*airline* **linha aérea** *(f)*
*airplane (US)* **avião** *(m)*
*airport* **aeroporto** *(m)*
*all* **tudo; todo** *(m)*, **toda** *(f)*
*allergic to* **alérgico a**
*allow (to)* **permitir, deixar**
*almost* **quase**
*alone* **só**
*also* **também**
*always* **sempre**
*ambulance* **ambulância** *(f)*
*America* **América** *(f)*
*American* **americano** *(m)*, **americana** *(f)*
*and* **e**

*Anglican* **anglicano** *(m)*,
  **anglicana** *(f)*
*animal* **animal** *(m)*
*anniversary* **aniversário** *(m)*
*answer* **resposta** *(f)*
*answer (to)* **responder**
*anticipation (thanking in)*
  **antecipadamente, desde já**
*any* **qualquer** *(mf)*
*apartment* **apartamento** *(m)*
*apparel (US)* **roupa** *(f)*, **roupas**
  *(fpl)*; **vestuário** *(m)*
*apple* **maçã** *(f)*
*apply for (to) (job, course)*
  **apresentar candidatura**
*appreciate (to)* **estimar**
*approximately* **aproximadamente**
*April* **abril** *(m)*
*Arab* **árabe** *(mf)*
*arm (body)* **braço** *(m)*
*arrival* **chegada** *(f)*
*arrive (to)* **chegar**
*artist* **artista** *(mf)*
*as far as* **até**
*Ásia* **Ásia** *(f)*
*Asian* **asiático** *(m)*, **asiática** *(f)*
*ask (to), enquire* **perguntar**
*ask for (to)* **pedir**
*at* **a, em**
*attachment (email)* **arquivo,**
  **ficheiro anexo** *(m)*
*attacker* **assaltante** *(mf)*
*August* **agosto** *(m)*
*aunt* **tia** *(f)*
*Australian* **australiano** *(m)*,
  **australiana** *(f)*
*auto(mobile) (US)* **carro,**
  **automóvel** *(m)*
*autumn* **outono** *(m)*
*available* **disponível**
*avoid (to)* **evitar**
*away: to go away* **ir(-se) embora**

*baby* **bebé** *(Eur.)* **/ bebê** *(Br.) (mf)*
*baby carriage (US)* **carrinho (de**
  **criança)** *(m)*
*baby changing room* **fraudário** *(m)*
*back (body)* **costas** *(fpl)*
*back: to be back* **estar de volta**
*backpack* **mochila** *(f)*
*bacon* **presunto** *(Eur.)* **/ bacon**
  *(Br.) (m)*
*bad* **mau** *(m)*, **má** *(f) (Eur.)* **/ ruim**
  *(mf) (Br.)*
*bad(ly)* **mal**
*bag* **saco** *(m)*
*baggage* **bagagem** *(f)*
*baggage conveyor belt* **tapete**
  **rolante de bagagens** *(m)*
*baggage reclaim* **recebimento**
  *(m)* **/ recolha** *(f)* **/ recolhimento**
  *(m)* **de bagagem**
*baker's (shop), bakery* **padaria** *(f)*
*balcony* **varanda / sacada;**
  **galeria** *(theatre) (f)*
*ball* **bola** *(f)*
*ballpoint* **pen esferográfica** *(f)*
*banana* **banana** *(f)*
*bank* **banco** *(m)*
*bar* **bar, botequim** *(m)*
*barbecue* **churrasco** *(m)*
*barber* **barbeiro** *(m)*
*bath* **banho** *(m)*; *to have a bath*
  **tomar banho**
*bathing costume* **fato de banho**
  *(Eur.)* **/ maiô** *(Br.) (m)*
*bathing suit (US)* **fato de banho**
  *(Eur.)* **/ maiô** *(Br.) (m)*
*bathroom* **casa de banho** *(f) (Eur.)*
  **/ banheiro** *(m) (Br.)*
*battery* **pilha** *(f)*
*be (to)* **estar; ser; ficar**
*beach* **praia** *(f)*
*beach chair* **cadeira de praia** *(f)*
*beach hut* **barraca de praia** *(f)*

beachwear **roupa de praia** (f)
beard **barba** (f)
beautiful **belo, lindo**
because **porque, por causa de**
bed **cama** (f); double bed **cama de casal** (f)
bed (child) **cama de criança** (f)
bedroom **quarto de dormir, quarto de cama** (m)
beer **cerveja** (f)
before **antes**
begin (to) **começar**
behind **atrás** (de)
beige **bege**
believe (to) **acreditar**
belt **cinto** (m)
better **melhor**
beverage **bebida** (f)
big **grande**
bill **conta** (f)
billfold (US) **carteira** (f)
bird **ave** (f), **pássaro** (m)
birthday **aniversário** (m)
biscuit **bolacha** (f), **biscoito** (m)
bite **mordida** (f)
black **preto, negro**
black coffee (no milk) **café preto** (m)
blanket **cobertor** (m)
blond, light brown **louro** or **loiro**
blowout (tyre) (US) **furo** (m)
blue **azul**
boarding pass **cartão de embarque** (m)
boat **barco** (m)
boiled **cozido**
bone **osso** (m)
book **livro** (m)
book (to) **marcar, reservar**
boots **botas** (fpl)
boring, annoying **chato**

born: to be born **nascer**
boss **patrão** (m)
both **ambos** (mpl), **ambas** (fpl)
bottle **garrafa** (f)
bowels **intestinos** (mpl)
boy, lad **rapaz** (m)
bracelet **pulseira** (f)
brakes **travões** (Eur.) **/ freios** (Br.) (mpl)
Brazilian **brasileiro** (m), **brasileira** (f)
bread **pão** (m)
break **intervalo** (m)
break (to) **quebrar**
breakdown **pane, avaria** (f)
breakdown van **pronto socorro** (Eur.) **/ reboque** (Br.) (m)
breakfast **pequeno-almoço** (Eur.) **/ café da manhã** (Br.) (m)
breath (to) **respirar**
bridge **ponte** (f)
briefcase **pasta** (f)
bring (to) **trazer**
British **britânico** (m), **britânica** (f)
broken **quebrado**
brother **irmão** (m)
brown **castanho** (Eur.) **/ marrom** (Br.)
brown (hair) **castanho**
Buddhist **budista** (mf)
building **edifício** (m)
bus, coach **autocarro** (m), **camioneta** (f) (Eur.) **/ ônibus** (m) (Br.)
bus, coach station **rodoviária** (f)
bus, coach stop **paragem de autocarros** (Eur.) **/ parada de ônibus** (Br.) (f)
business **negócio** (m)
business visit **visita de negócio(s)** (f)

businessman **homem de negócios / empresário** *(Br.)*, **comerciante** *(m)*

businesswoman **mulher de negócios / empresária** *(Br.)*, **comerciante** *(f)*

but **mas**

butter **manteiga** *(f)*

buy (to) **comprar**

by **por;** *(proximity)* **junto de;** *(transport)* **de**

by car **de carro, automóvel**

by oneself **sozinho** *(m)*, **sozinha** *(f)*

cab **táxi** *(m)*

cabin (ship, theatre) **camarote** *(m)*

cake **bolo** *(m)*

calculator **calculadora** *(f)*

call (reverse the charge) **chamada a cobrar** *(f)*

call (telephone) **telefonema** *(m)*, **chamada** *(f)*

camera (photo) **máquina fotográfica** *(f)*; *(video)* **máquina de filmar** *(f)* ; **câmara** *(f)*

camp bed **cama de lona** *(f)*

camper **campista** *(mf)*

campsite **parque de campismo** *(Eur.)* **/ camping** *(Br.)* *(m)*

can **poder, saber;** *(manage)* **conseguir;** I can't open this **não consigo abrir isto**

can, tin **lata** *(f)*

Canadian **canadense** *(mf)* **/ canadiano** *(m)*, **canadiana** *(f)* *(Eur.)*

cancellation **cancelamento** *(m)*

capital (city) **capital** *(f)*

car **carro, automóvel** *(m)*

card **cartão** *(m)*

card, form **ficha** *(f)*

carnival **carnaval** *(m)*

carrier bag **saco** *(m)* **/ sacola** *(f)* *(Br.)*

carry (to) **levar, transportar**

cash dispenser / cashpoint **terminal caixa** *(m)*

cashdesk, check-out **caixa** *(f)*

castle **castelo** *(m)*

catch (to) **apanhar**

Catholic **católico** *(m)*, **católica** *(f)*

cell phone (US) **telefone portátil, telemóvel** *(Eur.)* **/ celular** *(Br.)* *(m)*

cent **cêntimo** *(m)*; **centavo** *(m)*

central heating **aquecimento central** *(m)*

centre **centro** *(m)*

cereal **cereal** *(m)*

change (small change) **(dinheiro) trocado** *(m)*, **troco** *(m)*

change (to) **mudar;** *(money)* **trocar**

cheap, inexpensive **barato**

check (to) **verificar**

check (US) **cheque** *(m)*

check in (to) (airport) **apresentar-se;** *(hotel)* **registar-se** *(Eur.)* **/ registrar-se** *(Br.)*

check out (to) (hotel) **pagar a conta e sair**

check-up (medical) **consulta de rotina** *(f)*

cheerful **alegre**

cheers! (toasting) **saúde!**

cheese **queijo** *(m)*

chemist's (shop) **farmácia** *(f)*

cheque **cheque** *(m)*

chest (body) **peito** *(m)*

child **criança** *(f)*

Chinese **chinês** *(m)*, **chinesa** *(f)*

chips (potato) **batata frita** *(f)*, **batatas fritas** *(fpl)*

choose (to) **escolher**
Christian **cristão** (m), **cristã** (f)
church **igreja** (f)
city **cidade** (f)
clean **limpo**
clean (to) **limpar**
clerk **empregado, funcionário** (m)
clock: o'clock **hora(s)**
closed **fechado, encerrado**
clothes **roupa** (f), **roupas** (fpl);
  **vestuário** (m)
club **clube** (m)
coat **casaco** (m)
coconut **coco** (m)
code **código** (m)
coffee **café** (m)
coin **moeda** (f)
cold **frio**
cold (have a) **estar constipado**
  (Eur.) / **resfriado** (Br.)
come (to) **vir**
come back (to) **regressar, voltar**
come down (to) **descer**
come from (to) (originally) **ser de**
come in (to) **entrar**
come out (to) **sair**
come up (to) **subir**
complaint **queixa** (f)
computer **computador** (m)
congratulations! **parabéns!,**
  **felicitações!**
connect (to) **ligar**
constipation **prisão de ventre** (f)
consulate **consulado** (m)
contact lens **lente de contacto**
  (Eur.) / **contato** (Br.) (f)
cookie (US) **bolacha** (f), **biscoito**
  (m)
cookout (US) **churrasco** (m);
  **piquenique** (m)
cool **fresco**

corkscrew **saca-rolhas** (m)
corner (inside of angle) **canto** (m)
corner (outside of angle) **esquina** (f)
correspondence
  **correspondência** (f)
cost (to) **custar**
cost, price **custo** (m)
cot **cama de criança** (f), (baby)
  **berço** (m)
cot (US) **cama de lona** (f)
country **país** (m)
couple **casal** (m)
course (of studies) **curso** (m)
cradle **berço** (m)
credit card **cartão de crédito** (m)
crisps (potato) **batatinha de**
  **pacote** (f), **batatinhas de**
  **pacote** (fpl)
cross over (to) **atravessar**
crossroads, junction **cruzamento**
  (m)
cup **chávena** (Eur.) / **xícara** (Br.) (f)
cupboard **armário** (m)
currency **moeda corrente** (f)
Customs **alfândega** (f)

daily charge, rate **diária** (f)
dairy **leitaria** (Eur.) / **leiteria** (Br.) (f)
danger **perigo** (m)
dark **escuro**
date **data** (f)
daughter **filha** (f)
daughter-in-law **nora** (f)
day **dia** (m)
dear, expensive **caro**
debit card **cartão de débito** (m)
decaffeinated **descafeinado**
December **dezembro** (m)
deep **fundo**
delay **demora** (f), **atraso** (m)
delivery **entrega** (f)

dentist **dentista** *(mf)*
deodorant **desodorizante** *(Eur.)* **/
desodorante** *(Br.) (m)*
depart (to) **partir**
departure **partida** *(f)*
dessert **sobremesa** *(f)*
diaper (US) **fralda** *(f)*
diarrhoea **diarreia** *(f)*
diary **agenda** *(f)*
dictionary **dicionário** *(m)*
die (to) **morrer**
diet **dieta** *(f)*
different **diferente**
difficult **difícil**
digestion **digestão** *(f)*
diner (eating place) (US) **pastelaria**
*(f)*, **café** *(m)* **/ lanchonete** *(f) (Br.)*
dinner **jantar** *(m)*
direct **direto**
dirty **sujo**
disabled **deficiente** *(mf)*
disappear (to) **desaparecer**
disco, discotheque **discoteca** *(f)*
disease **doença** *(f)*
disembark (to) **desembarcar**
dish **prato** *(m)*
district, suburb **bairro** *(m)*
diversion, detour **desvio** *(m)*
dizzy **tonto**
do (to) **fazer**
doctor **médico** *(m)*, **médica** *(f)*
document **documento** *(m)*
dog **cão / cachorro** *(Br.) (m)*
dollar **dólar** *(m)*
door **porta** *(f)*
double **duplo**
downstairs **lá em baixo** *(Eur.)* **/
embaixo** *(Br.)*
dozen **dúzia**; half a dozen **meia
dúzia**
dressed, get (to) **vestir-se**

drink (beverage) **bebida** *(f)*
drink (to) **beber**
drive (to) **conduzir** *(Eur.)* **/
dirigir** *(Br.)*
driver **motorista** *(mf)*
driver's license (US) **carta de
condução** *(Eur.)* **/ carteira de
motorista** *(Br.) (f)*
driving licence **carta de condução**
*(Eur.)* **/ carteira de motorista**
*(Br.) (f)*
druggist (US) **farmacêutico** *(m)*,
**farmacêutica** *(f)*
drunk **bêbado, bêbedo** *(m)*
duty: on duty **de serviço**

ear (inner) **ouvido** *(m)*, (external)
**orelha** *(f)*
early **cedo**; (fast, before time)
**adiantado**
earn (to) **ganhar**
earrings **brincos** *(mpl)*
east **este, leste** *(m)*
easy **fácil**
eat (to) **comer**
egg **ovo** *(m)*
eight **oito**
eighteen **dezoito**
eighty **oitenta**
either… or… **ou… ou…**
elbow **cotovelo** *(m)*
elderly person **pessoa de idade** *(f)*
electronic **electrónico** *(Eur.)* **/
eletrônico** *(Br.)*
elevator (US) **ascensor / elevador**
*(m)*
eleven **onze**
e-mail **email, correio-e** *(m)*
embark (to) **embarcar**
embassy **embaixada** *(f)*
emergency **emergência** *(f)*

empty **vazio**
end (to), finish **acabar, terminar**
engaged (telephone) **impedido**
engaged (toilet) **ocupado**
engineer **engenheiro** (m),
  **engenheira** (f)
English **inglês** (m), **inglesa** (f)
English (language) (discipline of
  study) **Inglês / inglês** (m)
enjoy (to) **apreciar, desfrutar
  (de)**; (like) **gostar de**
enough **bastante**
enterprise, firm **empresa** (f)
environment **meio ambiente** (m)
escalator **escada rolante** (f)
euro **euro** (m)
Europe **Europa** (f)
European **europeu** (m), **europeia**
  (Eur.) / **européia** (Br.) (f)
everyone **toda a gente / todo (o)
  mundo** (Br.)
everything, all **tudo**
evident **evidente**
except **exceto**
exchange (foreign currency)
  **câmbio** (m)
excuse me! (drawing attention)
  **por favor!**; (asking to make way)
  **com licença!**
exercise **exercício** (m)
exit **saída** (f)
expense **despesa** (f)
explain (to) **explicar**
export (to) **exportar**
expression **expressão** (f)
expressway (US) **autoestrada** (f)
ever **alguma vez**
eye **olho** (m)

face **face** (f), **rosto** (m)
facilities (premises) **instalações,
  facilidades** (fpl)

facility **facilidade** (f)
factory **fábrica** (f)
faint (to) **desmaiar**
fall (to) **cair**
fall (US) **outono** (m)
family **família** (f)
far **longe**
fare (ticket) **passagem** (f)
fast **rápido**
father **pai** (m)
father-in-law **sogro** (m)
fax **fax** (m)
February **fevereiro** (m)
fed up **farto**
feed (to) **dar de comer**
feel (to) **sentir**
fever **febre** (f)
fiancé, fiancée **noivo** (m), **noiva** (f)
fifteen **quinze**
fifty **cinquenta**
fill (to) **encher**
filling station **posto de
  abastecimento / combustível /
  gasolina** (m)
find (to) **achar, encontrar**
fine (penalty) **multa** (f)
finger **dedo** (m)
finish (to), end **terminar, acabar**
fire **fogo** (m)
fire brigade **bombeiros** (mpl)
fire department (US) **bombeiros**
  (mpl)
fireplace, fireside **lareira** (f)
firm, enterprise **empresa** (f)
first **primeiro**
fish **peixe** (m)
five **cinco**
flight **voo** (m)
floor **andar** (m); **chão** (m) (ground)
florest **floresta** (f), **mata** (f)
flower **flor** (f)
flue **gripe** (f)

food **comida** *(f)*
foot (body) **pé** *(m)*
for **para; to**
for (time) **há**
for, during **durante**
forbidden **proibido**
foreign **estrangeiro**
forget (to) **esquecer(-se)**
fork **garfo** *(m)*
forty **quarenta**
four **quatro**
fourteen **catorze**
free **livre**; *(gratis)* **gratuito**
freeway (US) **autoestrada** *(f)*
freezer **congelador** *(m)*
French **francês** *(m)*, **francesa** *(f)*
Friday **sexta-feira** *(f)*
fried **frito**
fried egg **ovo frito** *(m)* **/ ovo estrelado** *(m) (Eur.)*
friend **amigo** *(m)*, **amiga** *(f)*
from **de**
front: in front of **em frente de**
frozen **gelado**
fruit **fruta** *(f)*
fuel **combustível** *(m)*
fuel station **posto de combustível** *(m)*
full **cheio**
full-time **tempo integral**
fun **divertimento** *(m)*
fuse **fusível** *(m)*

game **jogo** *(m)*
game (bird) **caça** *(f)*
garage **garagem** *(f)*
garbage (US) **lixo** *(m)*
garden **jardim** *(m)*
gas(oline) (US) **gasolina** *(f)*
gate **portão** *(m)*
gate (airport) **porta de embarque** *(f)*

German **alemão** *(m)*, **alemã** *(f)*
get up (to) **levantar-se**
girl **menina** *(f)*, **moça** *(f)*
give (to) **dar**
glad **contente**
glass (drinking) **copo** *(m)*
glasses, spectacles **óculos** *(mpl)*
gloves **luvas** *(fpl)*
go (to) **ir**
go back (to) **regressar, voltar**
go down (to) **descer**
go in (to) **entrar**
go out (to) **sair**
go up (to) **subir**
gold **ouro** *(m)*
good **bom** *(m)*, **boa** *(f)*
goodbye! **adeus!**
goodbye!, bye! **tchau! / chau!** *(Eur.)*
granddaughter **neta** *(f)*
grandfather **avô** *(m)*
grandmother **avó** *(f)*
grandson **neto** *(m)*
grant (to) **conceder**
grape **uva** *(f)*
grasp (to), seize **agarrar**
grateful **grato**
great! **ótimo!**
green **verde**
grey **cinzento** *(Eur.)* **/ cinza** *(Br.)*
grey (hair) **grisalho**
grilled **grelhado, na chapa**
group, party **grupo** *(m)*

hair **cabelo** *(m)*
haircut **corte de cabelo** *(m)*
hairdresser **cabeleireiro** *(m)*, **cabeleireira** *(f)*
hairdryer **secador de cabelo** *(m)*
hairspray **laca** *(f) (Eur.)* **/ laquê** *(m) (Br.)*, **fixador para cabelo** *(m)*
half **meio**

half (a) **metade** (f)
ham **fiambre** (Eur.) **/ presunto**
  (Br.) (m)
hammock **rede** (f)
hand (body) **mão** (f)
hand luggage **bagagem**
  **de mão** (f)
handbag, purse **bolsa** (f)
handkerchief **lenço** (m)
handy **prático, conveniente**
handy (to be) **dar jeito**
hanger **cabide** (m)
happy **feliz, contente**
harass (to) **perturbar, interferir**
harbour **porto** (m)
hard **duro**
hard-boiled egg **ovo cozido duro**
  (m)
hat **chapéu** (m)
have (to) (drink, medicine) **tomar**
have to (to) **ter de / que**
he **ele**
head (body) **cabeça** (f)
headache **dor de cabeça** (f)
headlight **farol** (m)
health **saúde** (f)
hear (to) **ouvir**
heart **coração** (m)
heat **calor** (m)
heavy **pesado**
height **altura** (f)
hello! **olá! / oi!** (Br.); (on phone)
  **está?** (Eur.) **/ alô?** (Br.)
help **ajuda** (f)
help (to) **ajudar**
help! (distress) **socorro!**
here **aqui**
hi! **olá! / oi!** (Br.)
hide (to) **esconder**
hike (to go walking) **caminhar**
Hindu **hindu** (mf)

hire (to) **alugar**
hit (to) **bater**
hitchhike (to) **andar à boleia** (Eur.)
  **/ pegar carona** (Br.)
hobby **passatempo predileto** (m)
hole **buraco** (m)
holiday (public) **feriado** (m)
holiday(s), vacation **férias** (fpl)
home **casa** (f); (going to) **para**
  **casa**; at home **em casa**
homeland **pátria** (f)
hope (to) **esperar, ter esperança**
hopefully **esperemos que sim**
horn **buzina** (f)
hospital **hospital** (m)
hostel **albergue** (m), **hospedaria**
  (f)
hot **quente**
hotel **hotel** (m)
hotel room **quarto** (m),
  **apartamento** (m)
hour **hora** (f)
house **casa** (f)
housewife **dona de casa** (f)
how long, for **há**
how much? **quanto?**
how? **como?**
hug (to), embrace **abraçar**
hundred **cem, cento**
hungry **com fome**
hurry **pressa** (f)
hurt (to) **doer**
husband **esposo / marido** (m)
hut **barraca** (f)
hypermarket **hipermercado** (m)

I **eu**
ice **gelo** (m)
ice cold **gelado**
ice cream, lolly **gelado** (m) (Eur.)
ice cream, sorbet **sorvete** (m)

*ice lolly* **picolé** *(m) (Br.)*
*ID* **documento de identidade** *(m)*
*idea* **ideia** *(f)*
*identify (to)* **identificar,**
  **reconhecer**
*if, whether* **se**
*ignition* **ignição** *(f)*
*ill* **doente** *(mf)*
*immediately* **imediatamente**
*import (to)* **importar**
*import duty* **direito de**
  **importação** *(m)*
*important* **importante**
*impossible* **impossível**
*in* **em**
*in, inside* **dentro**
*inconvenience* **incómodo** *(Eur.)* **/**
  **incômodo** *(Br.) (m)*
*Indian (from America)* **índio** *(m),*
  **índia** *(f)*
*Indian (from India)* **indiano** *(m),*
  **indiana** *(f)*
*indigestion* **indigestão** *(f)*
*individual* **individual**
*industry* **indústria** *(f)*
*information* **informação** *(f)*
*injury* **ferimento** *(m)*
*inland* **interior** *(m)*
*insect* **inseto** *(m)*
*insert (to)* **introduzir**
*inspection* **fiscalização** *(f)*
*instance, for* **por exemplo**
*insufficient* **insuficiente**
*insurance* **seguro** *(m)*
*intend (to)* **tencionar**
*interested* **interessado**
*interesting* **interessante**
*international* **internacional**
*Internet* **Internet** *or* **Rede** *(f)*
*interpreter* **intérprete** *(mf)*
*interrupt (to)* **interromper**

*introduction* **introdução** *(f)*
*introductory* **de introdução a**
*Irish* **irlandês** *(m),* **irlandesa** *(f)*
*island* **ilha** *(f)*
*Italian* **italiano** *(m),* **italiana** *(f)*

*January* **janeiro** *(m)*
*Japanese* **japonês** *(m),* **japonesa**
  *(f)*
*jewel* **joia** *(f)*
*Jewish* **judeu** *(m),* **judia** *(f)*
*job* **emprego** *(m)*
*joke* **piada** *(f)*
*joke (to play a), have fun* **brincar**
*journalist* **jornalista** *(mf)*
*journey* **viagem** *(f)*
*juice (fruit)* **sumo de fruta** *(Eur.)* **/**
  **suco de fruta** *(Br.) (m)*
*July* **julho** *(m)*
*jump (to)* **pular, saltar**
*jumper* **camisola** *(f) (Eur.)* **/ suéter**
  *(m) (Br.)*
*June* **junho** *(m)*
*jungle* **selva** *(f),* **mato** *(m)*

*keep (to)* **guardar**
*kettle* **chaleira** *(f)*
*key* **chave** *(f)*
*key / card (to open door)* **chave**
  *(f)* **/ cartão** *(m)* **(da porta)**
*keyboard* **teclado** *(m)*
*kidney* **rim** *(m)*
*knee* **joelho** *(m)*
*knife* **faca** *(f)*
*know (to)* **saber, conhecer**

*label* **etiqueta** *(f)*
*lack (to)* **faltar**
*landing (aeroplane)* **aterragem**
  *(Eur.)* **/ aterrissagem** *(Br.) (f)*
*language* **língua** *(f)*

*lantern* **lanterna** *(f)*

*laptop (computador)* **computador portátil** *(m)*

*large* **grande**

*last* **último**

*late* **tarde**; *(slow, too late)* **atrasado**

*later* **logo, mais logo**; *see you later* **até logo, até mais logo / até mais** *(Br.)*

*laugh (to)* **rir**

*laughter (burst of)* **gargalhada** *(f)*

*laundry service* **lavagem de roupa** *(f)*

*lawyer* **advogado** *(m)*, **advogada** *(f)*

*learn (to)* **aprender**

*leave (to)* **partir, sair**

*leave behind (to)* **deixar**

*left: on / to the left* **à esquerda**

*leg (body)* **perna** *(f)*

*leisure* **lazer** *(m)*

*lemon* **limão** *(m)*

*lend (to)* **emprestar**

*less* **menos**

*letter (message)* **carta** *(f)*

*lie down (to)* **deitar-se**

*life* **vida** *(f)*

*life jacket* **colete salva-vidas** *(m)*

*life preserver (US)* **colete salva-vidas** *(m)*

*lift (elevator)* **ascensor / elevador** *(m)*

*lift (free ride)* **boleia** *(Eur.)* **/ carona** *(Br.)* *(f)*

*light* **claro**; *(weight)* **leve**

*light bulb* **lâmpada** *(f)*

*lighter* **isqueiro** *(m)*

*like* **como**

*like (to)* **gostar de**

*like this* **assim**

*likewise* **igualmente**

*line, queue* **fila** *(f)*

*list* **lista** *(f)*

*listen (to)* **escutar**

*litter* **lixo** *(m)*

*little* **pouco**; *a little* **um pouco**

*live (to), be resident* **morar**

*liver* **fígado** *(m)*

*loan (to)* **emprestar**

*local cuisine* **comidas regionais** *(fpl)*, **pratos típicos** *(mpl)*

*log in (to) (computer)* **iniciar**

*log off (to) (computer)* **sair**

*log on (to) (computer)* **entrar**

*log out (to) (computer)* **encerrar**

*long* **longo, comprido**

*look (to)* **olhar**

*look after (to)* **olhar por**

*look for (to)* **procurer**

*look forward (to)* **estar desejoso / ansioso por**; *(letter writing)* **aguardar**

*look like (to)* **parecer**

*loose* **solto**

*lorry* **caminhão, camião** *(Eur.)* *(m)*

*lose (to)* **perder**

*lot: a lot of* **muito**

*love (to)* **gostar muito de; amar** *(someone)*

*love (to) (passionate about)* **adorar**

*luggage* **bagagem** *(f)*

*lunch* **almoço** *(m)*

*lung* **pulmão** *(m)*

*machine* **máquina** *(f)*

*mail* **correio** *(m)*

*mainly* **principalmente**

*make (to)* **fazer**

*make-up* **maquilhagem** *(Eur.)* **/ maquilagem** *(Br.)* *(f)* mall **centro comercial** (Eur) / **shopping** (Br.) (m)

man **homem** (m)

manage (to) **dar um jeito**; (business) **administrar**

manage (to) (to do something) **conseguir**

management **gerência** (f)

mango **manga** (f)

many **muitos** (mpl) / **muitas** (fpl)

map **mapa** (m)

March **março** (m)

margarine **margarina** (f)

married **casado** (m), **casada** (f)

match **fósforo** (m)

mauve **roxo / violeta, claro**

May **maio** (m)

maybe **talvez, pode ser**

me **me**; to / for me **para mim**

mean (to) **significar, querer dizer**

measure (to) **medir**

meat **carne** (f)

media **média** (mpl) (Eur.) / **mídia** (f) (Br.)

medicine **medicamento, remédio** (m)

meet (to) **encontrar**

meeting **encontro** (m); (business) **reunião** (f)

meeting point **ponto de encontro** (m)

menu card **ementa** (f) (Eur.) / **cardápio** (m) (Br.)

mess **confusão** (f)

message **mensagem** (f), **recado** (m)

microwave **(forno) micro-ondas** (m)

midday **meio-dia** (m)

midnight **meia-noite** (f)

milk **leite** (m)

million **milhão**

mind: do you mind? **importa-se?**

mind: I don't mind (it's all the same) **tanto faz**

mini-fridge **frigobar** (m)

minimarket **minimercado** (m)

minute **minuto** (m)

mirror **espelho** (m)

mislay (to) **extraviar, perder**

miss (to) (transport) **perder**; (be missing) **faltar**

mistake **erro, engano** (m)

mistaken (to be) **enganar-se**

misunderstanding **engano** (m)

mobile phone **telefone portátil, telemóvel** (Eur.) / **celular** (Br.) (m)

mobile video phone **videofone portátil** (m)

Monday **segunda-feira** (f)

money **dinheiro** (m)

month **mês** (m)

more **mais**

morning **manhã** (f); good morning **bom dia**

mother **mãe** (f)

mother-in-law **sogra** (f)

motorway **autoestrada** (f)

mountain **montanha, serra** (f)

mouse (computer) **rato** (m)

mouth **boca** (f)

much **muito**

music **música** (f)

Muslim **muçulmano** (m), **muçulmana** (f)

must **dever**

my, mine **meu** (m), **minha** (f)

name **nome** (m)

napkin **guardanapo** (m)

nappy **fralda** (f)

nationality **nacionalidade** (f)

*native town / city* **cidade natal** *(f)*
*near* **perto**
*nearby* **perto daqui, aqui perto**
*necessary* **necessário**
*neck (body)* **pescoço** *(m)*
*need (to)* **precisar**
*nephew* **sobrinho** *(m)*
*never* **nunca**
*new* **novo**
*New Zealander* **neozelandês** *(m)*,
  **neozelandesa** *(f)*
*news* **notícia** *(f)*
*newspaper* **jornal** *(m)*
*next (time)* **próximo, que vem**
*next, near* **próximo**
*nice, friendly* **simpático**
*niece* **sobrinha** *(f)*
*night* **noite** *(f); good night* **boa
  noite**
*nine* **nove**
*nineteen* **dezanove** *(Eur.)* **/
  dezenove** *(Br.)*
*ninety* **noventa**
*no, not* **não**
*noise* **barulho, ruído** *(m)*
*none* **nenhum** *(m)* **/ nenhuma** *(f)*
*no-one* **ninguém**
*north* **norte** *(m)*
*nose* **nariz** *(m)*
*nothing* **nada**
*November* **novembro** *(m)*
*now* **agora**
*number* **número** *(m)*
*nurse* **enfermeiro** *(m)*, **enfermeira**
  *(f)*

*Oceania* **Oceania, Oceânia** *(f)*
*October* **outubro** *(m)*
*of* **de**
*office (public service)* **secretaria**
  *(f); (room)* **escritório** *(m)*

*official, civil servant* **funcionário**
  *(m)*, **funcionária** *(f)*
*often* **muitas vezes,
  frequentemente**
*oil* **óleo** *(m)*
*OK!* **certo!, está bem!**
*old* **velho**; *I am … years old* **tenho
  … anos**
*omelette* **omelete, omeleta** *(f)*
*on* **em**
*once (at)* **já, imediatamente**
*one* **um** *(m)*, **uma** *(f)*
*only* **somente, apenas**
*open* **aberto**
*open (to)* **abrir**
*or* **ou**
*orange* **laranja** *(f)*
*orange (colour)* **cor de laranja,
  laranja**
*order (out of), damaged*
  **avariado / com defeito** *(Br.)*,
  **desarranjado** *(Br.)*
*other, another* **outro** *(m)*,
  **outra** *(f)*
*out, outside* **fora**
*owner* **dono** *(m)*, **dona** *(f)*;
  **proprietário** *(m)*, **proprietária** *(f)*

*padlock* **cadeado** *(m)*
*pain, ache* **dor** *(f)*
*painkiller* **analgésico** *(m)*
*pale (colour)* **claro**
*pancake* **panqueca** *(f)*
*pants (US)* **calças** *(fpl)*, **calça** *(f)*
*papaya* **mamão** *(m)*, **papaia** *(f)*
*paper* **papel** *(m)*
*parade* **desfile** *(m)*
*parasol* **guarda-sol** *(m)*
*parcel* **pacote, embrulho** *(m)*
*pardon?* **como (disse)?**
*parents* **pais** *(mpl)*

park **parque** *(m)*
parking **estacionamento** *(m)*
parking meter **parcómetro** *(Eur.)* **/**
  **parquímetro** *(Br.)* *(m)*
part: take part in **participar em**
partner (business) **sócio** *(m)*, **sócia**
  *(f)*
partner (relationship)
  **companheiro** *(m)*, **companheira**
  *(f)*
part-time **tempo parcial, meio**
  **expediente** *(m)*
party **festa** *(f)*
passenger **passageiro** *(m)*,
  **passageira** *(f)*
passport **passaporte** *(m)*
pay (to) **pagar**
payment **pagamento** *(m)*
peach **pêssego** *(m)*
pear **pera** *(f)*
pen **caneta** *(f)*
pepper **pimenta** *(f)*
per cent **por cento**
perhaps **talvez**
person, people **pessoa** *(f)*, **pessoas**
  *(fpl)*
pet **animal de estimação** *(m)*
petrol **gasolina** *(f)*
pharmacist **farmacêutico** *(m)*,
  **farmacêutica** *(f)*
pharmacy **farmácia** *(f)*
phone card **cartão de telefone**
  *(m)*
photocopy **fotocópia** *(f)*
photograph **fotografia** *(f)*
physically impaired **deficiente**
  **físico** *(mf)*
picnic **piquenique** *(m)*
pillow **almofada** *(f)* *(Eur.)* **/**
  **travesseiro** *(m)* *(Br.)*
pink **cor de rosa, rosa**

place **lugar** *(m)*
place (to), put **colocar, pôr**
plaster: sticking plaster **penso**
  **adesivo** *(Eur.)* **/ esparadrapo**
  *(Br.)* *(m)*
plate (eating from) **prato** *(m)*
plate, disc **chapa** *(f)*
platform **plataforma** *(f)* **/ cais** *(m)*
  *(Eur.)*
play (to) (game, sport) **jogar**
playground (children) **parque**
  **infantil** *(m)*
please! **por favor!, faz favor!**
plug **tomada** *(f)*
pocket **bolso** *(m)*
police **polícia** *(f)*
policeman **agente de polícia** *(m)*
policewoman **agente de polícia**
  *(f)*
pool **piscina** *(f)*
portable computer **computador**
  **portátil** *(m)*
Portuguese **português** *(m)*,
  **portuguesa** *(f)*
Portuguese (language) (discipline
  of study) **Português / português**
  *(m)*
Portuguese-speaking **falante de**
  **Português** *(mf)*; **lusófono** *(m)*,
  **lusófona** *(f)*
possible **possível**
post office **correio** *(m)* **/ agência**
  **de correio** *(f)* *(Br.)*
postcard **postal / (bilhete) postal**
  *(Eur.)* **/ (cartão) postal** *(Br.)* *(m)*
poultry **aves** *(fpl)*
pound **libra** *(f)*
power point **tomada de corrente**
practise (to) **praticar**
pram **carrinho (de criança)** *(m)*
prefer (to) **preferir**

prepare (to) **preparar**

prescription (medical) **receita** (f)

present, gift **presente** (m)

prevent (to) **evitar**

price, cost **preço** (m)

printer **impressora** (f)

priority, right of way **prioridade** (f)

problem **problema** (m)

profession, job **profissão** (f)

progress: to make progress **fazer progressos** (mpl)

pronounce (to) **pronunciar;** how to pronounce it? **como se pronuncia?**

proof of payment **prova de pagamento** (f)

Protestant **protestante** (mf)

pub **bar inglês** (m)

pull (to) **puxar**

puncture (tyre) **furo** (m)

purchase **compra** (f)

purple **roxo / violeta, escuro**

purse **bolsa** (f)

push (to) **empurrar**

pushchair **cadeirinha (de criança)** (f)

put (to), place **colocar, pôr**

put out (to) (fire) **extinguir**

query **dúvida** (f)

question **questão** (f)

question (enquiring) **pergunta** (f)

queue **fila** (f)

quickly! **depressa!**

quiet **calmo**

quiet (to keep) **estar calado**

quite **muito, bastante, completamente**

radio (set) **rádio** (m)

railroad (US), railway **caminho de ferro** (m) (Eur.) **/ estrada de ferro** (f) (Br.)

rain **chuva** (f)

raincoat **capa de chuva** (f), **impermeável** (m)

rare, underdone (food) **mal passado**

reach (to) **alcançar, atingir;** (arrive) **chegar**

ready **pronto**

receipt **recibo** (m)

red **vermelho**

refrigerator **frigorífico** (m) (Eur.) **/ geladeira** (f) (Br.)

refuse (to) **recusar**

remember (to) **lembrar(-se)**

remind (to) **lembrar**

remote control **controle remoto** (m)

rent, lease (to) **alugar**

repair (to) **consertar**

reply **resposta** (f)

report (to) **informar**

rescue services **resgate** (m)

residence **residência** (f)

rest (to) **descansar**

restaurant **restaurante** (m)

restroom (US) **lavabo** (m), **casa de banho** (f) (Eur.) **/ banheiro** (m) (Br.)

retired **aposentado** (m), **aposentada** (f) **/ reformado** (m), **reformada** (f) (Eur.)

return (ticket) **ida e volta** (f)

return (to) **voltar, regressar;** (item) **devolver**

right **certo**

right: on / to the right **à direita**

right: to be right **ter razão**

ring **anel** (m)

river **rio** *(m)*
road **estrada** *(f)*; **rua** *(f) (urban)*
roasted **assado**
robbery **roubo** *(m)*
rose (colour) **cor de rosa**
roundtrip **ida e volta** *(f)*
route **caminho** *(m)*
rubber **borracha** *(f)*
rubbish **lixo** *(m)*
rucksack **mochila** *(f)*
run (to) **correr**

sad **triste**
safe **cofre** *(m)*
safe **seguro**
safety belt **cinto de segurança** *(m)*
salad **salada** *(f)*
saloon (US) **bar, botequim** *(m)*
salt **sal** *(m)*
salty **salgado**
same: the same as **igual a**
sand **areia** *(f)*
sandals **sandálias** *(fpl)*
sandwich **sandes** *(f) (Eur.)*,
  **sanduíche** *(f) (Eur.)* **/ sanduíche**
  *(m) (Br.)*
sanitary towel **penso higiénico**
  *(m) (Eur.)* **/ absorvente feminino**
  *(m) (Br.)*
Saturday **sábado** *(m)*
sauce **molho** *(m)*
say (to) **dizer**; how do you say …
  in Portuguese? **como se diz …**
  **em Português?**
school, college **escola** *(f)*, **colégio**
  *(m)*
Scottish **escocês** *(m)*, **escocesa** *(f)*
scrambled egg **ovo mexido** *(m)*
screen **écran** *(m) (Eur.)* **/ tela** *(f) (Br.)*
sea **mar** *(m)*
seafood **frutos do mar** *(mpl)*

seashore **beira-mar** *(f)*, **litoral** *(m)*
seasick **enjoado, mareado**
seaside **praia** *(f)*
secretary **secretário** *(m)*,
  **secretária** *(f)*
see (to) **ver**
seize (to), grasp **agarrar**
seldom **raramente**
self-service **autosserviço** *(m)*
sell (to) **vender**
send (to) **enviar**
send for (to) **chamar**
separate **separado**
September **setembro** *(m)*
serious **grave**
service **serviço** *(m)*
service station **estação de serviço**
  *(f)*
seven **sete**
seventeen **dezassete** *(Eur.)* **/**
  **dezessete** *(Br.)*
seventy **setenta**
several **vários** *(mpl)*, **várias** *(fpl)*
shade **sombra** *(f)*
shame, what a shame! **que pena!**
shampoo **champô** *(Eur.)* **/ xampu**
  *(Br.) (m)*
share (to) **partilhar**
shave (to) **fazer a barba**
shaver **barbeador** *(m)*
shaving cream **creme de barbear**
  *(m)*
she **ela**
shellfish **marisco** *(m)*
ship **navio** *(m)*
shirt **camisa** *(f)*
shoelaces **cordões de sapato**
  *(mpl)*
shoes **sapatos** *(mpl)*
shop **loja** *(f)*
shopping **compras** *(fpl)*

shopping (to go) **fazer compras**
shopping centre **centro comercial
  (Eur) / shopping (Br.) (m)**
short **curto**
short, brief **breve**
show (to) **mostrar**
shower (bath) **chuveiro** (m); **duche**
  (m) (Eur.) / **ducha** (f) (Br.)
shower (rain) **aguaceiro** (m)
showing (cinema) **sessão** (f)
sick (fed up) **farto (de)**
sick (ill) **doente**
sick (nauseated) **enjoado**
sick: to be sick (vomiting) **vomitar**
side **lado** (m)
signature **assinatura** (f)
signpost **placa** (f)
silver **prata** (f)
since **desde**
single (hotel room, etc.) **simples**
single (ticket) **ida / simples**
single, unmarried **solteiro** (m),
  **solteira** (f)
sister **irmã** (f)
sit down (to) **sentar-se**
site (computer) **sítio** (m)
six **seis**
sixteen **dezasseis** (Eur.) /
  **dezesseis** (Br.)
sixty **sessenta**
size **tamanho** (m)
skin **pele** (f)
sleep (to) **dormir**
slow **lento**
slowly **devagar, lentamente**
small **pequeno**
smile (to) **sorrir**
smoke **fumo** (m)
snack **lanche** (m)
snack bar **pastelaria** (f), **café**
  (m) / **lanchonete** (f) (Br.)

snow **neve** (f)
soap **sabão** (m)
soccer **futebol** (m)
socket (electrical) **tomada** (f)
socks **meias** (fpl)
soft drink **refrigerante** (m)
soft-boiled egg **ovo cozido mole**
  (m)
sold out **esgotado**
some **alguns** (mpl), **algumas** (fpl);
  **uns** (mpl), **umas** (fpl)
someone **alguém**
something **alguma coisa, algo**
sometimes **às vezes**
son **filho** (m)
son-in-law **genro** (m)
sorry! **desculpe**!
soup **sopa** (f)
south **sul** (m)
South African **sul-africano** (m),
  **sul-africana** (f)
souvenir **lembrança** (f)
Spanish **espanhol** (m), **espanhola**
  (f)
speak (to) **falar**
spectacles **óculos** (mpl)
speed **velocidade** (f)
spell (to): how do you spell it?
  **como se escreve?**
spend (to) (money) **gastar**
spend (to) (time) **passar**
spoon **colher** (f)
sport **desporto** (Eur.) / **esporte**
  (Br.) (m)
spring **primavera** (f)
square, precinct **praça** (f),
  **largo** (m)
stadium **estádio** (m)
stairs **escada** (f)
stamp **selo** (m)
star **estrela** (f)

start (to) **começar**
station **estação** *(f)*
station (fuel, service) **estação de serviço** *(f)*
stay (to) **ficar**
steal (to) **roubar**
steward **comissário de bordo** *(m)*; **hospedeiro (de bordo)** *(m) (Eur.)* **/ aeromoço** *(m) (Br.)*
stewardess **comissária de bordo** *(f)*; **hospedeira (de bordo)** *(f) (Eur.)* **/ aeromoça** *(f) (Br.)*
stomach **estômago** *(m)*; *(abdomen)* **ventre** *(m)*, *(belly)* **barriga** *(f)*
stop (to) **parar**
stop (to) doing ... / being ... **parar de ...**
storm **tempestade** *(f)*
strawberry **morango** *(m)*
street, urban road **rua** *(f)*
streetcar (US) **elétrico** *(Eur.)* **/ bonde** *(Br.) (m)*
striped **listrado / às/com riscas** *(Eur.)*
stroller **carrinho** *(m)* **/ cadeirinha** *(f)* **(de criança)**
strong **forte**
student **estudante** *(mf)*
study (to) **estudar**
subject, matter **assunto** *(m)*
subway (US) **metro** *(Eur.)* **/ metrô** *(Br.) (m)*
succeed (to) **ser bem sucedido**
succeed (to) (in doing) **conseguir fazer; consegue abrir isto?** *can you open this?*
sugar **açúcar** *(m)*
suit (to), be convenient **convir**
suitcase **mala (de viagem)** *(f)*
summer **verão** *(m)*

sun **sol** *(m)*
sunburn **queimadura de sol / solar** *(f)*
Sunday **domingo** *(m)*
sunglasses **óculos de sol** *(mpl)*
sunscreen **protetor solar** *(m)*
sunshade (awning) **toldo** *(m)*; *(parasol)* **guarda-sol** *(m)*
sunshine **sol** *(m)*
supermarket **supermercado** *(m)*
supper **ceia** *(f)*
supply (to) **fornecer**
supporter (enthusiast) **aficionado, torcedor** *(m)*, **aficionada, torcedora** *(f)*
surgery **consultório** *(m)*
surname **apelido** *(Eur.)* **/ sobrenome** *(Br.) (m)*
swallow (to) **engolir**
sweater (US) **camisola** *(f) (Eur.)* **/ suéter** *(m) (Br.)*
sweet **doce**
swim (to) **nadar**
swimming pool **piscina** *(f)*
swimming trunks **calções de banho** *(mpl)*, **calção de banho** *(m)*
swimsuit **fato de banho** *(Eur.)* **/ maiô** *(Br.) (m)*

table **mesa** *(f)*
take (to), carry **levar**
takeaway (food) **para levar**
taken (seat, taxi) **ocupado**
take-off (aeroplane) **descolagem** *(f)*
takeout (food) (US) **para levar**
talk (to) **conversar**
tank (fuel) **depósito** *(m)*
tap **torneira** *(f)*
tax **imposto** *(m)*

taxi **táxi** *(m)*

taxi-rank **praça de táxis** *(f)* **/
ponto de táxi** *(m)*

tea **chá** *(m)*

teach (to) **ensinar**

teacher **professor** *(m)*, **professora**
*(f)*

telephone **telefone** *(m)*

telephone (to) **telefonar**

telephone directory **lista dos
telefones / telefónica** *(Eur.)* **/
telefônica** *(Br.)* *(f)*

telephone operator **telefonista** *(mf)*

television (set) **televisor /
aparelho de televisão** *(m)*

tell (to) **dizer, contar**

temperature **temperatura** *(f)*

ten **dez**

tent **tenda** *(f)*

terminal (bus) **rodoviária** *(f)*

thank (to) **agradecer**

thank you **obrigado** *(said by
a male)*, **obrigada** *(said by a
female)*

that (one) **aquele, esse** *(m)*,
**aquela, essa** *(f)*

that (thing) **aquilo, isso**

that, which **que**

the **o** *(m)*, **a** *(f)*

then **então**

there **aí; ali; lá**

there is / are **há**

think (to) **pensar**

thirsty **com sede**

thirteen **treze**

thirty **trinta**

this (one) **este** *(m)*, **esta** *(f)*

this (thing) **isto**

thousand **mil**

three **três**

throat **garganta** *(f)*

throw (to) **lançar, atirar**

Thursday **quinta-feira** *(f)*

ticket **bilhete** *(m)*; *(fare)*
**passagem** *(f)*

ticket (performance) **entrada** *(f)* **/
ingresso** *(m)* *(Br.)*

time **tempo** *(m)*; *what time …?*
**que horas …?**

time, occasion **vez** *(f)*

time: to have a good time
**divertir-se**

time: to take time **levar tempo**

timetable **horário** *(m)* **/ tabela de
horário** *(f)* *(Br.)*

tip (gratuity) **gorjeta** *(f)*

tired **cansado**

tissue (hankie) **lenço de papel** *(m)*

to **a, para**

toast **torrada** *(f)*

tobacco **tabaco** *(m)*

today **hoje**

toe **dedo (do pé)** *(m)*

together **juntamente; junto**

toilet **sanitário** *(m)*, **casa de
banho** *(f)* *(Eur.)* **/ banheiro** *(m)*
*(Br.)*

toilet paper **papel higiénico**
*(Eur.)* **/ higiênico** *(Br.)* *(m)*

toilet soap **sabonete** *(m)*

token **ficha** *(f)*

tomorrow **amanhã**

too **também**

too much **demais, demasiado**

tooth **dente** *(m)*

toothache **dor de dentes** *(f)*

toothpaste **pasta de dentes** *(f)* **/
creme dental** *(m)*

tourist office **agência de turismo**
*(f)*

tourist spot **ponto turístico** *(m)*

towel **toalha** *(f)*

tow truck (US) **rebocador,
reboque** *(m)*

town **cidade** (f)
town council **município** (m),
  **câmara municipal** (f)
town hall **câmara municipal** (f) or
  **paços do concelho** (m)
  (Eur.) **/ prefeitura** (f) (Br.)
toy **brinquedo** (m)
traffic **tráfego** (m)
traffic jam **engarrafamento** (m)
traffic lights **semáforo** (m)
train **comboio** (Eur.) **/ trem**
  (Br.) (m)
tram **elétrico** (Eur.) **/ bonde**
  (Br.) (m)
transfer (passengers) **transbordo**
  (m)
translate (to) **traduzir**
trash (US) **lixo** (m)
travel (to) **viajar**
travel agency **agência de viagens**
  (f)
traveller's cheque / check (US)
  **cheque de viagem** (m)
tree **árvore** (f)
trolley (airport, supermarket)
  **carrinho** (m)
trousers **calças** (fpl), **calça** (f)
truck **caminhão, camião** (Eur.) (m)
try (to) **experimentar**
Tuesday **terça-feira** (f)
turn (to) **virar**
turn: your turn **sua vez**, my turn
  **minha vez**
twelve **doze**
twenty **vinte**
two **dois** (m), **duas** (f)
two-way (ticket) **ida e volta** (f)
tyre **pneu** (m)
tyre, flat **pneu furado** (m)

umbrella **guarda-chuva** (m)
uncle **tio** (m)

underdone (steak) **mal passado**
underground train **metro** (Eur.) **/
  metrô** (Br.) (m)
understand (to) **compreender,
  entender**
underwear **roupa de baixo** (f)
undressed, get (to) **despir-se**
university **universidade** (f)
until **até**
upstairs **lá em cima**
urgent **urgente**
use (to) **usar**
useful **útil**
usually **habitualmente,
  normalmente**

vacant **vago**
vacation (US) **férias** (fpl)
vaccine **vacina** (f)
valid **válido**
vegetables **legumes** (mpl)
vegetarian **vegetariano** (m),
  **vegetariana** (f)
very **muito**
video **vídeo** (m)
view **vista** (f)
visa **visto / visa** (m)
visit **visita** (f)
visit (to) **visitar**
voyage **viagem** (f)

wait (to) **esperar**
waiter **empregado (de mesa)**
  (Eur.) **/ garçom** (Br.) (m)
wallet **carteira** (f)
want (to), will **querer**
wash (to) **lavar**
washroom (US) **lavabo** (m), **casa
  de banho** (f) (Eur.) **/ banheiro**
  (m) (Br.)
watch out! **cuidado!**
watch, clock **relógio** (m)

water *água;* drinking water **água potável** *(f)*
waterfalls **cataratas, cachoeiras** *(fpl)*
wave **onda** *(f)*
wave *(to)* **acenar**
way **caminho** *(m)*
way in, entry **entrada** *(f)*
way out, exit **saída** *(f)*
we **nós**
weak **fraco**
weapon **arma** *(f)*
wear *(to)* **usar**
weather **tempo** *(m);* fine weather **bom tempo,** *bad weather* **mau tempo**
weather forecast **previsão do tempo** *(f)*
Wednesday **quarta-feira** *(f)*
week **semana** *(f)*
weekend **fim de semana** *(m); at the weekend* **no / ao fim de semana**
weight **peso** *(m)*
welcome **bem-vindo** *(said to a male),* **bem-vinda** *(said to a female)*
welcome *(response to thanks)* **de nada**
well **bem**
well done *(food)* **bem passado**
well done! **muito bem!**
Welsh **galês** *(m),* **galesa** *(f)*
west **oeste** *(m)*
wet **molhado**
what …? **(o) que …?**
when **quando**
where **onde**
which? **qual?**
while, whilst **enquanto**
white **branco**
who? **quem?**
wholegrain, wholemeal bread **pão integral** *(m)*

why? **por quê? / porquê?** *(Eur.)*
widow **viúva** *(f)*
widower **viúvo** *(m)*
width **largura** *(f)*
wife **esposa / mulher** *(f)*
win *(to)* **vencer**
wind **vento** *(m)*
window **janela** *(f)*
wine **vinho** *(m);* red **tinto;** branco white
wine list **lista / carta dos vinhos** *(f)*
winter **inverno** *(m)*
wish *(to)* **desejar**
with **com**
with me **comigo**
without **sem**
woman **mulher** *(f)*
work **trabalho** *(m)*
work *(to)* **trabalhar;** *I work* **estou empregado** *(m),* **empregada** *(f)*
work *(to), function* **funcionar**
world **mundo** *(m)*
worried **preocupado**
worse **pior**
wounded **ferido**
wrap up *(to)* **embrulhar**
wrecker *(US)* **pronto socorro** *(Eur.)* **/ reboque** *(Br.) (m)*
write *(to)* **escrever**
wrong, incorrect **errado**

year **ano** *(m)*
yellow **amarelo**
yes **sim**
yesterday **ontem**
yoghurt **iogurte** *(m)*
you **você; tu**
young **jovem, novo**

zero **zero**
zone **zona** *(f)*

# Taking it further

Selected information on further learning opportunities, places to visit and other matters related to the Portuguese language and its speakers

## The Portuguese language and its world

See these web pages for the history of the Portuguese language, where it is spoken, local variations, etc.:

www.linguaportuguesa.ufrn.br/en.wikipedia.org/wiki/
Portuguese_language

The Instituto Camões website – www.instituto-camoes.pt – contains a wealth of material catering for all levels of competence in Portuguese as a foreign language as well as lists of literary works and literature on culture and other topics.

On www.cplp.org you will find a political, demographic, and economic profile of each country in the 'Community of Portuguese-Speaking Countries' (Comunidade dos Países de Língua Portuguesa – CPLP).

## Portuguese courses wherever you are

To find what best suits your requirements, do a web search entering the country / area / city where you would like to attend a course and one of the following requests depending on what you are looking for: Portuguese classes / Portuguese distance learning / Portuguese private tuition / Portuguese-speaking universities. This way you can get the latest on what is being offered.

## Places to visit

For options around the Portuguese-speaking world, do a web search on 'Places to visit in...' and slot in the destination of your

choice, for example: Angola / Azores / Brazil / Cape Verde / East
Timor / Equatorial Guinea / Guinea-Bissau / Macau / Madeira /
Mozambique / Portugal / S. Tome e Principe.

### News on-line

www.LusoNEWS.org

At this web address you will find daily news for different
Portuguese-speaking countries and communities. Just click on the
country you are interested in.

### Portuguese-language newspapers

www.kidon.com/media-link/

This web address provides extensive information on newspapers
written in Portuguese and published in different parts of the world.
Select the appropriate continent and then click the country of your
choice.

### Television

Watching TV can speed up your language learning process, as you
both hear and see how native speakers interact. Rádio Televisão
Portuguesa (www.rtp.pt) and TV Globo (www.redeglobo.com.br)
are two major sources of programmes in the Portuguese language.
Both have international channels. Depending on your whereabouts
in the world, you can access them via satellite. To see the online
programme guide go to these web pages:

www.rtp.pt/rtpi
www.redeglobo.com.br/globointernacional

Note on Portuguese-language web addresses:

Recommended sites are usually available in both Portuguese and English. If you key in your
query in English in the search box of a Portuguese page (**buscar** or **pesquisar**) the reply is
likely to come back in English.

# Index to grammar and problem words

The first number in each reference is the unit number followed by the section title or exercise number. If there is only one number, it is to the dialogue(s) at the beginning of the unit in question.

Examples:

2 refers to the **initial dialogues of unit 2** and respective comprehension questions (**2.1** and **2.2**)

**3:HTPI** refers to the **How to pronounce it** section in **unit 3**

**5:Ea** refers to subsection **a** of the **Expressions** section in **unit 5**

**7:CIa** refers to subsection **a** of the **Cultural information** section in **unit 7**

**13:HIWc** refers to subsection **c** of the **How it works** section in **unit 13**

**16:12** refers to **exercise 12** in **unit 16** and so on.

**PSG** refers to the pronunciation and spelling guide and **VG** to the verb guide and tables, at the end of the book.

*a* 2:HIWa, 2:HIWb, 2:HIWd,
  4:HIWe, 7:HIWd, 15:Ea, 21:HIWa,
  22HIWb, 23:HIWa
*à* 2:HIWd, 5:HIWb, 9:Ed
*a/an* 2:HIWb, 3:HIWc, 7:HIWd,
  15:HIWc
*acabar de* 19:HIWf
*achar, pensar* 23:Ea
*acreditar, crer* 24:Ea, VG

*adjectives, adverbs* 2:HIWa,
  2:HIWe, 3:HIWd, 4:HIWa,
  5:HIWc, 10:HIWc, 14:HIWa,
  17:HIWf, 18:HIWd
*age* see *index of topics*
*ago* 18:Eb
*aí, ali* 13:Eb
*ali, lá* 13:Eb
*alphabet* 11:4

andar a 15:HIWa
any 3:HIWb
aquele, aquilo 7:E, 12:Ed, 13:Eb
aqui, cá 13:Eb
-ar verbs 3:HIWe (see also verb
  tables)
articles 2:HIWa, 2:HIWb, 2:HIWd,
  3:HIWa, 3:HIWb, 7:HIWc,
  7:HIWd, 17:Eb, 20:HIWf
at, in 2:HIWd, 5:HIWb, 8:Ec, 8:4,
  13:HIWd, 23:HIWa
até 9:Ed, 23:HIWb
atrasado, tarde 15:Eb
augmentatives 13:HIWd

be (to) 4:HIWd, 18:Ea, VG
because 17, 24:HIWd
bem, boa, bom 12:HIWa, 10:HIWc,
  24:HIWa
best, most 18:HIWd, 24:HIWa
born 20:Ee

cá, aqui 13:Eb
can 4:CIa, 20:Ec, VG
command forms 12:HIWa,
  12:HIWb, 17:HIWb, 17:HIWc,
  17:HIWd
comparatives 14:HIWa, 17:HIWf
compound or perfect tenses
  18:HIWa
compound verbs VG
compound words 5:HIWc, PSG, VG
conditional 19:HIWa
conhecer, encontrar 20:Ed, VG
conhecer, saber 20:Ed, VG
conjugations 3:HIWe, 5:HIWa,
  8:HIWa, 9:HIWb, 10:HIWe,
  12:HIWa, 13:HIWa, 13:HIWb,
  14:HIWb, 15:HIWa, 17:HIWa,
  17:HIWe, 19:HIWa, 19:HIWd,
  21:HIWc (see also verb tables)

conjunctions 9:HIWa, 17:HIWa,
  17:HIWe, 19:HIWd, 19:HIWe,
  21:HIWd, 21:HIWe, 24:HIWd
continuous tenses 15:HIWa,
  18:HIWc
contracted words 2:HIWd, 5:HIWb,
  20:HIWa, 20:HIWd, 21:HIWa
costumar 14:HIWb, 19:HIWf
could you please 3:CIa, 4:CIa,
  19:HIWc
crer, acreditar 24:Ea, VG

dates, days see Index of topics
de 2:HIWc, 15:Ea, 18:HIWe,
  20:HIWa, 20:HIWd, 20:HIWe,
  23:HIWa
demonstratives, indefinites
  3:HIWb, 7:E, 12:Ed, 12:HIWd,
  13:Eb, 24:HIWb
diminutives 13:HIWd
doer 18:Ea, 24:HIWc, VG

é 4:HIWd, 10:HIWb (see also ser)
é que 10:HIWb
em 2:HIWd, 23:HIWa
emphatics 24:HIWa
encontrar, conhecer 20:Ed, VG
-er verbs 24:HIWe (see also verb
  tables)
esse, este, isso, isto 7:E, 12:Ed,
  12:HIWd, 13:Eb
esse/isso – you, your 13:Eb
está 4:HIWd, 10:Ec (see also
  estar)
estar 4:HIWd, 7:CIb, 18:Ea, VG
estar, ficar 4:HIWd, 21:Eb, VG
estar, ser 4:HIWd, 15:HIWa,
  15:HIWb, 18:Ea, VG
estar, ter 18:Ea, 23:Eb, 24:Ed, VG
eu queria 14:HIWc
ever 18:HIWa, 23:HIWb, 24:Ee

*faça, faz* 2:CIa, 3:CIa, 4:CIa, 10:Ec
  (see also *fazer*)
*faltar* 21:Ec
*favor* 2:CIa, 3:CIa, 4:CIa, 17:Eb
*fazer* 2:CIa, 3:CIa, 10:Ec, VG
feminine see gender
*ficar, estar* 4:HIWd, 21:Eb, VG
*ficar, ser* 4:HIWd
*for* 5:HIWb, 18:Eb, 23:HIWa
forms of address see Index of
  topics
*from, of* 2:HIWc, 5:HIWb, 23:HIWa
future (colloquial) 9:HIWb, 13:HIWc
future (emphatic) 13:HIWb, 13:HIWc
future (indicative) 13:HIWa,
  13:HIWc
future (in the past) see conditional
future (subjunctive) 17:HIWe

gender 2:HIWa, 3:HIWb, 4:HIWa,
  10:HIWc, 10:HIWd, 12:HIWc,
  12:HIWd, 18:HIWf
gerund see present participle
*gostaria, gosto* 8:HIWa, 19:HIWa,
  19:Ea

*há* 5:Ea, 8:HIWa, 18:Eb (see also
  *haver*)
*haver* 10:Ec, 13:HIWb, VG
hyphen, use of 22:HIWa, 22:HIWc,
  PSG

*if* 17:HIWe, 19:HIWe
imperative see command forms
imperfect (indicative) 14:HIWb,
  14:HIWd, 19:HIWa
imperfect (subjunctive) 19:HIWd
impersonal verbs 24:HIWc
*importar-se* 3:CIb, 13:Ea, 19:HIWc
*in, at* 2:HIWd, 5:HIWb, 8:Ec, 8:4,
  13:HIWd, 23:HIWa

*in, on* 2:HIWd, 5:HIWb
indefinites, demonstratives
  3:HIWb, 7:E, 12:Ed, 12:HIWd,
  13:Eb, 24:HIWb
indicative tenses 8:HIWa,
  10:HIWe, 13:HIWa,
  14:HIWb
indirect speech see reported
  speech
infinitive 3:HIWe, 15:HIWa,
  21:HIWc, 21:HIWd
inflected infinitive see personal
  infinitive
-ing 5:HIWa, 9:HIWb, 15:HIWa,
  18:HIWc
intensifiers 24:HIWa
interrogatives 9:HIWa, 10:HIWb,
  20:Eb, 24:HIWd
*ir* 9:Ec, 9:HIWb, VG
*ir* + gerund 15:HIWa
*ir* + infinitive 9:HIWb
-ir verbs 3:HIWe (see also verb
  tables)
*ir, vir* 21:Ea, VG
irregular verbs 3:HIWe, VG (see
  also conjugations)

*já* 9:HIWa, 23:HIWb

*lá, ali* 13:Eb
*leave (to)* 24:Eb
*lembrar* 9:HIWa, 24:HIWc
*let's* 17:HIWc
*levar, trazer* 21:Ea
*like (I would / should)* 3:Ea, 4:CIa,
  14:HIWc, 19:HIWb
*live (to)* 20:Ee
-lo 22:HIWc
*logo* 23:HIWb
looking forward 22:E
*love (to)* 19:E

mais de 18:HIWe
mais que 14:HIWa, 18:HIWe
mão 5:HIWb, 5:HIWc
masculine see gender
me, mim 21:HIWa, 22:HIWa
meet (to) 20:Ed
miss, missing 21:Ec, 24:Ec
morar, viver 20:Ee
muito 12:Ea, 18:HIWd
myself 9:HIWa

negatives 4:HIWb, 9:HIWa,
   17:HIWd
no 2:HIWd
-no 22:HIWc
no, not see negatives
nouns 2:HIWa, 2:HIWc, 2:HIWe,
   3:HIWa, 3:HIWd, 4:HIWa,
   5:HIWc, 7:HIWc, 10:HIWc,
   10:HIWd
numbers see numerals
numerals (cardinals, ordinals)
   3:HIWc, 7:HIWb, 8:HIWd,
   12:HIWc, 13:HIWe

o 2:HIWa, 2:HIWb, 2:HIWd,
   4:HIWe, 7:HIWc, 21:HIWa,
   22:HIWb
obrigado 2:CIa, 2:HIWa
of, from 2:HIWc, 5:HIWb, 23:HIWa
old (… years old) 7:CIb
on, in 2:HIWd, 5:HIWb
-or/ôr verbs 3:HIWe (see also verb
   tables)
orthography-changing verbs VG

para, por 23:HIWa
participles 3:HIWe, 4:HIWa,
   5:HIWa, 15:HIWa, VG
passear 19:Ed, VG

passive voice 15:HIWb
past participle 3:HIWe,
   15:HIWb, VG
pé: a pé, de/em pé 11:8, 15:Ea
pedir, perguntar 20:Ea, VG
pensar, achar 23:Ea
perfect tenses 18:HIWa
perguntar, pedir 20:Ea, VG
person 7:HIWa, 8:HIWb, 21:HIWc,
   24:HIWc
personal infinitive 21:HIWc,
   21:HIWe
play (to) 19:Ec
pluperfect (indicative) 18:HIWa
plurals 2:HIWe, 3:HIWd, 4:HIWa,
   5:HIWc, 10:HIWd
pode 2:CIa, 4:CIa, 13:Ea (see also
   poder)
poder 2:CIa, 19:HIWc, 20:Ec, VG
poder, saber 20:Ec, VG
por 5:HIWb, 15:HIWb
por, para 23:HIWa
pôr 3:HIWe, VG
possessive case 20:HIWa
possessives 4:HIWe, 5:HIWb,
   20:HIWb, 20:HIWc, 20:HIWd,
   20:HIWe, 21:HIWb
prefixes see compound verbs
prepositions 2:HIWc, 2:HIWd,
   5:HIWb, 23:HIWa
present (indicative) 8:HIWa
present (subjunctive) 17:HIWa
present participle 5:HIWa,
   15:HIWa, 18:HIWc
preterite (indicative) 10:HIWe,
   14:HIWd
pronouns: personal subject
   7:HIWa, 14:HIWc; object 8:HIWc,
   21:HIWa, 21:HIWb, 22:HIWa,
   22:HIWb; reflexive 9:HIWa

pronunciation 2:HTPI, 3:HTPI,
4:HTPI, 5:HTPI, 7:HTPI, 8:HTPI,
9:HTPI, 10:HTPI, PSG

que, qual 20:Eb
que, quê 24:HIWd
queria, eu queria 14:HIWc
queria, quero 3:Ea, 4:CIa, 12:Ea,
14:HIWc, 19:HIWb, VG
questions and replies 4:HIWc,
10:HIWa, 10:HIWb, 23:Eb

radical changing verbs VG
reflexive verbs 9:HIWa, 24:HIWc
regular verbs 3:HIWe, VG (see also
conjugations)
reported speech 18:HIWb,
19:HIWa

saber, conhecer 20:Ed, VG
saber, poder 20:Ec, VG
se 9:HIWa, 17:HIWe, 19:HIWe
ser 4:HIWd, 7:CIb, 18:Ea, VG
ser, estar 4:HIWd, 15:HIWa,
15:HIWb, 18:Ea, VG
ser, ficar 4:HIWd
sitting, standing 11:8, 12:5, 17:2
special verbs VG
spelling (general) PSG
spelling (old and new) PSG
spelling changes 2:HIWe, 5:HIWb,
10:HIWc, 22:HIWb, VG
subjunctive tenses 17:HIWa,
17:HIWe, 19:HIWd
subordinate clauses 9:HIWa,
17:HIWa, 17:HIWe, 19:HIWa,
19:HIWd, 19:HIWf, 21:HIWd,
24:HIWd
suffixes 13:HIWd
superlatives 18:HIWd

tarde, atrasado 15:Eb
te, ti 8:HIWb, 8:HIWc, 21:HIWb,
22:HIWa
tem 15:Ea (see also ter)
ter 5:Ea, 7:CIb, 18:HIWa, 24:Ed, VG
ter, estar 18:Ea, 23:Eb, 24:Ed, VG
than 14:HIWa, 18:HIWe
that, this 7:E, 12:Ed, 12:HIWd
time see Index of topics
to 3:HIWa, 23:HIWa
todo, tudo 12:Ea, 24:HIWb
tomara 18:HIWa, 21:HIWd
trazer, levar 21:Ea
tu 8:HIWb (see also you)

um, uma 3:HIWb, 3:HIWc

vai 9:Ec, 9:HIWb, 15:CIa
(see also ir)
verb tables: regular and irregular
VG
verbs 3:HIWe, 6:11, VG (see also
conjugations)
vez 9:Ed, 17:Ea, 23:HIWb
vir, ir 21:Ea, VG
viver, morar 20:Ee
você 8:HIWb (see also you)
vós 8:HIWb

walking, standing 11:8, 12:5,
15:Ea, 17:2
weather see index of topics
word order 2:HIWc, 2:HIWf,
4:HIWa, 7:CIb, 9:HIWa, 10:HIWa,
10:HIWb, 21:HIWa, 22:HIWa,
22:HIWb

yes 4:HIWc
you 7:HIWa, 8:HIWb, 9:HIWa,
21:HIWa, 21:HIWb, 22:HIWd

# Index of topics

The first number in each reference is the unit number followed by the section title or exercise number. If there is only one number it is to the dialogue(s) at the beginning of the unit in question.

Examples:

2 refers to the **initial dialogues of unit 2** and respective comprehension questions (**2.1** and **2.2**)

**5:Ea** refers to subsection **a** of the **Expressions** section in **unit 5**

**7:CIa** refers to subsection **a** of the **Cultural information** section in **unit 7**

**13:HIWc** refers to subsection **c** of the **How it works** section in **unit 13**

**16:12** refers to **exercise 12** in **unit 16** and so on.

**TIF** refers to the **Take it further** pages

*accepting / declining 7, 15, 21:5*
*accommodation 4, 4:E, 4:3, 5:Ea,*
  *5:Eb, 5:4, 23:6, 23:7*
*addresses 6:1, 7:CIb, 11:5, 22:CIa*
*advertisements (work / business)*
  *23:1 (property) 23:7 (study) 25:5*
*age 7:CIb, 11:10, 11:11, 20:Ee*
*agreeing / disagreeing 23:Ea,*
  *23:Eb, 24:Ea*
*ailments 3:4, 18:6 (see also*
  *chemist; doctor; dentist)*
*air travel 2, 2:HIWc, 2:3, 2:5, 16:9*
*apartment 4:E, 23:6*
*apparel see clothes*

*appearance see people*
  *(describing) (identifying)*
*appointments 17, 17:CI, 23:1*
*arriving 2, 2:3, 6:2, 6:3, 8, 9*
*asking for something 3:Ea, 3:CIa,*
  *3:CIb, 3:4, 4:CIa, 5:Ea, 13:Ea*
*asking the way 2, 2:4, 4, 4:6, 6:1,*
  *6:6, 9:Ec, 9:3, 12*
*automobile see car hire; driving*

*bank 2:6, 3:6, 21, 21:2, 21:3*
*barber / hairdresser 22:1*
*beach / sea 4:6, 11:8, 16:19, 16:20,*
  *19*

bedroom 6:9, 13:4, 23:6 (see also hotel)

belongings 2:HIWc, 2:3, 18, 18:4, 20:HIWa-e

beverages 3:Ea, 3:HIWe, 5:3, 5:5, 6:12, 13:3, 20:3

bill 3:Ea, 13:3, 16:4

birthday 11:10, 11:11, 23:HIWb, 24:6

body see people (describing); size (clothing and footwear); chemist; doctor; dentist

body (movement) 11:8, 12:5, 15:Ea, 17:2 (see also disabled facilities)

booking (hotel) 4, 23:5; (car) 6:4; (doctor) 17, 17:CI; (social / business) 17:CI; (business / work) 23:1

bus / coach 3, 4:6, 8:CI, 11:3, 16:8, 16:11, 16:12

business / work 7, 7:CIb, 23 (see also meeting people (social and business))

cab see taxi

café 3:Ea, 3:4, 13:3, 15

camping / caravanning 4:E, 5, 5:Ea, 5:Eb, 5:4, 22:6

car breakdown / damage 6:10, 18

car hire 2:3, 6:3, 6:4

carnival 19:5, 19:6, 19:7

cash 3:HIWe, 13, 13:Ea, 15:4

cash dispenser / cashpoint 3:HIWe, 21

celebration / party 21:5, 24:5

cell phone 3:HIWe, 18:4, 25:2 (see also telephone)

changing money 2:6, 3:6

check see cheque

cheers! (toast) 24:5

chemist 2, 3:4, 15:5, 17

cheque 3:6, 15:HIWb, 15:4, 21

children 7:CIb, 10:CI, 10:HWId, 19:Ec, 22:6

Christmas 11:10, 11:12

cinema / theatre 15:5, 24:1

clarification / pardon? 2:CIb, 3, 6:1, 11:4, 19:3, 20:7, 22:5, 24:2

cleaning (clothes) 5:4, 13:5, 24:3; (room) 13:4, 24:3

clothes 9:Eb, 9:4, 11:8, 13:5, 14, 14:5, 17:Ec; (accessories) 5:5, 14:Ea, 17:Ec

coach / bus 3, 4:6, 8:CI, 11:3, 16:8, 16:11, 16:12

colours 9, 9:Ea, 14:Ec, 14:5, 22:1

comparisons 14:HIWa, 17:HIWf, 18:HIWd

complaints 12:HIWb, 16:4, 16:5, 18:4

computer see internet and e-mail

concert 24:1

containers 12:Ec, 20:3

conversation / small talk 7, 10, 14:2, 14:5, 15, 15:2, 15:3, 17:Eb, 19

correspondence see e-mail; letter writing (social and business)

country / home town 7, 7:CIb, 10:4, 20:Ee, 20:5, 20:6, 23:3

credit card 3:HIWe, 15:HIWb, 15:4, 21

crosswords see word games

culture / sights 8, 19:3, 19:5, 20:4, 21:6, 22:4, 24:2, 25:1, 25:5, TIF

currency 2:6, 3:6

customs 2:HIWd, 6:2

CV 23:3

daily routine 9:HIWa, 10, 10:5, 14:HIWb (see also routine action / event) *date (of birth)* 10:Ea, 24:6 (see also birthday)

*dates* 10:Ea, 11:10

*day (parts of)* 8:Ec, 24:2

*days* 8:Ea, 10:Ea, 10:5

*decisions* 12:Ea, 14, 15, 20, 21

*declining / accepting* 7, 15, 21:5

*dentist* 6:10, 17:4

*describing yourself* see self; people (describing)

*diner* see snack bar / restaurant

*directions* 2, 2:Ea, 2:Eb, 4:6, 9:Ec, 9:Ed, 9:3, 11:7, 12, 16:16, 16:17

*disabled facilities* 4:E, 15:HIWb, 22:6

*disagreeing / agreeing* 23:Ea, 23:Eb, 24:Ea

*dislikes / likes* 8:HIWa, 10, 19, 19:Ea, 19:HIWb, 19HIWf

*doctor* 6:10, 15:5, 17, 17:4, 17:5

*drink* 5:5, 18:3, 20, 20:3, 20:4, 23:HIWa, 24:5

*driving* 2:3, 5:HIWb, 18:3 (see also car hire; fuel station; garage)

*druggist* see chemist

*Easter* 11:10

*eating out* see restaurant / snack bar

*electrical equipment* 5:4, 23:6

*e-mail* 2:7, 6:13, 22:5, 23:5

*emergency / first aid* 3:4, 6:6, 6:10, 15:5, 17, 17:Ed, 17:4, 17:5, 18:2

*employment (looking for)* 23:1

*entertainment* see television; cinema / theatre; concert; night club; stadium

*excuse me* 2:CIa, 4:CIb, 6:14

*fado* 24:2

*family / friends* 7:CIb, 10:CI, 10:HIWc, 10:HIWd, 20:Ee, 23:4

*feelings* 18:Ea, 18:6, 24:Ec, 24:Ed

*fine* 18:7

*first aid / emergency* 3:4, 6:6, 6:10, 15:5, 17, 17:Ed, 17:4, 17:5, 18:2

*food* 3:HIWe, 3:4, 5, 5:3, 12, 16:15, 20:7, 24:4

*footwear* 14, 14:5, 17:Ec

*forms / written messages* 3:HIWe, 6:9, 11:10, 11:11, 11:12, 13:5, 16:15, 21:5, 21:7

*forms of address* 1A:CI, 8:HIWb, 22:CIa, 22:CIb

*free time / holidays* 7, 7:CIb, 8, 8:Ea, 10, 19, 19:Ec, 19:Ed, 19:2

*fuel station* 4:6, 6:5, 13, 13:Ea, 18

*furniture / furnishings* 4:E, 6:9, 23:6

*future (talking about)* 9:HIWb, 13:HIWa, 13:HIWb, 13:HIWc; 16:2

*garage* 4:6, 13, 13:Ea, 18; (private) 23:7

*getting attention* see excuse me

*goodbye* 1C, 1C:CI, 15:CIb, 17:HIWe, 22:CIb, 24:Eb

*great!* 18:HIWa, 23:HIWb, 24:Ee

*greeting cards* 11:10, 11:11, 11:12

*greetings* see hello

*hair* 5:4, 8:5, 22:1

*hairdresser / barber* 22:1

*health* 17:5 (see also chemist; doctor; dentist)

*hello* 1A, 1A:E, 7, 15:CIa, 17:CI, 22:CIb

*help* 2:CIa, 6:14, 17:Ed, 17:6

*hi* see hello

*hiring (car, sunshade, etc.)* 2:3, 6:3, 6:4, 16:20

hobbies / interests 19, 19:HIWb, 19:HIWf, 19:2

holidays / free time 7, 7:CIb, 8, 8:Ea, 10, 19, 19:Ec, 19:Ed, 19:2

home / house 6:1, 7:CIb, 10:5, 23:6, 23:7

home town / country 7, 7:CIb, 10:4, 20:Ee, 20:5, 20:6, 23:3

homeland / nationality 7:CIb, 7:5, 20:Ee, 20:5, 20:6

hopes / wishes 17:HIWb, 18:HIWa, 19, 19:HIWd

hospital 2:HIWe (see also emergency / first aid; illness and accident)

hostel 4:E, 5:Ea, 22:6

hotel 4, 4:E, 4:3, 4:4, 6:8, 6:9, 13:4, 16:15, 22:6, 23:5

housework 24:3

ID 2:HIWc, 2:3, 4, 7:CIb

illness and accident 6:10, 17, 17:CI, 18:Ea, 18:2, 18:6 (see also emergency / first aid; doctor)

instructions / requests 12:HIWb, 12:2, 12:5, 13:4, 17:Ec, 17:2, 17:3

intentions / planning 19:Eb, 19:2, 22:6, 23:4

interests / hobbies 19, 19:HIWb, 19:HIWf, 19:2

internet 2:7, 5:7, 6:13, 22:5 (see also e-mail)

interrupting see excuse me; sorry (apology)

introductions 1B, 7:CIa, 7:CIb, 7:3

invitations 7, 21:5

job / occupation 7:CIb, 7:HIWd, 7:4, 23

job / profession 3:Ec, 7, 7:CIb, 7:HIWd, 7:4, 10, 23, 23:3

keep-fit / sport 5:4, 9:3, 15, 15:2, 19:2

layout / shape 9:Ec, 11:7, 18, 18:5, 23:6, 24:HIWc

leisure activities see hobbies / interests; sport / keep–fit; word games

letter writing (social and business) 21:7, 22:CIa, 22:CIb, 22:6, 23:5, 23:7, 25:5

likes / dislikes 8:HIWa, 10, 19, 19:Ea, 19:HIWb, 19HIWf

location 2, 2:Ea, 4, 4:HIWd, 4:6, 7:E, 11:1, 11:7, 12, 12:Ed, 12:4, 15, 16:16, 16:17

looking forward to 18:Ea, 22:E

lost property 18, 18:4, 19:7, 20:Ed, 21:Ec

map 3:CIa, 3:4, 6:1

married / single 7, 7:CIb, 11:10, 23:4, 23:5

material (made of) 14:Eb, 18, 18:5

meals 4:E, 5:HIWc, 7, 16:15, 20

measures / weights 12, 12:Eb

meeting people (social and business) 2:3, 8, 9. 15, 16:3, 20:Ed

menu 20, 20:7

mobile phone 3:HIWe, 18:4, 25:2 (see also telephone)

money 2:6, 13, 13:Ea, 13:2

months 10:Ea

name 1B, 4:5, 7:CIb, 7:HIWc, 9:5, 11:4, 22:CIa, 22:CIb

nationality / homeland 7:CIb, 7:5, 20:Ee, 20:5, 20:6

New Year 11:10
night club 15:5, 24:2
numbers 3:HIWc, 7:HIWb, 8:HIWd,
  10:Ea, 12:HIWc, 13:HIWe, 16:4,
  19:6

occupation / job 7:CIb, 7:HIWd,
  7:4, 23
opinions 23:Ea, 23:Eb, 24:Ea
order (out of) 12:2, 18:HIWc
ordering (breakfast) 16:15;
  (restaurant meal) 20; (snack)
  13:3

pardon? / clarification 2:CIb, 3, 6:1,
  11:4, 19:3, 20:7, 22:5, 24:2
parting words see goodbye
party / celebration 21:5, 24:5
past (talking about) 10:HIWe,
  14:HIWb, 14:HIWd, 16:2;
  18:HIWa
pastimes see hobbies / interests;
  sport / keep–fit; word games
pattern (design) 14:Ec, 18, 18:5
paying 3:HIWe, 6:4, 12:Ea, 13:3,
  15:4, 16:18, 21:2
people (describing) 8, 8:5,
  14:HIWa, 18:Ea, 18:HIWd,
  18:HIWe; (identifying) 9, 11:8,
  16:13, 18:5
personality see likes / dislikes;
  interests / hobbies; daily routine
pets 19:Ea, 24:3, 25:3
pharmacy see chemist
physical appearance see people
  (describing)
planning / intentions 19:Eb, 19:2,
  22:6, 23:4
please 2:CIa, 6:14, 6:15, 17:HIWe
points of the compass 11:1

Portuguese (learning and
  speaking) 6:1, 6:11, 14:HIWa,
  15:3, 16:7, 18:HIWd, 20:Ec, 23:1,
  25:1, 25:2, 25:3, 25:4, 25:5
positional words 2, 2:Ea, 4:6, 13:Eb,
  16:16, 16:17
post office 2, 4:6, 8:CI, 13, 13:Ea,
  15:5, 21:4, 22:CIa, 23:2
postcard 13, 21:7 (see also
  correspondence)
present, gift 24:5, 24:6
problems (hotel) 6:9, 13:4, 18:4;
  (other) 3:3, 3:4, 6:1, 6:10, 6:11,
  6:13, 16:4, 16:5, 18, 18:HIWc,
  18:4, 18:5, 18:7
profession / job 3:Ec, 7, 7:CIb,
  7:HIWd, 7:4, 10, 23, 23:3
public notices and signs 3:HIWe,
  3:3, 6:6, 16:6

quantity 5, 12:Ea, 12:Eb, 14:HIWa,
  15:HIWc, 18:HIWd, 18:HIWe,
  24:HIWb

receipt 5:Ea, 6:4, 16:18, 21:3
recipe 24:4
relationships see introductions;
  family / friends
repairs 6:10, 18, 18:HIWc, 18:4
requests / instructions 12:HIWb,
  12:2, 12:5, 13:4, 17:Ec, 17:2,
  17:3
reservations (travel, accommodation,
  etc.) 3, 3:Ea, 3:HIWa, 3:HIWc,
  3:HIWd, 8, 11:3
restaurant / snack bar 4:6, 5:Ea,
  13:3, 15, 15:5, 16:4, 20, 20:2,
  20:7
restroom see toilets
road accident 18:2, 18:5, 18:6

*routine action / event 8:Ea,*
*8:HIWa, 9:HIWa, 10, 10:5,*
*14:HIWb, 16:12, 17:Ea, 19:2*

*salutations (speech) see*
*hello; goodbye; (writing) see*
*correspondence*
*samba 19:5*
*sea / beach 4:6, 11:8, 16:19, 16:20,*
*19*
*seasons 10:Eb, 10:3*
*self 4:5, 7:CIb, 9:HIWa, 11:9,*
*20:Ee, 23:3*
*self-service see vending machines*
*shape / layout 9:Ec, 11:7, 18, 18:5,*
*23:6, 24:HIWc*
*shopping 5, 6:12, 12, 12:Ea, 12:3,*
*14, 14:5, 16:17, 16:18*
*sights / culture 8, 19:3, 19:5, 20:4,*
*21:6, 22:4, 24:2, 25:1, 25:5, TIF*
*signs see public notices and signs*
*single / married 7, 7:CIb, 11:10,*
*23:4, 23:5*
*size (clothing and footwear) 14,*
*14:3, 14:4*
*small talk / conversation 7, 10, 14:2,*
*14:5, 15, 15:2, 15:3, 17:Eb, 19*
*snack bar / restaurant 4:6, 5:Ea,*
*13:3, 15, 15:5, 16:4, 20, 20:2,*
*20:7*
*snacks 3:4, 13:3, 15*
*socializing see meeting people*
*(social and business); invitations*
*sorry (apology) 2:CIa, 6:14;*
*(empathy / sympathy) 5:CI,*
*11:10, 17:HIWa, 18:16, 21:Eb,*
*24:Ed*
*speed limits see fine; road accident*
*sport / keep-fit 5:4, 9:3, 15, 15:2,*
*19:2*

*stadium 15:5, 19:4*
*subway, tube see underground,*
*tube*
*swimming / water sports 9:3,*
*19:2*

*talking about yourself see self;*
*job / profession; job / occupation;*
*interests / hobbies*
*taxi 2:3, 3:Ea, 3:CIa, 6:10, 11:6*
*telephone 2, 3:HIWe, 3:6, 5:6,*
*7CIb, 17:CI, 21:5, 22:2, 22:3*
*television 5:4, 6:8, 23:6*
*thank you 2:CIa, 2:HIWa, 6:14,*
*6:15, 17:HIWe*
*theatre / cinema 15:5, 24:1*
*theft 18, 18:5*
*tickets (transport) 2:HIWc, 3,*
*3:Ea, 3:Eb, 3:5, 8, 11:3, 19:7;*
*(performance) 19:4, 19:6, 24:1*
*time (clock) 8:Eb; (at what time)*
*8:4, 15:5; (on time) 15:Eb, 16:3;*
*(how often) 8:Ea, 17:Ea, 17:4*
*(other) 2:Eb, 13:Ea, 16:1, 18:Eb,*
*23:HIWb*
*timetable (train, coach, etc.) 11:3,*
*15:5, 16:8, 16:10*
*toiletries 5:5, 6:9*
*toilets 2:3, 4:E, 23:6*
*train (surface / underground) 3,*
*3:HIWe, 4:6, 6:7, 8:CI, 11:3, 12:5,*
*16:10, 16:11, 16:12*
*transport (means of) 15:Ea, 15:2,*
*16:12, 19:7, 22:4*
*traveller's information 2:3, 4:6,*
*8:CI, 22:6*

*underground, tube 3:HIWe,*
*15:Ea, 16:12 (see also vending*
*machines; tickets (transport))*

vacation see holidays / free time
vending machines 3:HIWe, 12:2,
  13, 13:Ea

walking 4, 10, 12:5, 15:Ea, 17:7,
  19, 19:Ed, 19:3
washroom see toilets
water sports / swimming 9:3, 19:2
weather 10:Ec, 11:2, 13:HIWc,
  24:HIWc
week 8:Ea, 8:3

weights / measures 12, 12:Eb
wishes / hopes 17:HIWb, 18:HIWa,
  19, 19:HIWd
word games 6:15, 16:14, 18:7,
  19:Ec, 20:4, 25:2, 25:3, 25:4
work / business 7, 7:CIb, 23 (see
  also meeting people (social and
  business))
written messages / forms 3:HIWe,
  6:9, 11:10, 11:11, 11:12, 13:5,
  16:15, 21:5, 21:7